With best

Blanche & Charles.

Xmas 1957.

The King's England

A New Domesday Book of 10,000 Towns
and Villages

Edited by Arthur Mee

in 41 Volumes

NOTHING like these books has ever been presented to the English people. Every place has been visited. The Compilers have travelled half-a-million miles and have prepared a unique picture of our countryside as it has come down through the ages, a census of all that is enduring and worthy of record.

The Charming Village of Finchingfield

THE KING'S ENGLAND

ESSEX

London's North Sea Neighbour

EDITED BY

ARTHUR MEE

With 373 Places
and 153 Pictures

LONDON
HODDER AND STOUGHTON
LIMITED   ST PAUL'S HOUSE, E.C.4.

First published August 1940
Sixth impression 1956

It has not been thought desirable to
note in this volume the changes which
the war brought about in some churches
and other buildings

*Printed and Bound in Great Britain for Hodder & Stoughton, Limited,
by Richard Clay and Company, Ltd., Bungay, Suffolk*

The Editor is indebted to
HUGO NELSON TYERMAN
for his help with this book

For the pictures to
SIDNEY TRANTER, ART EDITOR

and to the following :

Messrs B. T. Batsford, Country Life, J. Dixon-Scott,
H. Felton, Humphrey Joel, A. F. Kersting, Photochrom,
H. J. Smith, F. Spalding, John Stone, E. W. Tattersall,
W. F. Taylor, and The Times; also to His Majesty's
Stationery Office, the Royal Commission on Historical
Monuments, and the Curator of the Colchester and
Essex Museum

PICTURES OF ESSEX

*Where the pictures are not on or facing the page given
they are inside the set of pictures beginning on that page*

PICTURES OF ESSEX

The Age-old Kingdom Between London and the Sea

A FLAT uninteresting county, it has been said, but what know they of Essex who say it? This county that faces the North Sea has stood four square against our foes from Caesar's day till now, and if it is dull what is it, we wonder, that has made its population grow from thousands into millions in these two generations?

It goes back with Kent to the very beginning of our story. Here are the first known heroes of our race, for the tale of Essex is older than Christianity.

And if we leave out London itself there are only two other counties as crowded with people as Essex is. It comes after Yorkshire and Lancashire, third county in population after the capital. It is its nearness to London that has made it so. The fact that Londoners can pour themselves into Essex so easily has transformed the whole county in our time, and living men have seen its population grow from over half a million until it is well within sight of two millions. There are over a million people in eight Essex towns alone, yet rural Essex remains much as it was, an agricultural county with shallow seas breaking in where pleasant little towns and pleasure resorts have grown up.

It is, of course, the great forest of Epping that gives an air of serenity and tranquillity to a piece of England the Industrial Age might so easily have spoiled. Once upon a time it was forest all the way from London as far as Colchester, but the woodlands fell back as the centuries came on, and Essex Forest became Waltham Forest, Waltham Forest became Epping Forest, and the menacing finger of Progress was pointing at the heart of all this natural glory when the City of London bethought itself of a chance to do a noble deed, and did it. It saved the forest from shrinking away entirely, and there are now preserved for ever 5500 acres of forest land, seven miles long; a piece of Merrie England left among us.

The whole of Essex covers 1524 square miles, with about forty organised areas of government and about 400 parishes. Though it is true that it is mainly low country with a crumbling shore and the peril of floods inland, it has hills rising 300 feet. One range of small heights runs from High Beech in Epping Forest to Danbury Hill between Maldon and Chelmsford, but the greatest general height is north-west, from where the longest rivers run, all bounding for the North Sea. Either they go south to the Thames like the River Roding and the River Stort, the Stort being a tributary of the Lea with which it forms the western boundary; or they go south-east like the Chelmer 46 miles long, the Colne 35 miles long, the Pant, a tributary of the Black-water, and the Stour, which separates Essex from Suffolk as the Thames separates it from Kent. There are two smaller rivers on the south, the Crouch and the Roach, which end in shallow estuaries used by yachts and small craft.

Essex has also a number of islands in her estuaries or off the coast, the most attractive being Mersea Island, which lies be-tween the mouth of the Blackwater and the mouth of the Colne; it is by this island that the biggest rivers meet the sea, the Chelmer, the Blackwater, and the Colne. On these three rivers stand three of the chief towns, Chelmsford, Maldon, and Colchester. Other islands are Foulness, the biggest of all, on the North Sea coast at the mouth of the Crouch and the Roach; Canvey Island; and Northey in the Blackwater, a few acres when its solitary inhabitant has his breakfast but hundreds of acres when he has his supper, or otherwise as the tides may be.

Essex has been closely linked with London since London be-came a city. The Essex bank of the Thames was one of the jumping-off grounds for the Roman conquest. Caesar had found British power centred at St Albans in his second expedition, and there he compelled the British chief to acknowledge his lordship; but even before then a Roman peace had been made in London and in Essex by the Celtic tribe known as the Trinobantes. Julius Caesar put their ruler on his throne at Camulodunum, the foundation city of Colchester which was to become the capital of the greater part of Britain for the next hundred years. It was arranged that they should pay tribute to Rome and the names of the rulers of Camulodunum were put on gold coins in Roman letters. It was here that Cunobelin held his court during the years when Our Lord was reaching his manhood in Palestine.

King Cunobelin was Shakespeare's Cymbeline, and he is interesting to us as the father of our first hero and our first traitor, for Essex now became the scene of what is perhaps the first dramatic human page in the history of our island. Cymbeline was the most powerful king in the island when he died, and was succeeded by two of his sons, Togodumnus and Caractacus.

Every schoolboy knows Caractacus, who became the most romantic figure in the island after his elder brother had been slain in battle, but few have heard of his youthful brother Adminius, who had been banished by his father and became a traitor in his exile. There was jealousy among the surrounding tribes, and Adminius encouraged the Romans to make war. They overcame the reigning brothers, and Caractacus, left alone by the death of Togodumnus, escaped into the mountains of Wales, where for years he kept the Romans at bay while the conquest of Britain went slowly on. In the end he was captured by the Romans and taken captive by the Emperor Claudius, marching with his family in chains through the streets of Rome.

Caractacus was brought before the tribunal for judgment, and who can forget his eloquent plea for freedom, which Tacitus wrote down in matchless prose and Bernard Barton has put into poetry? This is the historian's report:

If to the nobility of my birth I had united the virtues of moderation, Rome would have beheld me not in captivity, but as a royal visitor and a friend. I had arms, men, and horses; I had wealth. Can you wonder I was unwilling to lose them?

I stood at bay for years. Had I acted otherwise, where on your part had been the glory of conquest, and on my part the honour of a brave resistance? I am now in your power; if you are bent on vengeance execute your purpose. The scene will soon be over, and

3

the name of Caractacus will sink into oblivion. Preserve my life and I shall be to a far-off posterity a monument of Roman clemency.

Claudius played the man and struck the chains from the hero's hands, welcomed him and his family to the capital of the world, and gave them a palace. There they lived and died, while the Romans built up their British colony far away. The British city of Cymbeline became the capital of Caesar, and all went well until Nero's day, when occurred the greatest calamity that ever befell the Romans in the island, bringing deep dishonour on their name. The Roman Governor betrayed the trust of a king of East Anglia who left his wealth to be shared by his two daughters and the Roman emperor. Hardly had he been laid in his grave when the Roman soldiers seized his estates and assaulted the daughters of the widowed queen. She was Boadicea, and the story of her vengeance has written itself in the memory of our race.

She gathered her armies and led them with frenzied energy, burning down Roman Colchester and Roman London. But it was all in vain except to make the first great story of a British battlefield, and Boadicea laid down her life for her country. The Romans now made Colchester a famous stronghold, and even today this thrilling town has two miles of Roman wall with the sites of buildings recognisable from their tessellated pavements, their foundation stones, the vaults under the castle, and the ruins of a Mithraic temple, all within the wall. It is the best Roman town wall in England or in Britain, in spite of the damage and neglect that has robbed it of much glory.

The Roman mark is everywhere in Essex, which has three main Roman roads. Icknield Street runs from London through Romford and Chelmsford to Colchester, where it turns north to cross the Stour into Suffolk at Stratford St Mary. Stane Street joins it at Marks Tey, having come from St Albans to Bishop's Stortford, thence to run due east across Essex. The Via Devana from Cambridge joins Icknield Street at Lexden, having come by Castle Hedingham. Many other roads seem to be Roman. The road between Chelmsford and Braintree running as far as Gosfield is as straight as a ruler, another Roman-looking road crosses Stane Street at Great Dunmow, and another appears at Great Chesterford. There must be many more, for Roman tiles all over the county bear witness to the fact that Essex was a flourishing centre of Roman life. It is probable that no other county has anything like the number of Roman tiles we find built into Essex churches.

Two other scenes of Roman prowess guard the wide entrance to the Blackwater like twin fortresses. On Mersea Island are the remains of a round building 65 feet across, built by the Romans as a watch-tower or a lighthouse; and across the river at Bradwell are the walls and bastions of a fort much battered by the North Sea yet still revealing the solid strength the Roman builders put into it. Here is one of our forgotten scenes of pilgrimage, a thrilling place to come to.

Across the walls of the Roman fort the Saxons built their church, and there it stands to this day. It was when the Romans abandoned this country to its fate that the Saxon hordes came swarming in, making Essex their home and Colchester their capital. This Colchester had already had three dynasties when Alfred gave it its fourth and last. It has been a Celtic capital, a Roman capital, a Saxon capital, and was Saxon for 200 years until Alfred's grandfather Egbert merged Essex into Wessex, and came within an ace of making himself King of All England. Then came the Danes whom Alfred fought on many battlefields in Essex. At Witham is a fort built by Alfred's son Edward, and Ashingdon-on-the-Crouch is believed to be the site of the Battle of Assandun at which Canute defeated Edmund Ironside and became King of England. It seems to take us back into the dark night of history to think of a Danish king of England, and yet we have in this county (this county they say is so dull) a little wooden church which has stood since those days, the most remarkable Saxon timbers on English soil. It is the Saxon church of Greensted, and in it the body of King Edmund rested for the night when it was being carried back to the grave at Bury St Edmunds, from which it had been hurriedly removed.

There is nothing in all England like this little church where Edmund's body rested at Greensted, built of split oak trunks with the mark of the Saxon adze on them, each trunk with a tongue of wood to fit into its place. The pilgrim in search of Saxon England will come here first of all, but there are other astonishing monuments of those days. The truth is that no county in England can equal Essex in its surprising legacy from Antiquity, for it has not only its extraordinary assemblage of Roman remains and the unique church of Saxon timbers at Greensted, but it has the oldest door in England still hanging on its hinges, as well as one of the two or three Norman timber roofs still surviving. The door, made of plain oak with three iron straps, opens into Hadstock church; the roof, uncovered in our time, is at East Ham. Among other notable possessions from Saxon England, Essex has a remarkable triangle-headed doorway in Colchester, a splendid tower of five stages at Little Bardfield, double-splayed windows at Inworth, and Saxon work at Chickney and Strethall.

From those far distant times comes one of the historic memories of the ancient county, for it was at a battle between a Saxon earl and the Danes that there was sung a verse famous as the first hymn to contain a Christian prayer on a battlefield.

Essex has a fine array of buildings of all periods, and as it has no native stone it is rich in exquisite timber work. The Conqueror made the county a stronghold and lived at Barking Abbey while he built his town house on Tower Hill. He gave his followers great estates hereabouts, the Mandevilles having castles at Pleshey and Saffron Walden, and the great Norman De Veres building Castle Hedingham. Macaulay called them "the most illustrious line of nobles that England has seen," and they became Earls of Oxford until 1703, when the line ended with the death of the 20th earl, who bore the same name as the Conqueror's friend, Audrey. They made Castle Hedingham one of the finest structures in the land. Colchester Castle, with the biggest Norman keep in England, was another medieval stronghold, and still is a delightful spectacle in the heart of the city's old streets, nobly set in a great green space in the very midst of this thrilling Celtic, Roman, Saxon, Norman, English town.

Essex has few domestic remains of monasteries, but they include the striking gateway and tower at St Osyth, the fine Gateway of St Botolph's Priory at Colchester, the Prior's chamber at Prittlewell, and Beeleigh Priory. Some of the monastic churches still remain, as at Waltham, Little Dunmow, and the Hatfields. Waltham Abbey is almost enough glory for a county in itself, a masterpiece of Norman work.

Little Dunmow church has a lovely 12th century arcade, and Hatfield Peverel and Hatfield Broad Oak both have in their churches a nave used by the old monks, and parts of the central towers of those days. The work of the Normans abounds throughout the county, from East Ham in the far south where the Norman timber roof of the apse has been revealed in our time, to Sturmer in the far north where the Normans found a Saxon church and used it as their foundation. Hadleigh and Rainham churches are entirely Norman, while the doorways at Finchingfield, Middleton, South Ockendon, Little Totham, Stansted Mountfitchet, Great Bentley, and Margaret Roding display the rich variety of ornament beloved of Norman workers in stone. The massive square tower at Great Tey, with its courses of Roman red brick, gives a vivid impression of the strength of Norman building, and the round towers at Broomfield, Great Leighs, and Fyfield remind us of the many round watch-towers the Saxons erected in East Anglia. Copford is a fascinating example of Norman skill, for not only has it a Norman stone roof (with technical points of which the only other examples in the country are at Great Clacton and Chepstow Priory), but the walls of the nave, chancel, and apse are covered with original

5

paintings, valuable for their costume and armour. It is one of the richest possessions the Normans bequeathed to us.

The next building period to make its mark in Essex was the 14th century, and one of the notable designs is the round arcade of the Knights Hospitallers church at Little Maplestead, the latest of the round churches still standing in England and of remarkable beauty. At Waltham is an exquisite chapel.

Yet it is the 15th century which is best represented. The cathedral-like spire of Thaxted's noble church rises 181 feet, the church itself being two feet longer, and an exquisite place. Dedham Tower, 130 feet, is big enough to have a carriage-way below it, and Brightlingsea's flint and stone tower, on a hill overlooking the sea, rises 100 feet and has 32 niches on its buttresses. Canewdon Tower, all stone and 74 feet high, had once a beacon to guide sailors making for London. Saffron Walden has not only a splendid tower and spire, but arcades and porches of great beauty. Fifteenth century porches are at Ardleigh, Chelmsford, Great Bromley, and Fingringhoe.

But stone has always been a luxury in this county, which is mainly clay, and the delightful flint ornament is chiefly confined to the chalk belt, so that as we travel about Essex we cannot but notice how often timber and brick is used with delightful effect. Timber towers with shingled spires greet us at Blackmore and Stock, Bobbingworth and Navestock, while on many other towers a wooden belfry has been ingeniously fixed. Margaretting has a strong timber tower, and both its porches are of wood, much beloved by artists, who, however, regard Doddinghurst porch as a close rival to it.

The brick tower reached its zenith in the 16th century, and with their rich patterns and glowing colour these towers nobly enrich the village scene, but the best brickwork is in the great houses. Faulkbourne Hall is a perfect 15th century building which has been inhabited and well preserved since our sixth King Henry gave its owner permission to fortify it. To the Tudor Age belongs that magnificent fragment of an even more ambitious home, Layer Marney Hall with its eight-storeyed gatehouse. Gosfield Hall and Little Leighs Priory are smaller buildings of great charm, in the soft glowing brick of the Tudors. The National Trust's proud possession at Coggeshall, Paycocke's House, relies on timber more than brick for its beauty.

The two biggest old buildings in the county are New Hall, and Audley End. New Hall, near Boreham, was built by Henry the Eighth, whose arms are richly carved on its stone; Audley End was built by Thomas, Earl of Suffolk, grandson of Thomas Audley, Bluebeard's famous Chancellor, on the site of an abbey near Saffron Walden. King James declared that Audley End was too fine for a king, but might do for his treasurer.

The old town of Saffron Walden is the richest town in Essex for ancient buildings, having over 150 scheduled as monuments worthy to be preserved by the nation. A walk through this town is a joy not to be forgotten for the elaborately carved timber buildings and quaint plaster ornament abounding. In all Essex there are over 750 medieval domestic buildings, the oldest being the 13th century manor house at Little Chesterford. The pilgrim in search of these old places will be well rewarded at Chelmsford and Colchester, Great and Little Waltham, Kelvedon and Coggeshall, Newport, Witham, and Braintree, for none of these places has less than twenty medieval structures.

Of farm buildings with fine interiors Essex has great wealth, and it is renowned for its number of old barns. One at Cressing is a 16th century five-gabled barn, 160 feet long, keeping company with a smaller barn, built earlier beside a Knights Hospitallers home. There are many dovecots and about thirty windmills still left; the dovecot at Tolleshunt D'Arcy is a little gem in brick and tile.

The handiwork of the village craftsmen is seen in many magnificent examples such as the double-hammerbeam roofs at Castle Hedingham, Great Bromley, and Gestingthorpe, all enriched by carving; in the porch roof at South Benfleet, where much beauty is compressed into little space; and at High Easter

6

with carved beams and pierced spandrels in the 16th century roof. At Shenfield and Theydon Garnon are timber arcades, so rarely found in churches. Castle Hedingham has a lovely timber screen in striking contrast to the simplicity of the 14th century one at Bardfield Saling. A gem of the same kind from the 15th century is in the church at Abbess Roding. Castle Hedingham has quaint 14th century misereres, and there are delightful bench-ends at Hadleigh, Danbury, Rettendon, Shalford, and Belchamp St Paul. There are splendid font covers at Thaxted (15th century) at Littlebury (linenfold), at Takeley, and at Pentlow, where the font is Norman. Essex has one of our very rare medieval wooden fonts. It is at Marks Tey, where it has been since the 15th century and has unfortunately lost the seated figures from its niches. The oldest stone font is at Little Maplestead, coming from the Conqueror's time, and among other Norman fonts are two (at Eastwood and Shopland) which show by their arcading how the pointed arch evolved from the round. Althorne has a fascinating font with vivid figures which show that this little masterpiece was carved about the year 1400.

There are at least a dozen medieval pulpits in the county, that at Sandon being a beautiful example. Newport has a perfect lectern 400 years old, and also a 13th century chest which was used as a travelling altar, having inside the lid five paintings which are said to be the first paintings in oil by English artists. Other Norman paintings are those on the walls of Copford church and in a recess above the altar at Great Canfield, where the Madonna sits in a red cloak nursing her child. One of the most striking of later wall-paintings is a great figure of St Christopher at Layer Marney.

There are few churches in Essex without some interesting monument, and Layer Marney's church has three splendid figures telling the story of the tragic end of the ancient house. Sir William Marney lies in alabaster on the tomb where he was laid in 1360, and two Lord Marneys lie fashioned in a hard black stone on terracotta tombs, father and son, dying within two years and ending the line in 1525. Their tombs were fashioned by the Italian craftsmen who built their gorgeous home.

There are ten figures carved in wood in Essex churches, a good share of England's hundred. There are three at Little Horkesley, two at Little Baddow (one a lady in 600-year-old costume), a priest at Little Leighs, a knight at Elmstead, and three in the hilltop church at Danbury. One of these three is of exceptional interest because his coffin was found and opened, and in it the knight was seen lying perfect in form, immersed in a curious liquid which had preserved him for five centuries; flowers and herbs were floating about him, surely one of the strangest spectacles ever brought to light from the ancient past. Three Tudor Earls of Sussex lie at Boreham on magnificent tombs, there are splendid tombs of the Smiths at Theydon Mount and of the Petres at Ingatestone, and the last of the Fitzwalters, descendants of a Magna Carta baron, is seen at Little Dunmow. At Felstead lies Lord Rich, founder of the great family from which so many of our peers claim descent, and heir to so much of the spoils of the monasteries. His face is an actual portrait, and his richly carved monument is one of the most interesting in the county because it was designed by Epiphanius Evesham, the first English sculptor of great fame. Nicholas Stone has monuments at Writtle and Walthamstow; at Writtle an elaborate monument to Edward and Dorothea Pinchon with a reaper standing among the corn, at Walthamstow a wall-monument of Sir Thomas Merry and his wife. At North Ockendon is a tomb of great splendour erected for himself by Sir Gabriel Poyntz.

For brasses Essex comes next to Kent and therefore second county in England, with 300 of these enduring records of dress and armour. One brass is 14th century; it is at Chrishall, and shows Sir John de la Pole clasping his wife's hand. Another at Wivenhoe shows the Countess of Oxford in her heraldic cloak. At Chigwell is an archbishop in the splendour of his robes, and at Little Horkesley is Lady Marney between two husbands.

7

Essex has little glass, but the oldest, at Rivenhall, is exceeding rich and rare, for it is by a Norman craftsman showing a Madonna and Child. Here too is a 13th century knight on a richly apparelled horse, and there is 13th century glass with a lovely figure of St Helen at North Ockendon, and again with a king at White Notley. Glass of the 14th century has survived at Sheering, Harlow, and Beeleigh Priory; and of the 15th century at Margaretting, at Netteswell, and at White Notley.

This county so rich in its historic heritage, so famous for its ancient buildings, is rich also in noble names. We have seen that it has known the Conqueror, and Caractacus and Boadicea a thousand years before him. It has also known an ancestor of George Washington and a Mayflower man to whom America should be grateful, for he found supplies for the Mayflower. Washington's ancestor in Essex was his great-great-grandfather Lawrence, who was ejected from his living at Purleigh and lies in an unknown grave at Maldon. The Mayflower man was Christopher Martin of Billericay, who joined William Brewster's little community in Holland and was one of three who came to England to arrange for the voyage to the New World. He chartered the Mayflower and provisioned her, and one summer evening in 1620 he and his wife and two others walked down the hill from Billericay to join the ship at Leigh. Alas for them all, and for their high hopes! They crossed the Atlantic but perished from the sickness which ravaged the ship and slew one-third of the Pilgrims as they lay off the coast of Massachusetts.

Two heroes of last century come into the story of the county. It was from here that Livingstone went out to Africa; after being afraid to face an Essex congregation he faced all the terrors of the Dark Continent and fought with a lion. In a small burial-ground belonging to the Quakers lies the great Elizabeth Fry, to whom every country in Europe owes something for her valour in redeeming prisons from shame. Three heroes of our own century come into the roll of fame, for Jack Cornwell lies in the cemetery at Little Ilford, Captain Fryatt lies at Dovercourt, and Captain Oates was an Essex boy. It may be thought that Jack Cornwell belongs rightly to Westminster Abbey, and so he does; it was by some sad mistake that he was in his grave before the nation realised how great a thing he had done and how immortal his name was to become. It would be no more than justice that he should even now be laid to rest among our kings of men. Captain Fryatt was one of the bravest men ever shot by the German Army, who treated him as a pirate because he defended his little ship against a submarine. He rammed the U-boat, and, being captured afterwards, was shot, his body being brought home at the end of the war. Captain Oates was a boy at Gestingthorpe, where we found his aged mother still caring for the memorial to the boy who grew up to march with Scott and to walk out into the blizzard to give his comrades a new chance of life.

But Essex must be left to speak for itself in these pages. We have no space to speak here of her industries, which have grown to such great dimensions in our own century. Stratford has the great workshops of the LNER; Dagenham has the Ford works which are as near the miraculous as anything mechanical can be; Braintree and Halstead have the famous works where artificial silk was born; Barking has the marvellous power station; a great area of London draws its water from Essex waterworks; and those who eat oysters have a warm corner in their hearts for the estuary of the Colne and for the Blackwater with Brightlingsea, Colchester, and Maldon as the centres where the oyster fishery is mainly carried on.

Essex has London's nearest seaside resort at Southend, and popular holiday places are the well-known Clacton, Dovercourt, and Walton-on-the-Naze. She has also the port of Harwich, the only seaport between the Thames and the Humber that has a regular line of steamers to the Continent. It stands on a prominence overlooking the estuaries of the Stour and the Orwell. Strongly fortified, and capable of building small ships on its own account, the port's serious business is with Holland and

9

Belgium through Rotterdam and Antwerp. It has built Parkeston Quay on piles two miles up the Stour and is in close touch with this delightful river running between Essex and Suffolk—a Suffolk river though Constable crossed over to the Essex bank to discover some of his most charming scenes. Tilbury is the other great port of Essex, the first of the Port of London docks for incoming ships, with passenger facilities equal to any in the world, daily cargoes from all over the globe, four miles of quays, and nearly fifty miles of railways. The biggest liners on the ocean can come to its floating landing stage at any hour of day or night, whatever the tide may be. Tilbury is rightly famous for its travel facilities, but more famous still is it for its place in history, for it was in an hour of grave danger for England that Queen Elizabeth came here, mounted on a charger, and addressed her troops:

Let tyrants fear . . . I know I have the body of a weak, feeble woman, but I have the heart of a king, and of a king of England, too, and think foul scorn that any prince of Europe should dare to invade the borders of my realm.

It was a great speech made in a great place, and Essex has not lost the spirit which thus resounded across her ports and fields and hamlets three centuries ago. She is a bulwark of Old England still, growing more and more in numbers and in enduring strength.

Here Men Have Lived Since the Stone Age

ABBERTON. The Old Stone Age man lived here, and some of his stone implements are in Colchester's great museum. The cottages line two of three roads to the north of Peel Tie Common, a wild and rough expanse. The road to the west dips into a sudden valley and rises again to pass on one side a lovely wood concealing Abberton House, and on the other side, across a field, Abberton Hall with a homestead moat and ancient barns. Behind this old-world group lies the church, which has a small ironbound chest 400 years old and a 15th century font.

The church was built in the 14th century but restored in the last two centuries, so that only the lower course of the rubble walls of the chancel remains from medieval days. The nave has still two 14th century doorways, however, one used and one blocked up.

There is a fine view from the top of the red brick tower, which has stood since the early years of the 16th century; at its foot once ran the Roman road from Colchester to the sea. In the churchyard is a gravestone carved with the skull and crossbones in 1701.

Cromwell's Trusted Friend

ABBESS RODING. Elms line the deep lane which brings us to its small medieval church, with a thin lead spire on a modern tower. Here are almost the best screens in the county for a church of its size, a deep band of elaborate tracery carved in the closing years of the 15th century and filling a third of the opening below the low-pitched arches. The panels have tracery at both ends and rich ornament along the rail. The roof of the chancel is 15th century; the rich woodcarving on the canopy of the pulpit is 18th. The oldest possession of the church is a square Norman font, but its chief treasure is in the windows, which have medieval glass showing a bishop and a saint. The bishop stands with great dignity in his robes and mitre, his staff in his hand and two fingers raised in blessing—a little masterpiece said to have been saved from destruction by being buried in some time of danger. The saint is probably Margaret; she has golden hair and is shown thrusting her staff into the mouth of a dragon. Both figures are 15th century.

There are two brightly painted monuments to the Capel family with a span of 300 years between them, the older one showing Sir Gamaliel Capel kneeling with his wife at a desk with a cloth of green and gold, their nine children in Jacobean costume below; and the modern one in memory of Lawrence Capel Cure, who was rector here for 54 years. On his wall-monument is his gorgeous coat-of-arms in full colour. The old hourglass is still on his pulpit, half-full of sand; he must have turned it over many times, and perhaps heard the applause of his congregation as he did so, starting his fourthly and fifthly in those days of long sermons. On another monument a lady of Stuart times (Lady Lyckyn) is being crowned by two angels.

In this village John Thurloe was born in the year Shakespeare died; he rose to be Secretary of State to Cromwell. To him we owe most of our knowledge of the Commonwealth under Cromwell. He was one of the Commissioners sent by Parliament to treat with Charles Stuart at Uxbridge, and was Secretary of State during the Protectorate. A man of great ability, he played an important role in Parliament, but was chiefly valuable to the country as over-seer of home and foreign posts. So successful was he in detecting plots and plotters that it was said that Cromwell carried at his belt the secrets of all the princes of Europe. Sincere friendship linked the two men, Thurloe being one of the few to whom Cromwell un-bent. Thurloe revered and loved him, and would have had him king.

Under Richard Cromwell he was the one strong man of the nation, able, sincere, and selfless. When the Restoration came he was imprisoned for treason, but was released and took no further part in public life. Charles the Second desired him to return to his old position, but Thurloe answered that he despaired of serving him as he had served Cromwell, whose rule, he said, "was to seek out men for places, and not places for men."

He died at his chambers in Lincoln's Inn in 1668. Many years after his death his vast store of State papers was found hidden in a false ceiling of a garret above his room: letters, copies of Cromwell's speeches now first made known, and reports by spies. He betrayed no man, taking his secrets with him to the grave.

From Thomas of Leighton's Day

ALDHAM. Its houses and its church have parted company. The 16th century houses are still by the road but the church was moved about a hundred years ago, stone by stone, to a quieter spot near a thatched barn. They gave it a new graceful spire in moving it, but most of the church was 600 years old when taken to its new address. It has a beautifully carved timber porch of the 14th century. Time has been kind to the lovely ironwork on the door of the tower, for it has come down from 13th century days, when the famous Thomas of Leighton was shaping his wonderful iron grille over Queen Eleanor's tomb in Westminster Abbey.

On the site of the old church is the tomb of Philip Morant, rector from 1745 to 1770, to whom all who love Essex owe much. By the influence of his son-in-law, Keeper of the Tower Records, he was made editor of the first records of Parliament, covering the period from 1278 to 1413, but his chief title to fame is the History of Essex.

Old Glass

ALPHAMSTONE. In narrow winding lanes its houses are strung out, several of them 17th century and one a 16th century farm. The churchyard has a fine outlook over the Stour valley, and marks the site of a far more ancient burial-place in the Bronze Age. Urns dug up hereabouts are in Colchester Museum. From the wooden bell-turret three Tudor bells ring out, but the nave walls may be as old as the 12th century, and the south aisle and the chancel with its splendid sedilia are 14th. One of the porches has timbers 500 years old, and the other is about a century younger, but both the doors have been here since the time of Agincourt. There are two chests and a communion table, all about 300 years old, and a 12th century font bowl with a 17th century cover. The chancel has two of the low medieval windows which have long puzzled our antiquarians. They have kept their ancient iron grilles, and are believed to have been used at mass, when a bell was rung from them for the people outside to hear. In several windows is 14th and 15th century glass, including blue and gold roundels, fragments of suns and tabernacles, fleur-de-lys and cups. A sad tale is told of the old glass of the church being sold for what it would fetch in Sudbury market at the beginning of last century.

Roman Bricks and Medieval Timbers

ALRESFORD. A scattered little place on high tableland, Nature has endowed it with fine woods round Alresford Hall, and round the old farmhouse called Tenpenny Brook, which has timbers that have lasted 400 years. A little way off (a mile to the west) a few fragments of brick and tessellated paving mark the site of a Roman house; we have seen Samian ware and painted plaster from it in Colchester Museum. A long lane leads us to the little church standing with a cross to village heroes in the loneliness of the fields. The shingled spire of the belfry rises above the walls the Normans built, and there are Roman tiles set in the corners of the nave. Over the altar is a lovely William Morris window.

Costume on the Font

ALTHORNE. Charming here it is to see the white-sailed boats coming up the wide estuary with the flowing tide, and delightful to come to the church by the grassy lane. In the church is a gem which should draw every traveller this way—a font exquisitely carved about the year 1400, recording for all time the costume worn by kings and queens and ordinary people of that age. The panels of the bowl are cut deep to throw the figures in strong relief. Here is a seraph feathered from crown to foot, and stately withal; here is a royal prince at a font with a priest baptising him; in another panel stands a king with his queen beside him, plucking at her gown as if to curtsy.

The church is 14th century, the tower 15th, its embattled parapet enriched with flints in a trelliswork of stone giving it great beauty. On a nave buttress is a medieval scratch dial. An inscription below a portrait brass tells us that this is William Hyklott, who paid for the wall of the church; he is with two daughters, one dressed as a nun, and engraved with them are a delightful Madonna and Child.

ARDLEIGH. It must have been an ancient home of men, as it has enriched the great museum of Colchester with Stone Age relics; but we found it gay with flowers and glorious with cornfields, for it has great nurseries and many farms. Ardleigh Hall has fine medieval timbers. There is a timber cottage of the 15th century near the church, and many quaint buildings go back 300 years.

The splendid tower of the church is 15th century, and in it hangs a bell cast in the years that followed Agincourt. The flint and stone work of the south porch is medieval, but the three old niches above the richly carved doorway have modern sculpture, and in their spandrels are St George and the Dragon. Crowned lions flank the door and two beasts sit on shafts running up from the buttresses. The doorway itself has quaint sculptures of Adam and Eve, and the door, with traceried heads, has been on its hinges for 450 years. The church has fine tracery in the base of an ancient screen rich in carvings of foliage, grotesque heads, and dragons.

Bravest of the Brave

ARKESDEN. It lies in a winding valley and has its share of the old farms and cottages which are the pride of Essex. From a little bridge guarded by an ancient elm its green slopes up to a churchyard with a peace memorial on a great boulder between two handsome pines. Higher still stands the church, which has a 15th century tower rising from the massive Norman foundations. The building has been much restored, but is chiefly 700 years old, with double lancets in the chancel, fine round pillars in the nave, and an aisle added in 1500 by a wealthy London fishmonger. The font bowl is Norman, and stands on low arches not quite so old. A piscina in one of the aisles has been supported by a grotesque head for 600 years.

But the great attraction here is in the ancient monuments. A solemn 15th century priest lies in his robes in the chancel, in a double recess divided by a pillar with a lovely niche. He may have come from Walden Abbey in Bedfordshire, to which this church belonged for nearly 200 years before the Reformation; we see the abbey arms in old glass in the tower. A brass portrait shows Richard Fox of 1439 in armour with his dog, and beside him towers the Elizabethan monument of Richard Cutte, who lies with his wife under a rich canopy. His feet are on the heraldic beast of his crest, and hers rest on a red dog, but the quaint feature of the tomb is its recesses at the sides, six of them with figures of children, all named.

A boy of the next generation in this family, son of another Richard Cutte, is known to history as John Cutts, and shines in the glowing pages of Macaulay as he shone on the battlefields of the Duke of

Marlborough. He was born at Arkesden in 1661 and lived to be a great soldier. He fought Protestant battles wherever he had the chance and always, as Macaulay says, as the bravest of the brave. He is a European figure and was the first to lead the attack at the Battle of Blenheim, his last battle. So much at ease was he in the hottest engagements that his men called him the Salamander and Macaulay declared that he was unrivalled for bulldog courage, always the man for a forlorn hope. In peaceful life he made Steele his Secretary and Steele dedicated his first book to him. Perhaps it is to the honour of this courageous man that he was himself the butt of Dean Swift's abuse. He died in Dublin, and so is not among his ancestors in this village which gave him birth.

Just a century younger is a big monument to John Withers of the Middle Temple, with handsome busts of himself and his wife, by Roubiliac. A side chapel is in memory of Herbert Fearn who in 1916 finished a ministry of 47 years. Rich glass above its little altar shows the Madonna, St Michael, and St Alban.

The churchyard has kept some of its gravestones since the 17th century, one with a cherub and two skulls in foliage deeply carved.

Treasures from the Mounds

ASHDON. Here by the Cambridge border is one of the surprises of Essex, the Bartlow Hills. They are a group of mounds in two rows, the biggest 40 feet high and 150 feet across. In them a century ago were found walled graves containing treasures of enamel and bronze and glass, the last resting-places of British lords when England was part of the Roman Empire. We find a casket from these graves in the British Museum. Many old farms and cottages has Ashdon, some Elizabethan, some 17th century, and one, the old guildhall (now turned into cottages) built about 1500; it has an overhanging storey, ornamental brackets, and the original timbers in the roof. The rectory is 100 years younger.

The oldest timbers in the village are in the 14th century church, where a lovely chancel roof was set up about the time of Agincourt. It has a beam with pierced ornament and other carving. Both porches are 15th century, and so are a chest and a moulded roof-beam. The nave roof has early Tudor woodwork, and the big 14th century south chapel has its original timber roof resting on corbels

Ardleigh   **Old Houses in the High Road**

Ardleigh   **The Medieval Church Porch**

Boxted   Gathering in the Harvest

Great Bromley 15th Century Church   **Boreham**   Medieval Church

of a lion and a knight. On a chapel wall at the windows are stone carvings of a knight and a woman, each behind a shield. The Norman font bowl is on a 13th century stem, the altar rails were made beautiful by Jacobean craftsmen, and there are many fragments of glass about 500 years old, including an angel with golden wings. An altar tomb panelled with shields is in memory of the Tyrells of Henry the Eighth's day, and a tablet carved with fishes and scallop shells is to Richard Tyrell of 1566.

The Great Earthworks

ASHELDAM. The two groups of earthworks where the land rises above the marshes here were the bulwarks of our shores in ancient days. One has features of a plateau camp of the Ancient Britons; the other is remarkable, for its oval of 16 acres has the old hall, a great pond, and the church within its ramparts. The very tower of the church is itself a little stronghold, so thick are its walls, while Roman bricks border a narrow slit through which arrows could be shot. The church was made new in the 14th century, when curious headstops of monarch and monk were carved for the chancel doorway. Another mason then left his marks on the arch of the doorway in the nave, perhaps the earliest mason's mark in Essex. The altar table is from the days of Queen Elizabeth; it has the bulbous legs which gave tables so quaint an appearance in her stately halls.

ASHEN. From the street of this upland village we look over the Stour into Suffolk. Its flint tower was built about 1400, and the brick turret was new about 1520; but two of the bells (called Thomas and Alice) were made 600 years ago, and the third is 15th century. The church is small, but very old, the nave having been built by the Normans and the 13th century men. A porch of Shakespeare's day covers a doorway 200 years older, making a frame for a door with 13th century hinges.

There are two little pews 500 years old, a nave roof about the same age, a carved chair of the 18th century, and a curious panel of 1620 which tells us it has been the marrying stool and "so it shall be still." In the nave are brass portraits thought to be John and Frances Hunt, who would be alive when the victory of Agincourt was the talk of the land. John, in armour, stands on a lion; and looking up at Frances is a little dog with bells on its collar.

C   17

Two Men Divide All England

ASHINGDON. A narrow lane climbs past an old barn to trees clustering on a hilltop, and brings us to the scene over the great valley in which the course of history was changed before the Conqueror came. In the shade of these trees stands a church with Roman tiles in its walls, probably the very walls built by King Canute in celebration of his victory. His church was pulled down and built up again 600 years ago; its tower is 50 years younger than the rest of it, very quaint with a tiny saddleback astride the red tiles of the low pyramid roof. We enter by the timbered porch, under a 400-year-old roof, noticing a stone cut with a rough sundial; it may have told the time to the 14th century builders. The church is small, the nave 25 feet long, and the chancel 21. The nave and chancel roofs are 15th and 16th century.

One of the most captivating possessions of Ashingdon is the smallest, a silver penny with portraits of Canute and Earl Godwin. A 14th century window in the chancel has in modern glass a portrait of Stigand, the first priest on this hilltop, and the coin and the portrait recall the historic event in the valley of the Crouch below. This is what happened.

Where now flit the white-sailed yachts of the holiday-makers there lay 900 years ago the longships of the invading army of the Danish king. Canute had fought many losing battles up and down England and had been slowly driven back on his ships. Here he was at last with the King of England, Edmund Ironside, hot on his heels with all his host. To be able to embark in safety Canute had to stand and fight. As the decisive morning broke the Saxons drew up on the slopes of Ashingdon Hill. Canute marched his men to the level ground between this hill and the swampy plain by the Crouch; the Saxons charged down; and the Danes wavered and were about to turn; but at this critical moment the heart of the Saxon Ealdorman Eadric failed, and he fled with his men. So, in the words of the Saxon Chronicle, he betrayed his lord and king and all the people of English kin.

Then it was that fortune turned for the Danes, and Canute won his great victory. Instead of sailing home to Denmark, he followed Edmund Ironside into Gloucestershire where, close to the old

Saxon village of Deerhurst, they divided the kingdom and arranged for Canute's succession as King of all England. Canute did not forget the scene of his triumph, and four years after, in 1020, he built a minster here with Stigand as priest. Little could Stigand have foreseen, as he ministered in the little church on this hilltop, that as archbishop he was to crown the Conqueror, that five popes would excommunicate him, and that, deprived at last of his see by pope and king together, he would starve to death in a prison cell.

Treasures of Every Age

AVELEY. It has treasures of every age in its church, from the arcaded Norman font to craft work of our time. It is thrilling to see the Roman tiles picked up by the Saxons and used again by the Normans in these flint walls.

The Normans built the nave, and their round arches face the pointed arches of the first English builders. The tower is 13th century but its dwarf spire is modern. A Norman pillar piscina is sunk in the chancel wall under a carved recess of the 15th century, and the woodworkers of the next century gave the church its splendid screen. It has five openings with traceried heads on each side of the entrance to the chancel. In front are three other beautiful things in wood; the pulpit, the lectern, and a tiny prayer desk. The six-sided pulpit, dated 1621, has arches on its panels, and high above it hangs a great sounding-board, also six-sided and wondrously carved. The beautiful lectern was carved in ancient oak from Winchester. The litany desk was given in 1916 by the Sussex Regiment, "for blessings received during their stay in the parish." An elaborate chair of 1620 is crowned with the Dacre crest. On the altar front are three paintings by Sir Charles Holroyd, famous as a forceful etcher and a Director of our National Gallery; the blue dress of the Madonna is of exquisite texture, and the adoring shepherds are natural figures.

A stone with a raised cross was probably the coffin lid of Nicholas de Belhus, brought to rest here from the manor house next door. A Flemish brass shows Ralph de Knevynton under a canopy of rich design, his feet on a dog with a collar; it is odd to see him at prayer with a sword. He has been here since 1370, and his armour is of great value to students. There is a tiny 16th century brass in memory of the infant daughter of Edward Bacon. Inscriptions record the burials of the Barretts and the Dacres, who lived in Belhus, the magnificent 16th century home in a park three miles round. The side of the house which faces Aveley, and the gatehouse tower behind, are noble examples of Tudor architecture.

AYTHORP RODING. It is a tiny place and ever has been so. The church stands among the cornfields halfway between Sleepy Hollow Farm by the stream and the fine smock windmill looking down. A good example of a 13th century manor church, every window in it is still in the style of the plain lancet which replaced the Norman. The bell-turret was set on oak posts in the nave 400 years ago to shelter three bells which rang out to herald the accession of Henry the Eighth. We noticed that Henry Ludgater was rector here for 53 years of last century; he sleeps under the limes.

Round Tower

BARDFIELD SALING. It has one of the six round towers in Essex, particularly interesting because it was built in the 14th century and is therefore a late example of such a tower. The rest of this small church is also 14th century, but the tiny chancel may be a generation younger, perhaps because the Black Death fell on the land. There is attractive carving in wood and stone. Two gargoyles look down from the tower, the 15th century font is panelled on bowl and stem, and there is a 600-year-old screen of two bays. Particularly fine is the Jacobean pulpit, on which the old carver has very cleverly shown arches in perspective. Two elaborate panels of the 17th century are in the modern pews. The organ was the gift of Sir George Elvey, whose church music is sung everywhere, for he was the composer of the well-known tune for Come, Ye Thankful People, Come.

Woolpits Farm not far away has kept a little home of the birds since the 17th century. It is a brick pigeon house, with a weathervane swinging over a timber lantern on the roof, and clay nests still in the upper floor.

The Old Abbey and the Great Power House

BARKING. It stands for the tranquil Age of Saxon England and for our troubled Age of Power, for it has the great ruins of the Old Abbey and the biggest Power House in the land. Thrilling it must have been to see it in its days of fame when the Conqueror would come to seek the hospitality of the Saxon abbess while he built his town house, the Tower of London. Here the Saxon earls would come to swear him fealty. Every Toc H man must know that his church, All Hallows-by-the-Tower, is actually All Hallows, Barking, for it belonged to the abbey here at which the Conqueror stayed and of which we may see the ruins to this day.

It is a spacious place to walk in, and two 15th century towers look down on us as we wander in the footsteps of those who knew the abbey in its days of splendour—the gateway tower and the tower of St Margaret's Church. We walk within the space of these great walls, in and out of the passages and corridors, for the site is beautifully kept and we can trace the foundations of the vanished structure, which was first Saxon, then Norman, and refashioned in medieval times. Stones have been let into the green turf to show us how the abbey stood, but much of the ancient walls remain a few feet high. A part of the nun's church wall runs by the churchyard still. In this vanished church, 340 feet long, two queens have worshipped (the queens of Henry the First and of King Stephen).

The medieval gateway into this field of peace is a two-storeyed structure called the Curfew or Fire Bell Tower. It has a round arch built after the Normans, and above the archway is a chapel with a sculpture of the Crucifixion, showing the Madonna and St John at the foot of the Cross, John's head leaning in sorrow towards the Master. It is the work of a 12th century artist, probably a Norman. Here also is preserved a ring which is believed to have been worn by an abbess of Barking Abbey.

The great church which stands by the ruined abbey has grown from age to age. Its oldest stone was part of a Saxon cross, carved with interlacing scrolls; it is preserved as perhaps the one link we have here with the settlement founded by St Erkenwald, the first bishop to preach in St Paul's. There is also here a fragment of a black marble gravestone which came from the abbey with the name of a Norman bishop on it, Maurice. The chancel is the work of our first English builders but has in it a richly carved pillar piscina of the Normans, and in one of its chapels is a round Norman pier with scalloped capitals carved by one of the abbey's Norman craftsmen.

The arcades in the nave are 13th and 15th century, the font is

16th, and has a 17th century cover painted with flowers, birds, and butterflies. One of the tower arch piers has a most beautiful recess with medieval tracery and ornamental vaulting; it is a gem, and has a tiny niche in it for some mysterious purpose. The roofs come from the same medieval period, and on some of the beams above the nave are ancient paintings; we noticed a woman riding a panther.

One precious possession the church has recovered from the ruins of the abbey, the gravestone of the first vicar here. He died in 1328, and his memorial is one of those engraved stones which were the forerunners of brasses. It shows him deeply cut in the stone with his curly hair, his embroidered collar and cuffs, and his name and office in bold letters.

Of the four brasses here three are 15th century and one 16th; two show priests in their robes, one shows Thomas Broke and his wife with a son and daughter, and a hundred years later is John Tedcastell with his wife, four sons, and five babes in swaddling clothes.

On the chancel wall sits in armour, in a tent guarded by sentries, with a page holding a horse close by, Sir Charles Montagu, whose brother sentenced Sir Walter Raleigh. Among a group of 17th and 18th century busts is Francis Fuller of 1636 with three bright shields, John Bennett in front of the prow and stern of a warship, Orlando Humfreys with four cherubs, John Bamber of 1753, and Sir Crisp Gascoigne, Lord Mayor of 1753. One of the windows has a quay scene in bright colours, and another shows St Erkenwald holding a model of the abbey.

One of the attractive modern possessions of this old place is an array of carved and painted figures on the top of the south chapel screen, the Fishermen's Memorial. It is an interesting company with St Nicholas and the three children he saved from death, James and John with their fishermen's nets, Ethelburga (first abbess here), and two famous historic figures whose names must live as long as history. One is Elizabeth Fry, who is here because she lived close by and lies in the little Quaker burial ground not far away; the other is the immortal Captain Cook.

It was a few days before Christmas in 1762 that Elizabeth Batts stood in front of the altar of this church to be married to James Cook, who was then paying a flying visit home from his charting of American waters. They had six children, of whom three died as babies, the other three boys growing up to love the sea. Elizabeth said goodbye to her husband in 1776 and four years later news came to her of his death, which had happened 20 months before. She was to survive him for 56 years, years of great sorrow for her, for she outlived all her children and was alone in the world for 40 years. There have been few lonelier lives than that of the bride who stood in this place to marry a sailor who found a continent.

One or two odd things of great interest Barking has in its church. There is a Bible of Armada year on an 18th century table, a helmet hanging on the wall, a stone from the old abbey, scooped out and called the Nun's Bath, and an oyster shell with the date 1510 scratched on it, thought to be the date of one of the extensions of the church.

Barking is fortunate in having one of its finest old houses in the care of the National Trust, which has placed it at the disposal of the town for its museum. It is the 16th century Eastbury House, one of the architectural masterpieces of its day, a handsome structure with its gables and chimneys and turrets, and original garden walls with the old niches for beehives. There is a great painted chamber with wall-paintings of Elizabethan ships, one in full sail and one at anchor, and another old painting of an avenue of trees standing out from an elaborate painted background of panels and corinthian columns. The room above this gallery, which is 70 feet long, has a magnificent queenpost roof which is in a perfect state of preservation.

The museum so nobly housed has a fascinating collection. There is a Roman coffin of stone which is 17 centuries old, and a series of charming watercolours of old houses and views reveal the Barking of last century. Mr Frank Brangwyn has given prints of his Stations of the Cross, and the National Art Collections Fund has enriched the museum with a panel of 16th century Flemish glass. An English woodcarving of the 17th century shows the Sacrifice of Isaac, and (constant delight of Barking's children) there is a Georgian Doll's House which has been completely refurnished in the style of 1865. The ingenuity of a young artist who was too poor to pay for living models is shown in a group of coloured figures which he moulded and arranged for his painting After Waterloo. He was Charles Gogin, who died in 1931. Here, too, is one of the finest collections of armour in this country. Contrasted with examples of exquisite workmanship from the 15th century, we have a model of an Elizabethan soldier trailing his pike. There is an excellent series showing the development of Gothic armour, and also of the development of spurs. Among the spurs is an English spur from Bosworth Field; its wearer evidently caught his heel in the bole of a tree and the spur brought him down. Another famous battlefield has yielded something to this amazing collection—Agincourt, from which has come a sword made at Dreux, with gold ornament and a coat-of-arms on its hilt.

The museum has been the scene of some valuable loan exhibitions, the most attractive having been one illustrating Elizabethan England and another the Art of the Theatre. Eastbury House has indeed come again into its own, a treasure house of great dignity, worthy of the fine town of Barking.

Such is Barking old, with all its wonder of the past; what of Barking new, with all its wonder of the present? It has come to stand for great things in the life of the greatest city in the world, for it has one of our greatest power houses for electricity, and on the other side of Barking Creek is the main outfall of North London's drainage, 28 acres of brick-walled reservoirs and tanks, looking like some great work of the Roman Empire, built by the engineer who laid out the Thames Embankment. In these great tanks takes place the chemical purification of all this drainage, the water being pumped into the Thames and the rest shipped on vessels which are taken out to sea, where it is thrown overboard. The concrete supporting the floor of the reservoir is 20 feet thick and the reservoir can contain over forty million gallons at one time.

The Barking Power House, standing among the wastes of the river estuary, gaunt emblem of the energy driving the wheels of the 20th century, has the two biggest transformers in the world and the two biggest turbo-generators in England. These works are one of the causes of the great growth of Barking's population, which has risen from 14,000 a hundred years ago to about 80,000. Side by side on the Longbridge Road are two open spaces the town has provided for all these people, a 76-acre park and a swimming pool 165 feet long, holding over half-a-million gallons of water.

The Saint of the Miserables

THE name of Elizabeth Fry (who lived here and lies here) endures for ever with Florence Nightingale's; she is the saint of the prisons.

Her clarion call for mercy and justice to the miserable people in the prisons of her day rang through England and through Europe. Prisons were then sinks of suffering and iniquity, in which plague came as a great deliverance from anguish. Men and women, innocent and guilty, were herded like cattle in filthy dens; even girls and little children perished of disease in these noisome places.

Into this world of misery and shame Elizabeth Fry came as an angel from Heaven. She was an eldest child in the old Quaker family of John Gurney, the banker of Norwich, and she had been moved as a girl by the preaching of the Gospel. She married Joseph Fry when she was only twenty, and the fact that he did not share her great-heartedness made her all the more determined to give herself to some great cause.

She began preaching, and it is recorded that her beautiful voice melted the hardest men. Even as a child she had visited a prison with her father, and when she was 33 she happened to hear of the state of things at Newgate, where about 300 women and children were crowded into two wards and two cells. They had nothing to do. They had neither nightclothes nor bedclothes. They ate and slept, cooked and washed, in the same foul space. Even the Governor of Newgate was afraid to trust himself alone in this place, but Elizabeth Fry went into it, and her presence had a miraculous effect on these unhappy people.

She roused Parliament and persuaded it to appoint a committee to go into all this. She found work for prisoners set free. She exposed the exploiters and oppressors of these prisoners, and she went into prisons all over the land improving their conditions. She made it possible for public men to think of reforms such as had never occurred to Parliament or to public men; it was her trumpet that woke up the nation to one of the greatest horrors existing within it. Sydney Smith, who laughed too much, declared that the sight of Elizabeth Fry among these people moved him to tears—they clung to the hem of her garment, he said, and worshipped her as the only being who had ever loved, taught, or noticed them, or spoken to them of God.

She carried her work to the Continent, and its influence spread through Europe. She met rulers and princes; it was nothing to her whether she was entertaining the King of Prussia or having tea with a cobbler. She gave her life to miserable people anywhere, and it made no difference to her when her husband became bankrupt and found himself in poverty. She carried on, and she went about doing good until she died at 65 and was laid in this little burial ground of the Friends.

The Biggest Family in the World

BARKINGSIDE. On the border of Hainault Forest, and now part of Ilford, it is a big district with a church about a century old. By the gate we noticed a gravestone carved with a woman kneeling at an altar under the trees, and within the church is a memorial to an officer killed by Arabs in the Egyptian War. He was brought home and laid in St Paul's.

But this is Dr Barnardo's village, and it is his church in the lovely park that will attract the pilgrim. The Children's Church it is called, with room for a thousand girls, and its pinnacled tower is the guardian of their cottage homes scattered about the grounds. Here are fountains, dovecots, and old trees; fields for games; and workshops where they are trained to be good workers and good citizens. And here, under a lovely memorial designed by Sir George Frampton, lie the ashes of the founder. His portrait is on the pedestal of a mother and child, and three children are seated below. The monument is as simple and appealing as the man himself, and on it is this proud statement of his faith:

I hope to die as I have lived, in the humble but assured faith of Jesus Christ as my Saviour, my Master, and my King.

More than a hundred thousand homeless children have been snatched from the streets and given hope and life in Barnardo's Homes, perhaps the best known philanthropy within the British Empire. We must count Thomas John Barnardo among the men who shaped the social structure of society in the progressive 19th century. He was to be a missionary in China until he took Lord Shaftesbury down to our own East End one night, and Lord Shaftesbury said to him that perhaps his duty was not to the Chinese but to these children at home.

If he did not invent kindness to children, at least he was the first great champion of children who were homeless.

A homeless child before Dr Barnardo's day got his living as a

26

wild animal does, hunting and fighting for it, and often stealing it. Every policeman was his enemy, and he could be brought before a magistrate for sleeping in the streets. Yet he had nowhere else to sleep. Barnardo found eleven boys sleeping on an iron roof. It was a bitter cold night, and they wore wretched rags and no under-clothes. He found 70 street arabs sleeping under a tarpaulin. In doorways and empty barrels everywhere slept the most unhappy children in London.

Once Sir John Gorst visited an industrial school and saw among big brutal-looking lads a pretty baby of six. He asked what the child had done to be sent there, and learned that a policeman had caught the little one sleeping out under Covent Garden arches, and a magistrate had committed him to an industrial home for ten years. At the end of the ten years Sir John inquired for him, and afterwards wrote: "What do you think he has learned in that school? He has learned to darn stockings, and the darning of stockings is the only technical attribute which this boy has there attained! Under Dr Barnardo's care he would have been taught a trade and put in the way of becoming a prosperous man."

In 1894 a Departmental Committee was appointed to inquire into the case of Poor Law children. After two years the committee made recommendations of reform, and the chairman added that most of the reforms had already been put into practice by Dr Barnardo. Dr Barnardo's Homes were a century ahead of State institutions.

This wonderful man who went to the rescue of destitute childhood was pronounced dead by two doctors when he was two years old. *It was the undertaker who found that there was still a flicker of life!*

The delicate baby grew into a quick-tempered boy who was often in trouble at school, but before he was 17 he grew to feel that he must give his life to the service of others.

While he was at the London Hospital, training so that he might be a medical missionary, he did some work in Ragged Schools. Learning from the stories of the homeless boys that 85 per cent of them were reduced to misery through drink, the young student went boldly preaching temperance into the vilest parts of the East End. He was assaulted; his hat was often knocked into the gutter, his spectacles smashed, his clothes torn, and once two ribs were broken. Once when a band of roughs meant to give him a thrashing they were stopped by a prize-fighter who recognised the young preacher as one of the doctors who volunteered to nurse cholera when the scourge was terrifying the East End.

Dr Barnardo began by paying a working-man to house the first homeless boy he found; then he hired a donkey stable for half-a-crown a week to shelter more, and in a few years he had great village homes packed with children. He had once told a little boy there was no room in the Home for a few days, and a night or two afterwards the child was found dead in an alley. After that Barnardo made the famous declaration, *No destitute child ever refused admission.* In order to keep his vow he had to run into debt, and when he died the debt was £250,000, but it was wiped out as a tribute from a grateful country.

Dr Barnardo, founding his Home when he was still studying for his degree, continued to work like a slave all his life, seldom going to bed before three in the morning, and it is not to be wondered at that he wore his heart out at 60. "O Syrie," he said to his wife, "my head feels so heavy," and, dropping it on her breast, he died.

He had rescued 60,000 children. He had helped to make a new world. The whole country mourned for him, and volunteers came forward to carry on his mighty work. But during his life he had had to face scandal and lawsuits, and to battle against tremendous cares. Only a man of exceptional courage and indomitable will could have won his battle; only a man of extraordinary ability could have organised the Homes as he did. And only a saint could have loved loveless children so well that he could say "I have never seen an ugly child."

The Prison of St Paul's

BARLING. A very old place on a creek at the mouth of the Roche, its church belongs to St Paul's Cathedral, given to it by Edward the Confessor. The bishops had a prison in this remote corner of England, and 15 feet of rubble wall on Jail Farm is said to have been part of it. The fields are flat and open, and in one stands a wooden mill, its sailless cap like a dingy sunbonnet on a little Dutch lady. Not far away is the massive medieval tower with a slender shingle spire. We come into the church by a modern doorway set in a Norman arch; the other old doorway has been blocked up but still keeps two quaint heads five or six centuries old. The Jacobean pulpit has a great sounding-board, and among the things that are treasured here are ancient pewter plates, a 14th century coffin lid, and fragments of alabaster figures from a medieval reredos with traces of colour still on them.

The Ancient Door

BARNSTON. Up the hill and past some lovely white poplars we come to its church and hall, the one so small that it is not 20 feet wide, the other Elizabethan with fine windows, a central chimney with diagonal shafts, and in front a most noble elm towering up 100 feet. The church has a Norman nave, a Norman chancel rebuilt by the 13th century men, and a Norman doorway containing an ancient door with medieval hinges. One of the original narrow windows still lights up an old choir gallery, and outside other windows are quaint 15th century heads. From the 17th century the village has an oak chest, a carved communion table, and a tiny poor-box with many locks. Moulded timbers 500 years old rise from the nave to support a turret with a weathervane. A monument with three bright shields reminds us of Robert Scott, who was Dean of Rochester and came to lie here in 1620; and there is a family window to the Livermores of last century, a tribute to 15 of them, from little Martha who died in 1827 to an old lady who died in 1893. Another window has a few coloured bits from the 14th century among its modern glass. But the treasure of Barnston is its ancient piscina, the earliest double one known. It was made about 1200, and looks like a piece cut from a beautiful interlaced arcade.

BASILDON. It has a hill with fine views everywhere, and its church looks down from it, the tower capped by a little pyramid from which springs a vane with the initials of the man who made it, and the date: F. A. 1702. The doorway and the nave are 600 years old; the red brick chancel was made new in Queen Elizabeth's day. There are quaint carvings on the spandrels of the beams, showing a bear holding a ragged staff, and a dragon with a barbed tongue.

BEAUCHAMP RODING. Quiet and remote it lies, with belts of tall trees behind its thatched cottages. The 14th century church is in the middle of the meadows, its 15th century tower seen from afar. For 500 years two corbels have been a source of wonder to children here, one a beast protruding its ugly tongue, the other a long-winged angel whose head has been ruthlessly cut away. There is a stone panel of the scene in Gethsemane.

A Man of High Distinction

BEAUMONT-WITH-MOZE. It is set on a hill rising from a creek between Walton and Harwich, and a lane brings us to a fine little group of long ago—the red-tiled barns, the timbered house with charming Dutch gables, and the little church with the bellcot guarded by four angels. The chancel walls, a doorway, and a buttress or two, are 600 years old; the altar and the altar rails are 18th century. From the hill on which this small church stands is a splendid view seaward of the salt marshes worked in Norman days, and we may think that from those days till now no braver man has come this way than one who sleeps here.

He was Lord Byng, who died in 1935 one of the heroes of our race, as famous in the Empire as in the Motherland. He it was who led the Canadians to victory in the Great War, and his name will be for ever associated with Vimy Ridge. He had a great share in the final victory in France, and played his part in the years after the war as Governor-General of Canada and as Chief Commissioner of Police. He reorganised the London Police Force and suppressed many evils in the social life of the Metropolis.

One little tale we heard of him in this village where he sleeps and where he used sometimes to worship. During the war he was walking alone down a road which was being shelled when he found a sergeant treating a horse with great cruelty. Lord Byng was wearing a raincoat, and was without the braided cap which would have advertised him as a Brass Hat. He did not want deference just then; he wanted to see things from a subordinate's point of view. When he spoke to the sergeant about his ill-usage of the horse the man said that the brute would not come along. Lord Byng replied that the horse was terrified of the shells. "You get it down the road yourself," said the angry sergeant.

Lord Byng loved horses. He calmed this one and made it feel, in the magical way some men have, that it was safe with him, and then he led it down the road. But his care for the ill-used horse did not end when he handed it over, trembling and foam-flecked, at the end of the road, for he saw that the brutal sergeant was removed to an infantry unit where he would have nothing to do with animals.

BELCHAMP OTTEN. Seven centuries have each brought something new to its little church, which is guarded at the gate by a great walnut tree. The nave is 12th century, the chancel 13th, the porch and the chancel arch 14th, the font with its battlemented rim 15th, the little panelled pulpit 16th or 17th, the altar rails and the small gallery-pew 18th. So has the wheel of time turned within these ancient walls; and as if to surprise us still more there is a modern belfry resting on a 15th century cross-beam supported by two 17th century posts. The Norman south doorway is fine with zigzags and spirally fluted columns; and in several windows are interesting fragments of medieval glass, showing chiefly tabernacle work.

It is only a very small village, but it is rich in houses and farms from Stuart England, some timber-framed and some with old panelling.

The Man Who Inspired Shakespeare

BELCHAMP ST PAUL. It is St Paul because Athelstan, first King of All England, gave it to St Paul's Cathedral a thousand years ago, and it is interesting because it was the home of a man to whom Shakespeare must always have been grateful—Arthur Golding. There are pleasant houses round the green, 17th century farms and a 15th century church among the trees. There is also still left a wing of the house in which the Goldings lived, Paul's Hall. We see a brass portrait of William Golding at prayer in his armour in the church; he died in 1591 and has round him his six sons and four daughters.

It was Arthur Golding's translations from the classics that were of such great value to Shakespeare, who took other people's stories instead of troubling to invent his own. Arthur was born about 30 years before Shakespeare, but outlived him, and he brought up in this village a boy who was to be famous in the Elizabethan scene—the poet Earl of Oxford, Edward de Vere. Golding's own contributions to literature are his classical translations, his chief work being Ovid's Metamorphoses. It was from these translations that Shakespeare took the last speech he put into Prospero's mouth in the Tempest, so that he was using Arthur Golding's work in the last thing he wrote for the world.

Shakespeare's speech begins:

Ye elves of hills, brooks, standing lakes, and groves;

and Arthur Golding's speech begins:

Ye ayres and windes, ye elves of hilles, or brooks, or woods alone.

There is in the church a heraldic window in memory of this man who inspired Shakespeare, given by a direct descendant of his in New York.

The great sight in the church is its collection of ten old chancel stalls with tip-up seats finely carved in the 15th or 16th century. They have poppyheads with foliage, a king, and a monk holding a book. The altar table is Jacobean, an old font bowl is carved with a rose, and there is a monument to Edward Pemberton, who died in 1859 after preaching here nearly 50 years, his ancestors having preached from his pulpit in unbroken line for over a century.

BELCHAMP WALTER. Among its old houses are St Mary Hall, which was here in the 16th century and has something left of a house 100 years older; the 15th century Hopkins Farm; and Clark's Farm with a Tudor fireplace, carved bargeboards, and a gabled dormer window. Above the Belchamp Brook stands the church, its 15th century tower with a chequered parapet, the lofty nave 14th century, the chancel 13th. The roofs are 500 years old, and so is the south porch of timber and brick. The font has a round bowl with bands of ornament, the work of a Norman craftsman; and there is an arched recess beautifully carved with flowers and shields, probably the canopy of a tomb of 600 years ago and the entrance to a vanished chantry chapel.

Saxon and Norman

BERDEN. A very old village close to Hertfordshire, it has among its old houses Berden Hall, built in Queen Elizabeth's day and still keeping its wide staircase with a handsome balustrade. From Tudor days also comes Berden Priory, though it stands on the site of a 13th century priory and has two ancient coffin lids for doorsteps. Its well is covered by a 17th century building, and a big treadmill is still used to draw the water from the deep chalk below. In a square of elms stands the church, its medieval tower capped by a pyramid above the battlements. It is cross-shaped, the

Eastbury House of the 16th Century

St Margaret's Church   The Abbey Gateway

OLD BARKING

Walthamstow   Historic Salisbury Hall

Berden   The Elizabethan Hall

nave being the oldest part, with Norman work in its walls and Saxon masonry at the corners. The attractive chancel and transepts are 13th century, and on the chancel arch is the name of the man who built it, Geoffrey the Mason.

The windows and doorways have hardly changed for 600 years, and there are roofs that have been with them most of the time. A remarkable piscina of the same age is carved with the head of a woman wearing a wimple; and upside down in the east wall is part of a 13th century coffin lid set up as a bracket. Another ancient stone lid is in the north transept. There is much old woodwork about the church, some in the beautiful pulpit, some in the modern pews, and some on the back of the organist's seat. The traceried panels are probably from a medieval screen, and a door with six panels of linenfold came from Berden Hall. There are brasses of a 15th century man, William Turner, with his two wives, all rather squat figures on an altar tomb; and of Thomas Thompson of Shakespeare's day, with his wife and 13 children. High in the chancel is a tablet with the arms of an Elizabethan haberdasher, Thomas Aldersaie, founder of a school in his Cheshire village of Bunbury.

He Tried Sir Thomas More

BERECHURCH. It has what it still calls a maypole green (without the maypole) to remind it of the gaieties of days gone by, traces of a Roman road recalling days when merchants came this way to Colchester, and a fine church made new at the end of the 15th century. Its tower has a 14th century doorway and, still swinging in it, a door made up of linenfold and traceried panels by a Tudor craftsman. The font is 16th century. The magnificent hammerbeam roof of the Audley Chapel is richly carved with heads and flowers, with the arms of the Audleys below the wall-posts. The chapel was established in the days of Thomas Audley, who founded the family fortunes. He was town clerk of Colchester and rose to be Henry the Eighth's Lord Chancellor and to preside at the trial of Sir Thomas More. He took Berechurch Hall from St John's Priory at Colchester when the King and Thomas Cromwell broke up the monasteries. There is a splendid monument of Civil War days with Sir Henry Audley lying in armour in black and white marble, his five children kneeling.

D   33

The Tragedy of the Mayflower Pilgrims

BILLERICAY. It has quaint old buildings and tragic memories; the thread of English history runs through it. In a neighbouring wood the followers of Jack Straw were caught and massacred on their way home in the great Peasants Rebellion, a tragic chapter for a village; but it is the human tragedy of a little group of people who died for their faith that is so poignant here.

To walk down the High Street is like walking through 400 years. The village grew up round a chapel attached to Great Burstead, but it has left Great Burstead far behind, though its old folk are still buried with their ancestors in the shadow of that splendid church. Billericay's church is 18th century, with galleries all round, but it has a medieval brick tower with a crow-stepped parapet and pinnacles, and its bell has been ringing 600 years. Behind the church is a row of 16th and 17th century cottages, and in front of it is the Chantry House with timbers that must have been growing when the Conqueror came, for the house was built in 1510. One of the cottages has a medieval barn built with upright logs. In Chapel Street is a chapel founded in 1672, and its graveyard faces Mayflower Hall, which has a tablet commemorating a gallant company of village heroes, Christopher Martin and his wife Marie, her brother-in-law Solomon Prower, and their servant John Langerman. They sailed in the Mayflower on the most historic voyage of the modern world. There is still here for us to see something of the mill in which they ground the flour for provisioning this famous ship.

Christopher Martin was a boy on these hills in the days of Queen Elizabeth, when men were free to believe in God and worship Him in any way they pleased. The village had its bitter memories of Mary Tudor and her reign of terror, and old Widow Watts would tell little Christopher how her husband died at Chelmsford rather than deny his faith, and how her boys were willing to be burned with their father. Then there was the story of the three young girls of Billericay, Elizabeth Thackwell, Margaret Ellis, and Joan Hornes, who were burned at Smithfield one bright May morning for being Protestants. Joan had appeared before the Bishop of London and told him to his face that she began to learn the faith at eleven years old, and that she would continue in it, God helping her. Then, like another Joan a hundred years and more before her, she walked into the fire.

Christopher Martin grew up when these stories were being told in the village, and in time he married the Widow Prower at the altar of Great Burstead church. They joined a church in Chelmsford and in course of time crossed over to Holland and joined William Brewster and his friends at Leyden, where John Robinson was their minister. But there was ever the fear of a Dutch war with Spain, and at last their grim poverty, the temptations before their children, and their growing desire to spread the gospel in distant lands, stirred a spirit of unrest among them, and they set longing eyes towards America, the new-found world.

In the beginning of 1619 the little Dutch colony sent Christopher Martin and two others to England to arrange for the voyage across the Atlantic, and they came to the Thames, chartered the Mayflower, and set to work to provision her. One summer's evening in 1620 Christopher and Marie Martin, Solomon Prower, and John Langerman, walked for the last time down the hill at Billericay to join the Mayflower at Leigh. Christopher was the treasurer, and one of the most trusted of this devoted band, but, alas for the tragedy of human courage, neither he nor his wife, nor any of the Billericay people, survived to leave their names in the new world, for every one of them perished in the terrible sickness which slew one-third of the Mayflower's pilgrims in the first winter, spent on board the ship, lying off the coast where now stands the Massachusetts town of Plymouth.

The Lost Shrine

BIRCH. Its ancient shrine, shaded by trees near the hall, has been in ruins for three centuries. It is a mere shell and a broken tower, full of years and melancholy. Perhaps the herons know it well, coming over from a score of nests at Chest Wood. The big chancel is 600 years old, and so is the broken tower, though its upper brickwork is Tudor. The nave was built by the Normans, who, here as elsewhere, made good use of the Roman bricks so plentiful round Colchester. Here they are, in the pilasters, at the corners of the walls, and in the doorway. A 19th century church stands among trees by the green, and has nothing ancient; but it has a bright east window of the shepherds at Bethlehem, attractive modern carving of angels and lions and foliage on the desks, and panelling in classic style behind the altar. On the wall are stone flags in memory of an officer who died in a massacre at Cawnpore; and there are memorials to the Round family whose home stands in a fine park with a lake.

Khaki on the Brass

BIRCHANGER. Very impressive are the trees at the great house, a splendid clump of eight elms in a field, a lovely larch in the churchyard, and a superb cedar of Lebanon, 18 feet round the trunk. Birchanger Place has also a dovecot with plaster nests still on its walls. The church has lost the old round tower which would have made it one of a select little company of seven in Essex; but it has kept its Norman nave with two doorways, each with a tympanum, one carved with a horse. The chancel is a century younger, with four small lancet windows. We come in through one of the Norman doorways to see a 15th century font, seven benches as old, and a modern brass, interesting as being one of the first pictures of a soldier's khaki uniform on a memorial. It is to Jack Watney, a lad of 19 who fell in South Africa in 1901, and shows a figure in khaki in front of a machine-gun. The gravestone of a rector tells a moving little story of Advent Sunday in 1877. Walter Hatch had taken as his text the words "Come ye, and let us walk in the light of the Lord"; and only a few minutes later "God took him."

The Woman Died

BIRDBROOK. Some of its old houses have been here about 500 years with overhanging storeys resting on curved brackets. The church has something much older still, for in its walls are Roman tiles used by the 13th century builders. There are three striking lancet windows at the east, with stone heads keeping watch outside, and on the tracery of a 14th century window of the chancel is scratched the name of Thomas Cersey in ancient lettering. The lofty roof of the nave is 500 years old, and there is woodwork of the same time in the choir-stalls. The graceful altar rails are 18th century. In the sanctuary is a medieval coffin lid, and by the altar is something we have not seen before by any altar—a fireplace.

On a stone in the tower is recorded the remarkable experience of Martha Blewit who died in 1681 at the Swan Inn, which is still in the village. She married nine husbands, but the ninth outlived her, whereupon the parson of Birdbrook chose as his text at her funeral the words, "Last of all the woman died also." This same stone also records that in the next century Robert Hogan married seven wives, so that there were between these two people 16 marriages. A less exciting monument is to the antiquarian Thomas Walford, who went about England a hundred years ago and wrote a book called The Scientific Tourist.

The Belfry Timbers

BLACKMORE. Come to Jericho, for there is much to see. It is a house that has been made new, but stands on the foundations of one where Henry the Eighth often came. "He has gone to Jericho" his courtiers would say. A charming place is Blackmore, with cottages probably old enough for Henry to have seen, and fragments of a priory pulled down at his command. It was founded in 1152, but a few stones in the garden of Jericho House and parts of the church are all that is left of it. The west end of the church is Norman, with its doorway and the windows above, but it is concealed by a great timber belfry, one of the biggest and most remarkable of its kind in Essex. Built in the 15th century, it goes up in three stages to a shingled spire, rather like a pagoda. It has a west window of its own, with a wooden frame and tracery; and, remarkable as it all looks outside, it is more impressive still within, where the massive beams illustrate the masterly way the old craftsman built for all time. There is a porch which has kept some of its ancient woodwork, and in the aisle roof, looking towards the village, are attractive gables of the 17th century. In the nave medieval arcades join on to the Norman walls, and above, in a modern roof, are bosses that were here when Chaucer was writing his Canterbury Tales. Scattered about the walls are many stones and bits of carving from the Norman builders. The font is more than 500 years old, and there is a panel of 18th century glass showing the martyrdom of St Laurence. A medieval brass portrait shows a man very prim in his fur-trimmed gown; and on an altar tomb patched with brick lie Thomas Smyth and his wife from Elizabethan England.

In the churchyard sleep two Twogoods from Queen Anne's time, each with a skull and crossbones on his grave. A quaint inscription on another gravestone tells of Simon Lynch, who found rest here in 1660, after being much persecuted for fearing God and the King.

What John Ray Did

BLACK NOTLEY. It lies on the road running down the valley of the River Brain, and has quaint cottages, a little Norman church, and a 15th century hall with a barn of five bays. The church is curious for having neither tower nor chancel arch. The thick walls are pierced with the doorways, and there are great posts in the nave which support the bell-turret, with its shingled pyramid roof and a tiny spire. The most remarkable possession the church has is the ornamental ironwork on the door in the north porch; it is among the rarest old ironwork in this country, having been worked by Norman craftsmen. Soon after this door was made Walter de Wydenal was the parson here, and a marble gravestone under the belfry records his burial in Norman French. He may have used this dug-out chest, and may have seen the men at work on the curious oak frame of the sedilia. The most remarkable woodwork in Black Notley, however, is at Stanton's, a farm a mile away. The house has a 600-year-old hall with moulded capitals on its timber framework. The hall has been divided into two storeys and a 16th century chimney inserted, but the roof remains as it was in the 14th century.

There lies in the churchyard here, under a notable tomb with an obelisk and shields, a village boy who came back to his birthplace to die. He was the village blacksmith's son, John Ray, and was born in 1628. His father was able to send him to Braintree School and then to Cambridge, where John became lecturer on Greek and mathematics, and, taking orders, delivered sermons and discourses forming the basis of books which later established his reputation as a philosopher.

A born naturalist, he explored England, Scotland, and Wales, carefully describing and cataloguing his collections. Driven out of the University by religious difficulties, he visited the Continent with pupils, and renewed there the Nature studies begun at home. With Francis Willoughby, his most famous pupil, he published the results of their discoveries as to the rise and fall of sap in trees. Alone he worked out a system of classification in Nature which, preceding the more perfect system of Linnaeus, led Cuvier to say that Ray had laid the foundations of the science of zoology.

He was elected to the Royal Society and for many years announced his discoveries in the form of Communications to that famous body. His interests were wide, embracing the study of rare words and phrases surviving in our language: observations on mushrooms, maize, musk-scented insects, spiders, the air-bladder of fishes, the anatomy of the porpoise. His observations were clear and exact, and revealed for the first time many of the marvellous adaptations by which life maintains itself in the plant and animal kingdoms.

Later generations built on his foundations. From his data his successors proceeded to new discoveries, and to deductions which would have startled this wonderful pioneer. He spent the last 26 years of his life in Essex, active to the last as student and teacher, and, dying in 1705, he sleeps within hail of the spot where he was born.

BOBBINGWORTH. Thus it is written on the map, but Bovinger it appears on the peace memorial, and thus its people speak of it. It has a small green and much natural loveliness. Round the walls of the church is 16th century panelling, and the clerk's desk has more elaborate woodwork of the period. The pulpit is enriched with Jacobean carving. A big 17th century chest has four slots for coins. After having been used as a flower bowl in Netteswell for 100 years, the 15th century font was recognised as having come from some church and placed in the churchyard of Little Parndon. Here the rector of Bobbingworth was walking one day and suspected that it had been removed from the old pedestal on which a 19th century font stood. This proved to be the case and the old bowl was brought home to Bobbingworth.

The Idea That Made a Town

BOCKING. It has kept much of its ancient beauty and has not sold its soul to industry, but it shares with its neighbour Braintree the prosperity of the great industry in rayon. Here has been developed one of the great ideas of our time, artificial silk, and the fine factory is side by side with the church, old and new together. Bocking was a village when Samuel Courtauld began his work at the beginning of last century; little did he dream that the end of it would be, a hundred years later, the wizardry of transmuting trees into trousseaus.

The Courtaulds were Huguenot refugees driven from France to England in the 17th century. They produced, a hundred years after that, an industrious idealist who was successively silk-weaver, paper-maker, and miller in Kent and Essex, then going to America to die in the attempt to found a perfect community. It was his son Samuel who started his silk factory here. Samuel's brother George returned from America to join the little firm, which linked the manufacture of crepe to the silk business, reached almost worldwide fame, and built up the nucleus of the financial resources from which immense developments were to spring. Courtauld succeeded Courtauld.

Synthetic chemists had long dreamed of copying the silkworm whose caterpillar, eating mulberry leaves, transforms the result into a gummy fluid which, on entering the air by way of its spinnerets, instantly becomes silk. The first man to rival the silkworm was actually Sir Joseph Swan, who patented a process for the conversion of cotton into a sort of artificial silk to serve as the filament of his electric lamp, in the invention of which he beat the famous Edison; and a Frenchman took up the idea and established factories for the production of synthetic yarn by treating cellulose with acid. There were other efforts towards the same end, but the master process was found in that evolved, after 12 years of research, by two English chemists who sold the rights to Courtaulds. Today the rayon process marches with the accuracy and precision of a familiar experiment in a chemist's laboratory. They order their materials, treat them according to formula, and produce silks and fabrics with unerring accuracy. In a Canadian forest in any year of peace are certain spruce trees, 35 years old, which a year hence will be issuing from this factory ready to dress a bride from head to foot and to play a part in furnishing her home.

Such is the wonderful idea which has changed this place from an old-world village to a modern town. It has still a host of old houses, with overhanging gables everywhere. Standing out among them are the three gables of the old Woolpack Inn, built in Elizabethan times with rich beams carved with grotesques and foliage. Close by is Wentworth House, with a 17th century canopy finely carved over the doorway; and on the front of one of the inns there is a carving of a man with a wreath of fruit on his head. At Church End is Doreward's Hall, its splendid Tudor wing impressive with chequered buttresses and magnificent windows. There are farms and cottages that have been here 300 years and more. There is an old post windmill with sails 60 feet long, preserved for ever in a playground for the children; and there is the Deanery, with its 17th century gable and chimneys, so-called because the parson here has the title of dean, the living being what is called a Peculiar, under the authority of the Archbishop of Canterbury. Beside the Deanery is an old barn and a dovecot with 135 nests of lath and plaster, the dovecot interesting because it was built during the residence here of John Gauden, the bishop who imposed a forgery on the world. He created intense interest in a book which was attributed to Charles Stuart—the Eikon Basilike, which pretended to be an account written by the king of his long sufferings, but was actually written by Bishop Gauden. It is believed that a copy was bought the day after the execution, and the volume ran through about 50 editions, calling forth a reply in Milton's Iconoclastes. Gauden, a Bury St Edmunds schoolboy, left a charity to Bocking in memory of his years at the Deanery.

The church, a magnificent 15th century structure, is dwarfed by the factory, which almost touches the Tudor wall round the church-yard; the iron gates on the south side are a peace memorial. The tower is splendid, with pinnacles and double buttresses, niches with carved heads, and rich stone panelling round the base. The fine embattled porch shelters a door covered with ironwork of great beauty, the craftsmanship of a clever smith 700 years ago. The interior is worthy of the impressive exterior, having a remarkable set of old roofs, those of the nave and aisles being 16th century and those in the chancel and the chapels a little older. The bosses show leaves and shields and other carvings. The south chapel has a window with beautiful 14th century tracery, and the net pattern of that period is also seen in the east window, where each space has an angel in modern glass. The lights below are resplendent with portraits of saints and martyrs, among them St Augustine, balanced with a splendid figure of Charles Stuart. Another beautiful window is the gift of two American citizens, Francis and James Goodwin, whose ancestors lived in Bocking. The window shows the Annunciation, the Nativity, and the Epiphany, with Bertha, Ethelburga, and other English saints in panels above and below. There are two 17th century chairs elaborately carved, a handsome modern screen, and a Tudor funeral helmet; and on a windowshelf when we called was a clock-hand, saying: "From 1731 to 1859 from Bocking tower I told the hour." It had been turning for more than a million hours when it was taken down.

Peeping from under the organ are John Doreward (in the armour worn at Agincourt) and his wife in a horned headdress. Another brass shows Oswald Fitch of Shakespeare's time in his long cloak and ruff, and there is a monument of 1624 with a beautiful figure of Grisell Moore kneeling between fine columns.

Most of the church as we see it would be familiar to the three courageous Bocking people who perished for their faith in the cruel reign of Mary Tudor: Catherine Hut and Richard Spurge, murdered in the name of God at Smithfield in 1556, and William Purcas, who was burned at Colchester in 1557.

Bluebeard's Castle

BOREHAM. It is famous for a palace built by Henry the Eighth, still a great house, approached through a mile of limes. One of the finest homes in Essex, New Hall stands nearly 90 yards wide with two projecting wings and six bays. The splendour of the windows amazes us as we approach, and the spectacle of this wonderful façade brings up in the mind a picture of the pageantry of the days in which it came into being. It was part of the estate seized by the king from the father of Anne Boleyn after her head had fallen on Tower Hill, but most of the structure as we see it was built by Thomas Radcliffe, Earl of Sussex, to whom the estate was given by Queen Elizabeth. There is a eulogy to her under the stone sundial on the parapet, above the great doorway flanked by pilasters and decorated with stars and porcupines.

On a painted stone panel are the arms of Henry the Eighth supported by a greyhound and a dragon, and the stone has an inscription telling us that Henry built this magnificent work. One of his gateways with two fine arches is still here. New Hall is now a convent, having been converted into a home for refugees from

France in the 18th century, but into its history come many famous names. George Villiers, Duke of Buckingham, bought it for £30,000 and Oliver Cromwell for next-to-nothing, but Oliver liked it not and changed it for Hampton Court. The house thus passed to General Monk, who might have been King of England but brought back the Stuarts instead; having made the great sacrifice he lived here in splendour with his wife, the farrier's daughter.

Here, long before their days, Henry had celebrated the Feast of St George and Merrie England, and here his two daughters lived after him. Here Mary Tudor entertained Lady Jane Grey, whose death warrant she was to sign a few years later, and here Elizabeth spent five days as queen.

There is an old house called Porters built 500 years ago, two 16th century farms, and the 18th century Boreham House facing a long lake flanked by a double row of elms.

The church is mainly 13th and 14th century. It has a fine central tower standing much as the Normans left it, with Roman tiles framing their small windows, but with a 17th century parapet. The arch facing the nave shows the Roman tiles mixed with stones which the Normans used in their arch, and below them is a 14th century arch. In the thickness of the walls of one corner of the tower runs a spiral stairway to the belfry. We come into the church through a porch with much medieval timber in its walls, the porch carried on to the gate as a shelter for the congregation.

The church is rich in fine possessions. In the Sussex Chapel lie three bearded Earls of Sussex in elaborate armour, the first a favourite courtier of Henry the Eighth, the second a Chief Justice under Mary Tudor, the third a patron of letters and a soldier. Their swords are broken and they have lost the metal chains once round their necks, but each one wears the garter, and at the feet of each is an ape in a quaint hat, while behind their cushioned heads are oxen wearing collars looking like crowns. There is a brass portrait of Alse Byng, an Elizabethan lady in a close-fitting cap and puffed sleeves kneeling with her family of six.

The font is 14th century, with panels of painted flowers in vases; there is medieval craftsmanship in a screen of six bays in the tower and a screen with twelve heads in the aisle; and also from medieval days comes the scratch dial on a corner of the south wall.

A gift of the manor by Queen Elizabeth to a worthy servant made Boreham the home and last resting-place of the Radcliffes, Earls of Sussex. The family rising to power during the Wars of the Roses, the head of the house was made Baron Fitzwalter. His son joined the rising of Perkin Warbeck, and was beheaded. The title was revived in favour of his son Robert who, present at the coronation of Henry the Eighth and afterwards at the Field of the Cloth of Gold, was created Earl of Sussex. He died Lord Chamberlain of England and was buried here.

The third earl, Thomas, was the crowning glory of the family, soldier, diplomatist, scholar, and friend of learning, whose second wife, Frances Sidney, aunt of Sir Philip, founded at Cambridge the Sidney Sussex College. His father having seen Henry crowned, Thomas saw him into the grave. From early manhood he was engaged in State affairs, seeking a French bride for Edward the Sixth and witnessing his will; and he played a leading part in bringing about the marriage of Mary Tudor with Philip of Spain.

He took part in the coronation of Queen Elizabeth, who made him Lord Lieutenant of Ireland, his duty now being to impose the Protestant faith on that country. With insufficient forces, and his difficulties aggravated by the enmity of the Earl of Leicester, he achieved practically nothing. Returning to England he played with skill and clemency a difficult part in suppressing the Northern Rebellion, and was entrusted with two missions concerning the projected marriage of Elizabeth.

Highly trusted by the Queen, who had made him Lord Chamberlain, he accompanied her on triumphal progresses, and in 1573 received from her the gift of Boreham and other manors. Dying in 1583, he was succeeded by his brother Henry, fourth earl, who in the course of troublous days in Ireland was imprisoned and almost brought to bankruptcy in the service of the Crown. As Governor of Portsmouth he was responsible for equipping ships to fight the Armada. He died in 1593, and sleeps here. The fifth earl inherited family debts incurred in State service, and appealed for a post which would enable him to die abroad in the service of the Queen rather than languish in poverty at home. Although impoverished, he won fame as a scholar and friend of learning. Chapman dedicated a sonnet to him, prefacing the translation of Homer which was later to inspire the immortal sonnet of Keats. Present at the inauguration of Charles Stuart as Prince of Wales, and at his coronation, he died in 1629, and rests here with his ancestors. The title passed to his cousin Edward, and expired with him 300 years ago.

Friend of Mary Tudor

BORLEY. Its people look across the Stour valley into Suffolk from the churchyard, which has some remarkable clipped yews, like umbrellas with round frills and huge round bases. The church tower, like the chancel and the porch, is Tudor, but the thick south wall of the nave may be 400 years older. There is a bell old enough to have rung for the defeat of the Armada, a 17th century doorway made of wood, a 15th century nave roof with embattled wall-plates, and a little bench with two poppyheads carved 500 years ago. In the chancel we see Magdala Southcote of 1598 kneeling at a desk, and in the nave is the great canopied tomb, 14 feet high, of Sir Edward Waldegrave and his wife Frances, who outlived him by 38 years. At her feet sits a squirrel with its paws to its mouth, and kneeling round the tomb are three sons and three daughters. The canopy rises on six Corinthian columns. Sir Edward was a Tudor Master of the Wardrobe. As an officer of Mary Tudor's household he was put in the Tower in King Edward's reign for refusing to prevent the princess from celebrating mass, but was set free on account of his health. On Mary's coming to the throne he continued to serve her but objected to her marriage with Philip of Spain, so that his feelings were overcome by a pension of 500 crowns. On the accession of Queen Elizabeth he was thrown into the Tower again for allowing mass to be said in his house; and in the Tower he died, being buried in the chapel.

In the Shade of the Elms

BOWERS GIFFORD. It is still growing about the road to Southend. From this road a long and shady lane runs down the hill to the marshy levels recovered from the Thames, bringing us to a Tudor church with a quaint stone tower, a wooden belfry, and a six-sided spire.

A few things remain from an earlier church: two bells of the 14th century, a piscina of the 15th, a font with a coloured cover of the 16th, and a magnificent lifesize brass said to represent Sir John

Gifford, who died about 1340. Though the head and a leg are missing, the costume and the armour are preserved and are unique, showing us what a knight wore when the first ball was fired from a cannon. It is the third oldest military brass in Essex, and valuable to artists as an important link in our knowledge of dress.

Behind the choir-stalls is a memorial to a lady buried in the shade of the elms. She was Flora Mary Campbell, who died in 1915, and this is how her friends described her:

Ever the seeker after truth, a lover of science and nature, wild beasts and trees of the forests, the sovereign birds of the air, the flowers of the field, the fishes of the sea, the constellations of the heavens, she has at last attained unto the open vision.

Twenty years ago the church was restored and beautified by Sir Duncan Campbell, who owned Earls Fee, the old manor of the De Veres. On a wall of the nave is a tablet placed by him to Sir John de Vere, 15th Earl of Oxford, who bore the crown at the coronation of Anne Boleyn and now lies at Castle Hedingham. Another tablet recalls Aubrey, the last of the famous De Vere family which came over with the Conqueror. He is described as the noblest subject in England, and indeed, as Englishmen loved to say, the noblest subject in Europe. He died in 1703 and the title was not revived until Mr Asquith chose it.

Cromwell's Friend

BOXTED. Its church has Roman bricks in the walls and traces of Norman work, especially in the tower, which the Normans began and the Tudors finished. The aisles and some attractive windows are 14th century, the porch has fine beams in its roof, and a neat little medieval font is enriched with flowers and shields. Most beautiful is the reredos, painted in our own time by Charles Webb. In bright colours enriched with gold it shows the Nativity, with charming angel-children kneeling at the manger, a lovely figure of the Risen Lord, and His burial. A monument carved with an angel and a skeleton tells of a Boxted lady who married a kinsman of Francis Bacon. He was Cromwell's friend and supporter, Nathaniel Bacon, who served on Cromwell's Council of State and wrote a remarkable book on the English Constitution. He was laid to rest at Coddenham, Suffolk, in the year Charles the Second came back. Another monument tells in Latin verse the virtues of Sir

Richard Blackmore, who wrote poetry when he was not prescribing medicine for King William or Queen Anne. He was probably better as a doctor than a poet, though his poem Creation was praised by Dr Johnson. Among the vicars of Boxted was Robert Ingram, who died the year before Trafalgar after preaching here for 52 years.

He Tried the King's Judges

BRADFIELD. The dormer windows of its thatched cottages have peeps of the River Stour as it pours itself into the sea. For 600 years and more a bell in the tower has been summoning the people of the cottages to the 13th century church, ringing out its merry message, "I am cock of this flock." The bell is centuries older than the tower, which was set up in the 16th century, its cheerful builders giving each of its four faces a row of seven jovial heads.

St George in brilliant enamel greets us as we come through the 14th century doorway, and a glowing transept window tells the story of the first Easter morning. The 18th century pulpit has earlier carving fixed on it. In the chancel is the portrait in brass of Joan Rysbye, shown in the grand dress she wore in the days of the Armada; and there is a brass tablet to Elizabeth Grimstone, who lived at the handsome moated house a mile away, Bradfield Hall. One of its wings is 400 years old. Here was born Sir Harbottle Grimstone, who tried the judges who tried the King. Born under Queen Elizabeth, he lived through the dramatic reigns of the Stuarts to within a few years of the flight of the last of them. In Parliament he stoutly championed popular rights, helped to frame the Grand Remonstrance to impeach Archbishop Laud, and to vindicate the privileges of the House when Charles sought to arrest the Five Members. He knelt to Charles, imploring him to make peace with his people, and when that failed he left the country after the execution of the king, remaining abroad for several years. Returning to Parliament, he was elected Speaker in 1660 and was sent to Holland to recall Charles the Second, to whom he delivered the official speech of welcome in Parliament. A kindly, hospitable man, charitable to the poor, and tolerant in religion, he sleeps in St Michael's Church, St Albans.

Last of His Race

BRADWELL. It is the Bradwell near Coggeshall, with lovely cottages and an ancient hollow elm, and with great attractions

47

in the church, notable among them the striking monuments to the Maxeys, who were stout-hearted followers of the king when most of Essex was against him. On a fine altar tomb we see kneeling figures of Sir Antony Maxey and his wife of Elizabeth's day, together with Sir Henry and his wife of a generation later. A handsome monument close by was set up by another Henry Maxey to his father and two brothers, all brave Royalists in the time of the Civil War. Of the father, Sir William, we read that he was a man of Joshua's resolution, who would gather his family round him by five in the morning that he might bless them and read from the Prayer Book.

A delightful inscription of our own century tells of Henry Brunwin, lord of the manor. He was the last of his race, and his people had been connected with Bradwell for 700 years. The first of them were perhaps here in time to celebrate the centenary of the church, which shows us by Roman bricks and a little window that it was first built by the Normans. The chancel was rebuilt about 1340, when flowers were carved on the tracery of the windows; and they were 14th century craftsmen who made the porch, a little gem with fine timberwork and 14 traceried openings. It shelters a studded door of about 1500.

Pictures on the walls and window-splays are 600 years old, some of them covering up paintings older still. Among them is a saint with staff and wallet, a cross with a banner, the lamb in a circle, and a picture of the Trinity in which Our Lord is a small figure with a dove on His head. He is also seen in glory between two angels.

The medieval screen has lost some of its tracery but has kept the panelling behind its vanished roodloft. There are traceried panels from another screen, a Tudor helmet hanging on the wall, two little alabaster cherubs with fragments of old carving, and sturdy posts supporting a turret built at the time of the Great Armada. Some good modern woodwork includes a priest's desk carved with hares. There are tiles that have been here 600 years. A lovely one, framed on the wall, shows a pelican feeding her young. The font came here in Norman England as a square bowl carved with small chevrons. Tudor craftsmen shaped the bowl again with eight sides and set it up on an elaborate brick base with a design of leaves. Later the Jacobean cover was added, leaving it as we see it all today.

48

Bradwell-on-Sea　　　　**The Little Saxon Church**

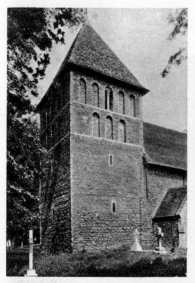

Corringham　　　Norman Tower　　**Little Bardfield**　　Saxon Tower

Clacton-on-Sea   The East Cliff

Southend-on-Sea   Clifftown Parade

The Old Walls by the North Sea

BRADWELL-ON-SEA. It is one of the forgotten wonders of our Motherland, with a story and a spectacle that must stir our hearts. We are here at the dawn of our history.

Here the Romans came and built a fort to keep the English back. They went away and the English came and built a church across the fort itself. The centuries passed, the Conqueror had had his day, the little church became a barn and was forgotten. The English builders set up their shrine about three miles away, 600 years ago, and from the 14th century till now its congregations have sung their praises and said their prayers within its walls.

Very old it has seemed to them, no doubt, as the generations and the centuries have gone by, and yet all the time there has been here this little consecrated barn built by the Saxons across the Roman fort, the citadel of God athwart the citadel of Caesar, one of the oldest surviving churches in England, far away in this forgotten corner of our land.

An enchanting little place, it has enjoyed its solitude for ages, a quiet pastoral life which even the Motor Age has not disturbed. It is true that the red brick tower of its 14th century church is only Georgian, but it is the newest thing we come to see. There are low plastered cottages, there is the brick cage which was the village lock-up with the whipping-post fixed to it, and there is a perfect mounting-block with an iron rod for the farmer's wife to take hold of as she mounted her horse to ride home from church. There is a timbered rectory, with one wing built before the Reformation and one to keep it company in the Adam style.

It is a captivating group that is gathered about the church, and in the church itself is a chancel arch with moulded capitals, a brass portrait of a Bradwell lady, Margaret Wyott, in the days of Henry the Eighth, and little faces carved in stone by a mason 600 years ago. There are, on the walls and on the font, men with their tongues out, grim men with set lips, and a priest to keep them company. It is all 600 years old, and yet how young it is for Bradwell!

Come away to the consecrated barn by a tiny cottage on the lonely peninsula, where the Blackwater River runs into the grey North Sea. It is an ancient solitude, haunt of rare birds, nothing but a lonely land until one day a traveller came more curious than most and noticed this old barn. He noticed its unusual height, the well-shaped stones, and the Roman bricks, the round window high up above the tower, which the farmer did not use. He noticed the high gables and the signs of arches at one end. He measured it and excavated round about, and found a porch on the west and an apse on the east; and there was no doubt at all that this traveller stood in the very church founded by Bishop Cedd 1300 years ago at what was then called Ithancester.

For all these centuries this little place had stood, drenched by the spray at high tides, its prayer and praise forgotten by the world, but not actually forgotten, let us believe, within these walls which echoed them so long ago and have stood here braving the storms of the North Sea, waiting for praise and prayer to come again. And they have come. The old barn is a church again, a service is held within its hallowed walls once every year, and it is one of the 4000 scheduled monuments of England that are never to come down.

There is nothing like it in all England, for it is unique as a Saxon building, 50 feet long, 22 feet wide, with walls over two feet thick rising 24 feet up to the eaves.

But let us think of the dramatic conquest of which this little building speaks, the thrilling irony of its site. When the great evangelist of the Saxons came, Bishop Cedd, he found here a Saxon community with their huts and barns, gathered about the derelict fort the Romans had built to keep the Saxons out.

Its walls were 12 feet thick, so jealous were the Romans of their little island. It was the Tilbury or the Sheerness of its time, and its great wall has been traced from one rounded corner to another rounded corner for a length of more than 500 feet, with two sides stretching seaward, one for 50 yards and one for 100. It formed a great quadrangle with two long lines parallel to the sea. The seaward line has been washed away by the waves, the sides running down to the sea are under the shore, the long inland wall can be traced exactly 522 feet. Only a fragment of this formidable work raises its head above the earth, a piece of wall and two bastions.

Thrilled by the arrival of a bishop in their midst, the Saxons set to work to build their church, and bravely they built it, for they set the church right across this 12-foot thick wall of the Romans, using the stones, red tiles, and pebbles lying about the ruined fort.

This is Bradwell. From this great wall the Roman Legions scanned the North Sea for the sea-rovers from the Elbe and the Schelde; it was their mighty refuge and defence. Now the sea covers their old home, the Roman Empire is no more, and the little church of the Saxons stands across the fort. Christianity has conquered.

We are all great travellers in these days, but who comes here? Few, very few; yet it is a sort of little Canterbury, and those who make this pilgrimage add a red-letter day to memory's calendar.

The Old World and the New

BRAINTREE. Its prosperity was founded on wool in the days of the Flemish weavers; today it hangs by a silken thread in Courtauld's giant factories. It was actually in Bocking that Courtaulds began a hundred years ago, but Braintree and Bocking are like neighbours growing into brothers, the Busy Bees of Essex. Their industries have sent out two names that are honourably famous beyond the borders of our land, for side by side with Courtaulds, makers of beautiful silks, are Crittalls, makers of beautiful windows.

The old world and the new keep company together, for in the narrow streets of Braintree are at least fifty buildings over three centuries old or more. It is delightful to walk among them, and delightful also to see the new development of this thriving town. The modern town hall in the market square, on which the town arms appear in rich colours, cost fifty thousand pounds and has a central bell tower and a dome with a bronze figure of Truth above it, the town's motto being "Hold to the Truth." Inside the town hall are panelled chambers with wall-paintings by Maurice Grieffen-hagen, an admirable series of local history subjects. Here also is a museum of Bygones, including a rare scold's bridle.

The Courtaulds have, of course, always been great benefactors of this town and its neighbour; among other things they have given are an Institute with a magnificent library, a fine hospital, and a delightful group of homes for nurses. The houses stand in a sunny space with a great fountain near them, the architectural scheme having been designed by Mr Vincent Harris, and the fountain having in its centre a figure of Youth by John Hodge.

Two Roman roads meet in the town, one coming from Colchester and one from Chelmsford, and Roman bricks helped to build the church on an ancient embankment. The nave and the chancel have Norman foundations but are mostly 13th century, like the tower to which a shingled spire was added in the 14th. On the walls outside are two surprising things, a washbasin and an inscription to a Tsar's physician. The basin was put here for the pilgrims crossing England in the 16th century; the Tsar's physician was Samuel Collins, a son of the rectory 300 years ago. In a faded gilt frame inside is another curiosity, a parchment roll of 1684 on which are written the names of 300 Braintree folk who died of the plague.

Miracle plays provided the money for widening the south aisle in the 15th century. At the same time the medieval vestry, with its curious head outside, was given its roof, and the little oak door was strengthened with ironwork. Woodcarvers of the 16th century fashioned the magnificent beams above the organ, with Michael and the Dragon on a boss, and the roof of the long chapel opposite, which has three older heraldic bosses over the doorway to a spiral stair. It led to the vanished roodloft and gives us a peep into the south aisle through a tiny window. This chapel was for years used as a school, and we noticed that the children had left their pencil scribblings on the arcade pillar. A beautiful modern screen fills one bay of the arcade, and on the wall is a modern brass portrait of Samuel Dale who doctored Braintree folk 200 years ago. He was noted as a botanist and was the friend of the better known naturalist John Ray. A modest tablet records that Bernard Scale, who died in 1852, was vicar for 57 years.

To Braintree belongs the story of the ironmonger's son Francis Crittall, who gave the world the admirable idea of steel windows. He was working in his father's shop when there came to him the vision which was to prove his key to fortune. His mother injured herself in struggling to raise a heavy wooden window frame, and Francis thought a lighter metal window frame would be much better. He started experimenting in a shed, and at 27 he had two lathes, a forge, shaping and screw-cutting machines, an emery wheel, a gas engine, and three workmen. The making of Crittall windows had begun, and the adventure was a great success. Business grew until Mr Crittall was rich enough to visit India, where he found a great new market for window frames which did not expand in tropical heat and could not be destroyed by white ants. He developed his works on model lines, and built a village for his people, with social halls and shops, and his own house among them.

He wrote a book on Fifty Years of Work and Play in which he told the beautiful story of how he fell in love with 17-year-old Ellen Carter and remained in love with her until their golden wedding day, and after that. All through their working lives they were together, and then Mrs Crittall passed away, and her husband went for a lonely cruise and came back to be laid in her grave. He was one of the backbones of the nation, the men who build up fine businesses and carry them on ungrudgingly whatever happens, sharing their prosperity with their people and seeking nothing mean.

It was a vicar of Braintree, one of the mystery men of the 16th century, who gave us our first English comedy. He was Nicholas Udall, headmaster of Eton in 1534 and vicar of Braintree in 1537. His comedy was called Ralph Roister Doister, and was in 5 acts divided into 27 scenes, with 12 characters. Udall's headmastership at Eton was cut short by his own misconduct, for which he was imprisoned. His second chance came with Braintree, for here his writings brought him the patronage of Catherine Parr, the lucky widow of Henry the Eighth. He was also befriended by Edward the Sixth, who made him a Prebend of Windsor, and finally he was employed by Mary Tudor to write dialogues for court festivities. It is said that as Princess Mary the queen had shared with Udall the labour of translating Erasmus. The last post held by Udall was the headmastership of Westminster School, which he lost when the school was amalgamated with the monastery. He survived the loss only by a month, and was laid to rest in St Margaret's Church.

The Immortal Airman and the Heroic Apprentice

BRENTWOOD. It has much of the old world still left, and its ancient school has memories of two immortal young Englishmen who gave their lives for England. Long famous as a coaching stage on the Roman road from London, Brentwood has a wide main street, fine old houses, gabled buildings from Tudor England, and attractive inns where there was much coming and going 200 years ago. One of the most interesting has a galleried courtyard with an overhanging upper storey and 500-year-old timbers. Another inn has an Elizabethan roof, and a room with a plaster ceiling panelled and enriched with birds and beasts and men in pleated skirts.

In a garden only a step from the street we come to what is left of Brentwood's old church, a chapel to Thomas Becket founded by one of the abbots of St Osyth. The lowest storey of its little tower is here, with some fragments of the nave, and the doorways suggest that the masonry still standing is 14th century work. There are two modern churches, one with a tall spire and at its entrance sculptures of Our Lord and the Evangelists, the Wise Virgins, and the martyrdom of Becket; the other (St George's) a 20th century memorial to an old vicar. It is a striking place and is not yet complete, designed by Mr Laurence King in the spirit of the new movement for making churches appealing to the new generation. It has a spacious sanctuary, processional aisles to the nave, and a lady chapel. Every seat has an unbroken view of the altar. The lighting is indirect and throws no shadows. One of the unusual features of St George's is an outdoor pulpit at the east end, facing the road; the pulpit has a canopy with a stone crucifix which can be automatically floodlit.

Brentwood is rightly proud of its public school, founded by Sir Anthony Browne in 1557. Its original charter was signed by Philip and Mary on a summer's day in that year, and the date 1568 is still over the door of the Big School, which remains from the ancient buildings. The fine group of modern buildings stretches from the London Road to Shenfield Common on the outskirts of Brentwood; they include a memorial hall built after the Great War, a spacious 19th century chapel extended in the 20th century, with three aisles, neat open rafters, dignified seats, and an attractive group of lancets in the east window.

Sir Anthony Browne, though he was Queen Mary's right-hand in the bitter persecution of the Protestants, founded his school to teach "virtue, learning, and manners," and it would thrill him with pride to know how well his school has fulfilled this high ideal.

It was from Brentwood School that there went out to join the RAF the young airman who wrote to his mother a farewell letter first published in The Times and afterwards in most of the newspapers of the English-speaking World. His name was kept secret, but everybody who read the letter of the unknown airman was deeply moved, and it was felt that it expressed nobly but with great simplicity the feeling of the nation at the time of the Deliverance of Dunkirk, where this young man fell. We are permitted to say that he was a scholar of Brentwood School, where his portrait (by Frank Salisbury) will hang for generations as an example of the character this school is making for our country.

We have no room to give the airman's letter, written before he set out on the raid from which he did not return, but in it he declared himself lucky to be the right age and fully trained to throw his weight into the scale for England. Those who serve England, he said, must expect nothing from her; we debase ourselves if we regard our country merely as a place in which to eat and sleep. He would have lived and died an Englishman and nothing else mattered. He had no fear of death and would have it no other way:

The universe is so vast and so ageless that the life of one man can only be justified by the measure of his sacrifice. We are sent to this world to acquire a personality and a character to take with us that can never be taken from us.

There is a marble obelisk on a green lawn at the cross-roads in memory of William Hunter, and tradition would have us believe that he was burned to death near the old elm in front of the school. He was a London apprentice in the days of Mary Tudor, and came to live with his father at Brentwood, where, finding a Bible lying on a desk, he learned to read it. They took him to Bishop Bonner for "meddling with the scriptures," and the bishop, liking him well, offered to make him a freeman in the City and give him £40 to set up a business if he would recant; but he said, "I thank you for your great offer; notwithstanding, my lord, I cannot find in my heart to turn from God for the love of the world." It was arranged that he should be burned, and on the day of the burning the sheriff's son came to this apprentice boy (who was 19) to bring him comfort, but could speak little for weeping. They brought him a letter from the queen promising him life if he would recant, but William rose and went to the stake, to which he was chained. He cried out, "Son of God shine upon me," and immediately the sun shone, and the people were much moved as he lifted up his hands in the flames.

A Ship for the Altar

BRIGHTLINGSEA. Almost entirely surrounded by the estuary of the Colne and its tributary creeks, it is a member of the Cinque Port of Sandwich, and its main business is still building boats. It is also a centre of the oyster fisheries.

Many narrow streets lead down to the quay from the broad street in which stand the modern church, an old timbered inn, and some quaint cottages. At high tide the quay is a lovely scene with trim yachts and sturdy smacks stretched seaward. In the High Street is Jacobes Hall, one of our oldest timbered buildings, the two steep-roofed wings of its banqueting hall with overhanging storeys.

The Beriffe family of shipping merchants bought the house from the Jacobes about 1400, and probably inserted the great beam across a fireplace in the hall, and the ceiling with its carved oak beams. In the angle between the west wing and the central block is a brick stair turret with a pyramid cap.

The old church stands on the hilltop a mile and a half inland, its 100-foot tower forming a landmark for miles by land and sea. A noble building, the church stands among tall pines, and speaks to us from its walls of the wealthy merchants and the humble seamen who dwelt in the town below for centuries and were borne here for burial. There are brasses of the days before Elizabeth, and for 60 years a tablet has been added to the walls for every sailor from this place who has perished at sea. There are now over 200 of them.

The earliest brass is of 1496, and shows John Beriffe in a long gown with belt and pouch, one of his three wives, and five sons and four daughters. On the floor close by are brasses of over half a dozen members of this family of merchants buried in the 16th century. Dame Alice, who died in 1536, stands with her daughter Margaret on a shaft and bracket of 1420, an old brass used again. John Beryff, mariner, in 1521, bequeathed "to the high altar for my tithes forgotten XXs, towards lengthening of the lady chapel 111-quarters of the ship called Trinitie, if God send her well home."

In the chancel is a huge marble monument erected over the grave of Nicholas Magens, who died in 1767. It cost £6000 and shows a great globe of the world, a laden ship, and a cupid seated on a Cornucopia, with an angel above.

There are many niches in these walls, some still with colour, but only one with its statue. Up the corner buttresses of the tower are 32 beautifully moulded niches, meant probably for sheltering saints, though the saints may never have been in them, for this lovely flint church was only finished just before the Reformation. There is an old sanctus bell and another bell of 1400, a coffin lid with a cross and traces of colour and gilding, a fragment of a Norman arch, old doors, old glass, and many architectural details of delicate craftsmanship.

A King's Bible

BROOMFIELD. Its soil has yielded up Stone Age weapons and many bits of Saxon England, but the oldest things visible are the Roman bricks used by the Norman builders of the church. They are in the nave doorway and in the tower windows, and they form the end of the Norman chancel which the 15th century builders extended. Parts of the church have been rebuilt in modern times, but the round tower has been standing 800 years, and is one of only six old round towers in Essex. It rises to a conical roof and a shingled spire with little gable lights. The font is about 700 years old; and hanging in the belfry is a clarinet, last used here in 1870.

The chancel is the last resting-place of Patrick Younge, a friend of Charles Stuart, who lies under a stone carved with his arms. He was the king's librarian, and died in the village; it is to him that Broomfield owes one of its treasures, a Bible Charles gave him.

The Careful Rich Man

BROXTED. With many fine trees and a windmill it stands out boldly a few miles from Thaxted. Its 13th century church has for companion a beautiful gabled house with one of its original Tudor chimneys, and standing by are two barns and a brewhouse from the 17th century. There are Roman tiles in the walls of the church, which has a wooden belfry, a 14th century doorway, and a 15th century aisle. A canopied niche facing the door is the beautiful work of a craftsman 500 years ago, with pinnacles and buttresses, roses and flowers, and two angel figures. The church has two fine things from the 17th century: a processional cross with flowered ends and raised bosses, and an oak pulpit with much elaborate ornament. A quaint inscription to an 18th century man, Thomas Bush of Westminster, tells in stately language how he judiciously bequeathed his fortune among his relatives in such manner as to place them above the cares but below the dangerous indulgences of life.

BULMER. Its finest possession has been in the church 500 years, a font beautifully carved and wonderfully preserved. It has an octagonal bowl and stands on a graceful panelled base. Seven of the sides have angels, double roses, and a shield bearing a thumbscrew; but the one we liked best shows a genial face between branches of grapes, with vine leaves coming from its mouth. The tower is 15th century and there are 14th century arches in the nave with a richly moulded doorway of the same age; but the chief interest of the building is in the 14th century chancel, which has a fine little arcade in the sanctuary wall, and a Tudor roof with canopied angels holding shields and the instruments of the Passion. In two windows is a little old glass. An opening outside one of the walls is blocked with bricks which appear to be Roman.

The Screen From a Lost Abbey

BULPHAN. In the flat country round the Langdon Hills, it has a few old houses and Appleton's Farm, very attractive with its upper storey overhanging both wings of a 15th century hall. Ivy-clad elms face the green where three roads meet, an old barn on one side and a lychgate on the other. The church has a handsome timber porch of about 1500, the bargeboards elaborately carved. The building has been made new, the medieval windows and the old doorway having been reset in the wall. The walls at the west end are plastered and timbered on a brick plinth forming a square of 24 feet, and within this area stand eight oak posts placed here 500 years ago to support the bell-turret. They are joined together by cross-beams with diagonal framing above, while cross-braces add to their impressiveness. In the turret is one surviving old bell which rings out the old year and a group of five tubular bells which ring in the new.

At the other end of the nave is a 15th century screen with two bays on each side of the entrance, their heads containing bold tracery.

It is a triumph of craftsmanship, and is said to have come from Barking Abbey, of which hardly a trace remains.

Nelson's Chaplain

BURNHAM-ON-CROUCH. A small town which has grown up by a quay on the River Crouch, it is thronged in summer days with lovers of yachting.

The church is a mile from the river, behind a green and by a farm. The seven great windows looking on the churchyard give the walls an impressive appearance. At the corners of the porch are two monstrous grotesques, and on a buttress is a medieval scratch dial. The font is the oldest possession of the church, a square Norman bowl, and a 14th century niche is the best example of medieval craftsmanship; its crockets and finial and a border of fruit are delicately carved. On the wall of the chapel is a tablet set up in memory of his family by Dr Alexander Scott, who was vicar of Southminster a few miles away. He is remembered because he lived through an hour of great emotion in our history, for he was the chaplain of the Victory, into whose ears the dying Nelson murmured, Thank God, I have done my duty.

Fine Doors and Windows

BUTTSBURY. Its small church stands lonely among elms and limes; by the path is a gravestone carved with a cherub fading away after 200 years. In a table tomb in the churchyard lies Thomas Tyrell of Charles Stuart's day. Two doors and two windows are the fine possessions here. Both doors have ornamental ironwork, one with hinges of the 13th century and tendril-like bands of great beauty forged in the 14th. The windows, long embedded in plaster, now admit the morning sunlight down each aisle. Their tracery has the graceful curves in which our 14th century architects delighted. In two later windows are fragments of medieval glass, and a bell of the 15th century rings from a last century tower. A local craftsman of great skill has given the fine candlesticks and oak panelling.

Roman Bricks in a Norman Church

CANEWDON. We may still trace the entrenchments, beyond the peaceful cottages, which remind us that hereabouts was fought one of the battles which changed our history and established on the throne our Danish king. Here it was that Canute, in the crisis of his fate, encamped his army before his last great fight with his pursuing adversary, Edmund Ironside. The English king, elated by his victories at Otford in Kent and elsewhere, pressed on determined to thrust the Dane out of the realm, but it was Canute who won the day.

The Roman bricks at the foot of the wall of this church were probably laid by men who saw that famous fight, and the village is believed to have been named after the victor. With the Normans came prosperity. There were six lords of manors here and the great size of the church bears witness to the needs of the 14th century, when the chancel, nave, and aisle were rebuilt. The tower is the chief glory of the building, with walls seven feet thick and rising 75 feet, dwarfing the huge elms. Three shields above the door tell something of our story: the middle shield shows the arms of France and England in the time of Henry the Fifth, and another the arms of the Bohuns. Mary de Bohun was the mother of the king, and it is said that Henry built this tower as a thankoffering for Agincourt. We ascend a hundred winding stairs and a hundred square miles of Essex lie spread before us, the little white yachts off Burnham gleaming in the sunlight, and on the horizon ships edging their way round Maplin Sands into the Thames, while the blue hills of Kent leap up to meet the southern sky. Small wonder that over 400 years ago they chose this tower as a beacon for ships at sea.

There are many treasures in the church over which to linger in admiration, and the wide 15th century windows give ample light. In the chancel wall are preserved painted shafts and painted niches, red and green and gold. Broken in two, a great altar stone rests on the floor of an aisle, four of its consecration crosses still visible. The 14th century arches of the nave rest on carvings in stone; we noticed the head of a woman, a bird, and a beast, and the shield of a family which came over with the Conqueror. The church has a wealth of woodwork. The roof of the nave has bold kingpost trusses that have lasted 500 years. A small ironbound box with strap-hinges was perhaps the money box from which the builders were handed their wages. There is one of the quaintest of old money boxes, its lid with a curiously hollowed surface.

Here, too, are interesting possessions in wood brought from

London after the Great Fire. One is an organ rescued from a chapel of old St Paul's; Milton himself may have pressed its keys. Another is a magnificent pulpit from a City church, with cherubs, foliage, and fruit in its panels which may very well have been carved in the workshop of Grinling Gibbons.

CANVEY ISLAND. A low-lying island of the Thames, six miles long and three broad, it has about 4500 acres of land, which some believe to be the Connos of the ancient geographer Ptolemy. The fields are a rich grazing ground, and were won from the river by a Dutchman who came here in 1621 and built a sea wall round it, receiving a third of the island in payment. There is still a pretty thatched cottage of that year in the older part of the village, and on the tombstones we read Dutch names; but nothing of the church of the Dutchmen remains, for the Dutch fleet raiding up the Thames in 1667 burnt it to the ground. The people replaced their lost shrine and the porch and some of the windows of the 18th century church are in the new one, a building all of wood, with a small belfry and spire. It has a window of St Katherine.

A Place to Hold Us Spellbound

CASTLE HEDINGHAM. Still in this 20th century it is like a piece of Norman England, clustering round its castle walls, and with Norman doors still swinging to and fro in its astonishing church. The ploughmen turned up a gold ring believed to have been worn by the countess who ruled over the nunnery founded in Norman England by the first Earl of Oxford. Castle Hedingham has an ancient stateliness which is not to be equalled in Essex, and hardly surpassed in the country.

For 600 years the Norman castle was held by the De Veres, Great Chamberlains of England, and the great keep they knew still rises on the slope of the hill, looking down on a compact little place with houses that have seen two or three centuries go by. This mighty keep, all that is left of the medieval castle, stands high on a mound of two acres which is surrounded on three sides by ramparts and a deep wide ditch. The ramparts extend one way for nearly 200 yards, enclosing the Georgian house and its garden, which are on the site of the outer court. The keep and the house are a charming picture, reflected with trees in a big lake.

We cross a Tudor bridge of four spans to the castle mound, and above us tower the smooth walls of a keep which is only a little smaller than that at Rochester and was probably designed by the same architect. The castle is 58 feet wide and nearly 100 feet high. It has two turrets and four storeys, the lowest with narrow openings in walls 12 feet thick and the top storey with windows under chevron arches in walls 8 feet thick.

An outer staircase of stone leads to the entrance on the second storey, its arch enriched with three rows of chevrons resting on scalloped capitals. The most striking feature in the entrance hall is the Norman fireplace with rich moulding; the smoke passed out through holes in the buttress. In a corner of the room is a circular staircase leading down to the basement and up to the audience chamber on the second floor, a splendid room with a fireplace and an eight window recess with chevron arches. There is a gallery within the wall, entered from the stairway through a richly ornamented arch and with arches opening into the hall, flooding it with light. But the most striking thing in the hall is the richly moulded arch sweeping across its centre to support the floor above. Resting on piers only seven feet high, it rises to twice that height in a noble span of 29 feet and is as perfect as the Norman masons left it. The top storey has lost its original floor, but its arches complete an ordered design which is one of the most perfect remaining from Norman times.

It was in King Stephen's turbulent reign that this castle was built by Aubrey de Vere, son of the Aubrey who came to England with the Conqueror. It was the stronghold of 17 Earls of Oxford, the best of them being John who fought for Henry the Seventh on Bosworth Field, and to Castle Hedingham came Henry in later years to be entertained with such pomp as exceeded all the bounds laid down by the law to check baronial power, so that the king fined his host £10,000 for his daring!

The Georgian house was built by Robert Ashurst, whose descendants the Majendies now live here. It is here that Miss Musette Majendie organised the Rover Scout Unemployment Camp which was the pioneer of many camps in Essex to train men and set them on their feet again. It is one of the most successful movements devised for giving idle men new hope and a new place in the world, a fit piece of work for this venerable place.

We are thrilled as we realise the wonder of the church which has kept company with the castle through so many generations. It comes from the end of the Norman era, although its red brick tower, fine with its parapet and pinnacles and turrets, is like a thing of yesterday, being 17th century. Above its west windows has been set a piece of ancient carving with the devices of John de Vere, the 13th earl; it runs round the top of the window and in it we see the gold whistle and chain of the Lord High Admiral, a boar grubbing for acorns under an oak, an ox crossing a ford, the Great Chamberlain's chair of state, and the familiar star on the shield.

As we walk round this ancient place we are captivated by the outside of the chancel. It has beautiful pointed windows with carved capitals on their shafts, a sundial is scratched on a buttress, the three windows on the east have a stringcourse linking their capitals, and in the gable above them is a magnificent wheel window with capitals on its eight radiating shafts.

And yet there is something more impressive than all this fine carving which delays our going indoors; it is something that should hold us spellbound, for there are three Norman doorways with three Norman doors in them. We have come upon no other group like this in all our tour of England, and there are very few Norman doors anywhere. One of the three doors is fixed in its place, the other two swing to and fro as they have swung to let in and out 25 generations worshipping in this church. The door that swings no more is set in an exquisite doorway with two orders of richly carved zigzag and foliage. The capitals of the four shafts of the doorway are also carved with foliage, and inside is the door, built of three massive battens with a hinge shaped like a big C by Norman smiths. The same smiths fashioned an animal on one of the ornamented straps of the south door, which hangs in an arch of three moulded orders, the capitals of the doorway being carved with the stiff leaves characteristic of the English style just coming in. The north doorway has been partly cut away but its Norman door still hangs in it.

Keeping company with these three Norman doors is a medieval one still hanging in the doorway the 15th century builders made for it, making a unique collection of doors which should bring many pilgrims to Essex.

Even after all this we must be thrilled with the splendour of this interior, for the fine clerestory windows light up the magnificent hammerbeams of the nave, and the clerestory itself is the greatest surprise of all, for it also is Norman. Up to their great height these Norman walls rise, five Norman bays on each side of the nave, and in the wall between two of the clerestory windows is a narrow doorway from which the priests would step on to the roodloft.

The screen that is here today was carved about 1400 and has six bays with fine oak tracery, the arches richly carved, the moulded cornice adorned with bosses. Beyond the screen in the chancel is a range of five handsome stalls carved while the screen was new; on them are the devices of the medieval craftsmen, shields and heads of wolves and leopards, a wolf carrying off what looks like a monk on a stick thrown over his shoulder, a fox with a distaff in its mouth, and so on.

But it is the roof of the nave (200 years younger than the plain roof of the chancel) which is the crowning glory of the woodcarvers who adorned the church. They were 16th century men and their roof has double hammerbeams. They were building this roof for the 13th Earl of Oxford, and proud he must have been of it, for the lower hammerbeams and the cornice are decorated with running foliage, crowned angels with outspread wings looking down from it. There is rich tracery in the spandrels, carved pendants and pinnacles, and scattered about are the star and boar of the Earls of Oxford.

At the east end of the nave the arch is pointed, and at the west it is round; the chancel arch must have been refashioned when the English builders were succeeding the Normans; the tower arch was reset as the Normans made it when the nave was shortened at the time the tower was built. Even the stoup is Norman here, its square bowl resembling a cushion capital richly carved with foliage and the head of a beast. It was probably carved by the men who shaped the figure of a woman with folded hands built into the wall over an altar.

Impressive in itself, the church has few impressive monuments, the chief one being the altar tomb which has been moved so that we see too little of it. On the side we can see kneel the four daughters of the 15th Earl of Oxford and his wife Elizabeth, who lie in black marble on the top, he in armour, she with a heraldic mantle. Very quaint these figures are, kneeling sideways in relief yet showing full face, with a harpy and a stag holding their shield-of-arms above them.

The Massive Norman Keep

A Castle Window

Hall in the Keep

Churchyard Cross

CASTLE HEDINGHAM

Chelmsford   **The Cathedral**

Chelmsford   **Essex County Hall**

There is more carving on the panelling of a cupboard in the tower, showing Daniel in the den of lions and Jonah beneath the gourd; it is probably 18th century. There is a panelled chest with three locks, a Jacobean altar table, and a painted memorial tablet from a vanished church on London Wall, brought here to keep green the memory of Dominic Van Heyla and his wife Wilhelmina, immigrants from Flanders in Shakespeare's day. One very beautiful thing here is framed on the wall, a beautiful embroidery of the Madonna.

In the churchyard the shaft and base of the 12th century cross have been set up in memory of the men of Castle Hedingham who did not come back from the war. It was found in the cellars of the medieval inn, the Falcon.

Here End the Chalk Hills

CHADWELL ST MARY. It rests on one of the finest gravel beds in England; and here end the chalk hills, from which we have a wide view over the reclaimed marshes round Tilbury, with the Kent hills rising behind Gravesend. The most charming house in the village stands at the cross-roads. Known as Sleepers Farm, it is a timber-framed building of the 15th century with a thatched roof. Much of its original woodwork remains, and it has a battered door of the 17th century. Fifty yards away stands the church, perhaps the successor of a church erected by St Cedd, missionary to the East Saxons, who, tradition says, baptised his converts in a well close by. The tower was built about the time of the Wars of the Roses. Its embattled parapet has brick and flint chequer-work, and quaint faces looking out. The doorway through which we enter is 15th century, but above it is the round head of the entrance made by the Normans. Across the nave is a plain Norman doorway, on which a mass dial was cut in the days before clocks.

The chancel has three works of art of great interest, an elaborately carved chair 250 years old, and two fine paintings, one of the Finding of Moses said to be by Caracci, the other Christ at the House of Simon Peter, a copy of the painting by Paul Veronese.

CHAPEL. A viaduct over 100 feet high and with about 30 arches here crosses the valley of the Colne, and a handsome little Georgian house with plaster panels is a neighbour for the church. Above the red roof of the church rises a wooden belfry with a short

F   65

spire, and its ancient door, swinging on the old hinges, brings us to a nave with 14th century walls. The pulpit and reading desk, about 300 years old, were used by Timothy Rogers, a great-grandson of John Rogers, the first victim of Mary Tudor's persecution. Timothy was a famous Puritan of Cromwell's time, and wrote the Jewel of Faith, a book widely read in his day.

The County Town

CHELMSFORD. It is the county town and has a cathedral, it stands on two rivers, and it has one of the finest of those wonderful spectacles of our 20th century, the towering masts of the Wireless Age. It has grown rapidly from a quiet agricultural centre to an energetic modern town, and it is its pride to have been the first of all our towns to light the streets with electricity.

To the last generation Chelmsford was a town with maltings, cornmills, breweries, and tanneries, serving the county and beyond by a short canal to the Blackwater, and conducting all this trade on the smallest draught of water of any river or canal in our island. To us it is a town of ironfounding and engineering works, of factories making ball-bearings and arc lights, and most of all it is the heart of that great wonder world built up by Marconi.

For miles in this level country the high Marconi masts draw the traveller's eye, their warning lights twinkling at night 450 feet above the town. They look down on great works covering 25,000 square yards, and on Marconi College where students come from everywhere to keep abreast with the latest developments in the miraculous wireless world. Their playing-fields have added to the delightful open spaces in which Chelmsford is so happy, thanks partly to Mother Nature who has sent her two rivers (the Chelmer and the Can) to mingle their waters in the city, and another little stream outside. Their banks are lined with willows and are very pleasant places. The Roman road to Colchester runs through the town at a point where the rivers were fordable, an 18th century bridge taking the old road over the Can, while our modern engineers have bypassed it on 550 yards of concrete arches.

The old village of Moulsham, with a few of its 17th century cottages left, has been drawn into the town. Here is all that is left of the old Friary which had become the home of King Edward's School when

66

its roof fell in in 1663. The school now stands in lovely grounds north of the city. The most famous scholar it has known was Philemon Holland, "the translator-general of his age." His first years were unhappy, for his father was a Protestant and had to flee to the Continent with Miles Coverdale when Mary Tudor was crowned. On his return the father became rector of Great Dunmow and sent the boy here to school. He wrote much, and the dull poet Pope made cynical fun of the groaning shelves on which his works stood. He would be very familiar with the overhanging timber shops and cottages in Moulsham Street, one of them still with a beam carved in the 15th century.

The heart of Chelmsford lies between its two rivers. It is a town of old and new, with a medieval church standing by the dull backs of the old Shire Hall, greeting across low roofs the splendid modern County Hall which governs Essex, and administers more than one area of Greater London bigger than Chelmsford. The County Hall fronts the pathway slanting through the churchyard and is striking with pilasters five storeys up, and below them (carved on flat spaces) the stone figure of a man carrying a scroll and a woman with a child in the rays of the sun.

Before the coming of the County Hall, with its five storeys of snow-white stone, the Shire Hall's 18th century front held sway in the streets, with four pillars crowned with a pediment on which are figures of Justice, Wisdom, and Mercy. The hall took the place of an older court which was infamous 300 years ago for its trials of witches and its persecution of nonconformists; it is recorded that one day in 1645 nine poor women were sent to the stake from here.

The City Council, too, is providing itself with handsome buildings, the first to be completed (in 1935) being the public library in Duke Street, with a great arch of white stone at its entrance. The whole of the ground floor is devoted to the housing of 32,000 books, and to lecture rooms, and above are the rooms from which the Mayor and his council govern the city. Close by is the peace memorial, a solid obelisk in stone rather like the Cenotaph in Whitehall; on the back in bronze letters are the words Our Glorious Dead.

Near the Shire Hall stands the Corn Exchange, and in the square outside is the bronze statue of a Chelmsford boy who grew up to be a judge and won fame by his courage in defending Queen Caroline.

He was Sir Nicholas Tindal, who became Chief Justice before he died; we see him sitting, and his statue is by Edward Baily. Where he sits once flowed a spring over which was a handsome conduit now at the other end of High Street. Here all has been changed save one or two inns, the Saracen in which Anthony Trollope used to write, and the Spotted Dog with its remarkable courtyard.

For relics of old Chelmsford we come to the mansion in the park at the London end of the town; it is known as Oaklands House, and stands in splendour amid lawns and cedars, a 19th century house filled with delightful things. There is a collection of 1000 British birds among which we noticed one of the only two needle-tailed swifts which have been captured in England. There is the collection of that remarkable man John Salter, a worldwide Nimrod who died in our time; very real are his stuffed beasts, especially the lion and a group of wolves. The lover of the story of Essex will delight in the flat stone on which the Bronze Age men sharpened their axes, the dug-out canoe in which they went fishing, the huge Roman vase found at Maldon, the Roman and the Saxon javelins from Witham. The art of medieval England is seen on ten panels from a screen of Latchington church with painted saints in red and green robes, and there is a small picture gallery where we found 80 water colours of Essex churches and houses by Bennett Bamford, a lovely Turner, and landscapes by those two immortals who loved this country-side, Constable and Gainsborough. Watching over the treasures in one of these rooms is the sculptured head of a priest who shepherded his flock in Egypt about 40 centuries ago. The museum is happily situated for the schools of southern Chelmsford, with their modern buildings and spacious playing-fields for nearly 2000 scholars. They are an honour to the city.

Chelmsford's church has been made a cathedral in our time, but time has conspired to hide it. One splendid thing it has done, for it has taken away the ugly railings round it and laid flat all the gravestones, an example we should like to see copied everywhere. By the churchyard stands the only house of dignity here, Guy Harlings, where the Provost lives; it has panelling 400 years old, and carved heads looking down on the hall from a Tudor frieze.

The church has stood about 500 years and has two fine things, a 15th century tower with a slender lead spire on an open cupola, and a richly panelled two-storeyed porch, the white stone of the panelling set in flint and continued as pinnacles. Much of the church has been rebuilt and the chancel has been lengthened. It has a clerestory supported by an arch which is perhaps unique, being divided in two with its centre spandrel made strong by upright stone bars. The most striking thing in the sanctuary is the elegant bishop's throne, with light tracery soaring towards the roof; it is in memory of the rector who became Bishop of Colchester in 1894, Henry Johnson, whose grave in the churchyard is marked by a tall cross. Looking down on the altar from a niche in the wall is a statue of Chelmsford's first bishop, John Watts-Ditchfield; it is a stately figure of this famous social reformer.

One of the screens is in memory of Frederick Chancellor, who was 93 when he died at the end of the Great War. He was the last original member of the Essex Archaeological Society, which gave this fine screen. His great book with hundreds of exquisite drawings of monuments in Essex churches has few equals in any county.

At the west end of the cathedral are four peace memorials: a golden bell to 44 Essex ringers, most of whom must have had a pull at the 12 bells here; a solemn figure holding a gun reversed in memory of 257 Essex yeomen; a fine window of St Michael between St George and St Nicholas in memory of 99 men of the parish; and an elaborate sculpture in memory of 55 Essex clergy and their sons who perished in the war and whose monument has these lines:

For unto them we know is given
A life that bears immortal fruit.

One pathetic tablet on the tower arch tells us of another hero, Scout Dawson of the Cathedral Troop, who gave his life at 16 while trying to save a Belgian Scout from drowning.

It may be thought that the cathedral lacks the grace of such a church as Thaxted, and the perfection in stone of such a church as Saffron Walden, but it had introduced when we called a fine note of colour in a series of modern windows by A. K. Nicholson; they represent the great psalm of praise. One of the older windows in the style of William Morris shows a group of angels as Faith, Hope, and Love, helping a pilgrim on the way to heaven. The 19th century pulpit has white and coloured marbles, and on the walls are the flags of the old Essex Militia, woven for the companies which marched about the county when Napoleon was expected.

On a big brass are the names of 41 Mildmays buried here from 1544 to 1798, and in the corner of a chapel is the great tomb of the founder of this vigorous line, Thomas. Henry the Eighth gave him the manor of Moulsham, and as his own good deed for the town he founded the grammar school; he had eight sons of his own to educate as well as seven daughters. He founded the almshouses, too, and as his wife died before him he himself probably built this rich tomb in which he lies with her.

The tomb is enriched with architectural features at that time being introduced from Italy, and the decoration carries the eye up to a golden ball perched on a Greek capital. The central panel is painted with heraldry, and at each end are sculptured groups of mourners, kneeling, Thomas himself with his sons, and his wife with the daughters. It was one of the sons who added to the tomb a decorated arch in honour of the "fifteen pledges which Thomas and Avice had of their prosperous love." One of the sons on the tomb was Walter Mildmay. As the father had grown rich as receiver of the surrender of the monasteries (when Henry the Eighth is said to have received 15 millions of money), so the son controlled the revenues of Edward the Sixth, and continued to serve Mary and Elizabeth. He was a pious man, and generous to education, for he founded Emmanuel College, Cambridge, and it was to this that Queen Elizabeth referred on meeting the Chancellor soon after. "I hear you have erected a Puritan foundation," said the Queen. "No, madam," said the Chancellor, "but I have set an acorn which, when it becomes an oak, God alone knows what will be the fruit thereof." Sir Walter does not lie here, but in the famous church of St Bartholomew the Great, which looks out on Smithfield, the scene of the burning of the martyrs in his day.

A neighbour of the Mildmays in the 17th century has his portrait engraved on marble in the south chapel; it is like a very curious brass and shows Matthew Rudd with two sons kneeling at prayer facing his wife and three daughters. On the desk between them are two books, and with a foot on each book stands Death, pointing a barbed shaft at these people.

The porch by which we come and go has about 20 heads looking down from the medieval panels of its timber ceiling, and above it is a library of books left to the church in the 17th century; we see them from the nave through open panelling of stone. In one of the books we read that miracle plays were performed in this wide nave as late as 1576.

Two sons of Chelmsford winning fame in the 18th and 19th centuries were Joseph Strutt and Wilson Barrett, one delighting his generation by his description of the people's pastimes, the other entertaining his generation on the stage. Joseph Strutt, born in 1749, was the son of a rich miller and became famous as an antiquarian, his chief work (many times reprinted since its first publication in 1801) being the monumental Sports and Pastimes of the People of England. Wilson Barrett, born at the Manor Farm here in 1846, started his career as a printer's lad, but soon migrated to the stage, making his first appearance at Halifax when he was 18 and remaining faithful to the theatre for 40 years, until a few weeks before his death in 1904. At his best in melodrama, he achieved many successes on the London stage, and Victorians vigorously applauded his performances, particularly in The Silver King and The Sign of the Cross—a play which drew crowded audiences for years to see Wilson Barrett and Maud Jeffries, a beautiful actress from Tennessee.

Older Than the Conqueror

CHICKNEY. Here, its walls askew, stands one of the oldest and most remarkable churches in Essex. With a couple of farms and a cottage or two, it is all there is of Chickney.

The church stands in an oval churchyard, a shape loved by the Saxons, and is much as the Saxon builders left it. Here are their nave and chancel, the chancel having been lengthened in the 13th century and the little tower added a century later. Stirring it is to look at these walls and feel that they were here when the Conqueror set foot in Sussex. There are doubly splayed Saxon windows in the nave, with doorways of the 14th century; and in the chancel two Saxon windows keep company with two of the 13th century. On two of the windows on the south side are several old scratch dials. The kingpost roof of the nave is 600 years old, and so is the chancel arch, by which is a curiously shaped peephole through which the altar can be seen. The 19th century restorers came upon the altar stone set in the chancel by the 13th century men, and here it is in position again, with its five consecration crosses. A splendid font to which the babies have been coming for 500 years is carved with canopies and angels and shields.

Close by stands a 17th century house which has kept some of its old panelling; and about a mile away is Sibley's Farm, built in the 15th century, a gabled house with overhanging storeys. It has a Tudor staircase, Tudor fireplaces, a Tudor barn, and one of the oldest dovecots in Essex.

Fragments of Rome

CHIGNAL ST JAMES. Fine wych elms cluster round its church, a simple building with walls thick enough to suggest that they were standing in Norman days; but older than anything else in the church are the Roman bricks picked up by the builders and worked into the walls. We come into the church by a 13th century doorway and find inside another doorway of much interest—that of the old roodstairs, which now lead to the pulpit. The oak arch of the doorway is carved in wood with the emblems of St James, a cockle shell and a fisherman's creel. The roofs are a hundred years older, adorned with leaves and knots and stars; and in a window of the same age are modern figures of St Michael and St George in red and silver and gold. Half a mile away stands the hall with its projecting upper storey. On a wall-plate within it has the name of the man who built it in 1552, John Mason.

A Church Without Stone

CHIGNAL SMEALEY. Brick Chignal it has been called, and not without reason, for we come here to admire the beautiful work of Tudor craftsmen who could make a church without stone.

The whole structure is brick, even the 16th century font. The tower has pinnacles and a high parapet; the doors have been swinging on their hinges since the days of Shakespeare; the pulpit is a century younger, and the Tudor screen is carved with leaves and tiny roses. There are two piscinas of brick shaped and moulded like stone, and three brick niches enshrining figures of Christ, a child, and a saint. The arcade and the aisle are of last century, and have not the rich warm glow of the Tudor brickwork. In two windows we see the oldest things in the village, oak leaves and foliage in glass

600 years old. Close to the church stands a 16th century house, still with an original chimney stack.

Archbishop and Busman

CHIGWELL. It is nothing like what Dickens called it, the greatest place in the world, but it has great charm in its woodland scenery, set in the valley of the River Roding between the two forests of Epping and Hainault. Chigwell has still the 17th century King's Head Inn which Dickens brings into Barnaby Rudge as the Maypole, and its grammar school has still the original building set up by Archbishop Harsnett, who was vicar here in 1631. There is a bust of him in the hall. William Penn, the founder of Pennsylvania, was a pupil at this school. The school hall rises to the full height of the building and is a fine place. The modern chapel has windows of four scenes from the Pilgrim's Progress, all the characters being shown as boys. Woolston Hall is a house with iron gates of the 18th century and chimneys of the 17th; Rolls is a fine house built round a 16th century block and has 17th century chimneys.

Avenues of clipped yews lead us to the old doorways of the church the Normans built; we come into it through one of their doorways, with cushion capitals on its shafts and a tympanum set in an arch of four orders. The nave and chancel are modern, but the aisle and part of its chapel were the nave and chancel of the Normans. The roof is 15th century. There are eight medieval posts in the west end of the aisle, with massive beams supporting a bell-turret above which rises a copper spire. There is a window of Ruth and Naomi, a sculpture of the Annunciation in the sanctuary, and two wall-monuments of the 16th and 17th centuries, the first to Thomas Colshill, who kneels in marble with his wife and two daughters, the second a glittering tablet to George Scott, who died at Woolston Hall. Two brasses are of remarkable interest for widely varied reasons. One is a tablet erected by the busmen of London to an old friend of theirs who lived here, George Shillibeer, described on the brass as the founder of their calling—and truly so, for he ran the first buses in London and introduced the word omnibus into our language. The other brass is one of the most famous in England, the last of the five we have showing an archbishop. It is in a recess in the chancel wall, and on it is Samuel Harsnett who rose from being vicar here to be Archbishop of York, but came back to

Chigwell to rest by the old church he loved. We see him on his brass, a fine bearded figure in full robes with his crozier and a book and with cherubs about him, shields-of-arms and the symbols of the Evangelists, and this unusual inscription: "Here lies Samuel Harsnett, formerly vicar of this church. First the unworthy Bishop of Chichester, then the more unworthy Bishop of Norwich, at last the very unworthy Archbishop of York." Remarkable characters were both these men.

George Shillibeer, born in London in 1797, left the Navy as a middy to learn coach-building. Setting up in business in Paris, he built two buses for a patron there, returned to London, and in 1829 placed on the streets the first omnibuses seen in England. Drawn by three horses, each carried 22 passengers, and plied between Paddington and the Bank of England at a shilling a head.

At first his only rivals were stage coaches, which covered the same journey in three hours at a cost of half-a-crown a passenger. Shillibeer furnished his vehicles with free newspapers and magazines, and dressed his conductors first in naval uniform and afterwards in velvet. In a year he had a dozen buses on the roads, and in spite of opposition from rivals, and from householders who felt that his buses vulgarised the streets, he prospered until, starting a service in opposition to the London and Greenwich Railway, he lost heavily, and several times had his property seized for licence fees.

This arrest of his industry ruined him, and the man who had transformed passenger traffic was driven off the streets. Later he invented an improved funeral hearse, which long bore his name. Beggared by his success in transporting the living, he retrieved his fortunes by carrying the dead. He died at Brighton but has lain here since 1866. All our buses sprang from his idea.

Samuel Harsnett, who has slept at Chigwell since 1631, was the son of a Colchester baker, who sent him to Pembroke College, Cambridge. His life was a succession of escapes and preferments. At the outset of his clerical career he denounced an aspect of Calvinism and was in turn denounced for Popery; made licenser of books for the Press, he narrowly averted imprisonment for passing a seditious work which he had not troubled to read. While Master of Pembroke and vice-chancellor of Cambridge University he was accused of over 50 offences, including absence from duty, slackness with accounts, and

Romanising tendencies; yet, although his resignation was inevitable, he still enjoyed the favour of James the First, and proceeded from the bishopric of Chichester to that of Norwich, and from Norwich to the archbishopric of York.

A high churchman, he offended many people in many places by his arbitrary conduct, and his relentless persecution of quiet men and women who dared to worship according to their conscience. He left writings to keep his fame alive, among them a treatise exposing those who professed to cast out evil spirits, a masterly production from which Shakespeare borrowed the names of spirits mentioned by Edgar in King Lear, and from which Milton derived ideas for L'Allegro. It was to mark his thankfulness for his advance from a vicarage to an archbishopric that he built and endowed his school here and gave the church a gallery for its scholars. His library he left to his native town. Dying in Gloucestershire, he was brought here in accordance with his wish to rest at his wife's feet.

Old Oak

CHIGWELL ROW. From its highest point we look out over the Thames valley to the Kent hills, and below us is the famous Hainault Forest where kings and abbots hunted and the LCC now reigns over 1100 acres of rolling fields and woodland. So close it is to London, yet all around is wild and natural, the nightingale sings in the thicket, and many big trees increase their girth undisturbed, though the giant of them all, the Monarch Fairlop Oak, fell a century ago, when it was 45 feet round the trunk and had 17 branches each as big as an ordinary oak.

Thomas Day, author of Sandford and Merton, used to come from his home near by to pay a formal call on the oak every first Friday in July, a practice started by his namesake Daniel, a Wapping pumpmaker who came here to collect rent. The pumpmaker gave his friends an annual feast of bean and bacon under this tent of leaves 300 feet round, and when he died in 1767 his coffin was fashioned from a fallen branch.

An avenue of limes and chestnuts leads to a house close to the 19th century church with a tower of our own century, and it seems fitting that this church among the trees should be graced with much fine woodwork. The east window pictures in lovely colours the opening of the Book and the worship of the Lamb. On the wall an arch-angel with grey-blue wings of enamel honours the names of the fallen.

Three Blasts

CHINGFORD. High on a hill overlooking the River Lea, it is famous among that great multitude which comes to visit Epping Forest. There are woods in which naturalists find rare treasures and a lake of much beauty known as Connaught Water, with a fine survival of the past close by. It is Queen Elizabeth's hunt-ing lodge, and was called a Standing, a place where spectators stood to watch the hunt. It has been transformed into a museum, and a rare old place it is, three storeys high, with one of the finest staircases in Essex, its stairs six feet wide and so easy to mount that we may well believe the story that Elizabeth rode up them on her pony. The timbers of the lodge are 16th century, the tapestry on the middle floor is 17th. One of the odd things we see here is the kind of wooden pipe which was used for carrying London's water up to the beginning of last century. It is a long hollowed-out trunk.

We meet an old neighbour of the Standing a mile away from the old church, Pimphall Farm. It is a timbered house of the 16th century with a barn of five bays not quite so old, and one of the best timbered dovecots in Essex. There is a quaint story of an Act of Homage by which this farm was held in olden time. It seems that the farm was given to a huntsman, probably by the king, on condition that the farmer did homage to the rector. This is the Act of Homage performed in 1659:

Samuel Haddon with his wife and two servants came to the rectory and blew three blasts with a horn, receiving from the rector a chicken for his hawk, a peck of oats for his horse, a loaf of bread for his hound, and a dinner for himself and his wife, his man and his maid. After dinner he blew three blasts and paid twelve pence, and so departed.

One other unusual monument we find at Chingford, an obelisk set up by the Ordnance Survey to mark the meridian of Greenwich, which was used until 1884 when a new zero line was adopted by international agreement.

There is an old church and a new one. The new one is on Ching-ford Green, with a font and a finely carved 17th century pulpit from the old church, and a table in the children's corner carved with animals; the old one is on a knoll a mile from the heart of the town.

Long neglected as a ruin, it has been well restored and has still a 13th century doorway, a medieval aisle and chancel, and Norman stones in the nave. The tower is 500 years old, and at the top of one of its beams has been placed a 13th century stone cross with a head on each side of the base. There is a 17th century chest with three locks, and two doors are still hanging on their 15th century hinges.

On a wall is a woman mourning at an urn in memory of John Heathcote, an 18th century man of science. There are many memorials to the Leighs. Sir Robert kneels in Jacobean armour, and Margaret kneels at prayer on another monument with a symbolical figure of Time. Mary Leigh, an Elizabethan lady, rests on the wall with a baby beside her. We noticed that Robert Lewis was vicar here half a century, through all the days while Napoleon was terrifying Europe.

David Livingstone Afraid

CHIPPING ONGAR. It is one of those small Essex towns instinct with the thrill of history. One after another there come to mind the moving scenes of its historic past. To some it will seem that the chief appeal of this long street with gabled houses and overhanging storeys is in a little room the passer-by is invited to look at, the room in the house of a pastor where David Livingstone lived, serving his probation before he set out on his lifework in Africa. The boy at the mill had come down from Blantyre and was training here with the minister, and there may well be those who remember hearing of the nervous young man who had hardly strength to lead his congregation at prayer, who gave out hymn after hymn while he summoned up courage to preach and then fled down the steps and into the street, afraid. Yet in the end he passed the test, and from here set out to carry on his preparation elsewhere for the work which was to win him immortality.

But far, far back we go beyond the fame of David Livingstone, for here is a mound crowned by a ring of living trees where once stood the wooden keep of a Norman castle, and there is little doubt that a castle stood on it before the Conqueror came, for in its walls is a medley of Roman tiles which strongly suggest that they were put here by the Saxons. On such foundations as they found the Romans set up one of their great strongholds. The mound is 230 feet across, encircled by a moat 50 feet wide, with the water still in it. On the town side was a courtyard with a rampart 80 feet wide, and even beyond this men have traced a rampart which embraced the whole of Ongar, a remarkable example of a town enclosure of feudal days.

Here lived one of the famous Norman barons, Richard de Lucy, Chief Justice in the reign of Henry the Second. He took the side of the king against Becket, and Becket excommunicated him. Weary of strife, the judge became a canon in a priory he had founded in Kent, Lesnes Priory at Erith, within whose quiet walls he died. Across the Darent, not far away from the ruins of Lesnes, are the ruins of the castle of another friend of the king excommunicated by Becket, William de Eynsford, who, also weary of strife, gave up this world and lived for the next, leaving his castle deserted, not to be lived in again for eight hundred years.

Richard de Lucy would see the church in the shadow of his high keep much as we see it now. The walls of the nave and the chancel are of the same rubble and Norman bricks as in his day. Through the little Norman windows the worshippers would see the keep against the sky. There are narrow Roman tiles outside these windows, and it is believed that Saxons put them there. There are Roman tiles at the corners of the walls and over a blocked-up Norman doorway; the light of a Norman window falls also on the gallery. A chancel window of a century later, a triple lancet, is one of the very early uses of brick by our English builders.

There is a captivating peephole in the chancel wall which faces this, a hole about 13 inches by 6, opening from a tiny chamber in the thickness of the wall. Outside the wall are hinges and the socket for a bolt, and above is a hole which seems to have held a roof beam. From all this it is supposed that this tiny chamber was the cell and the grave of one of those strange anchorites who shut themselves up from the world, immured in the wall with a little hole through which they could fix their eyes on the altar. The roof the anchorite would see is still above the nave, with a Norman corbel surviving from the earlier roof, and a carving on one of the timbers of a man with toothache. Through this roof in the 15th century they pierced a space for the massive timber belfry, and about 200 years ago they set on the spire the weathervane in the form of a pennon which still turns in the wind.

The pulpit is 17th century; it would be new when they laid here beneath the chancel Jane Pallavicine, the daughter of one of the less known Oliver Cromwells, the Sir Oliver whose claim to fame rests on his lavish entertainment of James the First. There is a monument by Nollekens to Sarah Mitford; the fashionable sculptor has given her angels on her tomb, one weeping and one placing a wreath. On the wall is one of those pathetic wooden crosses from the battlefields, brought from the grave of Henry Austin Noble, who died for us a month before the Armistice. There is a window to him with St Martin in it.

This is one of the rare places where the chapel appeals to us as well as the church, for the Congregationalists have been established in Ongar since 1690, and the most famous men of Ongar have been two Nonconformists—David Livingstone, who trained here for the ministry, and Isaac Taylor, who was pastor here. Livingstone must have known this chapel, and may have preached in it for his tutor-pastor, Richard Cecil, of whom we read in the story of Stanford Rivers. Isaac Taylor lies behind his church, and with him lie his wife and their daughter Jane, who (at their house at Lavenham, over the border in Suffolk) wrote at least one thing known to every child, Twinkle, Twinkle, Little Star. There is a tablet in the chapel to them, and though a schoolroom now stands over their graves we may lift up a panel in the floor and read their simple stone.

The Taylors of Ongar

IT was said of the Taylors of Ongar that it was impossible to be one of them and not write. They did more than write; they painted, engraved, and invented, and Sir Francis Galton cited them in his famous list as examples of the diffusion of hereditary talent. The line took its rise in a 17th century Worcester metal-worker and engraver, specimens of whose work are in the British Museum.

He was the father of the first Isaac Taylor, who, born in 1730, walked to London and worked as a silversmith until he proved himself an engraver of merit, whereupon he was entrusted with the plates for Goldsmith's Deserted Village. His son Isaac was educated at Brentford and then worked in his father's studio. After engraving plates for Shakespeare, the Bible, and Thomson's Seasons, he entered the ministry at Colchester, and arrived at Chipping Ongar at 51, pastor of the Congregational Church. Here he spent the last

19 years of his life, teaching his children and his flock, and writing biography, travel, and other books for the young, while his wife wrote moral and instructive lessons for children and parents. They had many children, among them the two girls and their brother Isaac.

The third Isaac, born at Lavenham in Suffolk in 1787, an artist with brush and graver, helped his father, illustrated his sister's books, and wrote books of his own, one on the Natural History of Enthusiasm. But it was the sisters, Ann and Jane, who immortalised the family. They wrote their early poetry in moments stolen from lessons. Not until 1804, when Ann was 24 and Jane 21, did their first volume appear. Bringing them fame and £15, it brought poetry for the first time to the lips of millions of children. In their Poems for Infant Minds were such familiar verses as My Mother and Little Star, with other pieces which have long been part of the nursery heritage of the world. Scores of editions were printed; the book was translated into foreign tongues, and soon children everywhere were repeating the lines of Ann and Jane Taylor. They wrote other books for children, tales, fables, and especially hymns, many of which are sung in all our churches. Jane died here unmarried in 1824; Ann became the wife of the Revd Joseph Gilbert, whom she accompanied to Nottingham, where she lived the last 41 years of her life.

In 1866 an odd thing happened, 60 years after Ann's poem My Mother had appeared. A writer in a literary weekly called attention to the last stanza in the poem and asked that it should be altered. These are the lines:

> *And when I see thee hang thy head,*
> *Twill be my turn to watch thy bed,*
> *And tears of sweet affection shed,*
> > *My Mother.*

> *For God who lives above the skies,*
> *Would look with vengeance in His eyes,*
> *If I should ever dare despise*
> > *My Mother.*

The critic, 60 years after, "in the name of all the children of England," proposed a change which should remove this threat of vengeance, suggesting that Tennyson should make the alteration. To everybody's surprise, however, Ann Taylor, then 84 and long forgotten under the name of Ann Gilbert, herself vigorously replied,

Chigwell
The 17th Century King's Head Inn

Chingford
Queen Elizabeth's Hunting Lodge

The Timbered Front with its Oriels

The Panelled Parlour

PAYCOCKE'S HOUSE, COGGESHALL

acknowledging the justice of the criticism, adding that it was "a favour now to have any critics at all," and drafting new lines ending:

> For could my Father in the skies
> Look down with pleased or loving eyes
> If ever I could dare despise
>   My Mother?

The Mound and the Moat

CHRISHALL. It is charming with thatched and timbered cottages 300 years old, a gabled farmhouse of Shakespeare's day, and a 15th century inn. It has, too, an ancient site that leaves us guessing, a mound surrounded by a moat still with water in it. Standing finely near a group of white cottages is the battlemented church, built by 15th century men who kept the thick Norman walls at the base of the tower, but made a fine new tower arch. On her tomb lies a stone lady with a perky dog at her feet; but the chief pride of the church must be in its brasses, one magnificent indeed. It shows John and Joan de la Pole of the 14th century, and, with its rich triple canopy, is one of the finest brasses in this country. John, wearing armour and a tunic, is hand in hand with Joan, who, with her pretty headdress and close-fitting gown, is a very captivating lady. At their feet are a dog and a smiling lion. Two other brasses show 15th century people, a lady with a high waist and a veil, and a man and his wife kneeling. For 600 years children have been baptised at this font; and there is a 16th century roof with Tudor roses over the north aisle, a fine modern kingpost roof in the chancel, pews with woodwork 400 years old, and lovely carvings of kneeling women.

CLACTON-ON-SEA. This seaside resort, one of the most popular and most visited holiday towns in Essex, has little to attract historians or antiquarians except its bracing air and its obvious cheerfulness, which even historians and antiquarians can sometimes delight in. Clacton is modern and proud of it. Everything here is designed to attract the holiday-maker and the convalescent, and the tree-lined streets and gardens, the parades and promenades, the Venetian Bridge and the fine cliff walks, are a handsome background for a wealth of entertainment which most visitors find irresistible. As an up-to-date seaside town Clacton is naturally proud of its band pavilion and winter garden, its swimming pool and model yacht lake, its pier 1150 feet long on which amusement literally runs riot, its facilities for so many kinds of sport, its seven theatres, five kinemas, and four ballrooms. Even the fine town hall is largely given up to social life. In Clacton, Play's the thing and Sunshine the Master of Ceremonies.

If we except the Martello Tower on the sea front the town has no antiquity to show. All its churches are modern, but its smaller neighbours and namesakes, Great and Little Clacton, have both kept their village aspect and their ancient churches. They are treated separately in this book.

The Man Who Saw Captain Cook Die

CLAVERING. Scattered about a brook which feeds the River Stort, it has in a meadow by the churchyard an acre of mounds with a dry moat round them, believed to have been the Roland's Castle in which Normans arriving before the Conqueror fortified themselves after incurring the anger of their Saxon hosts. On the hill is a windmill which has lost its sails.

The village has some delightful old cottages, and one by the churchyard gate is 500 years old and is said to have originally been built as an almshouse. Next to it is a house with carved Jacobean woodwork and wall-paintings of religious subjects. The clerestoried 14th century church has its original porch, and two fine arches in the tower and the chancel, supported by weird heads, are balanced by dignified nave arcades. The oldest possessions of the church are the 700-year-old bowl of the font and a stone figure of a knight in 13th century mail, lying in a recess. On a wall-tablet is Haynes Barlee, of grave features and curly hair, with his third wife, and to keep him company is a tablet in coloured marbles with a bust of his first wife, several children, and some skulls, and a bust of his second wife, "by whom he had a very plentiful fortune." There is another tablet in memory of the wife of William Wales, the gallant astronomer who sailed with Captain Cook and saw him die. He was one of that broken-hearted band who came home with the news a year later, and he settled down as mathematical master at Christ's Hospital. He took great interest in the condition of Society and was one of the first to conceive a census of the English people; but he found so much religious hostility to the idea that he gave up his researches. There are brass portraits of Thomas and Ursula Welbore and their six children in Elizabethan costume, and on another brass are three girls left motherless by Joan Smith in the 16th century.

The church is rich in treasures of 15th century glass, with scenes from the life of St Catherine, angels, Madonnas, the head of Christ crowned with golden thorns, and St Cecilia. All the roofs are 15th century, that of the chancel supported by finely sculptured heads, and a bishop and a company of grotesques sustaining the roof of the nave, which has fantastic bosses carved on its beams and seraphim watching from the sides. One roof has bosses of musicians playing, a priest in his robes, and an angel with an organ.

The high 15th century screen has panels of saints drawn in black lines on a white ground. There are over a score of medieval benches, two Tudor chests, and two 15th century chairs. But the masterpiece of craftsmanship here is the Jacobean oak pulpit, which, set on the stem of its medieval predecessor, is carved on each of its seven panels and has delicate inlay work of other woods.

House Beautiful

COGGESHALL. Who has not heard of Paycocke's House? It is ours for all time, still standing on the Roman road to Colchester. Look where you will in this quaint town and carved beams meet your eye; there are 99 monuments here scheduled by the Government. But among them all it is Paycocke's which stands supreme, a complete example of a richly ornamented merchant's house of Tudor days.

Its timbers overhang the road where all may see them, its upper storey with a frieze of running foliage on it and tiny heads, a shield with a merchant's mark of an ermine's tail, and the initials of Thomas Paycocke himself, who died in 1580. Both storeys are divided by buttresses into five bays. On the sideposts of an arch are moulded pedestals, and under canopies are two statues of a man with a shield and another man with a load on his shoulder. Indoors most of the rooms have elaborately carved ceiling beams, original doorways, linenfold panelling, and fireplaces carved with grotesque beasts.

Even older than Thomas Paycocke's House is the inn Thomas would pass on his way to church, called the Woolpack in compliment to the industry which brought wealth to this town. Its embattled beams have supported the gables 400 years, and one of its bedrooms has a handsome kingpost 500 years old.

The church was made new amid the great prosperity of the 15th century, and we know from the Roman bricks among the flint rubble of the walls that it was refashioned from an older church. A perfect whole in construction and design; its graceful columns and its great windows are delightful, especially the seven-panelled east window, which looks big even from the tower arch 40 yards away. The oak roof of the nave looks down from a height of 40 feet and its old and new timbers rest on canopied figures of the Apostles placed here last century. The font is 700 years old.

Engraved on brass is the portrait of Thomas Paycocke, and on other brasses are John Paycocke of 1533 with his wife, and William Goldwyre of 1514 with his wife. Two other civilians are shown in rich robes of the 15th century, and two unknown women in butterfly headdress. It was probably in their day that the pelicans and leopards and lions in the porch and at the priest's doorway were carved.

It has happened in our own time that the church of Markshall close by has been pulled down, many of its memorials being bricked up in the vaults, and the oak choir-stalls, the reading desk, and the brass lectern were brought to Coggeshall. Several memorials to members of the Honywood family have been taken to Colchester and can be seen in the garden by the Holly Trees Museum; they include one of Sir Thomas, who took a leading part in the siege of Colchester and was brother-in-law to Sir Harry Vane. Another of this family's monuments is now in the vestry here at Coggeshall; it is that of Mrs Mary Honywood, a well-known 16th century lady who lived to be 93 and died here, but was taken to Kent for burial at Lenham. A banquet was given to her by 200 of her descendants, and the gathering might have been much greater had transport been much easier, for she had a descendant for every day in the year and two over. She was a brave woman, with something of the spirit of Elizabeth Fry, for she visited prisons in Mary Tudor's time.

In a delightful pastoral scene on the other side of the Blackwater is a perfect little chapel of the 13th century; we come to it by a brick bridge which has been here 700 years, perhaps the oldest brick bridge in the country. Dedicated to St Nicholas, patron saint of travellers, the chapel stood at the gate of a monastery. It is of interest on its own account and also for the small pink bricks forming the arches of the windows, the piscina, and the sedilia; the bricks are also at the threshold of the doorway where they are cut and shaped into a pattern. These bricks are under two inches thick and are the earliest known in England since Roman days; it is believed that they were made at Tylkell on the north boundary of the county.

Fading away at the back of the sedilia in this little chapel is a consecration cross marking the place where the bishop put his hand on the wall 700 years ago. It was because the chapel was used as a barn that it escaped the fate of the great church of the abbey at the Dissolution. Not a stone of that church remains to be seen, but its Norman foundations have been traced and found to measure 70 yards long with a width of 80 feet across the transepts.

A group of farm buildings here is of very great interest. One dates from about 1200 and has roof beams 400 years old; and there is a 13th century wing connected by a two-storeyed corridor to a 16th century house built from the ruins of the monastery. The columns and arches we come upon as we wander through this quaint rambling house suggest that the old monks were building for all time.

Long after the monks had passed away there were four brave men at Coggeshall who died for their faith. Thomas Hawkes told the cruel Bishop Bonner that if he had a hundred bodies he would suffer them all to be torn in pieces rather than deny his faith, and he was burned in the vicarage field, raising his hands and clapping them together. With him were burned Thomas Osmund, a fuller, and William Bamford and Nicholas Chamberlain, two weavers. Another story of cruelty is suggested by an entry in the parish register, which records the death, in 1699, of the "Widow Common that was counted a witch." Several times had she been put in the river to see if she would sink, and it is thought that this cruel treatment was the cause of her death.

Very Heart of Very England

COLCHESTER. We walk about its streets and it seems that time goes back for 1800 years. All through these centuries this High Street has been here, and everywhere before our eyes are the bricks of Roman Colchester. They are here in hundreds of thousands, in arches and doorways and windows, bricks the Romans made, the Saxons handled, and the Normans used again; bricks that have seen the world go by from the Roman Empire down to ours, so that we feel here the spirit of Cowper's lines on Boadicea:

> *Regions Caesar never knew*
> *Thy posterity shall sway.*

Here have been found the ashes of the fires of Boadicea. Here is the vivid memory of that great chieftain who defied the might of Rome and the vivid witness of the regions Caesar knew.

Colchester was the first Roman city in the Island and has preserved for us a host of lovely things. Wherever we turn we find the touch of a Roman hand. Though much of the glory of the Roman wall has been lost, the wall skirts the town more or less consecutively for two miles, and is the most extensive Roman town wall surviving in England. In parts it has a very dignified appearance, but too often it runs along mean streets and poor backs.

The story which thrills us as we walk about these streets began before Caesar came to Britain. Here men were living in the Stone Age and the Bronze Age, and the things they made and the tools they used have been found. It became a place of importance, a British city, between the time when Julius Caesar came and went and the time when the legions of Claudius came and conquered. It was the city of Shakespeare's Cymbeline, and its name was Camulodunum. Cymbeline of Camulodunum was a prince of Britain, and the Romans called him King of All the Island. He reigned through nearly all the first half century of the Christian Era. He minted coins as fine as any British coin today. He built up an active trade between Britain and Rome.

It was a prosperous city that he built up when he moved his capital from Verulamium (now St Albans) in the year 3 AD, and we know exactly where it stood, for its site has been opened up with the making of the bypass road. It lies in the triangle formed by the bypass, the Lexden road, and the road to the station, most of the British dwellings having been found by the River Colne at Sheepen Farm. There is not very much to see, but here proud Cymbeline sat on his throne. His walls were defended by a dyke and long entrenchments which we can trace, for their outlines have been found by that new race of discoverers who reveal the mysteries of our old earth from their seats in the clouds.

All this was happening while Paul was on his journeys, writing letters to the Corinthians. Camulodunum flourished, and then there happened one of those pathetic tragedies of fate which more than once in our human story have changed the course of nations.

Cymbeline had several sons; the oldest was Adminius, and one of the younger was Caractacus. Every schoolboy knows Caractacus, the brave patriot who loved our Motherland and rather than surrender was carried captive to Rome and marched through the streets in chains, bearing himself so proudly, addressing Caesar with such eloquence, that Caesar set him free, too proud to chain such a hero. Perhaps few of us know his brother Adminius, for he rebelled against his father, went to Rome, and persuaded Caesar to send his legions to govern where Romans had so far only traded. There are few sadder tales of brothers than this of the two sons of Shakespeare's Cymbeline, hero and renegade.

So it was that the 400-year-old story of Britain as a Roman colony began; in the year 43 came Claudius with his legions. Cymbeline was gone; he was spared this bitterness, and his sons Caractacus and Togodumnus were left to defend the Island. It was in vain, for the legions were too strong for them. The Romans took the city of Cymbeline and settled there, strengthening the defences but sweeping away the huts of the Britons, building in their place substantial structures whose sites have been found.

The years went on; the Romans grew stronger and stronger, and then came another tragedy to change the course of things. What is now Norfolk and Suffolk was then the kingdom of the Iceni, and its king Prasutagus died. His queen was Boadicea, and the wise old man, fearing that Rome would swallow up his kingdom, appointed Caesar joint-heir with his queen and her two daughters. It happened that this Caesar was Nero, and his emissaries were as ruthless as he. The chivalry of the old king was nothing to them. They devastated his kingdom, whipped his queen in public, and assaulted her daughters. This was Nero's work in this place where we stand.

Then it was that Boadicea put herself into history for all time. She summoned her sorrowful people and raised an army to redress their wrongs. She came in a chariot to Colchester with her mantle of hair streaming down to her waist, a proud and valiant figure as we see her in bronze in the shadow of Big Ben; she is one of the noblest figures in the streets of London. Tacitus tells us in his history how the statue of Victory at Camulodunum fell down for no apparent cause, and there were ominous shadows of coming events.

Boadicea swept down on the Roman stronghold and took them by surprise, so that the small Roman garrison there retreated to the temple and the city was taken on the second day. It was a frightful revenge for a bitter wrong, and every living man, woman, and child in the town was slain. The victorious queen fought her way in triumph to St Albans and London, and there have been found both here and in London the ashes of her fires. We have been down in the foundations of All Hallows-by-the-Tower and seen the walls that were blackened by the fires set alight by this proud queen nineteen centuries before the Nazi barbarians burned down the church which had risen above them. Boadicea had slain 70,000 people when she slew herself in the sight of her defeated army—for in the end she was defeated, and the Roman city rose again, now at last on the site of the Colchester we know, a city of truly Roman splendour, the old British town close by being used for potters and burials. They made it an incomparable place, and even now the walls are the most perfect example in England of a walled town of those days. They are not equal to the marvellous walls of York and Canterbury and Chester, but those are medieval and these are Roman, and this Roman wall was built in the face of almost incredible difficulty, for there was no stone available on the spot and huge lumps of hardened lime were brought from the beach, cut into blocks, and on these foundations the walls were built up of bricks and rubble with the help of Roman mortar which set like iron. For three centuries no sea rover could enter this fortress.

Where these walls have been rescued from their mean surroundings they are magnificent. They ran about 3000 yards and were strengthened by round bastions of which two remain, waiting to be surrounded by the dignity a proud town should give them. It is thrilling to remember that within the walls have been found the ruins of about a hundred Roman structures (mosaics, pavements, foundations, kilns, and so on), the most remarkable of all being the temple below the castle and the Temple of Mithras in a meadow. We have come

MEAVONMFPOLFACI

The Roman Centurion of Colchester

Old Siege House in East Street

Number Three West Stockwell Street

TUDOR COLCHESTER

The South Front with the Domed Turret

The Massive Walls of the Norman Keep

COLCHESTER CASTLE

Roman Sphinx

Cavalry Officer Longinus

Pot showing Combat with a Lion

The Famous Colchester Vase with Gladiators and Huntsmen

TREASURED RELICS OF ROMAN COLCHESTER

upon one or two other remains of Mithraic temples, but this buried temple one minute from the streets of Colchester is far the most important survival in England of the days when Christianity was fighting for existence against the influence of the sun god Mithras, whom the Roman soldiers worshipped. We may look down into it through the railings in the middle of the meadow and may visit it from Holly Trees Mansion close by.

What is believed to have been the finest mass of this great wall is lost in a mean street, and is known as the Balkerne Gateway. It must have been magnificent, with guard rooms and four arches, but what we look upon today is an unimpressive arch railed round next to an inn, a lost piece of grandeur that should be saved from this indignity. Not far away, at a corner of the meadow which has the Mithraic temple, a fallen arch lies on the ground, its square bases erect beside it. It must have been part of a gateway, and seems to have been thrown down by force. It was set up in the first century of our era; how long it has been lying here no man knows.

Set in the midst of these Roman walls is the monument which links us with the Roman conqueror of Britain and the Norman conqueror of England, Colchester Castle, one of the most fascinating buildings in this country. It has something in it of the dignity of the White Tower of London, the Conqueror's Town House, and it was raised by Eudo Dapifer, the Conqueror's steward.

From its earliest days Colchester Castle was a royal stronghold and many famous people have lived in it by royal grant. King John was here on several occasions and after his reign the Bishops of London were the lords of the castle. The good Duke Humphrey held it from 1404 till 1447 and was followed by Margaret of Anjou, queen of the tragic reign of Henry the Sixth. In the 14th century part of the castle was made into a prison and it remained so until the middle of the 19th. To this place were brought many of the Protestant martyrs of Mary Tudor, and the Royalist leaders Sir Charles Lucas and Sir George Lisle were imprisoned in one of the dungeons before being shot outside the castle walls.

For all its grim story the castle keep is a cheerful sight with its rows of bright red tiles breaking up the mass of stone from Kent and Caen and Barnack, and the rough mass of Roman masonry. If we come to it in spring we find wallflowers clinging to its walls in lovely contrast with the rich green of the turf mound, which has the appearance of advancing like a wave against this massive place.

The keep is 151 feet by 110, covering a bigger area than any other Norman keep in England. It has lost much of its old height and has now but two storeys, unless we count the turrets, one with a flagstaff on its broken wall, one roofed with a low tiled pyramid, one with a quaint dome and a weathervane. High up by the dome grows a sycamore tree which is said to have been planted there to celebrate the Battle of Waterloo. Very trim is the front this building shows to those who hurry by, with big modern windows in the upper storey, and only a Norman doorway and a tiny window beside it breaking the face of the lower wall; but walking round we see that the Norman builders pierced the lower walls with windows between the buttresses.

We come in by the great Norman doorway, which has three depths of moulding in the arch, and carved capitals. We may still see the grooves for the portcullis. Just inside is a recess for the warder, and the eye falls on a sculpture of St Christopher, as if we were in a church; he has been here since the 14th century.

On a stone close by we read the only old inscription which is part of the castle; it is in memory of Roger Chamberleyn, a 14th century gaoler, and his wife. We walk on through a lobby into a great quadrangle with the great walls rising all round, the outer walls impressive with windows narrowing down to tiny slits outside. Here their arches almost fill the upper walls, narrowing as they go back, for the walls are very thick, some 30 feet.

There are two groups of vaults, one comprising dungeons with strong staples to which prisoners were fastened, the other group, underground, being part (it is believed) of a Roman temple dedicated to Claudius. On the ground floor are Roman mosaics found in the town, one with long-tailed monsters hunting. A staircase opposite the Norman doorway leads up to the first floor where at the east end we find the apse-shaped crypt of a Norman chapel which must have been an imposing sight when the building was perhaps twice as high as we see it now. The whole of the keep with its quadrangle has been roofed over and turned into a museum. There are few museums in England with such a wealth of Roman possessions, the proudest of all being the impressive sculpture of the Roman centurion holding his wand of office. His name was Marcus Favonius, and the monument was set up by two of his freedmen. The junior cavalry officer Longinus is here riding over a fallen foe, as he instructed his heirs to set him up, and above the arch under which he sits triumphant on his horse is a sphinx between two lions. There are splendid Roman vases, and on one, known all the world over as the Colchester Vase, are gladiators fighting, men attacking a wild beast, and a hound pursuing a hare and two deer. There are terracotta busts, toys, lamps, glass burial urns, mirrors, brooches, bracelets, keys and rings, and even cups for feeding babies are in this vast assortment of objects from the Roman world. There are objects also from Cymbeline's town, older than the Roman Empire.

For all the interest of Colchester since the Romans we come into the neighbouring museum, standing so pleasantly across at the entrance to the park, and known as Holly Trees Mansion from an avenue of holly trees. It is a Georgian house which has been made into one of the daintiest museums in this country, where we may not only walk about and see lovely things, but may sit down in a rest room, or sit at a table and write—an admirable touch of hospitality we have not found in any other museum.

We come to this beautiful place through 18th century iron gates, and in the hall is a bronze bust of the generous man who made this place, and Castle Park itself, into the splendid possessions they are, the first Lord Cowdray. The museum has an impressive collection, and is charmingly arranged. It has a fine collection of Bygones, especially of things of everyday use in the 19th century. It has military uniforms and Victorian dresses, and a jolly model of an old pedlar woman. It has old books, including one printed by Caxton himself, and a small sanctus bell which rang out on the Field of the Cloth of Gold. There is a heap of coins (671 of them) which are part of a hoard of 12,000 silver pennies found in a lead coffer under a house buried in the reign of Henry the First, and there are two receipts for £10,000 paid to Fairfax as the town's indemnity.

It was after the siege that two heroes of Colchester, Sir Charles Lucas and Sir George Lisle, were shot on the spot marked by an obelisk in the Castle Park. The siege had lasted 12 weeks when Fairfax pressed on the Royalist forces and ended it. Dogs, cats, rats, and horses had been eaten by the people, and not a crumb of food remained. Lucas and Lisle were led out to the spot marked by this monument, and Lucas was shot saying, "I am ready for you, rebels; now do your worst." Then Lisle was brought forward, kissed the body of his dead friend, and stood before the firing squad, which he invited to come nearer. "I'll warrant you we will hit you," said one, and Lisle replied, "I have been nearer you, friends, when you have missed me." They lie in St Giles's church, under an immense black marble stone which tells us that they were barbarously murdered in cold blood.

The little church stands by the garden wall of the abbey of St John founded by Eudo Dapifer soon after the castle was built. His work has vanished, but some of its medieval magnificence is here to see, for the 15th century gateway stands. It is one of the few great structures here with no Roman bricks in it; it is built of flint and stone, with corner pinnacles and a battlemented parapet. The abbey itself was demolished before the siege, but we can see the mark of a cannon-ball in one corner of the gateway.

Out of its ruins was built one of the loveliest little places in or about Colchester, the Mill at Bourne Pond. It has lovely windows and high chimneys, and a dormer set in the roof, and its chief attraction is its two gabled ends, charmingly shaped and in four stages, each stage adorned with pinnacles. The harbour is down at Hythe, the port of Colchester, where the North Sea flows up the River Colne; here many a freight must have been landed in Roman galleys and by Saxon and Danish boats, and here still the barges with their great red sails pass by.

The 12-week siege of the town ruined the great Norman church of St Botolph, but it left this massive structure the chief sight of the town next to the castle, if not the finest single spectacle the town has. Truly magnificent these ruins are, standing by the new church which is in the style of the old one. The west front is as the Civil War left it, the great central doorway finer than anything at the castle, and one of the aisle doorways still standing next to it.

Above them are tiers of narrow Norman arches, all simplicity itself compared with the great doorway, which has five depths of carving and six pillars. We walk through into the nave and are staggered by its stupendous piers, each rising like a mighty monument from the grass, some of the arches complete from the floor to the height of the roof, and all open to the sky. At the east end of the wall are three windows which show us three changing styles, Norman, 13th century, and 14th—the simple and massive Norman strength, the lightness of the Early English, and the elaborate Decorated style. This marvellous arcade has looked as we see it since the Civil War, but what we see men have looked on for 800 years, and the bricks of which this place is made are a thousand years older than that; they are Roman. There must be a hundred thousand of them in this impressive ruin.

St Botolph's has been the noblest of all Colchester's churches, for though the town has many they have little to attract us. We may run round them all very quickly. No traveller will miss the best church tower still standing in the town, with the fine triangular doorway looking on to a quaint narrow street leading to the town hall at one end and the abbey gate at the other, and in the middle of it, opposite the little Saxon tower, the old home of Queen Elizabeth's electrical wizard, William Gilbert.

This tower of Holy Trinity is one of the finest possessions of the town, and it has still hanging in it on its old hinges a door which may have been opened for Queen Elizabeth. The tower is built of Roman bricks and stands as the Saxons left it. The door by which we come in at the south porch has also been opening and shutting for 500 years, and has a fine rose for its knocker. Looking down into the nave is a fox carrying off a goose and a lion having a meal, and there are 15th century glass roundels in the windows. The font is also 15th century, and the church has one of the rare medieval mazer bowls, with a silver rim.

Here, in an unknown grave, lies the most renowned composer of those madrigals for which Elizabethan music was famous, William Wilbye. He lived in a house near the church for the last ten years of his life, and was buried here in 1638. Hardly any manuscripts of his are preserved, but his madrigals have been sung by every generation since his own. They are very beautiful and some of the best known are Stay, Corydon; Adieu Sweet Amaryllis; and Flora gave me fairest flowers.

But the chief interest in the church is the alabaster carving which tells us that here lies William Gilbert, the wonder man of Queen Elizabeth's court, her physician, who used to amuse her with electrical experiments. He was the first man who used the word Electricity, and perhaps the first man to have any practical knowledge of it. He lived across the street, where Queen Elizabeth is said to have visited him in 1579, and we may be sure he would point out this Saxon tower, and probably he opened one of these very doors for her. We may go through the archway facing the church and see the delightful white house in which Gilbert lived, with a bay window perched under its overhanging storey and three dormers in the roof. It is Tymperleys, a lovely little place.

Gilbert was one of the giants of learning in Elizabethan England. It was he who coined the word electricity. The ancient Greeks had discovered that amber could be made to attract other bodies; and Gilbert thought of extending friction to other things and found that what was true of amber was true of such substances as sulphur, resin, sealing-wax. He investigated magnetism and declared that the whole earth was one vast magnet, setting forth the truth, unproved until the advent of Michael Faraday two centuries later, that electricity and magnetism are two emanations of the same fundamental force pervading Nature. Francis Bacon, unfit to hold a candle to him in mathematical and physical knowledge, attacked the great discovery, but Gilbert was nobly vindicated by Galileo, who loved his book for the daring with which it traversed dogmatic and untested principles. "I extremely praise, admire, and envy this author," Galileo wrote; "I think him, moreover, worthy of the greatest praise for the many new and true observations he has made, to the disgrace of so many vain and fabling authors who repeat everything they hear from the foolish vulgar, without attempting to satisfy themselves by experiment." Gilbert, who grasped the relations between the earth and the moon, and realised that the moon is responsible for the tides, invented two appliances for finding the latitude by astronomical observation.

St James's church on East Hill was begun in the 11th century and stands near the Roman wall by the east gate. It belongs to all our three building centuries, and its tower has Roman bricks. The chapel and the chancel have their original roofs, and the tower and the vestry have 15th century doors. The font was new when the doors were hung. Hanging on the wall is a big picture of the Nativity by George Carter. There is a 16th century brass with portraits of John Maynard and his wife (she headless), and at the west end reclines Arthur Winsley, a remarkable figure meditating, wearing a cloak and holding a book in which we read "Go and do thou likewise." He founded 12 charity houses 200 years ago.

St Peter's church has a fine door which opened for the congregation in the 14th century and has still its old lockplate and the ironwork a medieval craftsman made for it—a precious possession suggesting the work of Thomas of Leighton Buzzard, who made the grille which protects the lovely tomb of Queen Eleanor in the Confessor's Chapel in Westminster Abbey. There is also a charming vestry door with its old ironwork, and under the vestry is a small vaulted chamber probably used as a charnel house. The fine oak pulpit was carved in the 18th century; near it in the floor is the stone of Sir William Campion, who was killed in the siege during the Civil War. The modern nave has 15th century arches and a group of monuments of the two centuries after that. Martin Basill kneels with his wife and 13 children on a marble tomb; George Sayer and his two wives are with their seven children, all elegantly chiselled and looking delightful in their ruffs. There are about 30 portraits in brass: William Brown with his wife and seven children; Agnes Leach with two husbands and nine children (1553); John Sayer of 1509 in an alderman's gown, his wife in her widow's veil with five children; another John Sayer kneeling at a desk; and Richard Sayer of 1610 with his two wives and two children in a quaint group. Over Richard Sayer's brass is an oak memorial to a Richard of the family which tells us that he was driven by persecution to seek refuge among the pilgrims in Holland, and went to America and died there in 1676. His son came here and died here, and this memorial was put up by his family in 1687.

In the High Street are the churches of All Saints and St Nicholas, All Saints with a 16th century tower faced with flints, an old door, and a fine lion and unicorn in spandrels; St Nicholas with a medieval bell, a Norman piscina, an altar table and three chests of the 17th century, and a painting which was the old altarpiece of the vanished church of St Runwald, a church dating from Saxon times which used to stand in the middle of the street.

St Martin's church has a 12th century tower with a ruined top mostly built of Roman bricks; most of the church is 14th and 15th century. Midway in the chancel is a rare and very beautiful timber arch six centuries old. There is a fine medieval font, a 15th century screen, and Jacobean chests, poorbox, and pulpit panels; but perhaps the most interesting possession of the church is the one so little seen, the ancient altar stone with five consecration crosses. Another ancient stone lying here is carved with what seem to be dragons.

The medieval church of St Giles by the gateway of the abbey is chiefly interesting for its 17th century wooden tower, a 600-year-old door, and the graves of Lucas and Lisle. Framed in oak are copies of the brasses from their coffins.

St Leonard's is at the Hythe, a 14th century church with a beautiful hammerbeam roof 400 years old, richly moulded, and well lit from the clerestory. Four angels which once held it up are in the vestry. The roofs of two chapels are a century older than the nave's. There are six old chairs, a mazer bowl of 1521 with a silver rim, and an Elizabethan cup with two bands of ornament, and two medieval bells still ringing in the tower, from which a remarkable clock face of stone looks down. It is as old as 1500 and has carved spandrels. Two heads which once supported the roof beam still project from the walls at the chancel arch. The windows are attractive with 24 big figures, among them Thomas Becket, Helena, Ethelbert, the Confessor, and Charles Stuart. The door by which we come and go is 500 years old and pierced with holes made by the bullets of the Parliament men in the Civil War.

The church of St Mary-at-the-Walls was new last century except for its 15th century tower, damaged in the siege and restored with brick; in the tower sits John Rebow, a 17th century merchant in a great wig. St Helen's chapel is a chapel no more, for the poor little place was disused when we called, yet in the 12th century it was attached to the abbey and was endowed with 14 acres of land.

Close by this disused chapel is one of the town's finest old houses, looking down on West Stockwell Street. The Angel Inn about 500 years ago, it has now been turned into offices and is admirably preserved by a firm of solicitors, having been restored by Mr Duncan Clark. It has a magnificent front with two gables and an overhanging storey, and its timbers and windows are charming. A little way off, down the street, is a simple house which was the home of Ann and Jane Taylor, beloved of children for Twinkle, Twinkle, Little Star, and many other rhymes. At the Marquis of Granby Inn on North Hill are 16th century beams with three queer figures carved on them

The Great Norman Arches of the Nave
ST BOTOLPH'S PRIORY, COLCHESTER

Medieval Gateway of St John's Abbey

Norman Doorway
of St Botolph's

Bastion of
Roman Wall

Saxon Doorway
of Holy Trinity

ANCIENT COLCHESTER

showing the costume of those days, and in the middle of the High Street is the captivating Red Lion, with a wealth of medieval timbers inside and out, with four roof gables, an irresistible interior, and a little courtyard into which at least 15 generations of travellers have come. The George Hotel, on the other side of the street, has much old work and foundations of the 16th century. Lower down, past Castle Park, is Siege House in East Street, a famous piece of Tudor England with a doorway in the first storey which seems to have been used for getting on to coaches. The house has lovely arcading on the front, fine faces on the brackets, and in the doorway is St George in one spandrel and the dragon in the other. The timbers are riddled with Civil War bullets, about 30 of the holes being ringed round with red paint.

Whatever may be hard to find in this old town with its winding ways, two things we never lose sight of, the peace memorial at the gateway of the park, and the elegant municipal tower which rises over all. The peace memorial, so superbly placed with the castle rising from the lawns behind it, is crowned by a bronze-winged angel with sword and laurel leaves, the stone pedestal having on one side Peace with the Dove, and on the other St George and his Dragon. It is a fine piece of work by Mr H. C. Fehr, the sculptor of the superb Middlesex Guildhall facing Westminster Abbey.

The Town Hall tower is elegant in the Italian style, crowned by a bronze statue of Helena, mother of Constantine, who stands with a sceptre and a cross 50 yards above the street, her face towards Jerusalem. Below her are four bronze ravens, and below these, but above the clock, are four sculptures of Engineering and Defence, Agriculture and Fisheries. On the front of the main building are six statues, four looking down on the High Street representing the Norman steward Eudo Dapifer, founder of the abbey; Thomas Audley, Henry the Eighth's Chancellor, Speaker of the House of Commons, and Town Clerk of Colchester; William Gilbert; and Samuel Harsnett, the Colchester boy who became Archbishop of York under Charles Stuart. Looking down on the side street are figures of Edward the Elder and Boadicea. The bell still hanging in the tower is probably 14th century, and rang out from the old Moot Hall which stood here.

Encased in bronze at the entrance are the names of 1263 Colchester men who fell in the war, and on the walls are 30 names of martyrs. There are busts of Mr Spurgeon and of a Colchester man who was Lord Mayor of London, and looking down on the stairway from opposite walls are jolly wooden statues of a Bluecoat boy and girl. The Great Hall has a rounded roof with fluted columns, a splendid organ, and fine portraits and stained windows. Among the pictures here is one by a local artist of the daughter of Jairus, and another of William Gilbert showing his electrical experiments to Queen Elizabeth. Notable in the collection of portraits are those of the first Lord Colchester in his robes as Speaker, Sir William Campion who was killed in the siege, Sir Charles Lucas, Sir George Lisle, Ireton and Fairfax, William Gilbert and Sir Thomas Honywood, and Lord and Lady Cowdray, she lovely in red and black, holding two roses, on a background of green. One of the interesting possessions of the Town Hall is a deed hanging on the wall; it is signed by William Gilbert, and is perhaps his only known autograph.

Another fine collection of pictures hangs in the Albert Hall, originally built as the Corn Exchange, which has in the lobby a bronze bust of William Willett, who spent much of his boyhood in the town; and among the pictures are works of local artists, and sketches and portraits by Constable, including one of his mother and one of the headmaster of Dedham School. There is also a portrait of the remarkable Mary Honywood, who lived and died at Markshall near Coggeshall and lies at Lenham in Kent; she left 367 descendants.

Such is Colchester, town of Shakespeare's Cymbeline, of the brave Caractacus and proud Boadicea, of the conquering Roman, the Saxon, and the Norman, and of the little electrical wizard of Queen Elizabeth. We should say also that it is the town of roses and oysters, for it is famous for both. Its oyster fishery belongs to the town and is managed by a Fishery Board. The town receives one-quarter of the revenue from the sales, and has a great feast every October at which 400 people are always found who can stand the sight of an oyster. But it is for more dignified and more enduring things that Colchester is known throughout the world. Its tale is written in the life of 20 centuries, and everywhere about us lies the witness of it. It is very heart of very England.

COLD NORTON. Its cottages are scattered on a slope above the River Crouch. Its church is of last century and has a few things from the older church, a brass showing a woman in the headdress of 1520, and an oak pulpit carved from the old beams in the roof. From the same ancient timbers comes the reading desk. Crouching apostles and saints with their emblems as corbels support the roof, a modern sculpture gallery; and three panels of glass with backgrounds of rich blue give a glow to the east window. Its central panel is a beautiful Crucifixion.

The Barn of Hungry Hall

COLNE ENGAINE. It is grouped round its church on a hill and has commanding views of the Colne valley. There are Roman tiles in the Norman nave, and a tower which was begun in the 14th century and finished 200 years later with two stages of brickwork. Its battlements and pinnacles project over a corbel table, and on one side is a shield with a mullet, the crest of the Earls of Oxford who were neighbours in the next village. We see the beautiful Tudor brickwork again in the porch, which has a stepped arch over the doorway with a new lead figure of St Andrew. The nave roof is 500 years old, and one of its corbels is a man who has been laughing all the time. There is a handsome modern eagle lectern, a fine 14th century piscina, and a brilliant east window showing the King of Kings and St Michael in a company of saints and martyrs and angels kneeling on the clouds. The church has a link with London and the Bluecoat boys. Its rectors are appointed by the Lord Mayor in his capacity as Governor of Christ's Hospital, and here on the wall are tablets to two who were headmasters of that school. In the 100 acres of Colne Park stands a tall column put up in 1791 by the famous architect Sir John Soane; and a mile or so away is Hungry Hall, which, in spite of its name, has a great barn of seven bays in which to store the winter needs of man and beast.

The Mitred Nero

COPFORD. It had an ancient ford at the river in the days when the Romans were in Colchester, five miles away, and today it has an ancient treasury without its equal in Essex (or perhaps in any village church), an array of wall-paintings which have been here 800 years. They are remarkable in size, in colour, in arrangement, and in the revelation of the costume of the 12th century; it is not too much to say that they remind us of the paintings in Italian Byzantine churches. We have seen few things more enchanting than this painted apse, one of the rarest legacies bequeathed to us by the Normans.

Here are priests and people and soldiers and saints and architecture and natural history of the time. There are Bible figures grouped with elaborate decoration, and dominating all else on the vault of the apse is a gorgeously arrayed figure of Our Lord on a throne encircled by a rainbow supported by angels. There are angels on thrones in the spandrels, and below are apostles under canopies. In the splays of the central window are the archangels Michael and Gabriel, and in the arch and on its face are the signs of the Zodiac and angels trumpeting. It is one of the most remarkable apses we have seen, a veritable masterpiece of antiquity.

There are more paintings on the walls of the nave and chancel, not so clear to see but recognisable as Samson struggling with the lion, soldiers in mail, Christ and the Centurion, and the Flight into Egypt. Most of these paintings are finely preserved, thanks to the whitewash which covered them for centuries.

The church stands remotely by the great house in the park, the house replacing that in which Bishops of London lived for generations. It has fine cedars about it. The apse whose walls are so wonderful inside is interesting outside for the flat Norman buttresses and windows with detached shafts. The buttresses and windows continue along one wall, and one buttress has been pierced high up for a door into the roof; the buttress has hundreds of Roman tiles, one of them the biggest we remember. The nave, chancel, and apse of the church are all the early work of the Normans, and the interior is remarkable for showing us the cut-off ends of the vaulted roof into which the buttress doorway gave entrance. The men who refashioned the church in the 14th century cut the vaulting away, replacing it with the splendid timber rafters we see. A hundred years later came the beams which support the bell-turret. At the end of the 12th century the south wall of the nave was pierced by pointed arches, two of them meeting in elaborate Norman windows of which one of the capitals remain; a third arch made in the 13th century took in the whole of a Norman window, the builders using its Roman tiles again.

This astonishing Norman church, with the apse practically as the Normans left it, has still the great square font they made, and some Norman timber in a door—an extreme rarity, for there is very little Norman timber left. The old chest and the screen are medieval. By the altar of this thrilling place lies that fearful figure Bishop Bonner.

Edmund Bonner was with Cardinal Wolsey through his decline and fall, and was present at the melancholy scene of the arrest. The master's catastrophe was the servant's opportunity; he insinuated himself into the confidence of Henry, vehemently vindicating the marriage with Anne Boleyn and writing of "the tyranny of the Bishop of Rome." Henry sent him to Rome to argue the case for the divorce, and the story runs that Bonner's language was so outrageous that the Pope threatened to have him thrown into a cauldron of boiling lead. Bonner's apologists challenge this story as an absurdity, but it is admitted that his manner to Francis the First of France was so intolerable that the most courteous of monarchs retorted that but for his love for Henry he would have caused Bonner to receive a hundred strokes. Sailing with the tide, Bonner was now an ardent Lutheran, and as such was appointed Bishop of London. With the accession of Edward the Sixth he wavered between Rome and Reformation, being imprisoned and released and again arrested. The advent of Mary Tudor restored his fortunes. He had no Lutheran scruples now, but inaugurated and carried through the terrible persecution whose horrors and vindictiveness brought him the title of the Mitred Nero.

Three of his victims were Latimer, Ridley, and Cranmer, but in three years 200 more Protestants, learned and simple, illustrious and lowly, men, women, and the young, were burned alive at his behest. Not content to pronounce their doom, he personally participated in their trials and tortures. He reviled them in opprobrious language; Thomas Tomkins, a Shoreditch weaver, he beat about the face; others he belaboured with his crozier. Ridley, when Bonner himself was in prison, had supported his mother and sister, giving them precedence at his table; now that his turn had come Bonner flung Ridley's relatives starving into the streets. Cranmer he humiliated by stripping him of his vestments and clothing him in rags.

Of all the men who hastened to Highgate to render homage to Elizabeth as she rode into London as queen, Bonner alone was denied the right to kiss her hand. She turned her face from him and drew back with a shudder. It is to his credit that, with the Reformation established, he did not again recant. Refusing to take the oath of supremacy, he spent his last ten years in prison and died there.

The Church Like a Fortress

CORRINGHAM. Thameshaven is its child, born almost yesterday, while Corringham has grown old for a thousand years. Much water has come down the Thames since this gracious place grew up among the lovely fields; and it has yet an old-world charm. We must love it for its group of old things, timber cottages and a 15th century inn keeping company with a glorious chestnut standing like a sentinel by the church. The tree is ancient but the church is older, for fragments of its walls were here before the Conqueror marched on London. The north aisle and the chapel are 14th century. The church tower is Norman and can have changed very little; it is immensely strong and has tiny windows but no buttresses, and its belfry has Norman arcading, with a roof like a hat too big for it. The tower arch has a keystone with a little head 800 years old. Among the treasures of this church so like a fortress are old bench-ends with carved panels; fragments of medieval glass with two angels and a dragon; two quaint old chests; and a fine oak screen with rich tracery, the work of a 14th century craftsman. The chapel has lost its brass portrait of Isabel Baud, who has been sleeping here 600 years, but the chancel has a civilian brass of 1460 and the brass portrait of one of its medieval priests, Richard Beltoun.

The Founder of a State

CRANHAM. Its graceful spire draws us from miles away to a church refashioned last century. It has some Tudor bricks in its walls, and there are others in the garden wall of the hall, which stands close by with a good cedar before it. It was here that General Oglethorpe came to live at the end of his adventurous life; and here they laid him to rest in 1785. The church has a marble inscription (covering most of the chancel wall) put up by his widow to tell of his life and virtues, and of the deed by which he will always be remembered, the founding of Georgia. We read, too, the quaint thought Alexander Pope had about him, that

> *One driven by strong benevolence of soul*
> *Shall fly like Oglethorpe from Pole to Pole.*

Entering Parliament for Haslemere, he came in contact with the horrors of our prison system, and, first of prison reformers, brought the matter before Parliament in 1729. Three years later he organised a scheme for the colonisation of Georgia, with the double purpose of relieving poor debtors and checking Spanish aggression. He took out with him John and Charles Wesley, and when Charles came home appointed George Whitefield in his stead. A high-souled Governor, Oglethorpe firmly banned both rum and slavery, a policy very difficult to enforce. Trouble with the Wesleys added to his burden, but he carried all before him, and came home bringing with him a number of Red Indian chiefs with whom, as with all their people, he maintained the happiest relations. War broke out with Spain, and his military conduct in the colony was such that after final victory Whitefield wrote that "The deliverance is such as cannot be paralleled but by some instance out of the Old Testament." Oglethorpe was poorly supported at home, where the Government refused to meet the bills they had authorised him to draw on behalf of the colony; and had he not made a fortunate and happy marriage, which brought him an estate at Cranham, he must have been ruined. It was this village therefore that saved a great reputation.

It was the Stuart rising of 1745 that ended his Georgian career. Sent North to fight under Wade, he was absurdly accused of excessive sympathy with the enemy, and though a courtmartial acquitted him, he lost his seat in Parliament and retired into private life, befriending scholars and making his house a centre of learning and happy society. Dr Johnson said to him, "I know no man whose Life would be more interesting; if I were furnished with materials I should be very glad to write it." That chance was missed, and Boswell, to whom Oglethorpe did give some details for the purpose, also let slip the great opportunity. Oglethorpe died suddenly at 89.

One Who Never Turned His Back

CRESSING. It is in delightful countryside not far from Braintree, and its history begins with the Knights Templars, the manor having been given to them 800 years ago. They lived at Cressing Temple until they were suppressed. The place was sacked during the Peasants Revolt in 1381, and in 1540 came the end with the Dissolution of the Monasteries.

While Elizabeth was still on the throne a great house was built on the site, and something of this Tudor manor remains in the Cressing Temple of today. There are two vast barns, one of brick and timber 40 feet high and 160 feet long, with a porch and five bays. This was for the wheat, and the smaller barn, 110 feet long, was for the barley. The church lies a mile away and has a Norman doorway with a stone above it carved by a medieval craftsman. The little gate into the churchyard is a memorial to a boy who gave his life in trying to save his sister from drowning; he was Clive Reginald Moss, aged 14.

An avenue of limes brings us to the church, which has a neat shingled spire on a wooden turret 400 years old. About us as we come in is a group of gravestones bearing a name famous in our history, one of them belonging to a General born in the delightful vicarage near by, Sir Evelyn Wood. He went from this vicarage to join the navy at 14, fought in the Crimea when he was 15, won the VC in India when he was 20, and altogether saw 50 years of fighting, during which he signed peace with the Boers after the defeat at Majuba Hill. Here with him lies his father Sir John Page Wood, who was chaplain to Queen Caroline, whose cause his own father gallantly defended. On a granite stone we read of one of these Woods those words of Browning that would do for all of them, "One who never turned his back, but marched breastforward," and inside the church hangs Sir Evelyn Wood's banner of the Order of St Michael and St George.

The 14th century church is small with no aisles. It has the original doorways and the original tracery in the windows. The nave has a fine roof, built in 1440, and huge timbers set up 80 years later support the bell-turret. There are a few fragments of medieval glass in the windows, and on a windowsill we found three heads carved in stone. A sad little tale lies behind the brass of Dorcas Musgrave, who sits pointing to her baby, which died with her at its birth in 1610. Both child and mother have huge ruffs round their necks, and the mother's hand rests on an hourglass; her sands had run out, though she was but 23. In a recess in the wall is a splendid monument to Henry Smith and his wife, who kneel at a prayer desk, he in Jacobean armour; their little girl is at prayer and their infant is in swaddling clothes. There are helmets on each side of the wall probably belonging to the Smiths, who lived in the magnificent Elizabethan house which succeeded that of the Knights Templars.

One of Our Vast Workshops

DAGENHAM. Here is one of the oldest and one of the newest wonders the Thames has seen. Below the marshes lies a submerged forest, and above them has arisen in our time one of the most remarkable industrial spectacles in England, the Ford Works.

This place on the banks of the Thames is one of the miracles of our 20th century, an example of what planning will do. In ten years its population has increased about ten times, the Becontree Estate alone covering four square miles of what was once green fields and has now about 30,000 houses.

Yet there must have been old people here not long ago who remembered seeing widows in this tiny village exercising their immemorial right by fetching a cartload of wood from the royal forest of Hainault, across Chadwell Heath, to their cottages by the church. A rural hamlet it was then; now a great estate stretches river-ward from Becontree, and an ancient gulf formed by a Thames flood 500 years ago has been transformed into a dock. Twenty thousand piles have been driven into the marshes and 100 acres of marshland have been turned into a workshop, resting on concrete foundations 80 feet thick. About 20 feet below these is a forest of yews whose branches were waving in the breeze a hundred centuries ago.

It was in 1929 that Mr Ford turned the first sod on his area of 500 acres, bounded on its Thames bank by a concrete jetty 600 yards long, at which ships of 8000 tons can berth. It is remarkable to look back and realise that an English engineer made all this possible long before a motor car was thought of, before any man had seen a railway train. For centuries the Thames had defied man and flooded its banks at every tide. The Abbess of Barking impoverished her abbey by striving to beat back the flood, and even as late as 1707 Parliament passed a bill taxing all ships using the river, in order to raise a fund to keep the waters back. In 1716 they found their man, Captain John Perry, who had been building waterways for Peter the Great in Russia. They gave him £25,000 to mend the wall, and he spent £40,000 and succeeded.

So it was that it became possible to set up here the first blast furnace in the south of England and the marvellous works that turn out motor cars by the hundred thousand. The factory took three or four years to build and has 32 acres under one roof, with a concrete floor covered by nine million wood blocks. There are two electric unloaders which are perhaps the biggest in Europe, discharging 300 tons of ore an hour, and the storage yard can hold 130,000 tons of ore and coal. At the long jetty by the Thames raw materials are unloaded at one end while the finished product is being loaded at the other, for delivery to the ends of the earth. The main factory has nearly 27 acres of glass in the roof and the windows (which open and shut electrically), a thousand ventilators, and five miles of rain gutters. There is a power station with a 30,000 kilowatt generator, and a blast furnace with stoves 100 feet high and 20 feet wide. There are 45 coke ovens producing 900 tons of coke in a day and a night, and altogether there are 6000 machines driven by 10,000 motors, with ten miles of conveyors for transporting parts. Over fifty cranes will lift any weight from one to 125 tons. One machine drills 92 holes in an engine crank-case in less than half a minute. The instruments for making measurements are checked to a millionth of an inch. There are 6000 electric light points, and the power-house generates electricity enough to supply a town of 180,000 people with light, heat, and power. Even the name of this vast place has its own statistics—the letters are 60 feet high and 140 feet long, and a flying man can see them 20 miles off.

A very different place this was when Elizabeth Fry came to live in a cottage here. She lived by the great gulf which is now the dock, and a kinswoman wrote of her singular retirement "living out-of-doors on the rich bank overflowing with grass and flowers, and watching the fine ships which seemed to float among the fields." Often looking at these ships must she have remembered the sad farewells she had made on Thames ships to women doomed by harsh laws to exile far away. Here she spent her last days, dying in 1845, and she lies a little way off in the Friends burial ground at Barking.

Dagenham's village church was built 700 years ago, and its chancel still remains, its old altar stone marked with two consecration crosses. In the chancel lies the man who helped to set Edward the Fourth on the throne, Sir Thomas Urswyk, Baron of the Exchequer in 1479; he lies in an altar tomb with a brass portrait of him in his judge's robes, his wife in a butterfly headdress, their nine daughters below them, one in the habit of a nun. Sir Thomas's feet are on a lion and he has a rosary.

On an elaborate monument of the 17th century stands one of the most contemptible men who ever rose to be a judge, Richard Allibon. He was born here in 1621, became a judge under James the Second, the last king of the dynasty whose tyrannical rule he stoutly supported. On his first circuit as a judge he complained that only three of the gentry had come to meet the judges, a fact which marked the public dissatisfaction at the appointment to the bench of a man entirely ignorant of law. He did his best to convict the Seven Bishops and bitterly complained of their acquittal at his next appearance on circuit. His death soon afterwards probably saved his life from outlawry. He was buried here near his grandfather, who had become a Roman Catholic, the grandson being the first Roman Catholic judge for 150 years.

By the church stands a medieval inn with a central hall and two modernised wings, and the vicarage with 1665 on the gable of the porch. The old home of the Earls of Pembroke, built in Queen Elizabeth's reign, is now the home of the local council, still with its dormers and gables and its panelled room.

Dagenham has had its martyr, Christopher Lyster, burned alive at Colchester with five others in Mary Tudor's Reign of Terror; and it has had two benefactors named Ford—Henry Ford whose millions have made it what it is, and an unknown Ford of long ago who left a thousand pounds for blankets and clothes for Dagenham's aged poor.

The Mighty Forest Buried in the Marshes

THE rivers of Essex are today mere streams compared with the rivers of 500 centuries ago; as they approach their wide estuaries they flow through marshland formed from soil brought down by their mighty forerunners. Along both banks of the Thames the marshes, little higher than the level of the sea, stretch far and wide, except for a few hundred yards at Purfleet and Grays, where the chalk breaks through their monotony.

The spring tides would often submerge them, and for centuries man has fought a battle with the waters blown upstream from the North Sea. The cost of embankments almost ruined the rich nuns of Barking, and it was not until the Dutch engineers came along in the 17th century that the Essex marshes could be profitably used by the farmer.

Since that time the marshes nearer London have become the sites of docks and industries, and another century or two will see London's great Port actually within sight of the open sea.

Romantic as is this victory of man over Nature, there is a great romance of Nature herself beneath the river and the ancient marshlands through which it winds its way to sea. Here beneath the waters, with the ships sailing above them to the ends of the earth, are the fallen giants of our ancient forests. Here and there on our coasts we come upon a fossil forest, as at Lulworth, with trees turned to stone, but beneath the marshes of the Thames are submerged forests with trees that are still wood, as when, perhaps fifty or a hundred thousand years ago, men dressed in skins would hide among them hunting hyenas and bears.

From one of these lost forests has come down to us a dramatic piece of news. We know that one day a wild pig, seeking food in a forest where Carmarthen Bay is now, was killed by a great tree falling. The pig lay dead beneath the trunk for ages, buried deep in leaves and moss each year until the mould piled up through centuries of time, while empires rose and fell, and the forest sank slowly in the sea. One day they found in the marsh, among the trees embedded in the peat, the tree which fell and killed the pig at Lydstep Haven near Tenby.

It is a forest such as this that lies today beneath the marshes of the Thames, both in Essex and in Kent. If we sail down to Margate from London Bridge we sail where birds once nested in the tops of trees. The trees are gone, and our most ancient river has piled mud and sand high above the verdant glades, so that all we see are mud flats and a waste of waters.

This estuary of the Thames, with the country round it, was once eighty feet higher than it is. Southend and Sheerness were then far from the sea, up-river places, and where their busy streets are now were wooded hillsides, over which the stag and the wild boar roamed and men sent flint-headed arrows after them. Then the Thames wended its way through green vegetation where now is sea as far as the eye can reach. After passing the Nore, the comparatively narrow channel of the ancient river took a north-easterly course through either Black Deep or Barrow Deep, submarine depressions believed to be the sunken watercourse of the Thames, and entered the North Sea several miles east of Clacton. The Medway was then a tributary of the Thames, rather like the Darent now, while a range of hills extended north-east from Sheppey and far out to sea.

Beneath the marshy tracts bordering the great river from London to the sea these trees can be recovered by anyone prepared to dig a dozen feet. For over 250 years this vast submerged surface of ancient Britain, with its fossil treasures, has been opened up at one place and another. It was so in the days of Pepys in 1665, when he wrote in his diary:

At Blackwall, in digging the late docke, they did, twelve feet underground, find perfect trees covered with earth, nut trees with branches and the very nuts upon them; some of whose nuts Johnson showed us; their shells black with age, and their kernell upon opening decayed, but their shell perfectly hard as ever. And a yew tree (upon which the very ivy was taken up whole about it) which upon cutting, we found to be rather harder than the living tree usually is.

From Woolwich to Crossness Point, under the entire area of Plumstead and Erith Marshes, are oak and alder trees, branches and roots in great quantities. Furniture has been made out of the oak. On each side of the Thames beyond Purfleet and the Darent the stumps of the trees may often be seen. Beneath the marshes of Rainham and Dagenham, are vast numbers of trees with roots, boughs, and bark covered with mould and clay to a depth of from seven to twelve feet; the latest older than the Romans, the lowest as old as the Stone Age. From Greenwich to Greenhithe on the Kent side of the river an old forest bed of yew, oak, and pine lies twenty feet below, and beneath this bed two of our ancient ancestors have been found, one a hundred thousand years old and one thousands of centuries older.

The Knight in His Coffin

DANBURY. It is over 600 years since the funeral processions of the three knights of St Clere drew all the neighbourhood up the deep fern-lined lanes to the hilltop church. It is over 600 years since the medieval craftsmen laid on their tombs these oak sculptures which are the admiration of all Essex.

Each of the three knights lies with his legs crossed and his feet resting on a lion, his face peeping out from the close-woven meshes of chain mail. Each wears a tabard with its folds realistically carved. But each knight has a different aspect, an attitude which may have some forgotten meaning. One is drawing his sword, the second is vigorously thrusting his sword back into a sheath which a little dragon is biting, the third has his hands folded at prayer.

The story of the embalmed knight of Danbury begins in 1779, when a lady of the manor, Mrs Frances Ffytche, died and a grave was dug for her near a recess containing one of the wooden figures. At about 30 inches below the pavement the workmen laid bare a huge flat stone under which was a lead coffin. There was no name on the coffin and the workmen hurried for the rector, who called a conference with his churchwarden and a Mr White, who has left a record of this discovery.

It was decided to open the coffin, in the great expectation of seeing the bones of the knight whose statue in wood they knew so well. Inside the lead coffin they found an elm coffin, firm and entire, and inside this was a shell three-quarters of an inch thick and covered with cement. The lid of the shell was removed and to the great surprise of all there lay revealed, not his bones, but a man in the vigour of youth, his flesh firm and white. He was clad in a shirt of linen, round the top of which a narrow piece of crude lace had been sewn with bold stitches. The man was five feet long, his limbs were in excellent symmetry, his teeth were perfect. The preservation of his body was due to a curious liquid which half-filled the coffin. Flowers and herbs in abundance, perfect in form, were floating in the liquor.

After some of the villagers had been to see this ancient inhabitant of Danbury the coffins were replaced, soldered up in the leaden cover, and lowered once more into the grave. Those who had seen the coffin opened had looked upon the perfect figure of one of these three knights, 500 years old.

The knights rest by the foundations of the Norman church they may have seen taken down, to be rebuilt in the 13th century and re-fashioned in the 14th, when the nave arcades and the tower were added. From the battlements of this tower springs a spire cased in copper, wooden shingles, and lead, a landmark for miles, for the church stands on the summit of a hill 365 feet high, in an old encampment used by the marauding Danes and possibly furnished with its rampart by the Romans, or inhabitants long before then.

There is carving 500 years old on four benches with moulded rails, and three poppyheads with weird beasts. Modern lovers of this church have carried on the medieval craftsman's idea, so that today all the pews are ornamented with lions and dragons. The gallery in the tower is a good example of 15th century woodwork; the balusters are Elizabethan. There is a 13th century piscina with quaint masks and neat 14th century niches on either side of the fine tower doorway. A helmet enriched with a lion rampant hangs in the aisle above the Mildmay tombs, and there is a brass almsdish of 1631 with Adam and Eve carved on it. In the lovely park at the foot of the hill the bishops of Rochester lived for 30 years, and the east window, with the Crucifixion, was Bishop Claughton's gift when he celebrated his jubilee. Hanging here is a piece of the wooden walls of Old England, an oak tablet cut from the battleship Britannia and inscribed with the names of the 250 men from the village who did not come back from the war. It is a lovely village they laid down their lives for, with old houses which have stood for generations looking down on England over commons on which dwarf oaks and stunted holly trees brave the winds from the North Sea.

Moated Halls

DEBDEN. It is rich in old houses and farms, some Tudor and some 17th century. Scot's Farm at Hamperden End has in one of its rooms a lovely frieze with lions' faces. Mole Hall, its moat still wet, has three original chimneys, a fine barn, and two timber-framed outhouses with oak staircases. Amberden Hall, some way off, also has a moat; and New Amberden Hall, for all its name, is 17th century. The great house is Debden Hall, which stands by a lake in a splendid park of 200 acres; it was built in the 18th century, and is said to be the successor of one that stood here in the Conqueror's day.

The church of this beautiful village is in a perfect setting, reached through a field rich in Spanish chestnuts. It has seen many changes, the 18th century having given it a new chancel and bell-turret; but it has kept a 14th century doorway by which we come to a nave with 13th century arcades. One of the aisles is 15th century; the other, with its porch, is a hundred years older. There is a Tudor chest bound with iron, a window with the Chiswell arms, and an elaborate modern altar tomb to Trench Chiswell, who rebuilt the chancel after it had been destroyed by the falling of the old tower. A tablet tells of Harold Fisher, a Haileybury boy who helped to defend Ladysmith, won the DSO, and lived on to die for us in the Great War.

A Tragic Witness

DEDHAM. It is just over the border from Constable's Suffolk, the near neighbour of Flatford Mill, with landscapes familiar to us because Constable painted them. Still a delightful little place in the valley of the Stour, it has many a cottage, shop, farm, and inn bearing witness to the days of its prosperity from the 15th to the 17th century. Then Dedham was an important centre of the wool merchants, and there stands on its outskirts still a wool merchant's house and factory of two storeys and attics, timbered and plastered, complete with courtyard and gateway. It is known as Southfields. The master weaver lived in one of the projecting wings, and the 400-year-old doors and the moulded ceiling beams are still in their place. The house is unique in the county.

Facing the church is the best of the old buildings of the High Street, an inn with stables built for horses which might have taken part in Tudor pageantry; it has a timber-framed stairway in its open courtyard.

Dedham has a church magnificent, built about 1500 by one of its princely merchants, Thomas Webbe, who lies in the north aisle on a richly carved tomb. He built his battlemented tower so that a carriage can pass beneath it, covering an area of 250 square feet and rising 130 feet to the top of its pinnacles, which spring from octagonal buttresses. Its vaulted roof is adorned with traceried panels, flowers,

Dedham   **The Cross**

Dedham   **Old Courtyard of Southfields**

Copford   Norman Paintings in the Apse

shields, and other devices. In the south porch the builders reset
the 14th century doorway and they gave the north porch two storeys
and hung in it a door which was one of the most perfect examples
of carving in Essex, with saints and angels in canopied niches.
Time has been unfaithful to it, but we can still trace the figures of
Christ and the Madonna.

We notice that two leaves of this door have been cut across, and
thereby hangs a tale. It was done in order that galleries could be
erected in the church in the days of King James and King Charles,
for in those times even this great church of Dedham would not hold
the people who came to hear the Puritan vicar, John Rogers. He
was for over 30 years one of the famous preachers of his age, and was
described by one who knew him as "the most awakening divine in
England." His tomb is in the churchyard, and in the chancel on one
of the walls, carved in a niche, is a bust of him in a skull cap, ruff,
and gown.

Near the bust of John Rogers is a stone with a fine little bronze
figure on the top in memory of a man who made it the delight of
his declining years to befriend the poor of Dedham. The old font
has been rescued from a hiding-place under the floor, and its figures
of angels, evangelists, and cherubs are sadly worn. It has a cover
with a pathetic interest because it was made from the timbers of the
Royal George; they were part of that bitter tragedy of 1782 when the
great warship sank off Portsmouth:

> *When Kempenfelt went down*
> *With twice four hundred men.*

She had gone down complete, heeling on her side, and it was of these
timbers we see at Dedham that Cowper wrote:

> *Her timbers yet are sound,*
> *And she may float again,*
> *Full charged with England's thunder,*
> *And plough the distant main. . . .*

The poet did not know that the timbers were rotten and that the
ship went down through the neglect of the Admiralty. The timbers
are a tragic witness to a cruel betrayal of our seamen. There are more
splendid timbers in the roof, fragments of old glass in the windows,
carvings on the font, mason's marks, and many attractive details

which hold our attention in this fine church, monument of an industry which has passed from this old home of merchant princes.

DENGIE. A Saxon village halfway between the Blackwater and Crouch and not far from the sea, it is a pleasant little place that has forgotten to grow up. There are Roman bricks in the church, and in the bell-turret are carvings of three ancient leopards. On a 16th century brass is a quaint group of children with their mother. There is a cup engraved in Shakespeare's day, and the stone reredos was carved by Edward Warmington, 44 years rector here until our own time.

DODDINGHURST. Its church, which keeps some 13th century work, has a little spire on a weather-boarded turret, inserted 400 years ago through the roof of the nave; and the wooden porch, one of the best in Essex, with 20 lights in the sides and original tiebeams in its roof, is also 16th century. There is a 13th century doorway with some of the delightful ornament of its time, a 15th century nave roof, a Jacobean chair, and some 300-year-old panels in a modern chest. The painted figures of Our Lord and Mary and John on the roodbeam are thought to be Italian work of the 17th century. A parson of some note here was Nehemiah Rogers, fervent Royalist and friend of Archbishop Laud, and remembered today chiefly for his writings on the parables. He was buried here in 1660. The old stocks stand at a corner of the common, and by the church is a tiny Tudor house in which the priest lived.

A Hero's Grave

DOVERCOURT. Here in this place, so linked with Harwich and with it transformed into a fortress in the Great War, sleeps one of the bravest heroes of that war, Captain Fryatt. The hub of the peninsula in the early days, it has been swallowed up by Harwich, but has still its wide green and some of its old cottages; 500 yards of breakwater, sea wall, and beautiful undercliff; and a church with two blocked Norman arches surviving in the nave. Most of the windows, the traceried font (once used as a cattle trough), and the doorway are 14th century, and the lower stages of the tower were built about the time of Agincourt. The church has a curiously interesting memorial, for the window in the tower with Our Lord and the

Centurion was given to it by the last German Kaiser in memory of many German soldiers who perished with ours in the ill-fated Walcheren expedition of 1810.

There is a 15th century brass of a man in a fur-trimmed gown, a poorbox made while men were still talking of the Armada, a floral cross on a 13th century coffin lid, and a great roodbeam on which stood a crucifix of which a very queer tale is told.

The story is that in the 16th century, before the Reformation, there was an idol called the Rood of Dovercourt which stood at the church door, with such power that no man could shut the door where it stood, so that it was left open for every day and night. It happened that one night three men went from Dedham in the moonlight, took the idol from its shrine, and set it on fire; so great a fire did it make that it "lit up one of the ten miles of their way home." But within half a year of the burning of the Rood the three men were hanged in chains.

That is as it may be; what moves us here is the grave of Captain Fryatt. When the Great War broke out he was 42, captain of the Great Eastern Railway steamer Brussels, and steamed regularly between England and Holland risking mines and submarines.

In March 1915 he shook off a submarine attack and three weeks later he was again assailed, this time passing from defence to attack, steaming straight at his enemy and ramming him. For this gallant feat he was thanked and rewarded by the Admiralty. On his voyage from Holland to Tilbury in 1916 his ship was captured by a German destroyer and Fryatt was taken prisoner. His log was examined and produced in evidence against him at a courtmartial held at Bruges. Fryatt was under Government orders. He sailed in uniform, and, being attacked, was entitled to resist by force, but his judges held that his conduct was unlawful, that he had no status as a combatant and was no better than a bandit. He was shot that night.

The event aroused deep sorrow and widespread indignation. At the end of the war the Germans reviewed the trial and declared that, while they regretted the haste with which the sentence was executed, the verdict was just and in accordance with their interpretation of the laws of sea warfare. Fryatt was remembered in honour by his countrymen, and in July 1919 his body was brought home and laid to rest at Dovercourt with full military honours. There is a worthy memorial to him—The Fryatt Memorial Hospital.

Commonwealth General

DOWNHAM. It lies on the hills above the River Crouch, the red medieval tower of its church standing out among the elms at one of its beauty spots. The church has been refashioned, and the 13th and 14th century doorways have been reset in the nave. A brass inscription in French has been saved from the old church, and a little old glass with some golden crowns has come from the 14th century. On an altar tomb in the tower is a name recalling a thrilling period of our history—Benjamin Disbrowe, whose father led the Parliamentary cavalry at Bristol, was General of the Fleet during the Commonwealth, and suffered at the Restoration because he was suspected of plotting the death of Henrietta Maria and Charles the Second. He was released, however, and lived to see his son refashion the Elizabethan gabled house of Fremnells, a mile away over the hills. It was at this house early in last century that the whole of the Desborough family perished of smallpox.

An interesting record of a vicar of Downham is on the wall of the tower, where we read that Peter Beauvoir was here for 61 years to 1821, so that he lived here through the longest reign of any king in England's history.

DUNTON. It is scattered on the lower slopes of the Langdon Hills. The arterial road to Southend runs between two of its oldest houses, Wayletts and Southfields. Wayletts is 500 and Southfields 200 years old. By an old farm is the red brick church in a great churchyard reaching out to a pond; in the churchyard is a 700-year-old coffin. At the west end of the church are the great beams the 15th century builders inserted to support the bell-turret.

The Vanished Tombs

EARLS COLNE. How are the mighty fallen! Here are old cottages in plenty, but the medieval priory founded by the Earls of Oxford has gone, and so have their splendid monuments. It was one of the delightful surprises of our countryside that we used to be able to open a door in a farmhouse and find four of their tombs.

They made one of the grandest groups in the county, decoratively arranged along a white wall with a wonderful oak beam set over them, grotesque faces looking out from its flowery carvings. Now, alas, Earls Colne has lost this great attraction, for the tombs have gone to Bures in Suffolk. Two by two the weepers stood in niches round the first of the tombs, on which lay the armed figure of Thomas de Vere, eighth earl, who died in 1371. Other niches completing the scheme came from the hidden side of the tomb at the far end, the earliest, made with its buttresses and pinnacles and lovely niches in the middle of the 14th century, though the mailed figure on it died in 1296. He was Robert, fifth earl, with a boar at his feet and angels at his head. Between these tombs lay Richard the 11th earl and Alice his wife, united no longer, for their tomb had been split so that we might see the full glory of each panelled side. Richard was in armour, his boar crest on the helmet under his head, his feet on a lion. His lady wore a dainty horned headdress and had two small dogs at her feet.

Their tombs were the greatest things these three earls left us, but King Richard the Second came here to clasp the dead hand of another de Vere whose meteoric career was the talk of all England. He was Robert, ninth earl, whom the king loved more than his throne, for he endangered the throne itself for this young man. He made him Duke of Ireland with despotic power and then could not bear to part with him and sent a deputy instead. Soon, however, the worthless earl was in danger of being tried for treason by his peers and Richard had to part with him, only to see him again when his body was brought to Earls Colne for burial, after he had been killed in a boar hunt. The king came to the village and the coffin lid was raised that he might touch his friend's hand again.

The star of the De Veres was even then in the descendant; yet it shines still in the parapet of the church tower on the hill. It is 200 years since the village blacksmith gave this tower a copper crown and a weathercock. The chancel and the nave roof are 14th century, but the rest is mostly modern. There are Jacobean chairs and an altar table in the chapel, where Richard Harlakenden kneels with his four wives on a small painted monument of 1602, but the chief treasure is a medieval paten engraved with the figure of Christ.

The Great Surrender

EAST DONYLAND. It is an old village running down a slope to the compact little hamlet of Rowhedge on the tide-swept banks of the River Colne. Ships are built on its quay, and small yachts moored in its creeks. But in this old place is no ancient church, only a modern one built of brick, its pews curving on an octagonal floor so that it looks like a chapter house. From the church that has vanished comes the brass portrait of Nicholas Marshall and his wife of Charles Stuart's day; we are told of his wife that she surrendered her soul "with alacrity of spirit." A neighbour they must have known, Elizabeth Marshall, sits with hand upraised expounding from a book, a sculpture in marble.

Roman Builders, Norman Joiners, Medieval Artists

EAST HAM. The ships of the world come to it, for its three docks (the Royal Albert, the King George the Fifth, and the Victoria) make up three sections of the biggest sheet of enclosed dock water in the world. The Royal Albert is a mile long and 500 feet wide, and the George the Fifth has 64 acres of water and 15 acres of warehouses. It was in the excavation for these docks that a canoe now in the British Museum was found, 27 feet long. It would be one of the earliest known boats on the Thames.

Across the river from here is a fine view of Kent, partly blocked by the six-mile embankment of a great sewer. Monstrous slag heaps such as are too often allowed to ruin our countryside make a grim background to the huge Beckton gasworks. One of our most industrial towns, it has little for the traveller to see, but its 70 or 80 miles of streets are fine and well kept, and planted with thousands of trees. There are 200 acres of open spaces, a Central Park of 25 acres, and Plashet Park a little smaller; it was the ground round Plashet House, the home of Elizabeth Fry when Plashet was a secluded hamlet. No trace of her home is left, but in our own time there has been discovered the rate-book of the house. The site itself is delightful with ornamental gardens. Near the Central Park is the memorial to the men of the Great War, whose names are on bronze tablets; there are 1669 of them. The Town Hall in the middle of the town (built of red brick with terracotta facings) has a fine clock tower, and inside are more memorials; one to four heroic men who gave their lives in trying to save one of their mates who worked for the council; another tablet is to 100 men who fell in the South African War, and with their names are Kipling's words, Lest We Forget. The technical college and grammar school is an impressive building, and there is a grammar school for girls, also nobly housed.

One of the most interesting old buildings in the town is Green Street House, at which Henry the Eighth stayed with Anne Boleyn. In those days the house was new, though the gables and cornices we see are 17th century. There is panelling of 1600 in the passages and in three of the rooms, and from the same time is the fine staircase with high wooden vases on its heavy balusters. There are 17th century doors and doorways, and two Queen Anne fireplaces.

Those who would read of these things may do so in a fine Carnegie Library, which has in its entrance hall a bust of the noblest woman on East Ham's roll of fame, Elizabeth Fry. She lived at Plashet House, of which only the grounds remain. Last century the Methodists raised a chapel to her memory in Plashet Grove, and St Stephen's church was built in her honour about the same time. The church is rich in modern woodwork.

The mother church of the town is Norman, and is of remarkable interest, having Roman bricks, Norman timbers, and medieval painting. The windows of the bell-chamber tell us the tower is only 400 years old, but it has a rare 14th century bell inscribed with the name of Gabriel, and shelters a fine Norman doorway with three pairs of shafts crowned by cushion capitals.

The Roman bricks in the walls must have come from a Roman settlement near the site, and Roman relics have been found in the churchyard—perhaps the biggest churchyard in England still in use. The bricks were used by the Normans, whose handiwork is in four windows and an archway. On the outside chancel wall is the stone frame of a 13th century doorway, and the medieval iron window fastenings of a hermit's cell. The doorway by which we come in has one scalloped capital carved by the Normans, and the porch has Tudor timbers in the roof. The nave has two Norman windows set in its thick walls, and one side has oak panelling carved with 17th century strapwork. The walls of the Norman chancel have a band of 13th century painting, and also 13th century are the red flowers on the walls of the Norman apse and on its deep window splays. It is above all this colour that we find the Norman timbers, a very unusual possession, found in only about a dozen churches in the country. They are heavy Norman beams, remaining as solid examples of carpentry in the original roof.

Along the chancel walls are remains of a lovely interlacing arcade of round arches with zigzag. Four arches are complete, but the others have been cut into for tombs, and for a Tudor doorway to the roodstairs. The apse has a 13th century bracket with a finely carved head which, with a Norman capital, has been fashioned into a pair of stone basins at which the priest would wash his hands.

The font has a quaint bowl given by Sir Richard Heigham in 1639, and in the chancel is a brass portrait of Sir Richard's wife, his family crest on a helmet hanging above. A wall-stone with a gilt cherub is to Sir Richard's daughter, and there is a brass of Hester Neve in Stuart dress. High on the chancel wall is a brightly painted monument with shields, pilasters, and obelisks giving it an air of dignity; in its arched recesses Charles Breame and his wife have been kneeling for over 300 years.

In a corner of the apse is the pretentious monument of a man who claimed to be an earl. It has its original iron railings, and eleven shields-of-arms. Above is an elaborate armorial achievement guarded by standing figures of Prudence and Hope, and below is an enriched recess with a carved helmet of red and black plumes set in front of a prayer desk. Here kneel Edmund Nevill and his wife Jane, a determined-looking woman with a red face and a coronet. In front of the tomb kneel their three sons and four daughters. The long inscription has in it a touch of defiance, proclaiming that Edmund Nevill, descended from kings and princes, was truly the 7th Earl of Westmorland. Actually his ancestor was Ralph Nevill, whose loyalty to Henry the Fourth has been vividly made use of by Shakespeare, but the 6th Earl was attainted for his attempt to release Mary Queen of Scots, and not even James the First would restore his title, so that the claim here is a bogus one.

In the churchyard is a stone set up in the days of the Commonwealth, but the most famous man buried here lies in an unmarked grave. He is Dr William Stukeley, the famous antiquary.

In the days when East Ham was a humble village William Stukeley paid a visit to his friend the vicar, Stukeley being then an old man who knew that his great labours were soon to end. As they wandered about the churchyard, gazing over the Thames marshes toward Shooter's Hill, the old man turned to his friend and said: "When I die may I have a grave under this green turf, and will you see that no stone or other memorial is raised above me?" Stukeley was the leading antiquarian of his day, and realised only too well how vain are pompous sepulchres. Born in 1687 at Holbeach in Lincolnshire, he went from the grammar school there to Cambridge, became a doctor, and practised; but his heart was in the ancient story of our land, and he helped to found the Society of Antiquaries, becoming its secretary.

Many and long were the journeys he made with his friends, and curious were his notes. He wrote 20 books which, with all the errors that will creep into books, have helped our antiquarians ever since. His friends called him the Arch Druid, for Stonehenge had cast its spell about him, and he had devoted months to exploring it. His theories are wrong, but even now people tell us, as he did, that the Druids sacrificed at this great temple. It is his error that persists. Stonehenge and Avebury are both far older than the Druids, if Druids ever did exist. But these errors are nothing, for they can be corrected. What is remembered of Stukeley is his unweary zeal and his intense love of the Past. In 1765 they brought him here by the Essex highway and over Bow Bridge, and laid him to rest in East Ham churchyard, levelling the grass so that none can point to the spot, and he lies unknown as he wished to lie.

The Ruin

EAST HANNINGFIELD. Far from any town it stands, on a ridge with long views every way. Wide grass borders to the highway give a charm to its neat cottages and the modern church has a prosperous look. The vicar's garden boasts the oldest well in the county, 480 feet deep. Close to the village are two Elizabethan farms with diagonal chimneys, but the church of medieval days is a ruin down the hill. It has given to South Kensington a wall-painting of great value, a treasure 600 years old showing Adam with his spade, Eve with her spindle, and Catherine with her wheel. For many years this painting was exposed to the open sky in the ivied ruins of the nave by the old chancel, now only used for funerals.

The Agincourt Soldier's Wife

EAST HORNDON. It is one of the places where the head of Anne Boleyn is said to lie, but we do not know; the story is that it was brought here for burial after the Calais headsman had severed it from her frail body. If the tale is true the head will lie in the red brick church on the brow of a hill which rises steeply by the Southend road. The church's bricks are very old, the chancel and its small chapel, the nave, and the two-storeyed transepts being 15th century, while the big chapel, the porch, and the tower are Tudor. The low tower owes its curiously stepped battlements to the men who set it up after it had fallen down 300 years ago. An odd feature of the church is an upper room in each transept; open to the church, they were the dwelling-rooms of the priest for over a century.

At the square Norman font the Tyrells were baptised for hundreds of years, one to grow up to fight for Henry the Fifth at Agincourt and to be three times Speaker, and another to suffer for his loyalty to Charles Stuart. There is a beautiful portrait of the wife of the Tyrell of Agincourt, cut by a master hand in grey stone on her tomb. In a few sweeping strokes the artist has drawn her restful and dignified face and form, giving her a horned headdress and a fur-lined cloak. On the shafts of her vaulted canopy are portraits of her ten children, each with the Christian name. One of these boys was the Thomas who lies in the small chapel on the other side of the chancel. His brass portrait has gone but his wife's remains. Were they the parents of the man who lies in the altar tomb in the transept? His brass shows him in armour and here are the brasses of his eight sons, but his name is lost. In the chapel lies the Royalist Sir John Tyrell, his gravestone recording how he was "once decimated, twice imprisoned, and thrice sequestrated," the first and last phrases, of course, referring only to his estates! The Tyrell arms are in 15th century glass in the east window of this chapel and two of their helmets have been here since the 16th century. The panelled chancel roof has bosses carved with flowers, birds, and shields; there are two poppyheaded bench-ends and a fine door 400 years old; and the carved pulpit is 17th century.

Paths across the fields lead from this lonely place towards the Tyrell home at Herongate and to East Horndon Hall, now a farm rich in oak beams.

EASTHORPE. Here the Normans, in building their church, picked up the tiles the Romans left behind them. They framed their windows with them. The medieval artists painted the window splays and their colour is not entirely faded. But the church has been transformed, the Norman apse has vanished, and the chancel has been lengthened. The stonework of the windows and the sedilia is decorated with medieval carving, and in one of the windows is 16th century glass of Our Lord preaching in Galilee.

There is an ancient cottage with an overhanging storey facing the church, and a timbered hall of the 15th century close by.

Island of Trees

EAST MERSEA. It is said that the Danes took refuge here in Alfred's day; and nearly a thousand years afterwards English troops were garrisoning the church during our wars with the Dutch and the French. There is still an ancient moat near the church, and close by is a lovely garden in the shadow of noble pines, a charming bit of Essex which we may see by opening a door and peeping in.

There is much to delight us on this island of trees and hedgerows, a patch of loveliness separated from the mainland by the Pyefleet Creek, which was famous for oysters in the days when Baring Gould was preaching here before he went to live in Devon. He put this village into one of his books, and ministered in the bare church that has been here 600 years. It has a 15th century font with a bowl resting on angels, fragments of glass painted in Chaucer's day, and a beautiful pulpit carved in Stuart times, still with its canopy and the stand of the old hourglass.

Dene Holes

EAST THURROCK. It has something that has puzzled antiquarians from Camden's day to ours. A very ancient place, it is squeezed between Grays and Tilbury, as the dormouse was squeezed between the March Hare and the Mad Hatter. We come down hill and by a few old cottages to the church among the oaks, in which a 14th century doorway brings us to a bit of Norman

England, a nave with two doorways through which the Normans came, and a chancel arch under which they walked to the altar. The chancel was made new 600 years ago, and has simple sedilia with beautiful capitals and a piscina with more elaborate ornament. The pulpit was made in 1700, and the modern reredos has tracery of the 15th century.

But the puzzling thing at East Thurrock is its group of the curious shafts known as Dene Holes, going down 50 feet into the chalk below Hangman's Wood. There are 70 of them in three or four acres, all about four feet wide, and nearly all ending in tunnels about 20 feet long. They may have been here a thousand or two thousand years, but why they were made is a mystery which has never been solved. Some think them merely quarries for chalk, some hiding-places; but no one knows.

The King Who Starved the Navy

EAST TILBURY. A tiny place, it was the ferrying centre to which the potters of Roman Britain brought their wares. Broken fragments of Samian ware may still be found in the mud of the shore, and covered up here are the foundations of the ferrymen's huts, all carefully explored and recorded years ago.

In the nave of the church is a blocked-up Norman arch, the earliest witness of Christianity here. It is possible that a Saxon church stood on this site, for Bede tells us how St Cedd, the Northumbrian missionary to the East Saxons, founded a monastery at Tilbury 1300 years ago. Three bold piers with carved capitals were set up in the time of Thomas Becket, when an aisle was added. The wide chancel arch is a delightful frame for the three lancets in the 13th century chancel, each one with a fine figure. The font is 400 years old and the handsome pulpit 300.

The patchwork walls of the nave tell a tale of the shame of Charles the Second, the starver of our navy. So mean was he that the Fleet was unable to ward off the Dutch warships which came up the Thames and battered down with shot and shell the aisle and the ancient tower of this church. The base of a new tower has been set up as a memorial to the men who with more patriotism defended London's river during the Great War. They lived across a field in a fort built by General Gordon in the days when he commanded the

Royal Engineers and was responsible for the defences of the Thames. His memory lingers here, and his name has been inscribed on the stones of the new tower. On the inside wall has been set the coffin lid of an ancient inhabitant; it has a cross moulded on it 700 years ago.

Here are memories of two famous authors, one remembered by every English-speaking boy and one known to the few elect. The little known scholar was Gervase of Tilbury, who was sent to Rome and grew up to teach law at Bologna. He was present at the famous meeting between Frederick Barbarossa and the Pope in 1177, and he was made Marshal of Arles, the town of splendour and ease in the days of Imperial Rome. The author known to every boy was Daniel Defoe, who worked at Tilbury (it is said in a tile factory).

The Wonderful Door

EASTWOOD. Here the lover of smith-craft will rejoice, for the ancient ironwork still gives strength to doors which have opened and closed for 20 generations.

Southend is swallowing up Eastwood, but toward the church still linger charming cottages built of wood and roofed with thatch. Rochford-way stands the old workhouse, with an upper storey projecting and a wing built in the days when Joan of Arc was driving our army out of France.

In front of a row of elms a border of grass creeps up to the churchyard wall, and two sycamores stand before a 16th century porch made beautiful with carved bargeboards on its gable. The roof of the church has a high pitch reaching up beside the wooden tower and covering both nave and aisle in its downward sweep. The tower has stood 700 years, supporting a slender spire, and is itself borne on a stone tower attached for some strange reason to the aisle. The door in the brick porch is one of the most wonderful doors in Essex. For six and a half centuries it has swung on these hinges, the planks held firm by scrolls and flowers hammered out of iron, yet when the smiths fashioned this piece of beauty they used once more the strap-hinges their grandparents had wrought for a still earlier door, with its boldly cut prayer of peace for those who come this way, and those who go. A door inside the church, equally beautiful, has been the companion of this all down the ages, and used to hang in the doorway now blocked up in the opposite aisle. There is notable ironwork on both doors, making them precious possessions for a village.

Close by is a masterpiece in stone, a Norman font with interlacing round arches encircling a tapering bowl. Norman arches older than the font are high up on the walls of the nave, one complete, the others only in part. In this aisle is a curious partition of oak, placed here in the 15th century to give the priest a private room. In the aisle roof is the trapdoor through which the priest used to climb up; it is still on its old hinges.

The chancel has a brass portrait of Thomas Burrough, who died three years before Elizabeth, and the wooden tower has two bells which have called the village to worship for over 500 years.

From Tudor Days

ELMDON. It is charming, tucked away on the chalk hills close to Cambridgeshire. Its tower, with quaint gargoyles 500 years old could tell a fine tale of village comings and goings. It saw the building of the Tudor cottages below, with their carved bargeboards and ornamental plaster bands; it saw the coming of an Elizabethan judge to sleep his last sleep here; and it has seen the rest of the church so refashioned that it is almost a modern building. Only one thing it has not seen—the making of the earthwork which hides in a grove of trees up the hill. The church has much ornament in the old style, including among its heads a monk and a demon; and it has kept a 15th century piscina with an elaborate arch and two longhaired heads. But the chief interest is in its ancient monuments, two brasses and an imposing altar tomb. The tomb is adorned with shields on the canopy and sides, and in it sleeps Judge Thomas Meade, who died three years before the Armada. One of the brasses shows a Tudor man in a furlined cloak, with his two wives and a group of children. Their names are not recorded; but we know that the four boys and eight girls on the other brass are the children of Thomas Crawley, who died in 1559 after founding a free school in the village.

To Bed Betimes

ELMSTEAD. It has old cottages where the roads from Harwich and Walton meet, inns that have seen many centuries go by, a timbered hall 400 years old, and a roughly built church enshrined in trees. Begun in the 14th century, the church has a chancel nearly as big as the nave, and an unfinished tower with red tiles peeping out oddly among the trees. Here are fine stone seats with a king and a bishop carved on them 600 years ago, and a tablet telling us that an old vicar buried his little son the year before the plague came to London. The epitaph tells us that as careful mothers put their babes to sleep when they would play the wanton too long, so Nature put this little one to bed betimes to save his youth from harm.

The chief possession of Elmstead is an old wooden figure, one of very few in Essex, showing a cross-legged knight with his feet on a woman, a strange piece of carving thought to be a memorial of Lawrence de Tony, who died about 1310. There are only a small number of these wooden figures in all England, probably a hundred.

From a Roman House

ELSENHAM. A Roman must have set up house here, for we find his red tiles in the church across the valley. The inner arch of one doorway is entirely made of them. They are in the 15th century tower, and were used in the walls of the chancel and the nave by the Normans whose simple carving turns the narrow south doorway into exquisite beauty. It has spiral shafts, and a tympanum repeating the pattern round the arch. A most curious thing is behind this tympanum, a Norman coffin lid with a patterned border and a raised cross, made for a Knight Templar who died about the time the doorway was made, but probably picked up from the chancel floor and put here to strengthen the tympanum by some casual workman when the 15th century door with its metal plate was put in. For 400 years a high-pitched brick porch has sheltered this old door and the older doorway.

High and narrow are the splayed Norman windows to the nave, but most of the light pours in through the lovely 20th century glass in the medieval east window, which we see perfectly framed in the Norman carving of the chancel arch. A mother and her step-daughter face each other on the jambs of this arch, their brass portraits made to match with twice as much lettering as picture. Though only four years passed between their deaths, early in the 17th century, their costume shows great changes. They were the wife and daughter of Dr Tuer, the vicar whose initials are on the Elizabethan chalice.

A Norman peephole to the altar is cut on one side of the arch, and red bricks frame the doorway to the old roodloft. The 15th century kingpost roof has been saved from the deathwatch beetle, except for one beam which it had almost completely devoured. The pulpit on an oak stem has Jacobean carving. In the chancel, where a fine double piscina was carved 700 years ago, are some coloured metal panels with portraits of saints, brought from France by Sir Walter Gilbey. Edward the Seventh used to come here to talk with this man who in his youth drove a coach hereabouts for a living, and in his old age drove the most splendid coaches in England for the joy of it.

Sir Walter lived in the big hall seen by the church against a dense background of trees, and by the road is a well in memory of his wife, with oak pillars supporting a gilded dome. A lover of horses, he wrote many books about them before he died in 1914.

The Old Plateau

EPPING. In the long and broad highway of this quaint market town is the very old and the new. A little before the road leaves the dense forest to skirt a wide common it passes Amesbury Banks, an ancient British plateau camp which some authorities claim as the scene of Boadicea's last fight with the Roman legions. The camp covers 12 acres, its six-foot rampart 800 yards round, and the ditch within 10 feet deep and 20 wide. On one side is a depression through which ran a stream which provided the water for the defenders.

A double avenue of elms marches with the road across the common into the town. The wooden pens for animals on market day, and the old coaching inns and cottages, give the place an old-world look, but the magnificent church is modern. Its splendid pinnacled tower stands apart from it, with niches from which look down statues of saints and angels and one who was neither: Augustine, Alphege, Alban, Theodore, Michael, Gabriel, Uriel with a trumpet, and Archbishop Laud.

There is a great triptych behind the altar, and a pulpit with statues of the Evangelists. In a chapel is a gem of modern craftsmanship, a jewelled aumbry of copper with angels adorning it. The glass in one of the windows tells the story of the church, showing Henry the Second granting the manor of Epping with the tiny chapel of St

A Vista at Chingford

Sunlight in the Glades

EPPING FOREST SCENES

Faulkbourne The Old Hall

Hockley The Old Church

John to the Abbot of Waltham, his jewelled crozier in his hand and a monk in a blue robe attending. In the scene is a dog, with other animals symbolising the neighbouring forest.

The Old Shovel

EPPING UPLAND. It lies in the undulating country between Epping Town and the River Lea, and has many farms which have seen the centuries go by. The 13th century church is almost hidden by the limes and pines clustering round it with quaint tombstones 200 years old lying in their shade. The church is 120 feet long and only 21 feet wide, the absence of a chancel arch emphasising its odd shape. The 16th century tower, enriched by a corbel table, has seven bells, one attached to the outside wall.

We come into the church by a 15th century door of broad oak boards; another door, in the tower, is old enough to have a wooden lock. There is a Jacobean chair, a font cover of the same age, and a group of seats with Tudor poppyheads; but the most fascinating possession is a square poor-box with a handle, called a collecting shovel. On the chancel wall is a brass portrait of Thomas Palmer in his robes as a Cambridge professor of Shakespeare's day. There are also memorials to the Conyers family, who commissioned James Wyatt, the destroying architect of so many churches, to build the new Copped Hall for them. Standing in a park of 400 acres, it is built in white brick and stone, one of the biggest houses in Essex.

Medieval Art Gallery

FAIRSTEAD. Few villages in the county are more remote; we come to it by a winding lane from lovely Terling. It has a shingled spire of the last years of Queen Elizabeth, set on a tower of 1200, pointing to the sky in the midst of limes, sycamores, and chestnuts. The capitals at its doorway have weathered the storms of over 700 years. But far older is some of the material in these walls, for there are Roman bricks halfway along the chancel showing where the Norman building ended and where our first English builders continued in the 13th century. The chancel arch has Roman bricks at the top, and in doorway, window, and wall these red bricks abound, mingled with pebbles and flints; it is as if the eager builders had said that any rough assortment would do, only let there be a church.

At least 700 years ago the wall over the Roman bricks in the chancel arch was made a picture gallery, and it is interesting to see that instead of painting the conventional Last Judgment the artists crowded several scenes in rows into their space. Next to the roof are Our Lord riding on the Ass; below are the Last Supper and the Betrayal (with Peter cutting off the ear of Malchus); in the third tier are Christ crowned with thorns, mocked, scourged, and brought before Pilate, while on the extreme right He is carrying His Cross. In a fourth row only two figures are at all clear. There are traces of later paintings on other walls and six red consecration crosses. There is a chest 700 years old, a dug-out nine feet long with two lids, 15th century benches in the nave, and in the belfry a bell which has been ringing for 600 years.

Four centuries ago a traveller would have seen a quaint figure roaming about these lanes. He was Thomas Tusser, the author who had come to test some of the 500 points of good husbandry of which he wrote. His theories met with very little practical success, and he confessed that Jack and Jill tithed so ill that he felt too heavily the burden of the daily pays and the miry ways. So Thomas returned to London, to die in a debtor's prison, a stone of Sisyphus which could gather no moss, as Fuller said, or, as the epigram says:

> *Tusser, they tell me when thou wert alive*
> *Thou, teaching thrift, thyself couldst never thrive;*
> *So, like the whetstone, many men are wont*
> *To sharpen others when themselves are blunt.*

The Unknown Knight

FAULKBOURNE. A house which is the pride of all Essex is standing here in a park of 100 acres of pines, elms, and chestnuts, and a cedar 19 feet round. So perfect is the brickwork of the house, and so elaborate the battlements, that it is not easy to believe that men lived here before the Wars of the Roses, but the king's grant for these very battlements still exists.

It was in the days of Agincourt that the timbered part of the house was built, and in the kitchen is the old six-panelled door and a serving door with its old hinge and iron knocker. Before Sir John Montgomery died in 1449 he rebuilt the front of the wing in brick, and his son Thomas is believed to have built the great tower. The corbel tables are the supreme beauty of it all, and there is an oriel window. The stair turret is remarkable, the steps and the newel being entirely of brick.

The small Norman church stands among the pines at a corner of the park; it is one of the few buildings dedicated to St Germain. The east wall of the chancel was rebuilt in the 13th century, portraits of men of the time being carved as headstops to the windows indoors and out. Inserted in a wall of the nave is a delightful brick window of the 16th century, and west of it is an original Norman doorway. The original priest's doorway opens into a vestry. In the 15th century bell-turret are two bells 700 years old, and above it is a weathervane of 1701 and a lead finial rising above a shingled spire. The roof, the font, and the door with three strap-hinges are medieval, and there are Tudor linenfold panels. The pews are modern, a credit to the craftsmen who made them from oaks grown in the park.

Far older than the oldest tree is the figure of a knight who was laid to rest here in the 13th century. He wears a flat-topped helmet and a long coat, and has in his hand a kite-shaped shield; the knights looked much like that at Runnymede. It is not known whom this battered stone represents. The more gorgeous armour of the Elizabethans is on the brass of Henry Fortescue, a member of the bodyguard of his queen; his children are below him in three groups, and his wife Mary is on a separate brass. The engraved silver cup used here was her gift, and perhaps she set in the chancel the helmet hanging there; it is of the period. A curious possession of the church is a barrel organ of 1830.

Old Brick, Old Timber, and Old Glass

FEERING. One of its houses, Feering Bury, has seen some famous figures under its roof. Here Queen Elizabeth came to stay; here came Bishop Bonner who sent the Protestant martyrs to their doom; and here came Bishop Ridley, the martyr to whom Latimer spoke that brave farewell which rings down the ages still. Still in the windows are Tudor arms, and there are two chimneys of the 17th century. In the village is an inn old enough to have been seen by all these people; and Houchin's Farm, with two storeys overhanging on brackets of grotesque figures, and a moat filled with water.

The fine brickwork of the Tudor builders gives the church a glow of warmth between the solid grey of the 14th century chancel and the 15th century tower. Parts of the nave are 700 years old, but the south wall has been refashioned in brick. There is a splendid porch with pinnacles, battlements, much ornament, and a vaulted roof, all medieval, as is the door with its fine ironwork. A 13th century coffin lid with a fine cross is the oldest treasure inside the church. There are scraps of old glass, some 600 years old and one with Queen Elizabeth's initials; one medieval chest and another of about 1600; and a canopied recess which is either the tomb of a benefactor or an Easter Sepulchre unusually placed in an aisle. The finest woodwork is on the pulpit, which has vigorous carvings probably by Flemish artists of 300 years ago. We see the Scourging of Our Lord, His drooping figure under the weight of the Cross, and the mocking of the Roman soldiers.

The Little Cromwells

FELSTEAD. Its fame is wherever the influence of our public schools has gone. It lies off the Roman road from Great Dunmow to Colchester, and has a fine little group of farmhouses and buildings. On one cottage in the heart of the village are the words, "George Boot made this house, 1596," and we must agree that he made it well, for its overhanging storey still rests on a moulded beam borne on carved brackets decorated with dragons and rosettes, and at one corner crouches a remarkable figure of a woman with cloven feet. Near by is the 17th century vicarage, and beyond is a charming group of almshouses made new in the old style with a small chapel in which we found an Elizabethan table with hinged flaps. The almshouses were founded by the Lord Chancellor who gave the village its chief pride, one of the most famous schools in England, older than Shakespeare. He was Lord Chancellor Rich, a melancholy figure in our history but a benefactor of this countryside.

His school has now about 300 boys, and the main modern building, with its towers and gabled windows, faces one of the finest cricket fields in Essex, on which is a pavilion built from the beams of old cottages that have gone. A cloister leads to the noble hall sheltered by a pair of lofty elms, and beyond is the gracious memorial building designed by two Old Boys. The school began in Tudor days in the delightful timbered and plastered building still standing in the heart of the village, the old schoolroom occupying four bays of the upper storey overhanging the street. The original roof beams are still visible. Next door is the 15th century cottage in which the schoolmaster lived, its three gabled windows projecting from the tiled roof.

In this small schoolroom four sons of Oliver Cromwell learned their lessons—Robert, who may have died at school; Oliver, the Captain Cromwell killed in battle; Henry, wisest and best of all the Protector's boys, and Richard, one of the pathetic figures of our history. To this school also came John Wallis, well known as a mathematician in the early 17th century. His amazing mathematical feats made him famous everywhere, and the rapid deciphering of a cryptical letter during the Civil War set him on the road to fortune, though indeed he was well off, his mother having bequeathed to him an estate in Kent. He is regarded as the chief of all the forerunners of Sir Isaac Newton in mathematics, for which he invented the symbol of Infinity. He would solve the most intricate problems in bed at night and startled even those who knew his great abilities by his wonderful ingenuity with figures, and his easy dealings with them. He knew Pepys, and one of his sad little notes was written to the diarist saying that till he was past 80 he could pretty well bear the weight of years, but he was now an old man, and his sight, hearing, and strength were not as they were wont to be.

There followed John Wallis as a scholar at this school that other mathematician whom we meet in the Poets Corner of Westminster Abbey, Isaac Barrow. Here he had his first lessons in mathematics, and it is no small tribute to this little grammar school that Isaac Barrow grew up to be the mathematical master of Sir Isaac Newton. That was the proud office he gave up in order to travel abroad, and he had great adventures, and when he fell asleep the last words on his lips were "I have seen the glories of the world."

Under the old schoolroom is a wooden arch leading to the ancient church, which has a Norman tower capped by a cupola set up about 1700, when the clock was made. Tiny Norman windows light the stair turret within the tower, which has a fine Norman doorway with a column on each side and two rows of zigzag ornament on its arch. We come into the church by a Tudor porch with a roof which still has its original rafters. The doorway into the nave was built about 1200, and has four columns with carved capitals. The south arcade is from the end of Norman days, the magnificent piers having foliage capitals. The tower arch is also Norman, though it has been restored with Tudor bricks. The chancel, and the fine rafters in its roof, are 14th century, and so is the grand roof of the nave, the clerestory, the north arcade, the walls of the aisles, and the much-worn font with its sculptured heads. Probably by these same 14th century craftsmen is the Easter Sepulchre carved with elaborate foliage and rich with pinnacles in which tiny arches are flanked by faces. There are two 500-year-old brasses, one with the portrait of Christine Grey in a veiled headdress, and the other showing a man magnificent in armour.

But the glory of this church is the great monument of Lord Rich. It is in a chapel built by him as the resting-place of his family, and his tomb is one of the most captivating pieces of carving in Essex. It is, moreover, a significant monument surviving from Tudor days, being one of the few works that are definitely known to be by our first eminent English sculptor, Epiphanius Evesham, whose work we have come upon in two or three places in Kent and in other counties. Here the sculptor has shown us a remarkable figure on a remarkable tomb. Lord Rich is leaning on his elbow in his robe of state, a living portrait of craft and guile with his long beard, and wearing a flat cap. The canopy over him rests on two black columns, and his coat-of-arms and scenes from his life are worked into panels behind him. We see him as a youth holding a cross and a document, Truth and Wisdom standing by him. A second panel shows him as Speaker in the House of Commons with Virtue and Justice behind him, and in the third, where his companions are Hope and Charity, he is represented as Lord Chancellor, carrying the Purse of State. We see him again engraved in black marble on the front of the tomb, riding on horseback, and, last scene of all, we see him on his funeral hearse elaborately canopied, with mournful watchers paying the last homage. The second Lord Rich kneels at a prayer desk let into the tomb, and as a background to the monument are pilasters framing the family arms supported by finely carved stags.

For all Cromwellians this church has much human interest, for here lies Cromwell's first-born son and here was married his last-born daughter. They could never have known each other. Robert

Cromwell died at Felstead when he was 18, a scholar in the old schoolroom; there is an exceptional tribute to him in the register by his friend the rector, who wrote, "Robert Cromwell, son of that honourable man Squire Oliver Cromwell. Robert was an uncommonly pious youth, fearing God beyond many." Like his three brothers who were pupils here, Robert would spend his leisure hours at Grandcourts, the 16th century home of the Bourchiers.

In a grave near by lies that Robert Rich who married Cromwell's youngest daughter Frances. His death was full of pathos, and her life crowded with romance. She is the subject of a remarkable group of marriage stories. It is said that Charles the Second was willing to marry her but that Cromwell would not agree to this plan of bringing peace to the kingdom, because, as he said, "Charles would never be such a fool as to forgive him the death of his father." Cromwell's chaplain, Jerry White, then made love to her, and, being caught by Oliver in the act, timidly protested that he was pleading for her support for his suit to the lady's maid, whereupon Oliver insisted on his marrying the lady's maid on the spot. The third marriage story is that Robert Rich, heir to the Earl of Warwick, fell in love with Frances and married her, so that she would have become Countess of Warwick in due time; but they were married in November in this church at Felstead and Robert Rich died in February leaving no issue. His widow now married into the Russell family, giving Sir John Russell several children, but burying him at last and remaining his widow for more than half a century.

Another figure still remembered here (pupil, master, and governor of the school) is Edward Gepp, a clergyman who spent most of his life at or near Felstead, retiring at last to Chaffix, a Tudor cottage at the end of the village. Here in our time he produced his Essex Dialect Dictionary, a rich fund of rural speech gathered from the neighbourhood. It is a careful and scholarly work, and the only book of its kind.

In the chapel of Felstead School is a memorial to 239 Felsteadians who gave their lives for England in the Great War; it is a fine screen made of English oak, designed and painted by Frank O. Salisbury. It has a statue of St George and the Dragon flanked by figures of Sir Galahad and King Arthur. The embattled cornice is carved with foliage, and on the back of the stalls below the screen are carved three wreaths for the Army, Navy, and the Air Force. Above it all is Mr Salisbury's beautiful window of Our Lord supporting a soldier in khaki, and on the panels are the names of the 239 fallen, among them the name of John Leslie Green, who was with the Royal Army Medical Corps in the Great War, and was awarded the VC for bringing a wounded man from the enemy's wire entanglements, dressing his wounds in a shell-hole amid a storm of bombs and rifle grenades, and bearing him to within reach of safety.

A Sinister Figure of History

RICHARD RICH, Lord Chancellor, who has slept at Felstead since 1567, was one of the sinister figures of Tudor England. It has been said that he made stepping-stones to fortune of the dead bodies of his benefactors. After a wild youth he became a foremost lawyer and was made Solicitor-General, making use of his office to visit Sir Thomas More and Bishop Fisher in the Tower and to betray both to death. Under a pledge of secrecy he extracted statements from Bishop Fisher which he treacherously used at the trial. When More was brought before his judges Rich put into his mouth words he had never uttered, leading More to declare that Rich, who had been a great gambler, was loose of his tongue, and such a man as no one could communicate with on any matter of importance.

Rich marched to power by servile flattery of Henry the Eighth, and was rewarded with part of the king's ill-gotten gains from the monasteries. Having worked with Thomas Cromwell, he now helped to manoeuvre his fall, and with his own hands he tortured Anne Askew in the Tower. In the troubled years which followed he supported whichever side seemed uppermost, betraying his friends in turn. He signed the proclamation for Lady Jane Grey and then came down into Essex and proclaimed Mary. He sent Roman Catholics and Protestants to their death. He rode with Queen Elizabeth into London, and was one of those summoned to discuss the question of the queen's marriage, but he was unworthy of his office, a base intriguer, one of the most selfish of men in spite of his benefactions.

Norman and Elizabethan England

FINCHINGFIELD. Part of its charm is set out round a big green dipping to the River Pant, which widens to add to the beauty of the scene. It is one of the rare villages not soon forgotten,

High Roding   Thatched Cottages in Main Street

Felstead   The Old School Buildings

Hatfield Broad Oak   A Corner of Broad Street

ESSEX HIGHWAYS

Finchingfield   **Old Houses by the Mill**

Terling   **The Smock Mill**

Shalford   **An Essex Pastoral**

Great Clacton   **The Old Village Church**

The Massive Tower and its Norman Doorway

The Impressive Interior with the Norman Tower Arch
FINCHINGFIELD CHURCH

a place where hardly a house or a cottage lacks charm, where the farms have seen four centuries come and go, and where the church is a feast in itself. Two roads wind over the hill from the green, one past an old windmill and the other past the Guildhall, a timber and plaster building with old casement windows and chimneys, and a fine kingpost truss in its roof. Among the other old houses are two from Elizabethan England: Parsonage Farm with five original doors and grotesque beasts carved on the eaves, and Cornish Hall, with a weather-boarded dovecot. But the pride of the neighbourhood is Spain's Hall in grounds of 100 acres, a lake formed from two mill-ponds, and a brick dovecot now cleared of its nests. A lovely old hall it is, with gables and splendid mullion windows, a porch rising the full height of the house to a gable of its own, and an original oriel window, all the work of our incomparable Tudor builders in brick. Even the rain-water pipes put up by the Kempes in the 17th century add their touch of beauty, having elaborate straps ornamented with leopards and cherubs and other things. Within the house is much old panelling lining the walls, and there are richly carved overmantels from the 17th century.

Yet Spain's Hall seems young when we remember the beginnings of the church boldly set on the hill, for it began in Norman England. Its striking western tower is crowned by a wooden lantern of the 18th century, but the masonry below has been standing 800 years with a splendid Norman doorway. The doorway is an arch of four orders, adorned with chevrons and zigzags and other rich patterns, and with corbel heads which we may imagine to be asking each other what has become of the vanished tympanum. The south porch has stone panels and beams and a handsome doorway, all from the 14th century; but a far rarer sight is the original double door still in use after 600 years. It is enriched with six traceried panels and quaint carvings of the Crucifixion, a pelican, a dove, and other figures cut from the solid oak.

The interior of the church is impressive, and we can well imagine its growth through the centuries. Here is a Norman tower arch from the oldest building of all. Here on the south of the nave are arches pierced in the 13th century, when the long narrow chancel and its entrance arch were built. Here on the north are beautiful 14th century arches, the same age as both the aisles and both the chapels. Above us are a 15th century clerestory, a 16th century nave roof, and a 17th century chancel roof with the names of Robert Kempe and John Glascock who set it up. So long does it take for a church to grow. Among the carved heads we noticed one with very long hair, several saints, a king, and a queen. The font has shields on its 14th century bowl, and angels just below. There is a very fine chancel screen carved in the 15th century with tracery and cusps and grotesques; and the side screen is even older, enriched on the cornice with carvings which include men playing pipes. Most handsome of the monuments is the 400-year-old altar tomb of John Berners in the south chapel. Heraldic shields are on the sides, and standing under canopies between the panels are beadsmen hooded and robed. John is shown in brass with his wife, both of them on the marble top of the tomb. He wears a tabard over his armour, and she has a heraldic mantle.

Passing to the chancel we see an 18th century altar tomb and a tablet with a bust, both to members of the Marriot family; and in the north chapel is a plain altar tomb to one of the Kempes 400 years ago. William Kempe, who lived at Spain's Hall in Charles Stuart's time, has a tablet rich with heraldry and festoons, and it is recorded that he was so much master of himself, that what others could scarce do by force and penalties he did "by a voluntary constancy"; he held his peace seven years.

A modern inscription tells us that Daniel Shed was baptised here in Stuart days, that he was one of the founders of New England in 1640, and that in his memory his descendants restored the church.

A fascinating relic on a window ledge in one of the aisles is a diagram of the old game of Nine Men's Morris. Did the village boys of Shakespeare's time shelter here, we wonder, playing this old game when the rain was falling in the churchyard?

Bricks of the Romans

FINGRINGHOE. A cheerful village on a slope of the valley of the Roman River is this, with thatched cottages and oak trees in a hollow by a pond. One of its roads runs down to a ferry across the estuary to the quaint village of Wivenhoe. Here lived the Romans; many of their red bricks are mixed with the flint and limestone rubble of the walls of the church. We come into this old place by a porch with sculptures of St Michael and the Dragon in the spandrels of its outer doorway; its inner doorway shelters a splendid 500-year-old door with the original iron handle. Stepping down into the church the eye meets on the Norman piers the paintings that stood clear in medieval times, and we can still distinguish Michael and a seated figure with long hair, wearing an ermine tippet. On the walls, too, are traces of painting of the 14th and 16th centuries. More definite are grotesque white faces grinning down from the dark beams curving round the white barrel roof. Resting on a bier of the 17th century is a hollowed-out chest much older than the date on it, and there is a great treasure of oak in the font cover, 500 years old, rising in three stages to a richly moulded terminal high above our heads. It has carving of the greatest delicacy. There is a brass with the portraits of John Alleyn and his little daughter, in Elizabethan clothes.

A Mystery Man of History

FOBBING. It is very compact with thatched and tiled roofs side by side, and an inn of the 15th century. The low hills on which the village stands are divided by a creek from the flat meadows reaching toward the Thames, which would still be marshes but for the river-wall built by Dutchmen 300 years ago. By the river stands a lighthouse on stilts.

The grey tower of Fobbing church is a landmark for miles, and by climbing the hundred stairs of the turret we can gaze out to open sea, or inland to the Langdon Hills, the heights of Essex. A round ring of stones above the 15th century west door shows us that the Normans started the tower, while a double-splayed window in the wall of the nave tells us of an earlier Saxon building. The door to the right of this window has remarkable strap-hinges 700 years old, and we notice their curious prongs. To the same period belongs the font, supported on eight pillars. A little barrel organ stands close by.

It is 600 years since the chancel, chapel, and aisle were added, the aisle being wider than the nave. A bearded king and a placid nun look down from the chancel wall, and inset in the wall is a stone inscribed in Norman French. The chapel has a gem of sculpture, Mary with the infant Jesus on her knees. Though it is but a fragment, we can realise how lovely it must have been when first placed by the altar. In the windows are fragments of old glass.

In one of the spandrels of the porch are the great head of a king and a seated man boldly opening a dragon's mouth.

Fobbing comes into history with the ill-fated rising of the labourers under Jack Straw, one of the mystery men of history, towering as a dragon for three weeks, and dying at the executioner's hands in the days of Wat Tyler and John Ball.

England was still in the Dark Ages, yet here was a marvel of organisation and cooperation which brought the men of Essex to East London at the very hour the men of Kent camped at Black-heath and the men of Hertfordshire at Highbury, while in all a dozen counties were in arms. Young Richard the Second rode to Mile End to meet the Essex men, heard their grievances, promised complete reform and pardon, and set 30 clerks to work writing out the necessary documents to implement his pledges. The rebels retired content to their homes, but as soon as quiet was restored, and concerted action by the peasants was no longer possible, the young king came upon them with an army and those who were not hewn down in the field were hanged.

Jack Straw left only a name. Associated with his rising was the immortal poem of Piers Plowman and the many writings of John Ball, who made Essex his centre, pouring out writings which were the direct forerunner of the political pamphlets of Milton and Burke.

FORD END. If we are looking for quaintness we find it here. Not in the handsome modern church with its figures of the evangelists on the tower, but some way off, at the hamlet of North End, where a famous little building has been standing 500 years. Black Chapel it is called, and as with its dormer windows it looks like a cottage the traveller might easily pass it by. It is a little church with a house joining on, parts having been added in the 18th century, though the nave and chancel are medieval, and so is the dwelling where the old priest lived. The walls are timber-framed, and there is a bellcot with a pyramid roof. Some of the nave beams are medieval, and look down on two very different fashions in furniture, benches from Henry the Seventh's time and box-pews from the 18th century. There are altar rails of the time of Queen Anne, whose painted arms hang over the tiny altar; a Tudor screen; and a barrel organ to remind us of the way they made music here 200 years ago.

Church, House, Inn, and Barn

FORDHAM. There are Roman bricks in the walls of its 14th century church, which was given a new aisle and a porch by the Tudor builders. A modern pulpit has little carved panels 300 years old, and there is a monument which shows us the head of a rector's son who died of smallpox in 1715. He was John Pulley, a captain in the navy, and we see him with his long curly hair and cravat. Below is a little carving of men-of-war with sail set on a stormy sea.

Close by, with a great walnut tree before it, stands Fordham Hall, part of it as it was in medieval days. It is not the only ancient house the village has, for there is a farm as old, a Tudor inn, and about half a dozen buildings of the 17th century, including a weather-boarded barn of seven bays.

Benjamin and His Daughters

FOSTER STREET. It is a quiet corner of our countryside but how far our thoughts run out as we stand by a grave in this hamlet, in the fields two miles from Harlow! For 200 years the Baptists of Harlow used this spot as their sacred ground, and so it is that a father and his two daughters lie here, Benjamin Flower with Sarah and Eliza. They lie in an altar tomb weathered and worn, a hundred years old and little known, yet as we stand by it we think of great crowds singing, and perhaps of a dire catastrophe, for it was Sarah Flower who wrote the words of Nearer My God to Thee and her sister who wrote the music. It has been sung for about 100 years in every church where English hymns are sung, and it was to its pathetic strains that the Titanic sank down into the waves.

Benjamin Flower was a London tradesman's son who failed in business and, taking a traveller's job abroad, found himself in Paris in the Revolution. He came home to edit a Cambridge newspaper, and, alone among provincial editors, he denounced the war with France. He was tried at the bar of the House of Lords for censuring the political conduct of a bishop, and for his daring he spent six months in Newgate. Here Eliza Gould visited him, she having also suffered for her Liberal opinions, and on his recovering his freedom she married him and they settled at Harlow, where he founded a printing business. They had two daughters, who found themselves motherless in 1810 and fatherless in 1829, and then devoted themselves to literature and music. Sarah wrote a religious drama called Vivia Perpetua, and many hymns set to music by her sister and sung at Finsbury Chapel. It is Nearer My God to Thee that has established her fame for all time, but her hymn He sendeth sun, He sendeth shower, with its refrain, Father, Thy will, not mine, be done, is typical of a character of singular charm and fervour.

Sarah married William Adams, a scientific man who devised a joint known to every railway engineer, the fishjoint which connects rails so that fast traffic can safely pass over the link. She died from tuberculosis in the year of revolutions, 1848. She was the last of the three to come to this grave.

FOXEARTH. A little village in the countryside Gainsborough knew so well, it is notable for a moated 15th century hall that is now a farmhouse, a 15th century cottage that is now a post office, and a medieval church much restored last century when the porch and tower were built, but still keeping some fine old woodwork. The chancel roof is 14th century, the roofs of the nave and aisle are 15th century, and the screen (with figures of Christ, the Madonna, and ten saints painted on its panels) is a treasure 400 years old.

FRATING. In good farming country, with cottages widely scattered, it has a small stone church with an embattled tower and a red and blue tiled spire. But in this tower are thin red tiles from Roman villas which stood here, some of them encircling a little Norman window peeping at us over the tiled roof of the 600-year-old porch. In the tower is a bell which was ringing at the time of Agincourt, and another which would ring with it at the coming of the Tudor dynasty. There is an Easter Sepulchre 400 years old, and the altar tomb in alabaster and black marble of Thomas Bendish, who died in the same year as Queen Elizabeth.

The Lighthouse Telephone

FRINTON-ON-SEA. We have read that here come the man who would forget his fame and the woman who is tired of the public's admiration. We do not know, but certainly here come thousands who love the cliffs and the sea. With roads laid out like a garden city and an open space known as the Greensward extending for a mile between the sea-road and the cliffs sloping gently to the beach, it is an attractive place. Its church has grown from one of the 14th century, with a brick porch added in the 16th, but it has few things of ancient days, though one of the chancel windows has two shields of 14th century glass. Here there was laid, from these splendid sands, the first telephone cable to a lighthouse at sea, first used on October 2, 1893.

Red Tower

FRYERNING. A little apart from the Roman road between London and Chelmsford, it has a sight not soon forgotten, a magnificent red tower standing out above a churchyard rich in pines and yews. It is a noble piece of 15th century brickwork, with handsome pinnacles, shapely windows and buttresses, stepped battlements, and tiny corbelled arches, a perfect tower of its age. There are red tiles on the church roofs, Roman tiles in the walls of the Norman nave and chancel, and wide-splayed Norman windows, some reshaped by a later age. The attractive little priest's doorway is 15th century, but the people's doorways are Norman, and one has a consecration cross. A striking Norman font is richly patterned with many designs. In the vestry is one of the best palimpsest brasses we have seen, mounted to show both sides. Its original engraving was of a 15th century lady in a horned headdress; but a little of the headdress is cut away to accommodate the plump face of Mary Berners, on the other side; she is wearing a handsome Tudor robe. There is a tablet to Captain Gordon Elton who died in the Great War after winning the DSO. It has these noble lines written 2500 years ago by the Greek poet Simonides:

> Yet being dead they die not; in the grave
> Though they be lying
> These be the souls to whom high valour gave
> Glory undying.

By the church is Fryerning Hall, a house with timbers almost as old as the church tower.

Roman Tiles and Norman Tower

FYFIELD. Its main street winds with the willow-shaded River Roding, and by this stream stands the church the Normans built in an ambitious way, with a central tower 17 feet square. Two of its stages alone remain, a wooden lantern and a short spire soaring

143

over them. There are Roman tiles in the nave, and peeping through an opening in the turret of the tower we see how the builders shaped these tiles into the round newel of the staircase. The Normans also fashioned the font. The 13th century men built the aisles and the handsome arcades, but the supreme beauty of the church is the work of 14th century masons. The chancel is rich in their craftsmanship. Four windows show the graceful lines of their tracery; the deep piscina and the pillared sedilia show their mastery of design, and their exquisite detail. On the sedilia are four perfect heads, a woman in a peaked cap, two men with curly hair, and a bishop. Headstops are over all the windows, and running round the east window is a rear arch with faces of people on one side and beasts on the other.

About a hundred years after this work was finished another mason set to out rival it. He had only to carve a niche for a statue, but its canopy, its ribbed vault, the bosses, and the little buttresses, are perfect. The timber screen with painted shields, erected in 1914, adds greatly to the beauty of the church.

GALLEYWOOD COMMON. A scattered village on the high ground south of Chelmsford, its glory is in its wild common, which we found a mass of living gold. The modern church stands on this wonderful gorse carpet, and its spire rises 127 feet high. A racecourse encircles the common and the church as well—an odd assemblage, though races were held at Galleywood long before the church came. Eight bells ring merrily in the steeple, which looks down on a churchyard beautiful with trees and flowers.

Here Lived a Very Gallant Gentleman

GESTINGTHORPE. Here lived a very gallant gentleman, though who could have imagined, seeing him as a little delicate boy walking in this pleasant wooded country, that he would live for ever as the matchless hero of Antarctica?

Three English explorers have passed mysteriously from the sight of men in our time: Irvine and Mallory were seen mounting up Everest and were lost in the clouds, Captain Oates walked out into the blizzard to give a better chance of life to Scott and his comrades. He was born in London while his mother was on holiday there, but this was the home of his boyhood, and the little 14th century church of

A Barge on the Chelmer near Chelmsford

The Blackwater at Little Braxted

TWO ESSEX RIVERS

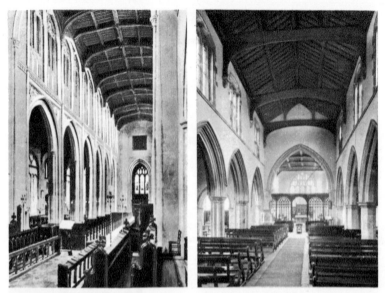

Saffron Walden

Newport

Great Bardfield

Stebbing

FOUR ESSEX INTERIORS

flint and red bricks, with a few Roman tiles in its walls, has a brass plate in the nave which says:

> *In memory of a very gallant gentleman. Died March 17, 1912, on the return journey from the South Pole of the Scott Antarctic Expedition.*
> *When all were beset by hardship he, being gravely injured, went out into the blizzard to die in the hope that by so doing he might enable his comrades to reach safety.*

Every week, we were told, an old lady, her years running close to the nineties, walked to the church to polish this brass in memory of her son. Well she remembered the time when he was so delicate that he was sent to South Africa for three winters. He knew this place well as a boy and his home is by the church, the 17th century house called Over Hall, which we see through the fine trees. It was faced with brick and partly made new in the 18th century, and has a dovecot 300 years old with a pyramid roof, four gables, and nesting holes for 500 birds. There is another dovecot at Moat Farm a mile away, a medieval house with its original doorway. The countryside of Captain Oates's boyhood is dotted with timbered and plastered farm houses—Park Farm with two original doorways and a 16th century chimney stack; Parkgate Farm, with the original roof of the hall; Edye's Farm, with its old doorway and the roof of the old hall still in its upper storey.

They are peeps of old England to stir the imagination of any boy, and we do not doubt that Captain Oates would often think of them in those last bitter days of his life. Like the farmhouses, the church has doors which have been swinging on their hinges for centuries, its west door and the door of the tower turret being both 400 years old. The magnificent hammerbeam roof of the nave has been as we see it for 500 years; so has the roof of the south aisle. The beams and wall-plates of the nave roof are carved with foliage and the names of Peter Barnard, Marget his wyf; and Thomas Loveday and Alys his wyf. Their children may have been christened at the medieval font, carved with an eagle, a bull, and a lion, all with wings.

From these medieval days comes a little glass in a window in the nave, showing a small crowned Madonna with her little Son on her knee, and the two richly traceried old bays worked into the oak chancel screen. There is an extraordinarily long dug-out chest with five locks, old paintings of Moses and Aaron, and a 17th century tomb on which John Sparrow kneels at a table in the armour of Charles Stuart's day. He wears a ruff and baggy breeches, and all about him are the weapons of war of his time, pikes and spears and muskets, helmets and a suit of armour, a red standard, and a drum.

Here Died a Very Gallant Gentleman

ALL the life of Lawrence Edward Oates would seem to have been a preparation for those hours in the Antarctic when he walked to his death in a blizzard to try to save his companions beset by hardship. Never was a greater example of the truth that no man can tell till the end of his life what has been the most important hour in it.

He was only 32 when he died, and up till the years of his Antarctic Expedition his chief expedition had been in the South African War, where he just missed the Victoria Cross. He was with the Inniskilling Dragoons in India when he wrote to Scott begging to be taken as one of his party on the Terra Nova. He was asked to come to London to talk it over, and, the two men recognising in one another a kindred spirit, the sailor took the soldier, who was to have charge of the ponies. Oates, rather shyly, asked Scott whether he would have a chance of going on the actual sledge party to the Pole. The Commander replied briefly that he intended to take the four fittest men, and if Oates proved to be one of these he would certainly go on with him. With this conditional promise Oates joyfully embarked. The record of the 900-mile sledge journey to the Pole is best told in the diaries of Captain Scott, found near the dead bodies of himself and his last companions. The most heartrending sentence in it is in the message Scott penned to England:

Had we lived I should have had a tale to tell of the hardihood, endurance, and courage of my companions which would have stirred the heart of every Englishman.

That hardihood and courage belonged to Lawrence Oates in full measure. He added to them an act of sacrifice which raised this simple soldier to a height at which he shines as an inspiration to the world.

Almost from the beginning the sledge journey to the Pole was dogged with mishap. The preparations were long and difficult after the party had reached their starting base. One of the questions hard to decide was whether to take ponies or dogs or both, and the decision to take ponies involved a delay of some weeks, because they could not stand the winter climate. The delay also caused another entirely unexpected misfortune, the character of which was only learned when it was too late. All unknown to Scott, while he delayed, Amundsen with his Antarctic party was starting on the same journey by a shorter route, and with more fitting equipment. Fortune favoured the Norwegian, and seemed to set its face against the English party from the first. They were behind their scheduled time and dared not pause for rest lest their food rations should not last. There was nothing but to go trudging on, hauling their sledges with agonising effort.

In spite of the heavy going over soft snow or crumbling ice they contrived to keep to nearly ten miles a day, but it was at terrible cost to themselves, and each began to ask himself how long he could keep the pace, and each to fear that his weakness might betray the others. What their nights were when they shivered, half-frozen and half-thawed, through brief hours of exhaustion, and when they seemed neither asleep nor awake, we hardly find it possible to think.

At last, when the lessening stock of food had lightened the sledges, they had only 27 miles to go; another two good marches would take them to their goal. On January 16 they had been marching about two hours when the seaman's eyes of Lieutenant Bowers saw something like a cairn of stones. But how could it be a cairn? Were they not the first to cross this untracked solitude? They marched on. Another half hour and there was a black speck far ahead. The bitter truth burst on them. With sinking hearts they came to a black flag tied to part of a sledge, and, drawing nearer, saw sledge tracks, marks of skis, and the footprints of many dogs pointing to and from the Pole. Amundsen had beaten them; the intrepid Norwegian had come and gone.

Our own hearts sink as we try to realise the bitter shock of disappointment to these worn and bewildered men. Had they indeed been the first to set their feet at the South Pole the exultation might have so raised their spirits that they would have set out on the return journey with bounding pulses and renewed vigour. It was not to be. They must face the miles back with the bitter consciousness that, though they had done their duty, it was not enough.

It was on the merciless journey back that Captain Oates broke down in body though his spirit triumphed to the end. His feet had been frost-bitten; he could scarcely stumble along; his iron will could not keep him in the traces of the sledge. He was left to sit on it while the others searched for tracks, and then to plod behind alone with his thoughts. He asked his nearest friend among them what he should do, and all the friend could say was "Slog on—just slog on," though both knew death was certain.

So Oates tried to battle to the end, though doubts came with every dawn and lasted through every agonising day. His hands were useless; his feet would barely support him. Try as he would he kept the party waiting. He came to the end of his endurance. He could not go on. He asked them to leave him behind in his sleeping-bag. But they would not leave him, though they knew his hours were numbered, and he struggled on a few miles more, when they camped. He awoke in the morning after a little sleep, and as he woke he knew what he must do. He struggled to his feet and limped out into the blizzard. He bade no goodbye; he said only: *I am just going outside; I may be some time.*

He was going out so that his companions should not be burdened with his company. The chance was faint, but his going might give them some hope of life denied to him.

Long afterwards, when the bodies of the others were found, a service was read over them beginning with the words: "The Lord gave and the Lord hath taken away; blessed be the name of the Lord." Over the body of Oates no service could be read, for the snow of the blizzard had enfolded it forever; but near the camp where he went forth into the swirling snowstorm a rude cross has been set up, and on it are the words: *Hereabouts died a very gallant gentleman.*

Red Earth

GOLDHANGER. It stands remote, close to the Blackwater estuary, and down by its sea-wall is a mound of red soil, one of 200 still seen beside the Essex estuaries, sites of potteries in days before history. In this mound Roman pottery was found in carefully constructed flues, and the experts say that here some potters settled in Caesar's day, working an already ancient site. There is no doubt that the Romans were here, for their bricks are in the church walls, set here by Norman hands. The deeply splayed windows of the Normans have now brilliantly coloured portraits of the saints. The bold tower, the chapel, and the three-bayed roof of the nave are medieval. In the chapel is the altar tomb of Thomas Heigham and his three wives; one of their portraits is still in brass on the tomb, showing her in Tudor costume.

The big churchyard, with its many chestnut trees, is a pleasant place to linger in on an autumn day, when creeper clothes the porch in a glowing mass of red and gold.

GOOD EASTER. A timber spire, soaring above the trees 100 feet high points the way to this delightful old-world place in the valley of the River Can. It may be proud of its past history, for in the Middle Ages it belonged to St Martin's-le-Grand, and Henry the Eighth gave it to Westminster Abbey. The nave and the chancel are 13th century, and the aisle with its fine arcade is from the 14th. An unusual feature of the chancel is the stone bench under the arcades along each wall. Among the small treasures of the church are a carved chair of Cromwell's time, a tiny coffin lid of the 13th century, and (not so small) an old bassoon used in the choir 100 years ago. High on the wall above, resting on a corbel, is a dog's head with its tongue lolling out, the crest of the owner of the 16th century helmet above it. Margaret Norrington, whose brass is in the aisle, may have seen this great man's funeral.

On the patch of green by the church is the old whipping-post.

The Infamous Chancellor

GOSFIELD. Beautiful with its heritage of parklands, it has welcomed a queen in her glory, housed a treacherous Chancellor, and sheltered a fugitive king. Its cottages blend harmoniously with the scene, some backing on the grounds of its great houses, Gosfield Place and Gosfield Hall.

The hall, with a charming lake of 50 acres, stands in grounds rich in cedars, tulip trees, and spreading shrubberies. Here came Queen Elizabeth as the guest of Lord Rich, of whom we read at Felstead. Wealthy from the spoil of the monasteries, he owned a great part of the county, including the hall which Sir John Wentworth had built. Two wings of Wentworth's house remain with their stately chimneys and splendid windows, and an entire floor is occupied by what is called Queen Elizabeth's Gallery, over 100 feet long.

There was an earlier hall here than Wentworth's, the home of the Rolfs, who 500 years ago built the church in a corner of the park by the lake, where the 17th century vicarage keeps it company, shaded by a great oak. The tower with its lofty arch is 15th century; so are the double doors in a doorway over which a queen and a bishop keep watch in the modern porch; so are the nave and chancel. The north chapel, a century younger, was converted in the 18th century into a raised chamber for the owners of the hall. An altar tomb of 1440 has a brass portrait of Thomas Rolf in the robes of a sergeant-at-law. There are only three such brasses of the period, and this is the most famous of the three for its perfect detail.

In the private chapel, its walls decorated with shields, its ceiling elaborate with plaster foliage, is the monumental tomb by Schee-makers showing the fine figures of John and Anne Knight, he in Roman costume, resting his hand on her shoulder, she touching her brilliantly coloured shield.

A beautiful window in the tower, with St Elizabeth, St Catherine, St George, and the story of the Good Samaritan, is to George Courtauld and his wife, founder of the great silk firm which bears his name. The sanctuary window, with scenes from the life of Christ, is in memory of Susannah Courtauld, who died at the hall in 1879. In a chancel window are fragments of red, blue, and yellow 15th century glass. There are two other fine tombs, one of which has coloured and enamelled shields, and the chancel walls have Tudor linenfold and friezes carved with grotesques and mermaids.

Hippos and Rhinos

GRAYS. Kent's chalk crops out in this little place by the Thames: here men have found in quarries, in the silted-up bed of a lost river older than the Thames, remains of early elephants, rhinos, and hippos, as well as the shells of the freshwater mussel now extinct in England. There are a few Roman tiles in the floor of the church (rebuilt last century), with a few 13th century arches, and a 15th century font; but that is almost all, save for a Tudor screen in the tower arch and brass portraits of two Tudor ladies with six daughters of one of them.

On a wall is a tablet recalling a tragedy of the Thames when a

schoolmaster and his boys were drowned in trying to escape from
fire on the training ship Goliath.

Romans and Saxons

GREAT BADDOW. Here men have lived for thousands of
years; their Stone Age and Bronze Age hoards have been
found. Its old houses crowd together in winding streets, some backing into the raised churchyard. This churchyard comes into our
history, for when the church was new it was a gathering-place of the
peasants in their ill-fated rising of 1381.

The most striking feature of the church is the 16th century brickwork of the aisle, and the clerestory springing into view behind. The
aisle has a neat crow-stepped parapet, and above the five windows
lighting the nave is a corbel table running under the parapet, above
which are six cone-shaped pinnacles. A leaded spire rises from the
tower, a bell under a little roof of its own jutting out from it.

The oldest things the village has are a few Roman tiles in these
walls; they must have been handled by Saxons in a building long since
gone. The two arcades and the wide chancel arch give distinction
to the church, and there is a touch of humour bequeathed to us by
the carver of a bridled head from which one of the arcades springs,
a warning against slander. The pride of the church is the Jacobean
pulpit. Its elaborate canopy has pinnacles and pendants, and the
pulpit has carvings of many beautiful devices. On the chancel wall
is a brass portrait of Jane Paschall, who was laid to rest here a few
years before they set up the pulpit. She is a fine figure in Elizabethan
dress. Two more ladies share the only other striking monument,
Amy and Margaret Gwyn, sisters who died in the middle of the 18th
century, their portraits being on a marble oval below a cherub.

Here the scholar poet Alexander Barclay came in 1546 as rector.
In 1508 he translated Brant's Ship of Fools into English verse, and
then became a monk of Ely, where he translated a life of St George.
Scholars owe a special debt of gratitude to Great Baddow, for here
also was born Richard de Baddow, who in 1326 founded the Hall
which became famous as Clare College at Cambridge.

The Beautiful Stone Screen

GREAT BARDFIELD. It has been a little town with a market,
and is lovely still with old cottages and shops, a tower windmill

known as Gibraltar, and a fine church, with the hall on the hill above the Pant valley. The hall is mainly from Cromwell's time, but has a Tudor wing. Two 17th century buildings in the grounds are a splendid barn and a timbered dovecot, the dovecot having a pole with a revolving frame and ladder to give access to any one of the 14 tiers of clay nests.

Place House, at the top of High Street, is another old house, with an overhanging storey and a bracket carved to tell us it was built in 1564. In a window are the arms of the Bendlowes family, and an inscription saying that William Bendlowes was a lawyer in the days of our two Tudor Queens. His altar tomb is in the church, with a brass portrait of his wife, his own having gone; and above is the remarkable chancel roof the Bendlowes family gave in 1618. Its two heavy tiebeams are richly ornamented, and the grotesque carvings of the corbels include a curious centaur. The chancel has two stone grotesques which have been 600 years at the corners of the gable outside. The lowest part of the tower was built a few years before Magna Carta, and its small lead spire was added about the time of Queen Anne. The rest of the church is a very good example of 14th century building, with handsome windows outside, a wonderful old door to let us in, an impressive array of columns in the nave, and a rare treasure at the entrance to the chancel.

The old door is a double one, and has been swinging on its hinges since the church was built. Grey with age, it shows in strong relief the trefoil panels and traceried borders cut into its solid oak. Thrilling it is to think of village people passing through it every day while the greater part of English history was being written. But rarer still is the stone screen built into the moulded chancel arch, a vivid example of the way the 14th century craftsmen loved to beautify their churches. The screen has a splendid central arch rising to a finial with a crucifix of stone, the carving on the underside of the chancel arch completing the frame in which the crucifix is set. Smaller arches rise to support statues of John and the Madonna; and in all this rich beauty everything but the statues themselves is the work of the old craftsmen.

A little 14th century glass still left in the windows shows canopied heads and figures of St Stephen in blue and purple, St Laurence with his gridiron, and a Crucifixion. The west window has shields of the

Mortimers, the famous Earls of March; and a beautiful modern window shows St Helena with her cross, St Anne teaching Mary to read, and two scenes from the life of St Augustine of Hippo. It is in memory of Rose Helen Kirwan, who gave the church its handsome font and cover.

High up in one of the aisles hang two funeral helmets which belonged in the 17th century to the Lumley family from Great Lodge, a great brick house, with a cupola rising from its long tiled roof.

The Faithful Family

GREAT BENTLEY. Here is a village green of 42 acres, with roads crossing it and ducks and chickens popping out from gates of cottages as they have done since Norman children played their games on this great place.

There is a pond by the green with 17th century houses behind it, and round the corner is the big churchyard. Passing through its gate we make our way under an avenue of lopped poplars to a timbered porch of the 14th century, with a carved Norman doorway inside.

We may see here too how deftly the Normans used their axes in carving the chevrons, the sunflowers, and the other rich ornaments of the doorway which also has two medieval sundials on the other side. To right and left above this door are the narrow round windows of the same age. The chancel was lengthened and the solid tower added 600 years ago. It was only in our own time that the roof of the chancel and the nave were revealed, and both are splendid examples of timber work of five hundred years ago.

The village has a pathetic memory of the bitter days of Mary Tudor's reign. There lived here a family of three, William Munt, his wife Alice, and their daughter Rose, who belonged to a little group of people who used to gather together to read the Bible. There was a Judas among them, a priest named Thomas Tye, who left the group and reported its practices to Bishop Bonner. The agents of the torturers met Rose Munt and tried to shake her faith by putting her hand in a candle flame, but Rose declared that if she were compelled to burn she would be given the strength to bear it. William and his wife were over 60, but Rose was 20, yet when the three were thrown into prison she went there singing. In their death this little family was not divided, for all three were burnt together in Colchester.

The Refugees

GREAT BRAXTED. It has the mark of a family of the Low Countries who fled to the freedom of Elizabethan England from the terrible Duke of Alva. They were the Du Canes, who acquired wealth by promoting the wool industry of their fellow refugees and bought the great house here, in a park which they made a paradise. Its 500 acres are crowded with magnificent trees, their noble branches reflected in a lake of 14 acres. The churchyard, with a lordly cedar, is ringed round by all this natural glory, and approached from the road by a long avenue of wizened yews.

On these hills lived the Romans, and the Normans used their bricks to shape the windows of the church. The lancets in the chancel and in the walls under the wooden turret were added in the 13th century; one of them has a medieval sundial scratched on it. The roof of the 15th century porch has timbering resting on stone corbels, two angels and two human folk.

The American Window

GREAT BROMLEY. A pleasant little place in the valley of the Frating Brook, it has a splendid church showing how wonderfully well the medieval workers in wood and stone could add beauty to the work of earlier days. The church is 15th century. The glorious tower with its pinnacles and great buttresses, and the clerestory with 14 great windows over 14th century arcades, were built in 1500. The high-pitched double-hammer roof with its richly moulded beams and curved braces belongs to the same period. The wall-posts of this lovely roof terminate in canopied niches in which saints stand on stone corbels carved with angels. The capitals of the piers in the nave are carved with oak leaves and grotesque beasts, one swallowing a man and one attacking a woman. There were many brasses on the stones in the floor but only two remain, one of William Bischopton, who died in 1432, and the other of John Hubbard, buried in 1537.

Here in our own century has been placed a window by American descendants of Gregory and Simon Stone, who left Great Bromley in 1634 to settle in the new land then growing up to be a New World. The window has a delightful picture of the ship which bore these courageous emigrants across the broad Atlantic, and in its scene is a stately figure of a Red Indian.

Perhaps best of all is the porch through which we come to see all this. It has a lovely doorway and a charming parapet, with big windows and walls of knapped flints in elaborately traceried stone panels; and it is a masterpiece of 15th century building.

The Mayflower, the Zeppelin, and the Martyr

GREAT BURSTEAD. Through the Romans, Saxons, and Normans its history brings us to a dramatic event of our own time. In this lovely hill country ancient Britons were at home before the Romans came; their earthenware has been found in a burial ground, with the coin of a British king and coins of three great Caesars: Trajan, Hadrian, and Constantine.

In this place of ancient memory lies a Saxon king, the 7th century Sebert; he lies in the great churchyard, in which an ancient yew is flourishing. The bold tower is 600 years old and has a shingle spire springing from the parapet. The Normans built the nave and one of their windows remain. There are two medieval porches, both with fine timber roofs and one timber-framed with a carved bargeboard. In this porch are the stone heads of a king and queen and a carving of Gabriel bringing the good news to the Madonna.

The font, the roofs, the doors with their ironwork, one of the bells, and a little of the glass, have all come down to us from the hands of medieval craftsmen, and their work is also on a splendid array of oak pews.

Older than all these possessions is the huge dug-out chest with seven iron hinges, in which they kept the village documents guarded by three padlocks. It is possible that there were kept in this trunk the wages of the men who transformed the simple Norman church into the place we see.

There is a lovely oak reredos, and over the tablet of the Commandments is a golden-winged cherub so superbly wrought that it is believed to have come from the workshop of Grinling Gibbons. In the sanctuary are two carved Jacobean chairs.

Two events that come into our history belong to Great Burstead, one to the chancel of this church and one to the village itself. In the chancel one winter's morning in 1607 stood a little wedding group. Christopher Martin was marrying Marie Prower, looking forward to great happiness in this Essex countryside. But, alas, the spacious days of Queen Elizabeth were gone, and the tyranny of the Stuart days had come, and they were to sail away in the Mayflower in search of freedom to worship God. Christopher was the treasurer of the ship, one of the inspirations of that immortal company of voyagers, and it is sad to have to record that within a month or two after reaching the new-found world of liberty they and their servant died from the hardships they endured. Their names are in the register here, and a few pages before is the name of Elizabeth Watts, a widow. Her husband was one of the heroes of the village, and one of the victims of the cruel reign of Mary Tudor.

The event of our own time which will not soon be forgotten was the coming down of a Zeppelin in the Great War. The Zeppelin was the L32, one of 12 raiders which came over Essex in the reign of terror of the autumn of 1916. Two reached London, killing 29 and injuring 99, but one never arrived and never returned home. Two airmen attacked the L32 and crowds of excited people saw the running fight. Soon a glow like that at the end of a cigar appeared at the end of the Zeppelin and suddenly the great airship was enveloped in flames. It came down burning from a height of 8000 feet, the second Zeppelin brought down in England, and in this churchyard where lies a Saxon king lie the men who perished with her.

Long before the Age of Zeppelins was the age of torture by fire in Smithfield and one of the bravest of 72 Essex victims of Queen Mary's persecution was Thomas Watts of Burstead. He was a prosperous draper here, a student of the Bible and a preacher. Married and with six children, and knowing the danger he was in, he sold all the cloth in his shop and gave his possessions to his family and much to the poor.

One day in the summer of 1555 he was brought before Bishop Bonner, and after three examinations was condemned to death and sent to Newgate. In June he was taken to Chelmsford and lodged in an inn with four other Essex men waiting to be burned. It is recorded that they had supper together and then joined in prayer, and that afterwards Thomas Watts prayed alone and left them to say farewell to his wife and his six children. "Let not the murdering of God's saints cause you to relent," he said to them; "I doubt not He will be a merciful Father unto you." Two of his boys, not bearing to leave their brave father, pleaded with him that they might be burned with him, but they were led sorrowfully away. For 44 years his widow lived at Burstead, and when they laid her to rest, in a grave by the yew tree still growing near the porch, the rector sat down and wrote in his register these words:

Elizabeth Watts, widow of Thomas Watts, the blessed martyr of God, who for witnessing suffered the martyrdom in the fire at Chelmsford in the reign of Queen Mary, was buried this 10th day of July 1599, having lived a widow after his death and made a good end like a good Christian woman in God.

A Superb Norman Building

GREAT CANFIELD. Behind the church and cottages of this quiet and charming place is a dense clump of trees. They spring from a mound 50 feet high and 280 feet wide, over which the walls of the castle keep of the De Veres rose high in the days of the Normans. Beyond it are the ramparts of the outer defences, which covered seven acres, and all round this great fortress we can walk in a dry moat 45 feet wide at its base and filled in ancient days by water from the River Roding. Aubrey de Vere, Great Chamberlain of England 800 years ago, dwelt here in a castle, probably built of wood, of which nothing remains. But the church by the moat has lost little of the beauty he gave it.

This little shrine is one of the most perfect Norman buildings in Essex. Save for the extension for the bell-turret added in the 13th century its walls stand as the Normans built them. Both the doorways are richly carved, and in one the mason surpassed himself, the tympanum being filled with zigzags converging in circles, as if flashes of lightning had been transfixed in stone. So hard a stone did he choose that the tiny eyes still peep from the faces he carved on the capitals of the shafts. Two birds peck the bushy beard on one face and rolls of ribbon flow from the mouth of the other. On one of the posts are five fylfot crosses, one of the earliest of Christian symbols and known to early man, carved on prehistoric monuments found in Italy, and something like the swastika.

The interior of the church is designed in a masterly way, the chancel arch perfect as a frame for a group of arches over the altar. A nearer view reveals a wall-painting as rare as it is lovely, a primitive masterpiece as old as any in our National Gallery and the work of an English artist. The painting shows a Madonna in a yellow robe nursing an infant Jesus; she sits serene on a throne raised on a dais, and experts declare that she was seated quietly here when Robert de Vere set out from the castle hard by to go to Runnymede.

The preservation of this painting is due to an act of vanity. On a side wall is an elaborate monument of Sir William Wyseman, holding the hand of his wife. When the monasteries were dissolved this family became all powerful in Great Canfield, so that there was no one to say nay when they decided to use the niche as a background for this monument. It was not till recent times that it was removed and the wall-painting found.

John Wyseman with his wife and their ten children are kneeling at prayer. He had grown grey in the hard business of auditing the accounts of Henry the Eighth, though he seems to have made a fortune for himself. Here, too, is his daughter Agnes with her husband John Fytche, who stands proudly with his head high and the date of Armada year on his tomb.

Rail, Road, and River Meet

GREAT CHESTERFORD. It was an important Roman village before it was an English one, and has sent Roman coins and pottery to Saffron Walden's museum. Every traveller from London to Cambridge knows it, for here the road and railway come together by the River Cam. Its embattled tower is modern, but the church is ancient and has some weird heads on its walls, a winged dragon sprawling over one of the buttresses. The interior is impressive with stately arcades of the 13th century, aisles and a chapel a little younger, and a south chapel of the 16th century. Many quaint carvings in wood and stone are on the corbels in the roofs. We see angels and crowned heads in the chancel, and grotesques in the nave and south chapel; but the best roof of all is the Tudor one in the south aisle, one of its corbels a longhaired head with a collar round its neck. There is a 15th century font, a 16th century chest, and two chairs and a communion table from the 17th century. The attractive modern woodwork includes neat screens, choir-stalls carved with kneeling angels, and a lectern formed by an angel with a sword. A lovely Madonna and Child shine from a 700-year-old window in the chancel. Here in brass is Agnes Holden, who founded a chantry not long before chantries were swept away. Her dress with its big cuffs is in the fashion of Henry the Eighth's time. Another little brass figure is full of pathos, showing a son of Lord Howard de Walden in swaddling clothes. He is described as Mr John Howard of 1600, and we read that his time on earth was 12 days.

Sycamores and pines give beauty to the churchyard, which has by its entrance one of Great Chesterford's charming houses. Timbered and plastered, with a gabled storey overhanging, it is thought to have been built in the 15th century, though a 17th century date appears on the plaster. A little way along the lane is another overhanging house of about 1600, and a quarter of a mile off is Manor Farm, built about 1500, with a wing added a generation or two later. On its beams inside are bosses carved with a rose and a pelican.

John Knox's Son

GREAT CLACTON. A place of great antiquity, it is Roman, Saxon, and Norman. Saxon graves have been found, and Roman tiles stand out among the flints and stones of the Norman church. In the village is a thatched cottage of the 17th century and an inn with timber-framing and moulded ceiling beams of the Elizabethan age. From a bend of the wide road a fine avenue of 16 lime trees runs through the great churchyard to a Norman doorway under a Norman window. The doorway in the other wall has 12th century pillars. The font, with carvings of two angels and of three seated figures, is about 500 years old, contemporary with the massive stone tower, on which is set a timber belfry with a dumpy spire. The student of architecture will delight in the traces of rare vaulting in the roof of the nave.

A tablet on the wall tells us that Eleazor Knox was vicar to his death in 1591. He was born at Geneva in 1558, when his father was living there in exile, his father being the immortal John Knox.

Marching to the Promised Land

GREAT DUNMOW. It is a quaint old town along the Roman road from Bishop's Stortford to Colchester, by the River Chelmer. It has a marketplace with a steep-roofed town hall 400 years old; a wayside pond in which Lionel Lukin, the designer of one of our first lifeboats, is said to have made his experiments; the 16th century house of Bigods with old thatched barns and an Elizabethan summerhouse; and cottages nestling close to its church.

A very interesting corner is this, with the great 14th century tower shading a 16th century vicarage with a timbered and plastered front, and there is near the church a 400-year-old house with a timbered clock turret and a cupola containing a bell of 1651. Over one of the windows of the gabled front is a woman's bust which has survived the weather of three centuries.

Much interest is there for us before we go inside the church—a monkey and a lion carved on the tower above a window, an imposing array of monsters as waterspouts, a coffin lid 700 years old, and a band of Roman tiles above a window.

We come into the nave by a pinnacled porch of the 15th century, through a doorway of the 13th, and we may call on our way in the upper room of the porch, which has still its original door; the room has a beautifully carved niche, and is remarkable for extending as a wooden gallery, from which we may see the nave and aisles. The gallery has been here 500 years, being as old as the clerestory windows.

The church is rich in possessions, having a font and a chest of the 14th century and another chest of the 17th, two Jacobean chairs, and a 13th century coffin lid. There is a brass portrait of Philippa Glascock, a subject of Queen Elizabeth, and on the wall is a carved oak tablet in memory of one of our heroes who fell at Gaza, "marching to the Promised Land." One of the windows is full of jewelled fragments of the 14th and 15th century. There are Flemish panels in other windows of 11 apostles, and in the tracery of two other windows are 12 Old Testament figures.

Hanging on the wall are two framed charters, one granted by Philip and Mary, their seal broken and the crown floating in air over their heads in a little drawing, the other by Elizabeth with the seal perfect, and the crown firm on her head in a drawing.

The church has two heroes. Thomas Bowyer gave his life for his faith in the terrible reign of Mary Tudor, and the vicar we found here (Edward Noel Mellish) won the VC in the Great War. He was a Saffron Walden schoolboy and joined Baden-Powell's Police in South Africa, where, besieged in a farmhouse by the Boers, he broke through and returned to his comrades with the good news that help was on the way. He came back from South Africa to work among the poor of Deptford, and the Great War found him on the battlefield again, walking out among the wounded, seeing three killed as

Great Waltham   Old Houses Near the Church

Writtle   Round the Village Green

Margaretting
Medieval Timber Porch

Feering
Tudor Brick Porch

Prittlewell
12th Century Doorway in Priory

Great Canfield
Norman Chancel Arch

he dressed their wounds, bringing ten men back to the trenches; and at last he received the VC, the first chaplain to win it in the war.

GREAT EASTON. Its oldest possessions are the Roman tiles in the walls of the church, but next in age comes what is left of a Saxon fort, a mound about 20 feet high surrounded by a dry ditch. It is in the grounds of Easton Hall, an old house with Tudor chimneys and a wing with 15th century roof timbers. The hall is close to the little green where a tall peace cross stands proudly, and is only one of Great Easton's old homes. Another opposite the green has a beehive and other devices worked in plaster; others of the 16th and 17th centuries line the lane; and by the footbridge over the River Chelmer is a timber-framed farm with Tudor chimneys, its next-door neighbour a perfect 15th century house with traceried bargeboards.

Norman builders fashioned the nave of the church, which has walls so thick at one part that it is believed to have had a central tower. Two of its five bells are 15th century, and all are doomed to ring in an unattractive wooden turret set up 100 years ago. The chancel is 13th century and has kept its ancient piscina and scratch dial. The vestry is built round a Norman doorway.

Odd Story

GREAT HALLINGBURY. It was the home of a man very anxious to die and of one who saved Parliament from a sudden end. In a wooded countryside near Bishop's Stortford, it has an ancient camp called Wallbury above the River Stort. Protected by a double rampart, it covers about 30 acres and must have been here before the Saxons came. Near Latchmore Common is a charming thatched cottage 300 years old, and in the walls of Hallingbury Place is good 16th century brickwork. Here for centuries lived the Parkers, who sprang into fame 600 years ago. One was admiral of the fleet which won our first naval victory, the Battle of Sluys; another was Henry, the eighth Baron Morley, who served Henry the Eighth at his court, was a student of the New Learning, and an authority on Italian literature. But the most famous of all the family was William Parker, Baron Morley and Lord Monteagle, who has been sleeping here since 1622 and is remembered for bringing Gunpowder Plot to light.

The Morley tombs have perished, and all we see is a collection of brass inscriptions brought together with a quaint figure of Death inside the 15th century tower. It is the only part of the church not rebuilt, except for a very remarkable chancel arch made almost entirely of Roman bricks. It was made about the time the Normans came, and there is a window as old. A doorway older than Agincourt is still in the porch, and a piscina unusually high in the nave shows that in the old days there was an altar in the roodloft. The head of the piscina is also of Roman brick.

Kept in the church are two Tudor helmets, one of them inlaid, and an ancient British burial urn, about a foot wide, dug up from the floor where it had lain almost since history began. Among the modern possessions is a beautiful mosaic of the Walk to Emmaus.

Both tower and chancel must have been familiar to old John Brand in Queen Elizabeth's reign, one of the queerest characters a village ever had. So queer was his story that it came to be written in the church archives, and there it is told how his troubles began one Christmas Eve, when an angel of the devil appeared before him in a vision and showed him plainly where he would find Mother Pryor's money. He found it, £7 18s; but that was not the end, for three months later the same angel came and told him it were better to kill himself than to marry the widow he had in mind. Determined to take this advice, John Brand began on a Monday by taking a dagger, and was only saved by his friends. On Wednesday he put a sack over his head and plunged headlong into John Pryor's pond, seven feet deep. The next Sunday he "took rat's-bayne and drank it in a messe of potage at his dinner, which pained him so, and could not die. So he took a hay halter and hanged himself upon an oak beside his house, and lieth buried at Hangman's Oak."

It is one of the oddest village stories we have come upon, handed down from the days when people everywhere were superstitious.

The Man Who Surprised Guy Fawkes

COINCIDENCE as strange as any novel was responsible for the way in which the Gunpowder Plot was revealed and prevented from taking effect by William Parker, fourth Baron Monteagle and eleventh Baron Morley, who sleeps in this old church.

Bred a Roman Catholic, he was imprisoned for complicity in

rebellion, but was active in bringing Jesuits to London to disturb the Protestant peace. But he changed his religious views, and wrote to King James stating his desire to be admitted into the Church of England. James marked his approval by summoning him to sit in the Parliament which was due to meet on November 5, 1605. In doing so the King unconsciously saved himself and his two sons.

An entirely new situation was now created in the mind of one of the chief conspirators, Tresham, who was Monteagle's brother-in-law. At all costs Monteagle must be preserved against the impending massacre. Catesby would not hear of Tresham warning Monteagle, but it is supposed that, without positive breach of confidence, Monteagle was warned to take serious notice of information that he would receive. At any rate, Monteagle ostentatiously gave a supper party, and there, in the presence of all the guests, a note, mysteriously brought, was conspicuously delivered into his hand at the supper table.

Monteagle gave it to an attendant, who was in the confidence of all the conspirators, and bade him read it aloud. The material part of the letter ran as follows:

I would advise you, as you tender your life, to devise some excuse to shift your attendance at this Parliament, for God and man hath concurred to punish the wickedness of this time. And think not slightly of this advertisement, but retire yourself into the country, where you may expect the event in safety, for, though there be no appearance of any stir, yet I say they shall receive a terrible blow this Parliament, and they shall not see who hurts them.

There was neither address nor signature. The man who had read the letter aloud to the company was now free to go and warn the conspirators that the plot had been published, while Monteagle took the letter to the Lord Treasurer as he sat at supper with other lords at Whitehall.

Accompanied by the Lord Chamberlain, Monteagle proceeded to the cellars of the Parliament House, where they saw a man standing by a heap of faggots. It was the unshakable Guy Fawkes.

Monteagle became a national hero as the saviour of the dynasty and of Parliament itself. He was rewarded with a grant of land worth £200 a year and a pension of £500 which he lived 17 years to enjoy.

GREAT HENNY. Much of its tower is Norman, and one of the bells has been ringing 500 years. The church was refashioned in the 14th century, and given a new brick porch 200 years later. In the opposite doorway a 15th century door is still opening and closing. There is a sanctuary chair 300 years old, finely carved, and a table in the vestry as old. A chest thought to have come from Italy in the 16th century is now the altar of the children's chapel; and on the chancel wall are brass portraits of William Fyscher, his wife Anne, and their 15 children, all in the costume of Henry the Eighth's day. With windows jutting from its thatched roof is the quaint village hall, a pair of cottages transformed for this good purpose by the men of the parish themselves. One who must have loved all these things in the 18th century was Jacob Brome, rector for 57 years.

While the Great War was Raging

GREAT HOLLAND. A small compact village on high ground, it has a quaint inn and cottages shaded by pines and rook-haunted elms; and it has from its churchyard a view of the sea over the sloping fields. A massive 16th century tower of red and black bricks is all that remains of the old church, but the modern interior is pleasing, and one corner of it must always be a solemn place to the village, for it was built while the Great War was raging. It is the vestry, where we read on a tablet these words of courage written in our Motherland's darkest hour:

> To the Glory of God and in complete confidence that victory will be given us, this vestry was added as an act of faith and thanksgiving. August 1917.

God's Soldier

GREAT HORKESLEY. The Roman road runs through it from Colchester, straight and wide, past timber-framed cottages and one of red-brick with a distinction all its own. Homely enough now, it goes back to the days before the Reformation, when it was the home and chapel of a priest. On the roof are stepped gables, and in the wall is a delightful little stone doorway, enriched with carvings of leaves and shields. One of its rooms has a tiny piscina with a Tudor rose, designed for the water to run away in the petals.

Just before the Roman road dips to cross the Stour into Suffolk is a splendid church, in company with a cricket green, many fir trees, and a rectory almost hidden by a magnificent cedar. Roman bricks form a corner of the nave; and still left from Norman days, are a window above the tower arch and a rare pillar piscina with a scalloped capital. Nearly all the building, however, is 14th and 15th century—the fine tower with animal heads including an open-mouthed goat, the roofs with some of their old timbers and a wooden figure holding a shield, the porch enriched with lovely tracery and sheltering a 500-year-old door with ironwork looking even older.

Master craftsmen in stone must have been here in those medieval days, their skill showing in many dainty heads outside the windows, floral designs on the south doorway, shields with bells and chalices on the arcade, and a little carving we liked of a lady in a 15th century hat. Scratched on one of the nave buttresses is a sundial.

The chancel has linenfold panelling and a chair carved in the 17th century. Just as old are a table in the chapel, and a splendid pulpit with arches and vines and a handsome wooden pillar for the parson to hold as he climbs in.

A tablet to a soldier in the South African War has an epitaph from Shakespeare, as short and fitting a memorial as a warrior could have. It comes from Macbeth:

> *Siward. Had he his hurts before?*
> *Ross. Ay, on the front.*
> *Siward. Why, then, God's soldier be he!*

Old Organ and Old Oak

GREAT LEIGHS. Here, in a lovely churchyard with a valley curving round, is one of the six round towers of Essex, built by the Normans on a foundation possibly Saxon. One of its five pilasters comes down to a doorway decorated with zigzags, and higher up the wall is pierced with 13th century windows. The Normans built the nave too, and it has kept three of their windows and a doorway in which the 14th century builders made a new entrance. The opposite doorway is 15th century, and so are eight pews with traceried ends. The font is 600 years old; its panelled stem a century younger.

But it is in the 14th century chancel, with its beautifully traceried east window, that the traveller will want to linger, for here are two splendid pieces of carving by the old artists in stone. One is a canopied recess where perhaps the man who built the chancel lies, its pediment a mass of lovely vine leaves. The other is the group of three sedilia and a piscina finely and delicately wrought, with dainty pinnacles, rich buttresses and gables, and leaves in great variety.

A very unusual brass here shows the body of a 15th century priest with the head of a 14th century man joined on to it. The head of the priest was broken off and lost, and the other one comes from a stone close by. It has vivid eyes and a turned-down mouth. Another curiosity is an old barrel organ of ten pipes, with a carved frame and a neat label to tell us it is the patent of Mr William Phillips.

Near the church is Lyon's Hall, much altered since it was built 500 years ago; and at Moulsham Hall is a living thing probably older, the Court Oak measuring 25 feet round.

A Saxon Stone and a Norman Apse

GREAT MAPLESTEAD. The Normans set its church on high, and its cottages run down toward the River Colne. Some of them are 15th and 16th century, the gabled-fronted Warden's House, home of the chaplain to a Diocesan House of Mercy, having a chapel of its own. Dynes Hall, a Queen Anne house with an Elizabethan wing, stands in 500 acres, and has a timbered and plastered dovecot with a gabled roof.

The tower stands on its Norman base, with Norman windows below and 13th century windows in the belfry. Its brickwork is 17th century, the time when the arch was built into the nave. The body of the church is wider than it is long. The choir is 700 years old, and we owe a debt of gratitude to the English builders for not pulling down the little Norman apse with its entrance arch and its three Norman windows. The apse is very tiny, being only six feet wide. It is probable that a stone fragment we found on a windowsill is older still, for it may be Saxon. The font is 14th century.

There are two interesting windows and two remarkable tombs. The small east window has a figure of Christ risen, with a Roman soldier sleeping, and a window given by the village children shows the hermit St Giles holding a wounded fawn, the hunter kneeling in front of him while a red-cloaked man holds his horse. The tombs are both 17th century. On one lies Sir John Deane in armour, with his feet against the muzzled head of a bear, his wife with four daughters and two sons about him on a shelf. On the other tomb is Sir Drue

Deane, lying like Sir John, with his mother standing on a pedestal in a loose shroud as if blessing the son at her feet.

GREAT OAKLEY. With a few houses 300 or 400 years old, it lies two miles west of Hamble Water, while the narrow church stands farther inland and is reached by an elm-lined valley road running by Ramsey Brook. Two sycamores guard the churchyard gate and oaks and chestnuts grow in profusion. A blocked Norman window above a 14th century doorway tells us how long a church has been here; the square font with 20 round-headed panels has been in use all through the church's history. Up in the chancel is a doorway of 1500 now closed for ever, enriched with carvings of angels, crowns, and heads. The east window is filled with portraits of saints and angels, and strikes a delightful colour note seen through the pointed chancel arch.

Set in a Ring of Chestnuts

GREAT PARNDON. It lies in undulating country carved out by Todds Brook, the medieval church on high ground in a ring of stout chestnuts. Just inside is the lovely font, tall and slender and rich in carving, floral bosses enriching its panels, flowers breaking out from the lower moulding, and cusped panels gracing the sides of the stem—a treasure for so remote a church.

In the chancel is a brass of a civilian who died in Armada year, one Rowland Ramston; and in a window are the arms of Lord Burghley, his greatest contemporary, who also died that year. In the same window are gems of 15th century glass, the head of a woman with tears in her eyes, and an angel's head on which is set a cross. Three windows of modern glass are brilliantly coloured, one showing Queen Victoria kneeling in her youth before the King of Glory; one showing Edward the Seventh in a similar scene, peacemaker kneeling before the Prince of Peace; the third showing the donor, who lived to be 90. He was Joseph Todhunter, who passed away having seen four sovereigns and paid these tributes to two. A splendid St George between two blue-winged angels is in the memorial window to this good old man.

GREAT SALING. Its church is a 14th century building much restored, with a traceried font and some roof beams of the

15th century, a panelled chest 200 years younger, and a monument with the kneeling figure of Bartlet Sheddon who died in 1823. Shining in the tower window is a red-robed St James, to whom the church belongs. Among the elms stands Saling Hall, a noble building of 250 years ago, with two gabled wings.

The Stone Carvings

GREAT SAMPFORD. It has a 14th century church built by the Knights Hospitallers, its great attraction being the chancel, which has two splendid features: the beautiful tracery of the great window, nearly filling the wall above the altar; and the series of arches on the side walls, each with a seat for one of the old knights. On the north are 11 of them, divided by a handsome priest's doorway; on the south are 15, one for the piscina and one pierced for a doorway into the oldest part of the church, a 13th century chapel. With their carved arches and clustered columns these chancel arcades have great beauty. One old treasure may have gone, for the rough stonework at the base of the chancel arch suggests that one of the rare stone screens snch as are still seen at Great Bardfield and Stebbing once stood here.

There is much to see as we walk about the church, inside and out. We notice two fierce goats standing out from the chapel gable, the niches in the buttresses, and the consecration crosses, formed of dark cut flint. The 14th century tower has a stair turret of Tudor brick, and the nave has six fine columns supporting a 14th century clerestory, in which a window was cut in the 15th century to light the roodloft. There are roof beams, a porch, and a fine tomb recess all 600 years old; and on an archway of the same time are some of the best stone carvings in Essex. One of the capitals has two monkey heads and rich foliage; the other shows a cowled head, pigs with lolling tongues, and the head of an owl with its feathers delicately suggested.

The handsome stem of the font is 14th century, but its plain bowl is 15th. There is a panelled Tudor cupboard, a 17th century chest bound with iron, and a beautiful six-sided table. The best modern craftsmanship is in the wooden lectern, a splendid eagle on rocks, with a pillar resting on lions. It is in memory of Robert Eustace who died in 1905 after 55 years as vicar; we read his name again on a tiny cross in the shadow of the tower, the grave of his little child.

Great Sampford has a three-cornered green, a big pond, and many houses 300 years old. One, The How, has kept its moat complete. White House has old fireplaces and a handsome staircase. Tindon End, some way off, has a panel with the date 1684, and some carved Tudor stones lying in the garden; but it is famous for another reason: it was the home for many years of John McAdam, the Scotsman who re-made our English roads.

The Thames Policeman

GREAT STAMBRIDGE. It lies almost within hail of the barges plying on the River Roche, and has an old timbered inn which has seen its 500th birthday, and a church that has seen about twice as many years.

The quaint 15th century porch has fine beams in its roof, but more remarkable is the wall to which it is attached, for it was standing before the Conqueror set foot in our land. As high as the arm can reach, Saxon masonry supports the tower, and high in the chancel wall are the stones which framed the head of a Saxon window. Three pointed arches show that the Saxon building was enlarged about 1300. The tower and the bold font are 15th century. There is a window in memory of Emily Keightley, who left this quiet rectory to give her life to the children of Ratcliff Highway. She died in 1905 and is shown with three little friends, while on each side are medallions with scenes in the lives of Christ and St Martin.

Here was born in 1745 John Harriott, who reclaimed Rushley Island from the sea and added it to his native county. He spent the last years of his busy life as magistrate, and promoted a police force on the Thames a generation before we had an organised force on land.

The Tower Above the Cottages

GREAT TEY. A huge Norman tower, 18 feet square and with many windows, proclaims to us from afar that we are drawing near a place which was a centre of busy life in ages past. This massive tower has Roman bricks in it, large and small; in the walls and in the arches of the windows we find these relics of Roman Britain, looking down on a great churchyard and towering above 16th and 17th century cottages.

In the neighbouring fields are farms with roofs and timbering of the 15th century, whose owners worshipped in the Norman church when splendid buildings clustered about the central tower. One pier remains of them all, buried in a modern wall; only the beautiful 14th century chancel and transept, indeed, remain to share the splendour of the tower, for the Norman nave and aisles were pulled down in our own time.

The outer walls of the chancel have beautiful tracery in the east window, and there is neat carving of heads and grotesques on many projecting stones, the most remarkable being a crocodile and a climbing monkey. The stones on which the gable rests are carved with grotesques and ballflowers, while a bishop and a bearded man look down on all who enter by the lovely priest's doorway.

Two of the tower arches are Norman but the side arches have mouldings of the 14th century. Both the piscinas are of that time, one elaborately carved and the other backed by part of the Norman altar top with three consecration crosses on it. The font has been here 500 years and has heads on its bowl. On four 15th century poppyheads in a reading desk are a crowned head and a kilted man playing bagpipes. On a 17th century chest are paintings of a man and a woman. The fruit and flowers on some medieval woodwork has been copied in a modern window.

Beacon Hill

GREAT TOTHAM. Very ragged looks our Essex coast on our maps; would you see it spread out as it is, come to Beacon Hill at Great Totham, and gaze seaward.

The cottages of this small place, great no more, range along a group of roads at the foot of this fine viewpoint, while the island of Osea, which belongs to it, lies away out in the Blackwater estuary. The churchyard is a place of charm, with trim lawns and roses surrounded by limes and pines, while a creeper climbs the porch of the red-tiled church. Here are one or two windows of the 14th century, and among the timbers of the roof are many that were hewn 500 years ago. A modern shingle spire rises from a wooden turret. In the chancel are portraits in brass of two Elizabethan Elizabeths, wearing ruffs. There are fragments of 16th century glass, and near the pulpit is a huge clock quaint enough to raise a smile however dull the sermon may be.

GREAT WAKERING. It has a rough common and the wide stretch of the Maplin Sands; and the long street has a small church of the Peculiar People as well as the parish church, which is remarkable for its age and for having a two-storey building which in the 15th century was attached to the Norman tower. It was added to shelter the priest who came to minister here from Beeleigh Priory. A projecting wing holds the stairway to the upper room. The nave has Norman windows and the chancel has lancets 700 years old, restored in olden times with Roman cement from some building of the time of the Caesars.

The Tudor Age

GREAT WALTHAM. It has not only a treasure-house in its church but is exceptionally fortunate in the number of old houses it has kept, the Historic Monuments Commission having noted more than 80 within the bounds of the parish. A rich heritage they are from the century that saw the coming of the Tudors, from the days of Queen Elizabeth and Shakespeare, from Cromwell's time and Charles the Second's.

Here is an Elizabethan house with ornamental plaster on its tall chimneys and original fireplaces; here an inn from the 15th century. Only a few minutes away is a lovely house with four gables, Hyde Hall, built about 1600, still with part of its moat and a thatched barn older than itself. And just outside this delightful village is the deer park of the Langleys, a house with amazing fireplaces and over-mantels and panelled ceilings in two 17th century rooms. In its grounds is a huge chestnut tree 300 years old. Langleys was the home of the Everards, whose monuments are in the church; but since 1685 it has belonged to the Tufnells, whose memorials we also see, good friends of Essex churches for over two centuries.

Watched over by a colossal pine in the churchyard, this church would thrill any lover of the old and beautiful. The tower, nave, and chancel were built by the sons of men who came to our shores with the Conqueror and have stood more than 800 years. Roman bricks are at the corners of the walls; others were used by the Norman masons in shaping windows now blocked. But there are Norman windows still shedding their light in the tower, and a neat little door-way about as old leads to the turret stairs. The tower arch is a little younger, about 1200.

The Tudor Age gave the church its clerestory, a graceful nave arcade, a porch, and some handsome roofs. The nave roof is enriched with angels and roses and faces; and the roof added to the 14th century aisle has bosses with shields and grotesque faces. The screen is modern, but the ancient furniture is still here. Some 30 seats have been in use 500 years, carved at the ends with tracery. We see a chair of the Stuart Age with a Tudor panel, carved with a helmet in a wreath. We can open a door with rich ironwork that has been opening since the 15th century, and go through its ancient doorway to the vestry, and see panels of a Tudor pulpit. We can look at the reading desk and see some delicate woodwork from the medieval screen. On the wall is a picture of an old wall-painting that has gone, showing Christ in Majesty with the angels adoring. There is a heraldic glass from the 14th and 17th centuries.

There are brass portraits of an unknown 16th century civilian; of Thomas Wiseman, one of his two wives, and some of his children, all as they were about 1580; and of Richard Everard and his wife in Jacobean costume. The arms of other Everards are on the chancel floor; but the best thing they have left behind is the great monument Sir Anthony was erecting when death took him in 1614. On it he and his wife lie, resting on their elbows, with shields round about. On pedestals on the floor in front lie two little boys in each other's arms and a third alone.

Little can be told of Sir Anthony's life, but it can hardly have been more thrilling than the crowded hours of little Hugh Everard, who perished on the Goodwin Sands when he was only 16. Leaving Felstead at 13, he helped to escort King William to Holland, and two years later was fighting against Spain. He died in 1703, and his memorial has a relief of a sinking ship.

A Brother's Memorial

GREAT WARLEY. Nature has been lavish in her gifts to this place and man has added to them in full measure down the ages, and still is adding to them. The heart of the village is on a hill-top from which we look down on woodlands rich in pines and oaks and silver birches, with avenues of chestnuts meeting. Round the green on this hilltop stand ancient dwellings, the 15th century post office, with two gabled dormers in its roof, and Wallets, a lovely medieval house much added to in succeeding centuries. It has two wings with overhanging storeys, an Elizabethan chimney, and a panelled room of about 1600.

The modern church of St Mary lies halfway down the hill in a churchyard like a garden, with neat lawns, grassy banks, rose-decked pergolas, and a sundial. The dove on the spire looks out on a scene of perfect peace. This church was the lord of the manor's memorial to his brother, and on a tablet over the door we read:

> *So might I toiling morn till eve*
> *Some purpose in my life fulfil,*
> *And ere I pass some work achieve*
> *To live and move when I am still.*
> *I ask not with that work combined*
> *My name shall down the ages move,*
> *But that my toil some end shall find*
> *That man may bless and God approve.*

A tablet to the lord of the manor himself (Mr Evelyn Heseltine) has this brief but fine eulogy:

> *His Life an Inspiration—His Memory a Benediction.*

The building, the pews, and the choir-stalls were designed by Mr Harrison Townsend, while Sir William Reynolds-Stephens designed and made the objects which make the interior unique. He is famous, of course, for the sculpture at the Tate Gallery of Elizabeth playing chess against Philip of Spain, and his work here is as symbolical and as pleasing as that famous piece. Marbles, metals, and coloured woods are all used by the sculptor to express the symbolism of the life of faith. The three-stemmed font supports two bronze angels. Six ribs encircle the nave roof, lilies decorate walnut panels on the walls, while the rose of sharon on a green ground fills the springing arches; both lilies and roses are in aluminium. The front of the pulpit is in the shape of a cross; trees support its arms, and the whole is of oxidised bronze and copper. Of copper also is the lectern, flowering branches upholding a brass book-rest. Behind the pulpit and the lectern is the screen, the most interesting thing in the church. Expressing the idea of the text "the fruit of the Spirit is Love, Joy,

Peace, Long-suffering, Gentleness, Goodness, Faith, Meekness, Temperance," the screen is formed of flowering fruit-trees in brass, which spring from a marble base, each bearing an angel representing one of these virtues. In front of the organ is a little angel, and on its case are metal reliefs illustrating Benedicite.

Crowns of thorns encircling rose of sharon form part of the altar-rail, where we stand in admiration of the decoration of the apse. A great vine springs up behind the altar, tendrils and grapes showing in relief against aluminium. In the centre of the reredos Christ stands with hand upraised in blessing, trampling a serpent under foot, while panels on each side show the Nativity and the Entombment, and on the wall round is carved a choir of angels. It is all very beautiful, and everything in the church leads up to the simple figure of Jesus. Every window, too, has its place in the Christian message expressed so reverently in every detail.

Most beautiful of all is the memorial to the men of Great Warley who gave their lives in the Great War. Sir William Reynolds-Stephens has carved, as the reredos, two angels looking on at Our Lord after Calvary, a snow-white marble relief called the Gateway to Life.

Night of Terror

GREAT WIGBOROUGH. Those who live here still thrill to the memory of the events of one of the dark nights of terror in the first years of the Great War. It is in the tower that we are reminded of it, for on the tower arch hangs a piece of the girder of a Zeppelin which fell on these fields below on September 24, 1916. Framed in metal from it is a printed record of that dread event, telling how the crew surrendered to the village constable after firing their monstrous machine, and how statesmen and generals came to Wigborough to see this new enemy of the air, which at that time was striking terror at the hearts of our people. We have lived through the Battle of Britain since then, but few villages can have known a more thrilling day than that on which a plain policeman received the surrender of this Zeppelin crew.

The oldest house here, Hyde Farm, was begun 500 years ago. Some of its original timbers support the tiled roof, while from a chimney peers forth a gargoyle which came from Little Wigborough. A lane leads us up the hill to the church, set in a ring of ancient elms.

Across the valley we see Peldon church dominant on its hill, the tiled and thatched roofs of a farmstead in the hollow breaking the green curve of the meadows. It is hard to believe that John Ardley and John Simson, who roamed these sun-bathed fields as boys, ended their lives in Mary Tudor's fires, an English terror centuries older than the German Zeppelin.

The stone tower was rebuilt after an earthquake in 1884, but a battered door in its turret is 500 years old; so are many of the timbers in both porch and nave. An old niche of great beauty faces the entrance, and the font, with roses on its bowl, may have been carved by the same 16th century craftsman. A bright note is given to the chancel by a reredos with five paintings of Fra Angelico's heavenly makers of music.

The Giants of Yeldham

GREAT YELDHAM. At its heart stands the huge Yeldham Oak, 30 feet round and perhaps 1000 years old; and in its beautiful churchyard is a hollow elm. They are the grand old men of this pleasant place, the oak probably twice as old as the oldest of Great Yeldham's charming houses.

One of them is Spaynes Hall of the 17th and 18th centuries; another is an inn going back to 1500, with a Tudor chimney-stack, a fine door at the back, and woodwork 300 years old; and a third is beautiful Yeldham Hall, built of timber and plaster in the 16th and 17th centuries, and still keeping its old panelling and balusters.

Older than most of these houses is the church, which comes from the 14th and 15th centuries. Its tower has angels on the parapet. Its porch is the lowest storey of an earlier tower which was either never finished or partly pulled down. It has an outer doorway with much beauty from the 14th century, and a Tudor room above. The door itself is 600 years old, and has kept its ancient handle and a long iron strap. A little doorway in the nave wall was meant to lead to the turret of the unfinished tower. On the 15th century screen are remains of a painting showing a bishop and a lady with a crown. The pulpit is Jacobean, and there are two chests and a carved chair from the 17th century. Timbers 500 years old are over the north aisle. In the 15th century south chapel is a brass showing Richard Symonds of 1627, kneeling with his wife and looking up at a cloud with the word Jehovah. Their six children are at another desk below. In the vestry, we found a picture of old George Hardy, who knew every stone of this ancient place, for he was singing in the choir for three-quarters of a century.

An old timbered dovecot, seen from the road, has a pyramid roof.

The Wooden Walls of Old England

GREENSTED. It is a shrine of universal pilgrimage, unique in its sylvan setting and unique in one of its possessions, a wooden church with Saxon timbers built into its walls. It is the Saxon church in which St Edmund's body rested on its last journey.

Even if its timbers were not so captivating for their great age (1013), the picture of this primitive church would draw the pilgrim to it. Its 19th century dormers, its neat porch with a red-tiled roof harmonising with the low roof of the nave, the little shingled spire on the wooden tower, and the red brick of the chancel wall, draw us into this rugged churchyard where roses bloom amid cypress trees. Giant survivors of the forest make a perfect background for a church whose walls stand much as they were when the monks of Bury St Edmunds, having, in their fear of the Danes, carried the body of their saint for safety to the walled city of London, brought it back and rested it in this forest sanctuary on its way.

Here are the oldest wooden walls of Old England; come close to them and run your fingers along the shaped timbers and feel the marks of the adze made by the Saxon carpenter. The trees they felled to build this church were growing when the Romans came; they felled a score of oaks and split each trunk in three, using the outer beams as a palisade and the central planks for the roof and the sills. It is interesting to see how these Saxon carpenters made this place. Roughly adzing off the upper ends of the uprights into a thin edge, they inserted them into a groove in a beam running along each side of the nave. They fixed their bases on a wooden sill, but a century ago they had so rotted that a dwarf wall was placed below them, their height being reduced by about a foot. There are 21 logs on the north wall with three extra ones where a door once stood, and 16 logs on the south, through which wall we enter. The Saxon nave is 29 feet long and 17 feet wide. The original roof was thatched and

The Sylvan Setting of the Ancient Church

The Oldest Wooden Walls in England

GREENSTED'S SAXON SHRINE

Hadleigh   The Ruined Castle Towers

Hadleigh   The Norman Church

was lighted from a window in the timbers of the west wall and from others in the chancel.

The church was much refashioned in the 16th century when the chancel, the beautiful priest's doorway, and the charming tower and belfry were added. A small painted panel of the martyrdom of St Edmund shows him wearing a crown but clothed in a loin cloth and bound to a tree pierced with arrows shot by soldiers, one of whom wears Roman armour. The panel is probably all that remains of a 15th century screen, and keeping company with it is another medieval portrait of the saint in a roundel of the west window; it shows his crowned head.

One possession the church has more curiously linked with the martyrdom of St Edmund, the wooden covers of a Bible and a prayer book, made from the timbers of what is believed to be the actual tree under which Edmund was martyred. The tree was growing at Hoxne in Suffolk and had become a giant nearly 20 feet round when it fell 100 years ago. Tradition had long fixed on this as Edmund's tree, and it is remarkable that when the tree fell a Danish arrowhead was found in the trunk. The arrow is still in existence.

The fine lectern on which this interesting Bible rests was carved in our own time by a local craftsman, from an oak growing at Greensted. It is a skilful piece of craftsmanship, likely to go down the ages with the 18th century pulpit, the medieval piscina, and the odd stoup cut 700 years ago in one of the great timbers of the wall.

Home of Two Queens

HADLEIGH. Its fame is in its Norman church and in the ruins of the home of two queens. Save for a few windows and doorways, the walls of the apse, chancel, and nave of the church are almost as the Norman builders left them. It is a joy to pass from the busy highway into this lovely old place. The chancel arch is only 18 feet high and not 11 feet wide. The font has foliage carved in the 13th century, and there is other carved stonework in niches. But the pride of the church is a painting of Thomas Becket on the splay of a window, made by an artist who may have seen him. It is from the years between 1170, when he was murdered, and 1173, when he was canonised. In the windows are modern portraits of Ethelburga, first

Abbess of England's first nunnery (at Barking) and the Evangelist of Essex, St Cedd.

Here in a field on the brow of a steep hill stand the ruins of Hadleigh Castle, with glorious views over the estuary of the Thames and of the coast of Kent merging into the horizon. The massive towers are magnificent, their walls being nine feet wide at the base, and the whole ruin covers about an acre. It was Hubert de Burgh who first built a castle here and Edward the First gave it to his queen. Rebuilt in 1365, it was made into one of the most remarkable Essex strongholds, and Henry the Eighth chose it as a home for his unwanted queen, Anne of Cleves. The ruins of this home of queens have been assured of lasting fame whatever may happen to them, for John Constable, who immortalised the northern boundary of Essex, came to admire and paint this lovely scene on its southern shore.

The Oldest Door in England and its Companions

HADSTOCK. We are on the borders of Cambridgeshire, and from the churchyard is a wonderful view over the thatched roofs of the village to the downs and woodlands beyond. Close by is the timber-framed manor house, with the original chimney-stack built in Shakespeare's time, and not far away is a farmhouse a century older, with a projecting storey and three terracotta niches in the walls.

All this has its own beauty, but it is to the church that we must come if we would feel ourselves back in the old world, for here is one of the oldest churches in the county, into which we come through the oldest door in all England. This door of Hadstock church has been opening and shutting for about a thousand years. Had the Conqueror come this way he would have found it swinging on its hinges. It is the only Saxon door we have come upon in our tour of 10,000 towns and villages. It must be the door the Saxon carpenter hung when this church was built. We do not know exactly when that was, but it is believed that the church may have been built to celebrate the victory of King Canute over Edmund Ironside in 1016.

The nave and one of the transepts remain from the Saxon building, though there is evidence that they were repaired or refashioned after the falling of a central tower in the time of Magna Carta. The other transept, with its original gable cross, is 14th century, and the present tower is 15th. In the walls of this 500-year-old tower, however, is something older than the Saxon door, a number of Roman bricks.

We come to the wonderful doorway through a 15th century porch, and open with a thrill this plain oak door with three iron straps riveted through it. If we have been to Saffron Walden and called at the museum there we shall remember a piece of human skin which was found under these straps of iron, the skin of a sacrilegious Dane which was nailed to the door in the days of King Canute; it is one of the brutalities which were practised in those days.

Above the doorway is a blocked-up Saxon window, and there are two other windows between a doorway and the tower, 15 feet up from the floor, both still with their Saxon window frames. It is almost incredible that these timbers should have survived in the door and windows of this little church. We have come upon half a dozen Norman doors and about the same number of Norman roofs in our tour of England, but nowhere except at the timber church at Greensted have we found Saxon timbers still in their place.

As if all this were not enough, Hadstock has three other ancient doors, one 700 and two 600 years old. They are all in the tower, and the oldest leads into the churchyard, the other two leading to the stair turret and the belfry. Still another wonder, a remarkable ladder, has been in use for 500 years, its rungs cut in a curious shape; and under the tower arch are the remains of a 15th century screen on which one of the spandrels is carved with the quaint scene of a fox dressed as a priest, standing in a pulpit and seizing a goose by the neck. Here, therefore, are timbers from the 11th, 13th, 14th, and 15th centuries, a unique collection. The lectern is a dainty piece of work in oak, its stem carved by a Tudor craftsman (and therefore probably adding another century to this remarkable collection of timbers).

Here Rose a Great Family

HALSTEAD. Built about a hill overlooking the Colne, it is a prosperous place, famous for its silk and crepe. For nearly a century it has had its town hall and its library; it has fine public gardens, and in its wide High Street are charming gabled shops and houses.

One house, with a carved hammerbeam truss in its roof, formed part of a 15th century chantry founded by Bartholomew, Lord

Bourchier, member of a family figuring in the Law, the Church, and Literature, and giving Shakespeare characters for two plays. We stand in the presence of many of them in the church; we see the house in which they lived.

The town grew up 600 years ago about the clerestoried church which crowns the hill, its 19th century tower replacing one that fell. A majestic eagle watches from a buttress of the pinnacled north porch, which has a 15th century window in an upper room. Angels look down from the timbers of a roof 500 years old. The church has a bell which has been ringing since about 1400, and an earthenware pot, used since 1658 for the refreshment of bell-ringers.

Among the memorials are a marble tablet with a 17th century brass portrait of Elizabeth Watson and her six children, one in swaddling clothes; a tablet of 1720 to Sir Samuel Tryon, last baronet of his line; an 18th century tablet to Elizabeth Holmes, who gave £4000 for the benefit of industrious townsfolk; and another to John Manistre, a Dorset rector who left £2500 to be spent in bread for 21 people—*Dissenters excepted!* If a man does not agree with the rector he shall not eat.

But the finest monuments are those of the Bourchier family. In the floor is the splendid 15th century brass of Bartholomew, Lord Bourchier, showing him in his armour with his two wives. On a low 14th century tomb, under canopies with angels, and instinct with pathos and solemnity, lie John Bourchier in his armour and tunic, with two monks and a dog at his feet, and his wife with two nuns and a dog at her feet. He was a judge under Edward the Second. His wooden shield is under the canopy of a handsome altar tomb, rich with cusped panels, arches, and spandrels, with an angel and a cockle shell, elaborate with heraldry. On another tomb is the judge's grandson John in armour, his head resting on a helmet with a Saracen's head as a crest, and his wife in a 14th century headdress with angels supporting her head, and dogs at her feet; they seem to say to us

Peace, good reader, do not weep,
Peace, the lovers are asleep.

Stanstead Hall, the old home of the Bourchiers, still has its moat filled with water, and beside it a fine 15th century barn of 11 bays, with aisles. The house is mainly Jacobean, with its original chimney-stacks and octagonal turrets.

Here rose a family which for two centuries produced scholars, lawyers, ecclesiastics, and soldiers. In the church are three generations, but the line gave rise to Thomas Bourchier, the 15th century cardinal who figures in Richard the Third. He crowned Edward the Fourth and Elizabeth Woodville, and then, in an evil hour during her widowhood, induced her to let her little second son leave sanctuary to join his brother in the Tower, so yielding him up for the horrible murder by Richard the Third. Richard having waded through blood to the throne, Bourchier crowned him, and he crowned his successor when Richard fell like a dog on Bosworth Field, launching the Tudor dynasty on its magnificent way.

But of all the family we owe most to John Bourchier, second Baron Berners. Scholar and soldier, he beguiled the tedium of his Governorship of Calais by bequeathing us a veritable literary treasure, his incomparable translation of Froissart. We had at the time only one fine prose work, Malory's Morte d'Arthur, and that a marvellous fairy tale. Bourchier's was history, and helped to found our serious literature. Dying in 1533 desperately in debt, he left us a rich gift which, if it has ceased to bring profit to publishers, has never ceased to bring delight to readers. Four centuries after his death a new edition of his masterpiece was issued at 25 guineas.

Old Brass

HARLOW. A little old-world town of much delight, it has a church full of fine things, a manor house of great interest, and a fine little Tudor chantry-house with a lovely porch and 16th century glass illustrating the months. The oldest parts of the manor house are Tudor, but it is the successor of a house given by Edward the Confessor, 900 years ago, to the Abbots of Bury St Edmunds. In a corner of the garden is a granary built by the Normans, still with its Norman doorway and windows, and with a kingpost roof of the 15th century. It was built as a chapel, the private shrine of the old abbots, who rested here on their journeys to London.

We can come to the church by an avenue of great limes or by another entrance near one of the most magnificent copper beeches in Essex. The church is in the shape of a cross, which is uncommon in this part of the county; and, though it has fragments of medieval work and a Norman window, it has been rebuilt more than once. Destroyed by fire in 1708, it was raised again in a poor style; and was finally rebuilt with a tower and spire and a fine peal of bells.

A coffin lid with a raised cross is thought to mark the grave of a rector buried in 1326, John de Stainton.

Most of the old monuments are in the transepts, a wooden tablet 250 years old in memory of a Bishop of Ely, a curious wooden monument with Faith, Hope, and Charity on pedestals in memory of John Wright in the 17th century, and sculptures of Alexander Stafford and his wife Julian at prayer. She it was who in 1630 founded the almshouses by the lychgate, still with their original bargeboards and a nail-studded door. A wooden panel which she may have seen has the Lord's Prayer in a beautifully carved border.

Under the lectern are brass portraits of a 15th century couple and their nine children; but the great collection of old brasses is in the north transept, mounted on a board on the wall. They show over 30 figures of men and women and children, all alive in Tudor and Jacobean England. One is Robert Druncaster, secretary to Henry the Seventh; another is Thomas Aylmer with his family of 12; and a third is William Sumner of 1559, a link with the old order, for he was the last tenant of the Abbot of Bury. Two Elizabethans are here with their children, and a third is shown with Death holding a dart beside him, perhaps because he was a park-keeper and died while shooting a deer. John Gladwin is a grim-faced old man of 95, with an inscription telling of his tedious lawsuits; Robert Lawson wears a fur-lined robe; Francis Reve and his wife are kneeling; and there are big figures of Richard Bugges and his two wives, he in armour with a lace collar and a walking-stick.

A lovely little sculpture by William Theed shows a baby on a cushion in memory of John Perry Watlington who died in 1862. One of the windows is to his kinsman, the first Bishop of Melbourne. In the vestry is a 600-year-old glass panel of the Madonna, and in a big transept window is glass of many periods, 14th century canopies, Tudor badges, and scenes from Solomon's life, lions holding shields, a portrait of Queen Anne, and a head of Charles Stuart with his martyr's crown coming down from the sky. Another transept window has two angels of about 1700. The fine west window has modern figures of Bible characters. A splendid Italian chest stands on the floor below, fashioned in the 17th century with poker-work panels and carvings of cupids, grotesque animals, and armed men.

The church has memories of several heroes of the battlefield. We read of General Sir Godfrey Thomas who won the DSO by his gallantry near Arras in 1917; of Sir Evelyn Wood, VC, who died here; and of Colonel John Neville Marshall who won the VC a few days before the Armistice, leading parties of men under intense fire to repair a broken bridge, and falling as he rushed across it at the head of his battalion. Here was born the writer of one of the hymns that have sung their way round the world, Nearer My God to Thee. She was Sarah Adams, and lies with her sister (who wrote the tune for the hymn) and their father in a graveyard two miles away, used by the Baptists of Harlow for 200 years. It is at Foster Street.

A Gateway to the Continent

HARWICH. One of our Gateways to the Continent, it shares its fine seaviews and its thrilling memories with Dovercourt, where sleeps one of the bravest of our brave. It has the oldest light-house in Essex and one of the oldest in England, built before Winstanley thought out his plans for Eddystone, and now transformed into a dwelling-house above the mile-long promenade.

The narrow streets of this old town are grouped on a low promontory where the Orwell and the Stour pour into the sea, and its memories are of men and ships. On the green close to the Redoubt is the old crane of the shipyard, and a shipyard bell cast in 1661; the crane was worked by men walking inside big wooden drums. By the coastguard station is the old naval yard established by Cromwell and often mentioned by Pepys. In the church register, which began with the second year of Queen Elizabeth, is the birth of Christopher Newport, a seaman who shared in Sir Walter Raleigh's settlement of Virginia, and the same register has a record of the marriage of Christopher Jones, the Master of the Mayflower, which bore the name of this town on her timbers, the letters still visible in the famous barn at Jordans in Buckinghamshire. In this harbour Nelson's fleet would ride at anchor under the shelter of Languard Point. This quay saw the coming and going of our Dutch and German kings, though the quay today is too small for our big steamers, which use

Parkeston Quay two miles up the Stour. The wharves and other quay buildings of Harwich rise on 12 miles of piles and concrete cylinders driven into the bed of the Stour.

Harwich has preserved the inn (the Three Cups) where Nelson stayed, with the fleur-de-lys on the Tudor ceiling of one of the rooms, and in Market Street is the Royal Oak, its upper storey leaning over the narrow way, and next to it a house with the date of Armada Year between two griffins at a doorway; there is a man in Tudor costume on one of the doorposts, and on its opposite post is a woman with a mirror and a shield. The oldest possession of the town is the Norman font in the modern church, which has also on its chancel wall brass portraits of John Rychemond with his two wives in Tudor dress. Facing them is a bust of Sir William Clarke, Charles the Second's Secretary for War, who fell in a sea fight and was washed ashore to be buried in the old churchyard. A tablet on the wall tells us of the burial in 1808 of Charles Cox, agent to His Majesty's Packets which sailed from this port in the Napoleon wars and founder of the bankers of British officers in succeeding wars. Here in a chapel hang flags that braved the breeze in the Great War, carried by Harwich pilots from ship to ship. Below them are the names of 12 pilots who went down in those four years, and with them on the peace memorial are the names of the men of Harwich and one nurse who never came home again.

In the Great War Harwich and Dovercourt were like a fortress and no strangers were allowed within the limits. Since the days when Harwich men sailed with Francis Drake and Thomas Cavendish in the first two English voyages round the world there have been no braver deeds at sea than some remembered here, for the Harwich Mine-Sweeping Flotilla held the record of enemy mines swept up in any theatre of war. There is a handsome stone and bronze memorial to the memory of the men who were lost, and, of course, to the memory of Captain Fryatt, who lies at Dovercourt. He was one of the bravest of all the men who laid down their lives for Britain.

Out of the Great War there has come to Harwich a transportation wonder that is all too little known, the ferry from here to Zeebrugge. The arrival of the ferry is one of the most interesting sights of Harwich. The broad-beamed monster can be recognised far-off by the lofty twin funnels as the boat comes slowly up the navigation channel of the estuary until it is opposite the land end of the railway line, when it swings round, makes a right-angled turn, and creeps in stern first between the terminal berths, constructed so as to fit the shape and size of the ship, with hardly a foot to spare. It is a master-piece of manoeuvring. The ferry can operate whatever the state of the tide. An adjustable bridge secured at the shore end is lowered by a gantry with electric winches, the platform of the bridge being swung between two vertical girders so that it automatically takes the same list as the ferry when traffic is moving on or off. Each of the Harwich ferries has four sets of lines, which will take 45 wagons with 20-ton loads. The boats are about 360 feet long, with engines of 3000 horse-power, and goods can be loaded on them at a factory in England and taken over this ferry to almost any country in Europe. It follows that Harwich has a most cosmopolitan appearance, for here are trucks from almost anywhere on the Continent.

Three Monuments of Three Centuries

HATFIELD BROAD OAK. It lies south of the thousand acres of Hatfield Forest, now in the keeping of the National Trust, where we see a lake and the famous Doodle Oak from which the village takes its name. Once a market town, it saw our Norman and Plantagenet kings come riding to the hunt, and has kept many of its 16th and 17th century houses with quaint gables and carved wood-work, nodding above the spacious street. It grew beside the priory founded by Aubrey de Vere about 1135, and prospered with it. But of the priory's greatness little is left but part of the precinct wall, the old fish-ponds, and an impressive church once the nave of the priory church.

Its 15th century tower, 80 feet high, has taken the place of a central tower of which we can still see some of the piers, Norman workman-ship like most of the north wall. A chapel by this Norman wall was rebuilt in two storeys in the 15th century, its windows high up to look over the cloister roof below. The nave arches, the chancel arch, and a turret on the south side are all 14th century; and about 100 years younger is the south porch with an embattled parapet, fine windows, and a sundial with two faces. The chancel roof is modern, but has four angels 500 years old; the aisle roofs are 14th century.

There is a 15th century screen, a Litany desk with an oak figure of a priest carved in Chaucer's day, and a curious font cover with a patchwork of carving from three centuries. From the 18th century comes a very fine candelabra with 36 ornamental branches, and a medallion of Richard Chamberlayne. The nave has a little gallery of 14th century corbels, among them portraits of Richard the Second, Thomas Duke of Gloucester, Eleanor de Bohun, Edmund Langley, John of Gaunt, Robert Earl of Oxford, and Bishop Braybroke, who was a stout defender of the parson's rights against the monks. Some of these helped to build this nave as a place of worship for the people. The chancel is enriched by a panelled reredos of the 18th century, said to have been carved by a pupil of Grinling Gibbons; and about as old are two chairs and the handsome altar rails.

To the south is a library built in the 18th century to shelter books given to the church in 1680. Among them are Matthew Prior's poems, an Aldine Aristotle of 1498, a Vinegar Bible, and rare theological books. It is a curious room full of interest, and among its treasures is a brass showing the head of a 14th century woman, a relic from the priory and perhaps a portrait of Lady Margaret Beryngton. There is a parish doctor's bill with other old documents, a 17th century chest with carving and poker-work, old stones from the priory, and a clarinet last played within living memory by an old man who died at 93.

Three monuments of three centuries are in the church. One shows cherubs and the arms of young Sir John Barrington, who died in 1691; another is to Lady Ibbetson of 1816, notable for being the work of Flaxman; and the third is a remarkable sculpture of Robert de Vere, the third Earl of Oxford. He is here in armour and a longcoat, his head on a pillow held by two worn figures, his shield ornamented with diaper work, and at his feet two monks who seem to be reading at a desk. It is all the work of a sculptor more than 700 years ago, for the earl died in 1221. He was not only a friend of the priory his ancestor founded, but one of the 25 barons appointed to see that King John honoured the seal he had put to Magna Carta.

Old Glass

HATFIELD PEVEREL. Its church is the nave of the Norman priory church, to which has been added a 15th century aisle,

Chrishall
Sir John and Lady de la Pole, 14th century

Great Bromley
William Bischopton, 15th century

TWO FINE OLD ESSEX BRASSES

187

a modern aisle, and a Tudor vestry of brick. The west doorway, a little window, and an arch over the altar are all Norman. A handsome building it is, the interior bright enough to display its old possessions. Part of a 15th century screen stands in the aisle, and Tudor craftsmanship of wood and iron is in the vestry door. There are two carved chairs of Charles Stuart's days, and three remarkable 14th century bench-ends with traceried panels, poppyheads, and heads of men and women, a king, and a queen. Traces of colour are still to be seen on window-splays, niches, and columns; one column has a much faded scene of the Crucifixion painted about 1400.

There is old glass of every century from the 14th to the 18th, an unusual array. The oldest shows leaves and canopywork; there is a Tudor rose among other fragments; the arms of Queen Elizabeth and a shield showing the three mitres of Evesham Abbey; and some Flemish glass at its best in a window with James and John and a woman on her knees. It is said that much of the glass here was brought by John Wright, a London coachmaker who restored the church in 1760. He lived close by at the 18th century house called the Priory, and is believed to lie in a vault, which was once the wine cellar. A handsome modern screen encloses the pews belonging to the house.

The church has an altar tomb of the 16th century, and a brass showing John Allen of 1572 kneeling with one of his three wives and a group of children. But the most interesting monument is a sculpture lying on a windowsill, a man with his feet on a lion and his hands clasped over a heart. He is thought to be a 13th century man, but there is a tradition that the figure is that of Ingelrica, the English wife of Ralph Peverel, the Norman knight who founded the priory here.

The village post office and many of the cottages are 17th century, and so are two fine windows at Toppinghoe Hall, a mile and a half away. Its barn is a century older, and was part of an earlier hall. At Mowden Hall Farm is a tall dovecot of two storeys, with brick walls over a foot thick.

The Witchcraft Men and the Queen

HAVERING-ATTE-BOWER. Kings and queens have walked here, and wherever we turn we come upon their memory. Here came Edward the Confessor seeking solitude, praying even that the nightingales might be silent. Here Edward the Third invested little Richard as his successor, and from here Richard as king set out for Pleshey with a band of men to trap his uncle Gloucester. Here, too, lived and died Henry the Fourth's queen, Joan of Navarre, who sleeps at Canterbury.

The portrait of Joan on her tomb at Canterbury shows her as a woman of outstanding beauty, yet she was regarded as a witch, having been accused by her confessor of plotting the death of her stepson Henry the Fifth. Duchess of Brittany when her husband died, she became Regent for the eldest of her eight children. In 1403 she married Henry the Fourth, was crowned at Westminster, and was voted a dowry of 10,000 marks a year. When the king died Henry the Fifth seems to have continued to love his stepmother, though at Agincourt her son Arthur fought against him and was brought captive to her door. Four years later, however, came this horrible accusation and the Council deprived the Dowager Queen of all she possessed, taking her from Havering-atte-Bower to the security of Leeds Castle in Kent and Pevensey in Sussex. The charge appears now to have been a gross piece of injustice and corruption. Henry the Fifth on his deathbed wrote a letter setting his conscience free from blame for having taken the queen's dowry, and so Joan was set free and what remained of her dowry was returned to her. For the remaining 15 years of her life she was held in high honour by Henry the Sixth.

Historians have always wondered why, in those days when witchcraft was a dread reality, the queen was never brought to trial. An examination of her household accounts (preserved at the Record Office and at John Rylands Library) reveals that Joan was exceedingly well furnished with food, luxuries, and servants during her three years of restraint; and it is now believed that the charge of witchcraft was trumped up so that the Exchequer, almost emptied by the wars in France, should receive the benefit of her dowry, which was a very substantial sum in those days.

The oldest site identifiable on which these royal homes stood is at Havering Park, where an 18th century house with a tower hides in a splendid group of trees. It was the place for the queens when their kings were hunting in Hainault Forest, and the last king to come was Charles Stuart, who was here to meet his wife's mother, the notorious

Marie de Medici. She hoped to settle in England, and Parliament could only be rid of her by a gift of ten thousand pounds.

It is possible still to make out the terraced walks of the royal gardens, and there stands in Pyrgo Park an oak 20 feet round which, if its story were true, would be one of the most famous trees in England, for the story is that under this tree Queen Elizabeth sat when they brought news that the Great Armada had gone down. We cannot vouch for it.

The big village green is on high ground from which the hills of Kent are sometimes seen. Beside the oldest of its elms are two relics of village life long ago, the stocks and whipping-post of about 1700. The church by the green is a handsome 19th century building, with heads of lions in the porch roof under the tower. The chancel is enriched with panelling, the font is Norman, and there is a memorial showing a sorrowing woman and a scene in a harvest field. The oldest gravestone is that of Thomas Cheek, who was Lieutenant of the Tower and died in 1688, the year of the Revolution which doomed the Stuart dynasty for ever.

HAWKWELL. The timber bell-turret of its little church is about 500 years old and has a quaint spire, borne on massive beams and curved braces which are a striking feature in the west of the nave. The door with its strap-hinges and cinquefoil handle-plate is a fine example of wood and ironwork of the 15th century. In a window to those who did not come home from the Great War are vigorous figures of St Nicholas and St George.

HELION BUMPSTEAD. A small village with some fine old timbered houses, we remember its church as a symphony in green, green everywhere from the ivy outside to the pews, the pulpit, and the organ within. The chancel and its arch are 700 years old, and the nave may be older still, though it has a 16th century clerestory. A consecration cross is still on one of the buttresses. The south arcade is 14th century, but was altered in the Tudor Age, from which time comes a chest with three locks, and part of the south aisle roof. The font is 15th century, and so are a number of carved wooden panels to be seen about the church, on the door, on two modern benches, and on the beautiful pulpit. More fine old woodwork is in the fronts of the handsome chancel seats and in pews in the aisle, one of which has wonderful tracery with little hanging flowers and faces. By the font we found two benches of the 17th century, and altogether the old woodwork of this small place is its chief delight.

Ruffian and Hero

HEMPSTEAD. Here was born a ruffian and here lies a hero. The ruffian was Dick Turpin, born at the 17th century inn and baptised at the 14th century font; the hero, who lies under an altar tomb, is William Harvey, immortal throughout the world for his discovery of the fact of the circulation of the blood. Turpin was a butcher's apprentice who grew up a thief and was hanged at York for murder, a despicable fellow unworthy of any of the romance which has been woven about him.

There are majestic oak trees hereabouts, and it was sad to see in a field a tremendous ruin of one of them. It is recorded that in 1801 it stood 100 feet high and 50 feet round its trunk. A little ring of trees in the heart of the village is known as Turpin's Ring, it being believed that it was once an enclosure for cock fights.

Hempstead Hall about two miles away, built in the reign of Queen Elizabeth, has beside it a moat enclosing an island reached by a wooden bridge with timbers in it 300 years old.

The church on the hill has a fine new tower overlooking the village; it was built up last century by the Royal College of Physicians as an honour to the memory of William Harvey, who sleeps in the vault among his people. On a wall of the Harvey chapel is a huge black and white monument to Harveys from 1661 to 1710, and 13 remarkable lead coffins with modelled faces on them contain their bodies in the vault below.

The great Harvey himself looks down from a niche, his little beard giving dignity to the solemn face on this very lifelike bust. Two white medallions by Roubillac have portraits of an 18th century William Harvey and his wife, and there is an urn on a pedestal in memory of still another William of a generation earlier. A memorial in which the foliage on the pinnacles finishes in little heads is to the memory of Sir Eliab Harvey who sailed in the Fighting Téméraire on the heels of the Victory into Trafalgar Bay. He lived to tell the tale and was laid to rest here in 1830. He must often have looked up at the splendid funeral helmet used by one of his ancestors in the 17th century; it hangs in the nave outside the chapel, a hand rising above it grasping a crescent.

The nave has a group of brass portraits of the 15th and 16th centuries; a civilian of 1480 and another with his wife of a few years earlier, and still another civilian with his wife and their nine children buried here about 1530. Thomas Huntingdon is magnificent in armour with his wife in a pedimental headdress of 1498, and on the biggest and best brass is William Mordaunt in a fur-trimmed cloak with a group of his ten sons.

We open a 15th century door into the 17th century vestry and find a big chest of the 16th century, three centuries meeting in this room.

A Momentous Discovery

WILLIAM HARVEY, discoverer of the circulation of the blood, was born at Folkestone in 1578 and was buried at Hempstead in 1657. After King's School at Canterbury and Caius College, Cambridge, he studied at the great medical schools of Italy, which were then the best in Europe. Among his masters was Fabricius of Aquapendente, discoverer of the valves in the veins which favour the flow of blood in one direction. Returning to London, he practised as a physician, numbering Francis Bacon among his patients. At 37 he was appointed lecturer on anatomy and surgery at the College of Physicians, and it was there that, in the course of his ordinary lectures, he gradually developed and expounded his views on the circulation. The revolution in knowledge did not reach the world for another 15 years, when Harvey published it.

As a court physician he accompanied Charles the First through a great part of the Civil War, and was once reading to the two princes under a tree on the battlefield when a cannon ball fell near him. Happily he lived to print his momentous secret, but the publication of his discovery called down fierce hostility upon him from professional and lay critics alike. His practice dwindled almost to nothing; his house was pillaged and his papers burned. He committed all his worldly affairs to his brother, contented himself with study, and managed to leave a comfortable estate to the College of Physicians at his death.

He had pioneer predecessors, but the mastery of the great secret of the circulation of the blood was entirely his own. Servetus had

Earls Colne   Alice, Countess of Oxford

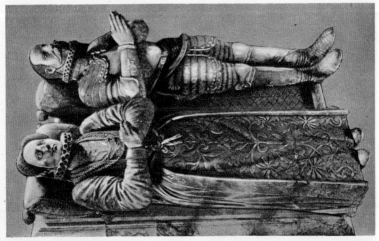

North Ockendon   Sir Gabriel and Lady Poyntz

Elmstead   The Wooden Knight

THREE FINE ESSEX MONUMENTS

Buttsbury (13th Century)   Hadstock (Saxon)

Heybridge (Norman)   Eastwood (13th Century)

ANCIENT CHURCH DOORS

described the passage of the blood from the right side of the heart, through the lungs, to the left side, but nobody before Harvey knew that the muscular contraction of the heart is responsible for pumping the blood. The wisest of his rivals imagined that the swelling of the heart attracted the blood to it, and that when the body drew "nutriment," in the form of blood the heart collapsed. It was Harvey who first introduced the law of mechanical science into biology.

HENHAM. With wide greens about its roads and pretty cottages with long gardens, it is a delightful place. One of the most charming of the thatched cottages stands by the churchyard, from which rises a handsome tower with a lead spire. The wide nave and the chancel of the church are 13th century, the 14th century built the tower and added the aisles, the 15th built the high chancel arch and the attractive porch. Tiny fragments of glass have been in the windows 500 years, one a shield with emblems of the Trinity; but the great attractions here are the old carvings in wood and stone. A beautiful bit of work on one of the capitals shows two angels censing the Madonna and Child, and on the same 14th century arcade are a leopard's head and a dragon. From the 15th century come the fine font with richly carved shields in its panels, the high screen, a niche with traces of its ancient colouring, and, finest of all, the oak pulpit with its little buttresses and pinnacles and traceried panels. The elaborately carved book-rest is 17th century. There is a monument to Samuel Feake, Governor of Fort William in the 18th century. It has a vase carved with an East Indiaman.

Mill Farm has kept and restored a windmill from the 17th century.

Strength and Grandeur

HEYBRIDGE. A busy little spot by the River Blackwater, it has a narrow winding street with houses looking across the water to the spires of Maldon, and a plain church of its own that might be mistaken for a barn. It has seen changes in its 800 years, but remains one of the most remarkable churches of its size in Essex. It impresses us with strength and a touch of grandeur, and stirs us to think of the years that have gone since its Norman builders were putting Roman bricks in its walls and round its windows. It is without aisles or chapels, and its nave seems to be without a tower, for there is no arch. But from the outside we can see the lower part of a west tower, which has become part of the nave. It must have fallen centuries ago, for the timbers supporting its pyramid roof have been here 500 years. There are three Norman doorways, and even the 15th century one is under a Norman arch. Two of the doorways have ornament and are high and narrow; and in one is a door with hinges as old as the foundations, sturdy smithwork that has withstood eight centuries of wind and weather. There is a fragment of a panelled Norman font near the rood stairs, and a 15th century bell come down to rest.

One of the things that strike us here is the odd effect the medieval builders have given by changing their minds when they began to make a clerestory; there seems no other explanation of these windows suddenly cut off by the roof beams. But the roof is a fine one, enriched with 15th century carving of foliage and shields.

There is a gravestone with a cross boldly carved 700 years ago, a recess in the sanctuary, where Thomas Freshwater has been kneeling with his wife since William of Orange landed, and a tiny man and a delightful little lady; he is John Whitacres of 1627, a quaint figure in brass; she has been in the tracery of a chancel window since the 13th century, graceful and stately in spite of her small size.

Tennyson Before His Fame

HIGH BEECH. It is the jewelled crown of Epping Forest; it was the beauty of it that attracted the greatest English poet of the Victorian Era to come here to live. It has little that man gave it save a few cottages and isolated houses and a modern church, but has the solitude of a noble beech wood Nature gave it, and we walk in it as in some great cathedral. In the tranquillity of these green shrines and grey altars our ancestors have walked for many generations, and here Tennyson loved to walk. He lived here through the first three years of the Victorian Era in which he was to be a shining figure.

It had been a painful farewell to Somersby, where the Tennysons had been living at the rectory, but things were financially difficult and they decided to come nearer London, and lived here till 1840, when they went into Kent. The poet had lost one pleasant brook at Somersby and was to find another at Boxley, but here in Essex it was Epping Forest that was his delight. He took a practical interest in furnishing the house, and we are told that he did not forget the kitchen things, and that he bought pretty and inexpensive furniture. There was a pond in the park on which he would skate in his long blue cloak. He loved to go to his friends in town; and, coming back in the evening, would often notice "the light of London flaring like a dreary dawn."

It was in these days that he was engaged to Emily Sellwood, but they were too poor to marry; he was even too poor to travel, and one of the letters he wrote from here regretted that he would never be able to see the Eternal City and the dome of St Peter's. There was a night when a great thunderstorm broke over High Beech, and the poet always remembered two experiences of this storm. One was that a friend saw a great fire ball come up the valley and burst over Tennyson's pond "like 50 batteries of cannon"; the other was that when Tennyson went up to his mother's room he found her on the floor, crying, "Oh, I will leave this house—the storms are very bad here."

These were his very early days, before fame and fortune found him. He longed in vain to see the Lincolnshire coast, but "the journey is so expensive and I am so poor." Yet he enjoyed life here, and here he lived in his imagination in the past and in the future. It may have been the thought of the submerged forest under the Thames Marshes that led him to write:

> *There rolls the deep where grew the tree,*
> *O, Earth, what changes thou hast seen;*

at any rate he wrote it here in Essex when working on In Memoriam, and here he wrote The Talking Oak and Locksley Hall; here he

Dipped into the future, far as human eye could see,
Saw the Vision of the world, and all the wonder that would be;
Saw the heavens fill with commerce, argosies of magic sails,
Pilots of the purple twilight, dropping down with costly bales;
Heard the heavens fill with shouting, and there rained a ghastly dew
From the nations' airy navies grappling in the central blue;
Far along the worldwide whisper of the south wind rushing warm,
With the standards of the peoples plunging through the thunderstorm;
Till the war-drum throbbed no longer, and the battle-flags were furled
In the Parliament of Man, the Federation of the World.

Here also he heard the bells of Waltham Abbey which inspired him to write perhaps the best known of all his verses, Ring Out, Wild Bells.

Marshal of Calais

HIGH EASTER. Its ancient cottages jostle at the gate of the churchyard, in which stand the Norman walls which were here before any of them. They make a charming group with overhanging storeys and high-pitched roofs. The noble 15th century tower of the church is stocked with gargoyles and heads of strange beasts to drive away evil from these pleasant highlands. There are Roman tiles set in herringbone fashion in the east wall of the chancel. The spandrels of the doorway of the tower have quaint carvings of a horseman with a woodman on one side and a winged beast on the other, while at the apex an angel holds a shield. Minstrels playing flutes act as stops to a modern window over the door, and angels form stops to the fine tower arch windows, carrying the eye up to the splendid 16th century roof in which every beam is moulded. There is running foliage on the embattled tiebeams, and the bosses of its arches are carved with faces of men and beasts and the device of Sir Geoffrey Gate, made Marshal of Calais by Henry the Seventh. Sir Geoffrey may have kept one of the keys of the 14th century chest, which is still held together by its ornamental ironwork, and members of his family were baptised at the handsome 14th century font. The east window is in memory of Edward Francis Gepp, who died in 1903 after having been vicar 54 years. Old Edward Porter knew this Norman chancel even better than he, having sung in the choir for 70 years. There are mason's marks on some of the pillars here, and a medieval scratch dial by the south doorway.

Immortal and Forgotten

HIGH LAVER. Here lies a quiet Englishman whose fame lives for his gentle virtues, John Locke. He lived for ten years in the home of the Mashams here, and in the church is this rare epitaph to his memory:

Stay, traveller; John Locke rests here. Do you ask What manner of man was he? He replies that he lived content with his own middle rank. Had he good qualities? They are less than can serve for praise to him or an example to you. Let his faults be buried with him. If you seek an example in morals, you have it in the Gospel. Would that no evils existed.

He lies by the porch of a church that has been made what it is through the centuries, with bricks from Roman houses in its walls, put there by the Normans. The 18th century tower has still the tiny sanctus bell which rang 600 years ago; here is the font at which children were being christened then. There is a 15th century family portrait in brass showing Edward Sulyard in armour, his wife Myrabyll in a flowing skirt, and their four boys gazing at a sister. The old chest has a heavy lid which must often have been lifted by Samuel Lowe, whose monument is on the wall; he was the rector who buried John Locke.

In the altar tombs of the churchyard lie the Mashams, Locke's friend Lady Masham among them. She studied under him, and Locke said of her, "You will not find many men to whom she is not superior in wealth of knowledge and ability to profit by it." Close by her lies the notorious Mrs Masham of the court of Queen Anne. She built up for herself tremendous influence, supplanting the great Duchess Sarah, and intriguing with such power that she overthrew a Government and sought to restore the Stuarts. Succeeding in one plot, she happily failed in the other, and she lies here forgotten after all the fame of her day, while fame has come to quiet John Locke sleeping a few yards away.

The Philosopher of the Quiet Life

HE was a Somerset man, born at Wrington in 1632, son of a Puritan lawyer who held a captain's commission in the Parliament army. Passing from Westminster School to Oxford, he was lecturer there in Greek and Rhetoric.

Studying medicine, and declared by Sydenham to be one of the most gifted doctors of the age, he was denied his medical degree, largely for political reasons, but acted as physician to Lord Shaftesbury, who procured him public employment, made him tutor to his son and grandson, and involved him in his own fall. For four years Locke lived in France, then returned with Shaftesbury's new lease of power, only to seek flight afresh when his patron was finally overthrown.

Making Holland his home, Locke had the company of illustrious sympathisers. By an illegal order he was deprived of his status at Oxford, and had to go into hiding to escape arrest on political charges. It was while he was a fugitive that he wrote his first

Letter on Toleration. After six years of exile he returned, following the Revolution in the train of Queen Mary and Dutch William, and now, but for his incurable asthma and the constant threat of tuberculosis, he might have held high office in the State.

A Fellow of the Royal Society and friend of Sir Isaac Newton, he lived for the last 14 years of his life at High Laver with his friends Sir Francis and Lady Masham. By this time his fame was firmly established. He had published two Treatises on Government, the first demolishing the doctrine of the divine right of kings, the second a declaration of the social compact as it seemed to him, the government of the people in the interest, and for the good of, the governed. In these he laid the foundations of civil liberty, as in Toleration he had laid the foundations of religious liberty. It was on the philosophy of John Locke concerning these vital issues that the British Empire grew to political and spiritual freedom.

The Essay on Human Understanding came at about the same time, when he was 57, the fruit of twenty years of study. It was the most brilliant exploration of the mind and its processes that had then been attempted. He shows that knowledge is not innate, but is derived from experience, which he vindicates by our ideas of space, time, infinity, substance, power, identity, and so on, leading to the conclusion that knowledge is limited to two certainties—of our own existence, by Intuition, and the existence of God by Demonstration, intuitive certainty making it plain that creation is the work of an eternal God.

His masterpiece was followed by treatises on the Reasonableness of Christianity and on Education, the second of which is the foundation of modern educational reform, seeing education as the formation of character, as that which moulds or modifies the soul or the mind.

His closing hours were solaced by the presence of Lady Masham. To the clergyman who had administered the last communion in his room he said that he died in perfect charity with all men, and in communion with the Church of Christ, by whatever name it was distinguished. Lady Masham was reading the Psalms to him when he gently interrupted her, saying that the end was come, and a few minutes later he fell asleep.

Three Windows

HIGH ONGAR. The village has a row of timbered cottages and the church two Norman doorways, one of them a beauty. It is amazing to realise that an axe could create such loveliness from stone. The arch is richly carved and encloses four rows of stones in the tympanum, each one differing in design. Narrow Norman windows still help to light the nave, but the lancet windows of the chancel show that the east end of the church was entirely rebuilt in the 13th century. The three windows in the east wall are of great dignity, two with 16th century heraldic glass in rich colouring; on one of them are the arms of Jane Seymour below the golden crown her royal Bluebeard set on her head, and the other has the arms of Henry the Eighth himself. There is a brass in the floor of the nave with a civilian in the dress he wore when Henry came to the throne. There is a Jacobean pulpit and a memorial pew of 1700 with carving copied from two bench-ends close by it. One of the Earles who were rectors last century preached from this pulpit for 58 years.

HIGH RODING. It has many gabled and thatched houses in its street, and a great pond between the churchyard and an old farmhouse. The church has been here 700 years, and the ironwork on the doors is as old as the stones. The doorways are small, and we may wonder how they carried in the massive medieval font, with delicately carved panelling. The pulpit has kept it company most of the time. There was a rich scene of colour in the window by the pulpit when it was new; all that is left now is an angel swinging a censer vigorously in the smallest of the tracery lights.

Victory for Canute

HOCKLEY. Its houses are on a hill between a great wood and the valley of the Crouch. We may imagine the Saxons fleeing for safety into the depths of this wood before the vengeance of Canute's Danes, who on the slopes below had won for their leader the crown of England. The round hillock in the valley was the home of still earlier dwellers in our Motherland, for pottery and a coin of the Roman Emperor Diocletian have been found in it. It was Diocletian who resolved to stamp out Christianity, but one of the first things done by King Canute was to found a church on this hilltop. No Saxon work is traceable today, for the oldest thing we see is the marble font, brought here about the time of Magna Carta, when most of the present church was built. The three round pillars between the nave and aisle have the conventional foliage of that time; the nave roof is 14th century, with well-moulded capitals and kingposts. The curious-looking tower was begun 600 years ago, the lower stage being square and solid; but where the buttresses end it becomes octagonal, with battlements surrounding a small spire.

Charles Stuart's Postman

HORNCHURCH. William of Wykeham sitting in his robes looks down from a turret in its splendid tower. He found here a 13th century church and is believed to have designed this tower for it himself; he sits on it with his arms extended in blessing. Above him a copper-covered spire rises 120 feet, sheltering a peal of eight musical bells.

The village has lost the brass with the portrait of a famous man who came here long before William of Wykeham—Sir Boniface de Hart, a canon of Aosta, lying in this English soil so far from his home. He is here because our powerful King Henry the Second, courting the favour of Frederic Barbarossa, the greatest of the Holy Roman Emperors, sent envoys to speak with him, and they passed over the Great St Bernard Pass. There they were cared for by the monks of the Hospice, and in return for the kindness of the monks Henry founded the only religious house in England attached to this famous Hospice of Savoy. The church of the hospice was served by foreign priests and their London house gave its name to the little Savoy Hill that runs down from the Strand to the Thames. In course of time Sir Boniface came from Aosta at the foot of the pass to reign as prior at Hornchurch by the Thames, now on the borders of Greater London, and here he died and was buried in 1330.

The church stands on the highest ground between the River Rom and the Ingrebourne; it has the stone head of a bull with copper-sheathed horns gazing out from its gable. There is still here a 13th century coffin lid with a cross for one of the first men buried here.

Coming through a porch as old as the tower, we swing open a door that is older still; William of Wykeham himself may have opened it. It brings us into a church with fine carving in stone, flowers in a panel above a graceful pier, and roses carved 500 years ago on the piscina. The chapel is lighted by glass 500 years old with a portrait of Edward the Confessor, the head of Our Lord in glory, and a head of Mary which has been wrongly set on the figure by a restorer.

Under the arch dividing this chapel from the chancel is a tomb of great beauty in which William Ayloffe has lain 400 years, and high on the chancel wall is a group by Flaxman, in which two women are mourning for Richard Spencer and his wife, whose faces are delicately carved. Kneeling under marble curtains are Richard Bealestone and his wife, buried here on the eve of the Civil War. Lying here also is a man linked by his scholarship with one of our kings, Humphrey Pye, letter-writer for King James; he is with his wife, carved in alabaster on the wall. In the tower is a quaint group of people in black, the 16th century family of Francis Rame with his wife and their ten children. There are portraits in brass of the two wives of William Drywood in quaint Elizabethan hats, and a portrait of their kinsman Thomas Drywood with his wife. Two brass tablets nearer our time awaken deep memories, for one is to Joseph Fry, whose mother was the angel of our prisons, and the other is to 769 members of the Sportsman's Battalion who offered their lives for their country in the war, were trained as soldiers at Hornchurch, and left this place to see England no more.

Here, as we have seen, lies a letter-writer for King James; but here lies one of the great pioneers of letters, a man who started the distribution of letters for King James's son on a scale King James never dreamed of. He was Thomas Witherings, who started the Post Office. We read of him on a black tablet with a tiny carving of a skeleton, which tells us that he organised the delivery of letters for Charles Stuart and that he died on his way to this church one Sunday in 1651.

In 1633 he was granted a patent as postmaster for foreign letters. There were already regulations for the carriage of Government letters, and in the reign of King James Lord Stanhope was Master of the Posts and Messengers, receiving 100 marks a year and all "avails and profits" in addition. In postal affairs generally, however, there was hopeless confusion, because merchants were allowed to use messengers of their own. Witherings soon proved himself a far-sighted organiser. He speeded up the mail between London and the

Continent so that he was able to point out to the king that his subjects could receive a quicker and surer reply to a letter from Madrid than ordinarily from Scotland.

Thomas Witherings accordingly drew up a new scheme which was embodied in a Proclamation, and after that a letter to Edinburgh took three days instead of nearly a month. Witherings made it a rule that the speed of the letter post should be seven miles an hour in summer and five in winter, and he also introduced registration and postmarks; in his own words:

Every postmaster is to keep a faire paper book to enter the packets in, and shall write upon the labell fastened to every or any of the packets the time of receit thereof.

Even with royal support it was impossible to carry out great reforms without hostility, and in 1640 this energetic organiser was accused of misdemeanours and his office given to a London merchant. A long wrangle ensued in Parliament and the courts, during which the mails were often seized, and the postal revenue fell to £5000 in 1643. Witherings was worried almost to death, and he actually died on his way to a service at Hornchurch in 1651. In the church we may still read what his friends thought of him, the

Chief Postmaster of Greate Britaine and foreign parts, second to none for unfathomed policy, unparalleled, sagacious, and divining genius; witness his great correspondence in all parts of the Christian World.

The Village Hero

HORNDON-ON-THE-HILL. Its delightful houses take us into another age, jostling each other with their thatched roofs. A timbered inn has overhung the road for 500 years, the 400-year-old market hall is a club for the village folk, and Arden Hall has a square brick dovecot of the 17th century. But an avenue of lime trees brings us to the quaint porch of a church older than all the houses, for we come into it through a Norman doorway to find the light falling through two Norman clerestory windows. The nave arcades are 13th century, with fine piers carved with leaves and flowers. The splendid chancel roof is 15th century, probably the work of the carpenters who set up the huge beams crowning one of the four bays to support the timbered belfry. The font, of unusual design and simple beauty, is 600 years old.

A great hero of this village was Thomas Highbed, who walked into the fire for his faith in 1555. He was apparently a man of some note, for the Record Office in London has a complete inventory of all his goods, chattels, and farming implements.

HUTTON. It lies on the road from Brentwood to Billericay, but its delightful church is down a lane, by the limes in which the rooks have a village all their own. So thoroughly was the church restored last century that little remains of its medieval walls, but most of the wooden porch of the 14th century has been replaced on new dwarf walls. The beam over the outer arch is carved with trefoils, richly traceried heads make beautiful the four windows in the sides, and there is a bargeboard of great beauty. The roof of the nave is as old as Parliament, and is continued over the tiny aisles, resting on the original clustered columns. A brass of about 1525 shows an unknown man in armour with his wife and their 16 children. The church also has a splendid modern screen with oak statues of St George, Joan of Arc, Sir Thomas More, and Bishop Fisher. Another imposing piece of craftsmanship is the high font cover, with a relief of a woman clinging to a rock; it is a memorial to a Mrs Hamilton who perished in a wreck.

A Great Modern Church

ILFORD. It has come into London, of course, and its 138 square miles is packed with 200,000 people; but only 100 years ago the River Roding was running through green pastures here and Ilford folk were going to service in the little medieval chapel of the Hospital of St Mary. It keeps its old chapel still, and it vies with the great new church in its appeal to pilgrims.

Among many other churches which have grown up are St Mary's with an apse and a spire, and St Clement's with its imitation Gothic; but the great monument of our time at Ilford is Sir Herbert Baker's brick church of St Andrew's.

Ilford is now the controlling centre of half-a-dozen places (Chadwell Heath, Seven Kings, Newbury Park, Barkingside, Goodmayes, Aldborough Hatch, and part of Becontree, the LCC's great estate) and it has a town hall which ranks among the best civic buildings of outer London. It has also 1000 acres set aside for a great airport. Among its old places is what is left of the Hospital of St Mary, the little chapel kept in repair by the Marquis of Salisbury, who maintains the chaplain and provides for the six poor people who took the place of the lepers centuries ago. It is 15th century, and the oldest building in the town.

We come from the Roman highroad by a charming gateway to find their one-storeyed homes facing each other across a courtyard, with the chapel looking on. Their homes were new two centuries ago, and the chapel was made new in the 17th and 19th centuries, but the chancel remains wholly medieval, a tiny place 16 feet wide with glass in the windows three or four centuries old, showing the Madonna and St Elizabeth as gems of colour in the tracery. An old stone priest who is thought to be John Smythe, master of the Hospital 500 years ago, lies in his robes under a new canopy. The panelled back of his old tomb being now in a wall. There is a big modern painting of Christ on the Road to Calvary.

Sir Herbert Baker's great church is set on Ilford's highest point, with spacious streets about it. It is somewhat like Sir Herbert's cathedral at Pretoria, and is 145 feet long and 80 feet high, with a small graceful spire of oak and lead. The copper-domed roof of the baptistry, rising between two entrance arches at the west end, is crowned with a bronze figure of Peace by Charles Wheeler, and the apse at the east end has Gabriel sounding his trumpet, designed in tiles by Henry Holiday.

The interior with its seven bays is like a basilica, with barrel roofs over narrow aisles lighted by round-headed windows, their arches all different. The baptistry recess has a roof in brick and tile suggesting great beams of light radiating from a panel of the Dove, by Phoebe Stabler, the architect's gift to the church.

In the roof of the nave are six beams each weighing a ton. The roofs of the chancel and the soaring apse are of barrelled and vaulted brickwork, and the apse windows have exceptional grace. But the gem of the stained glass is a window in the north aisle showing the Madonna crowned. In this green and blue jewel Carl Parsons surpasses all his other windows here, but those on either side of the Madonna, one of Christ the Carpenter, the other of Solomon the Builder, are delightfully apt, for this chapel is the gift of the church's own builder, Alfred Griggs, whose proud opportunity it was, as Mayor of Ilford, to hold his civic inauguration in this church of his own building. The chapel is a memorial to his parents and his brother Horace, an Ilford lad who meant to be a priest but gave his young life as a soldier. In one window we see him as a student at Oxford, in another as an officer in France, and the altar, lectern, and litany desk were all made with his hands for the church hall when he was quite a boy.

The wave of enthusiasm which set this fine church on the hill broke into a hundred gifts for it, and they are everywhere, so that the church has become a storehouse of memories. Remembered above all is Dr Edgar Jacob, the bishop who left his diocese of New-castle to organise the church in this fast growing suburb of Greater London. The church is his monument, as it is also the monument of a group of fine modern craftsmen. Its beautiful woodwork was designed by Laurence Turner, the noble altar triptych by Colin Gill; the fine altar linen was done by a lady who worked at it for years and died a year or two before the church was consecrated.

We found another band of enthusiasts carrying on the health activities of Ilford in a 17th century house in Valentine's Park, home of the vine from which Hampton Court's famous great vine came. The parent stem died some years ago, but its offshoot bears its wondrous harvest of over a thousand pounds of grapes every year.

One more modern church here, St Peter's, we found at Aldborough Hatch near Barkingside, and it is interesting because it has in its walls some stones from old Westminster Bridge, the bridge on which Wordsworth stood when it seemed to him that *Earth has not anything to show more fair.*

Servant of Four Kings

INGATESTONE. A landmark for 200 years, its windmill is still at work crushing oats and beans with stones turned by wooden cog-wheels, the wooden cap swinging round to the wind on a massive brick tower. The red-roofed houses of the old town crowd on the narrow road, and behind them looms another landmark, the 15th century church tower of black and red bricks and white-capped pinnacles, which dwarfs the little nave and the three gabled roofs. There are Roman bricks set in the walls by Norman builders.

Under the arch between the chancel and the chapel he built, Sir William Petre lies on his tomb with his wife, a stately alabaster figure in armour, looking up at the coat-of-arms suspended above him. Delicate ironwork rails off this ornate pillared tomb, a fine example of Elizabethan craftsmanship.

Sir William lived through 67 years of the 16th century, serving Henry the Eighth and his three children on the throne. He grew rich as one of the destroyers of the monasteries, and it is said that his reward was as much as 36,000 acres. Yet he is remembered as a man of great moderation, and one of the stories told of him is that of a French official at Boulogne in 1550 who said, "Ah! we could have gained the last 200,000 crowns without hostages had it not been for that man who said nothing."

Sir William's youngest brother Robert appears as a kneeling figure on a wall in the chapel, and a portrait in relief shows Captain John Troughton wearing a sash across his richly ornamented armour.

A brass tablet tells us of a distinguished soldier of three centuries later, Algernon Wood, who went through the Boer War and the first Gallipoli campaign, and was shot dead in a Gallipoli trench within a fortnight of being awarded the DSO.

The noblest of all the monuments here is one raised by the second Lord Petre to his wife and parents; it is a masterpiece in black and white, almost filling the west wall of a chapel built for it. Three generations are here, the grandparents (the first Lord Petre and his wife) kneeling opposite each other in the central bay, both in rich fur-lined cloaks, the grandchildren carved in relief along the base, eight boys and four prim girls in full skirts and fashionable Stuart hats, and their father, a very dignified figure in one of the side bays, looking towards the wife whose death started the building of this superb monument.

Their old home, Ingatestone Hall, with its many delightful stepped gables, was altered in the 18th century but has still a pleasant look of Elizabethan days about it, and is now a Roman Catholic retreat.

His Life for His Friend

INGRAVE. It lies two miles from Brentwood by the lovely woodlands of Thorndon Hall and a medieval farm with a timbered house. The church is one of the rare 18th century buildings, with a big tower, and in it are some treasures from the lost churches of this and a neighbouring village. From old Ingrave church came the Tudor font and a 17th century communion table; and from West Horndon came the most beautiful things Ingrave has to show—a stately brass of Margaret Wake, who died in 1466, and a magnificent group of Sir Richard FitzLewes and his four wives. Sir Richard, who died in 1528, wears a rich tabard over his armour and his head rests on a crested helmet. Three of his wives wear heraldic mantles which give them great dignity. There are roundels and ermine, bugle horns and a dancing goat, and other quaint heraldic devices.

A bitter fate was soon to befall this family. In a few years time, so the story runs, John FitzLewes was burned to death with his bride on the night of his wedding, and his wealth passed to his sister, who became a ward to Henry the Eighth, he giving her in marriage to John, the son of the first Lord Mordaunt. They lie in one of the lovely tombs at Turvey in Bedfordshire.

Thorndon Hall and its 1500 acres passed to the Petre family who came here from Ingatestone in the reign of Elizabeth. In its 18th century Roman Catholic chapel lies James Radcliffe, the romantic Earl of Derwentwater who perished on Tower Hill in 1716. His was a tragic story.

When James the Second, flying in haste from the throne of England settled at St Germain in France, the second Earl of Derwentwater and his wife (a daughter of Charles the Second) joined him in exile. There in 1689 was born their son James Radcliffe, to spend his childhood with the young James Stuart, known in history as the Old Pretender. James Radcliffe came to England in 1710 and lived in his ancestral homes at Dilston in Northumberland and on Lord's Island in beautiful Derwentwater.

Five years later the Stuarts raised their call again, summoning their friends to the hopeless task of regaining the throne for them. Radcliffe was wise, and he hesitated, but the king's sister he had married accused him of cowardice, threw her fan at his feet, and cried: "Pick up that fan and give me your sword. I will take the field and you can stay at home."

Stung to the heart, the earl picked up the fan and solemnly handed it back to his wife; then, drawing his sword, he cried, God Save King James, and set out for battle and the grave. With a small group of retainers he eluded the officers who already had a warrant for his arrest, and joined the Jacobite Army. He fought with great courage at the battle of Preston, but was taken prisoner and carried to the Tower. There was a great trial in Westminster Hall, and he was condemned to death. So gallant was his bearing that he won the admiration of all, and his friends made great efforts to save him, £60,000 being offered to Sir Robert Walpole for his life, while his wife, in her remorse, went on her knees to King George the First to beg for his life. But there was no mercy for this tragic youth; he died in the cause of the companion of his childhood, one of the last of a faithful host sacrificed for a faithless House.

The Saxon Follows the Roman

INWORTH. Here lived Saxons on a Roman settlement, among the lovely hills and valleys of the Blackwater country. In the church, hidden by trees on a hilltop, are many Roman tiles, set in the walls by the Saxons. They give colour to the corners of the building and frame the Saxon arch of the chancel. The double-splayed windows, which the Saxon archers found so useful for defence still admit the slender shafts of light through the thick walls, and one glows with a mass of fragments of rich glass of the 14th and 15th centuries, a kaleidoscope of rare beauty. The church has charming woodwork. From the year 1500 come the well-moulded wall-plates of the porch, and the door within it. There is a richly carved seat just inside, and much fine medieval carving in the flowing curves and spandrels of the screen. Right and left of the chancel arch are remains of wall-paintings 700 years old. It is a little difficult to read their meaning, but a tower, a boat with a striped sail, and a few people, can be picked out of these fading picture stories.

Mr Spurgeon's Village

KELVEDON. For about a mile it runs along the Roman road to Colchester from London, and under the road at the foot of Feering Hill the Blackwater flows through a five-arched bridge. We may wonder how many villages in England there are with sixty national monuments in them, for sixty old houses in Kelvedon are scheduled for preservation by the nation.

In this historic little place was born last century a boy who grew up to make his name known wherever men listen to sermons or read them, Charles Haddon Spurgeon, for whom no church or chapel in the world was too big to hold his congregations.

Marks Tey
Wooden Font

Little Dunmow
The Prior's Chair

Chignal Smealy
Brick Font

Newport   13th Century Portable Altar

Blackmore   Thomas and Margaret Smyth

Layer Marney
Lord Marney

Ingatestone
Sir William and Lady Petre

Theydon Mount   Sir William Smith   **Little Easton**   Sir Henry Maynard

FIVE ESSEX MONUMENTS

The 600-year-old tower of the church is joined on to Norman walls with Roman bricks in them; the tower has grotesques at the corners and we noticed a very comical face grimacing on the walls. Indoors the capitals on two nave columns are very beautiful with stiff leaves carved 700 years ago, among the best of that time in Essex. The roof, well lit up by clerestory windows, is magnificent 15th century work and has supporting it richly carved figures playing hautboys and holding shields, crowns, and books. The church has what is called a weeping chancel, built a little aslant, it is said, in keeping with the legend that Our Lord bowed his head on the Cross. In the vestry is a quaintly carved panel of Esther on her knees before Ahasuerus; it is 16th century, and was brought from one of Kelvedon's old houses. The best window has the Annunciation by Louis Davis, recalling Rossetti's masterpiece in the National Gallery.

Charles Haddon Spurgeon of Kelvedon, son of a minister, preached his first sermon at 16; at 18 he was a Baptist pastor; at 20 he was offered a pulpit in London; and a few months later all London was talking of him.

No chapel could hold the throng which crowded to listen to his sermons; he filled the Surrey Gardens Music Hall, and in the end they built him his own great Tabernacle. It cost £31,000, and every penny had been subscribed when he had been preaching there a month. Three times a week he preached, and nearly 7000 people pressed in every time to hear him. He spoke at the Crystal Palace at the time of the Indian Mutiny and 24,000 came to listen. But this was nothing to the size of his unseen congregation. He had the biggest unseen congregations before the days of wireless. Once a week a sermon of his was printed, till the sermons ran into thousands and their copies into a hundred millions, read all over the world.

For half a century a shop in Paternoster Buildings existed on the sale of these sermons at a penny each. They were reproduced in newspapers; they were translated into many languages. But when his publishers sent a boy late one night through a snowstorm to deliver the proofs of one of them he could spare the time to write asking them "please to blow somebody up for sending the poor little creature here late tonight in all this snow, with a parcel much heavier than he ought to carry," and then he added: "There was no need at all for it. Do kick somebody for me, so that it may not happen again."

Wit and homely speech forced home the fervour of his sermons. He was no actor carrying people on a wave of emotion, but a deep thinker whose printed word would send a man down on his knees. But his creed was that of the old Puritans, as narrow as the gate of heaven seemed to him. Yet Spurgeon's sermons were not bought only by Nonconformists. High Churchmen and Low, Roman Catholic and Evangelical, read them, sure that no sermons they could preach were as rich in thought as these. The city man and the shop assistant, the coalheaver and the duchess, bought his penny sermons as now they buy their penny papers; and just as the crowd waits outside the kinema today so they would wait outside Spurgeon's Tabernacle at the end of last century.

On his tomb at Norwood it is said that he "being dead, yet speaketh." For years that was true; and still his sermons are read, and there are many to say that none are finer yet. But his influence has died down like the lull after a great storm, and we are left wondering at the power of this man.

KELVEDON HATCH. It has two churches, but the old one is forsaken and has sent some of its treasures to the new. The old church was refashioned in the 18th century and stands by the woodlands of Kelvedon Hall. It has kept a few old brass inscriptions, a quaint one of 300 years ago telling how Richard and Anthony Luther were such truly loving brothers that they kept house together for 40 years "without anie accompt atwixt them." Ringing in the little red spire of the new church is the medieval bell from the old one, and also here is the tall 14th century font, with tiny carvings of flowers and fruit, a mitre, and a captivating little head of a man with well-combed hair. The font cover is an elaborate piece of ironwork wrought by hand last century, and both pulpit and screen are excellent examples of the same craftsmanship. From the road to Ongar we glimpse the delightful timber and plaster house where the rectors used to live, built perhaps 300 years ago.

Remarkable Timbers

LAINDON. The village nestles below the round knob of a hill which Nature seems to have left for the little church that has crowned it for 800 years. The tall shingled spire on a wooden tower is a landmark for all who travel on the main road to Southend. Climbing the steep lane, we find that a quaint timbered house of two storeys was added 300 years ago to the west end of the church, serving then as the village school and now as the rector's room. The wooden porch of the church has been rebuilt, but has still the two original archways, one having a dragon and a scallop shell carved in one spandrel, and a beast pierced by a cross in the other. The woodwork within is remarkable. Massive posts support the tower, the roofs of the nave and chancel are splendid 15th century work, and there is carving on the wall-plates. The nail-studded door has been hanging about 500 years. The font is two centuries older. There are portraits in brass of two of the priests who ministered here in the 15th century, John Kekilpenny and Richard Bladwell. Among fragments of old glass in the windows we noticed a fleur-de-lys growing out of the head of a leopard; it is 400 years old.

LAMARSH. Its cottages are dainty, its tower is rare and ancient, one of the six round towers in Essex and one of only three known to have been built by the Normans. It was partly restored about 250 years ago. The odd-looking spire with its little dormer windows is modern, but one of the lancet windows is 12th century. The nave walls may be Norman, but the chancel was refashioned 600 years ago. There is 15th century woodwork in the ten bays of the screen. Tudor builders added the brick porch, which shelters a doorway and a handsome door just as old. Fine trees surround Daw's Hall, a 16th century house with a 14th century crowned head carved on a boss over one of its doors.

Gems of Glass

LAMBOURNE. It is at the edge of the ancient forest of Hainault, and from its high ground above the River Roding it looks across to Epping Forest running along the horizon. On this high ground stands the church, with two Norman doorways through which we pass no more. It is the glass of the east window that strikes us as we come in, a modern scene of Bethlehem in memory of Lord Lambourne. In another chancel window are small gems in quieter tones, a group of five panels brought from Basle, painted about 300 years ago. They represent the choice between Good and Evil, the Adoration of the Wise Men, the Incredulity of Thomas, Christ and Peter on the sea, and the Shepherds. A nave window is in memory of a man who loved to ride about these uplands, and lived to ride in that last wild charge from which he never returned, against the Russian guns at Balaclava. He was George Lockwood, aide-de-camp to Lord Cardigan.

Engraved in brass are the portraits of a Tudor mercer with his wife and their family of nine sons and ten daughters; and there is a wall-monument to Thomas Winniffe, who became Dean of St Paul's and Bishop of Lincoln, and retired here during the Commonwealth. The pulpit is of his day, and some of the old stalls. There is a gallery of 1704.

Lambourne Hall was built in Queen Elizabeth's day on the site where lived a warrior bishop who fought in Italy for the Pope and crushed the peasant rising against the taxes of Richard the Second. He was Henry le Despenser, of whom perhaps the best that can be said is that he was loyal to Richard after his fall.

Essex Heights

LANGDON HILLS. It is named from the heights on which it stands; there is nothing higher than its 386 feet in a line due north between here and the North Pole. The views all round are wonderful, pleasant woods, sloping meadows, and waving cornfields lying immediately below, with the Thames marshes in the distance and the blue downs of Kent on the horizon. It was one of the sights that thrilled Arthur Young, who wrote of it. Almost at the top is the lofty tower of the new church, from which peals some of the finest music of bells in Essex.

A tree-shaded lane winds down to the charming place in which the villagers worshipped in olden days. Deserted and forlorn for years, it is a fine example of the work of the Society for the Protection of Ancient Buildings, which has restored this rare church rebuilt in the brief revival of Gothic in the days of Charles Stuart. Delightful is the moulding of the red bricks framing the east window, flanked by moulded niches. The altar rails have turned balusters and are Jacobean and the three-decker pulpit is in the same style.

Peace

LANGENHOE. An earthquake shook its old church to the ground, an incredible thing to come upon in this secluded place.

The new church of last century has an imposing tower, from which peep out some of the ancient gargoyles which survived. Many of the stones of doorways and windows were also used again, and the 500-year-old doors were rehung. From the old church, too, comes the font, with flowers carved on each of its eight panels; and a quaint chest and a carved chair have seen three centuries.

Very peaceful now is this place so stricken in 1884, the church rising again in the long grass of the churchyard, a group of ducks on a pond outside a farm gate breaking the silence of the fields:

> *Four ducks on a pond.*
> *A grass bank beyond,*
> *A blue sky of spring,*
> *White clouds on the wing:*
> *What a little thing*
> *To remember for years,*
> *To remember with tears!*

Unique in England

LANGFORD. Langford Hall has been here since the 17th century, but it is young compared with the church close by, a building of great interest to lovers of old and rare things. Almost certainly it was here in Saxon England, and until the 19th century restorers destroyed some of its character it can have changed little in 900 years. This church is almost unique in England in having a western apse, which is believed to be a survival from the first centuries of Christianity, when a separate baptistry was often built at the west end of a church. The apse has three little windows high up, with wide splays inside. Each is about two feet high, but only seven inches wide. One of the original doorways is here, its inner arch also splayed to allow the door to swing. Through a pane of glass in the plaster wall we can see the rough masonry of the Saxon builders. There is a 15th century font and a double piscina of the 13th century that has lost its pillar. Marks on the chancel floor indicate the foundations of an eastern apse, so that Langford has made itself famous and unique by saving the west apse and losing the east.

Here Constable Would Sit

LANGHAM. Its tower on the hill is memorable in the story of British art, for on the top of it John Constable would sit and work, having climbed the ladder which is still the only way up.

He had been to school at Dedham, a mile or two away, and was friendly with John Fisher, the rector here, who offered to make him schoolmaster in the village. He is said to have painted one of his pictures of the lovely Stour valley from this tower; and it was another John Fisher, a nephew of the kindly rector, who became one of his lifelong friends.

The tower was ancient when Constable first saw it, for it was begun in the 13th century, carried up in the 14th, and completed with a brick parapet and pinnacles by Tudor builders. The nave has Roman bricks used again by the Normans, and the chancel a little pointed window of about 1200. The interior is dominated by the work of the 14th century men, from its nave roof to its arches and many of its windows. They fashioned the tomb recess with its three quaint heads, and the grotesque monsters with flowing manes on the little priest's door. There are some coffin lids 700 years old, a timber almsbox possibly older, and two Tudor bench-ends richly carved with crowns and lions and solemn angels. A modern lychgate is touchingly dedicated to a mother in memory of her care and teaching; and among the church's neighbours are Langham Hall, a modern house with old panelling on its walls inside, and Church Farm, a 17th century house with a two-storeyed porch.

One of the most delightful houses hereabouts is Valley House of the 16th century, with a staircase wing and a most attractive porch added a few decades later. The porch has four big brackets carved with spiral ornament, and the staircase is fine with exquisite balusters, rich newel posts, a series of carved vases, and a quaint figure of a woman. Not soon forgotten is Valley House, with its buttresses and windows and triple chimney-stacks, all making a fine array.

LANGLEY. Its cottages, thatched and timbered, stand back in their gardens beside the path to the church; and its hall, from Cromwell's days, is carrying on as a farm, with the original bargeboards still on its gables. From the churchyard we look far over undulating country rich with woods. Some of the tower is 600 years old, and so is its pointed arch, but the nave was first built 800 years ago and has kept its Norman doorway. The roof has a double hammerbeam carved in the 15th century, and all round the tops of the walls are deeply carved wall-plates grey with age.

The Tudor Age rebuilt the chancel in red brick, but it has the arms of the Stuarts in glass over the altar.

Rich Brass

LATTON. A charming place, it shares a wild common with its big neighbour Harlow, but has a medieval church of its own in the park of Mark's Hall. It has fragments of Roman Britain in its walls, bricks handled by the Saxons and the Normans and worked into this 15th century church.

Between the little chapel and the chancel the founder lies in an altar tomb, richly panelled under a carved canopy. He is Peter Arderne, and on the tomb is his brass portrait showing him in his judge's robes, his wife beside him in a rich horned headdress. On the floor are brasses of other Ardernes, a man in armour and a woman in a veil. More magnificent is the dress of Frances Frankelin, laid to rest here in 1604. The brocaded silk, engraved in brass, is a work of art, and the brasses of her son and daughter show the lovely clothes the children wore then. There is Jacobean costume on the brasses of Emanuell and Margaret Wollaye close by. On the walls of the chancel are two monuments of another family flourishing here 300 years ago, James Altham and his wife kneeling in alabaster in front of a prayer desk, their three sons and eight daughters in a row below.

But it is the little chapel of which we may have a peep over Peter Arderne's tomb which brings back olden times. Heads of strange beasts guard its windows outside, and inside a wagon roof curves down to coloured and gilded mouldings, under which frescoes can be traced on the walls. Over the arch of the tomb many faces remain of a Nativity scene; wings of angels appear on the splays of a very narrow peephole, and above it the sculptor has suggested the Almighty appearing in a cloud. On another wall is a painting of St Christopher at the ford. A handsome chantry chapel this must have been in the dying days of the medieval age.

A curiously roofed barn a mile away recalls that time of change. Within is all that is left of Latton Priory, lovely 14th century arches of the monastic church; yet so deserted had it become that it is on record that its last prior, John Taylor, walked out of it in 1534 and that it then fell into secular uses.

The Flag That Flew at Jutland

LAWFORD. A deep valley divides its roadside cottages from those remote on the hill where the church stands above the gleaming waters of the Stour. By the gateway of the church is the gateway of the park of Lawford Hall, a timbered house of Armada days, with oak mullioned windows in its wings and 16th century roundels in its windows. One of the roundels has a delightful figure of St Quirinus in armour and another has St Richard of Chichester in his cope. Standing by great lime trees and ivy-covered elms, the 15th century church tower looks venerable. The timbered porch has stood 600 years with a face looking down from the middle of the roof.

It is the white ensign that meets our eyes as we come in, a thrilling one, for it flew at the battle of Jutland on the destroyer Abdiel. The village peace memorial has these fine words:

> When the Almighty shook the nations and scattered kings, these Lawford men gave their lives for freedom and justice.

The chancel is famous hereabouts for the marvellous detail of its delicately carved stonework, all the work of a 14th century craftsman. Each of its eight side windows is beautiful with tracery, no two alike, and some of them have fragments of old glass. Above these windows are richly carved arcades with owls and an amazing chain of quaint figures performing a vigorous Morris Dance, some holding each other by the leg or the hair, some playing musical instruments, some with flutes or birds or squirrels. There is a superb sedilia below the windows, ending in a priest's doorway opening out behind a buttress. The delicate carving below the curves of the arches is magnificent, and, though battered by time, still holds us by its beauty, with tiny figures in the spandrels, crowned heads, and musicians above the priest's door.

In an arched recess kneels Edward Waldegrave and his wife Joan, both as they were in the days before the Armada; he died when Lawford Hall was new. On a tablet we are told that Dean Merivale was rector here for over 20 years last century; he is remembered by two sorts of people—by sportsmen because he rowed in the first university boat race, and by scholars because he wrote a famous history of the Roman Empire.

Little Baddow   A Picturesque Lock

Danbury   The Village Pond

Woodham Ferrers
Bicknacre Priory

Little Leighs
Priory Gatehouse

Upminster   St Laurence's Church   **Leigh**   St Clement's Church

Hornchurch
The Graceful Medieval Church

Fryerning
The Magnificent Brick Tower

Great Dunmow   The Ancient Church and the Tudor Town Hall

Layer Marney   The Marvellous Gatehouse

The Broken Dream

LAYER MARNEY. Who sees it once does not forget it ever. Here for 400 years has stood one of the most imposing buildings in England, the gatehouse of the home Sir Henry Marney planned for himself in the place where his ancestors had lived from Norman times. Alas, he had ancestors but no descendants. He died before his wonderful house was finished, and the next year died his only son without an heir.

Sir Henry Marney was one of the trusted friends of kings, Privy Councillor to Henry the Seventh, traveller to the Courts of France and Italy, Captain of the Guard and Keeper of the Privy Purse. So it was that he persuaded the king's architect, Girolamo de Travizi, to design his new house. He made it one of the amazing sights of Essex. The gatehouse is of brick and terracotta, the black bricks forming a pattern among the red. It stands 80 feet high, turrets of eight storeys flanking two great windows above the archway. The lower turrets climb beside them, while two square turrets rise to the full height behind. There are transomed windows, Corinthian capitals, and Italian scroll work, and the parapets are richly decorated, those of the turrets with little dolphins. The two remaining fluted chimneys, equal in beauty to those at Hampton Court, are a fitting crown to this marvellous place.

On each side of the gatehouse are wings two storeys high with fine windows and doorways, and fitted with splendid fireplaces. But the place was never finished, for the dreamer of this magnificence, made a baron in 1522, was borne to rest in 1523 in the church he had built beside the house. He is on a splendid tomb by the tomb of his son John, his features chiselled in fine black Cornish marble by an Italian sculptor. Near them is the elaborate tomb and armoured figure of Sir William Marney who died in 1360, and round this tomb, silent watchers since Sir Henry refashioned the church, sit carved leopards on spiral posts, grasping shields with Marney badges.

There are two beautiful screens in the church, the chancel screen with rich tracery of the 15th century, the other with Tudor linenfold. The pulpit, too, is linenfold with a 17th century canopy, and a bookrest finely carved. On the wall is a painting of St Christopher carrying the Child, and in a window of the Marney Chapel is fine heraldic glass. Tower and turret, porch and walls, are all embattled, fitting well into this scene, and in front of it all the Green slopes away toward the coast beyond a lovely garden.

LEADEN RODING. The cottages are at the cross-roads; the church has stood since Norman times by a farmstead nearer the River Roding. It has a doorway the Normans made in the nave, and a chancel leading out of it with no intervening arch, built in the 13th century. The 14th century font has the staples into which the cover was padlocked so that witches should not steal the water for their magical rites; the font cover was adapted for the staples in the 17th century, reminding us that the Reformation did not reform away the old belief in witchcraft. Many a sermon against witches would be preached from this perfect little 16th century pulpit. It stands on a trumpet-shaped stem and its eight narrow panels have tracery at the top and quatrefoils below.

Sentinel of London's River

LEIGH. It stands on a hill which may justly be called a sentinel of London's river, and the imposing tower has been a landmark to seamen for 400 years. Figures holding shields look down from the original roof of the church on the oldest portraits in Leigh, the ancestors of her most famous sons. There are two brasses on the same stone with 26 portraits in all, Richard Haddock, his wife, and their 10 children, with his son, his two wives, and their 11 children, all in Tudor costume. In one century this family gave two admirals and seven captains to the navy, and the family still cherishes a cap which Charles the Second took off his head and put on the head of Richard Haddock after a battle in which his ship had been wrecked. There are brasses in the chancel to Richard Chester, a master of Trinity House in the 17th century, and to Captain John Price of Queen Anne's day. Another master of Trinity House has a painted bust here, showing him in his ruff as he was in Civil War days. He is described in pompous language as the great instrument of God's glory and the Commonwealth's good, restorer of Navigation almost lost, whatever that may mean. We may be sure he would be at the funeral of William Goodlad, who died a year or two before him after having been commander of the Greenland fleet for 20 years. There is a tablet placed here by four sons in memory of another seaman, their father William Brand, who commanded the

Revenge at Trafalgar; *all four sons lived to see the centenary of the battle.*

It is said that the Mayflower called at Leigh for provisions, and it may well be so, for her flour was milled at Billericay not far away. In one of Leigh's old buildings is a loft which two centuries ago was the meeting-place of smugglers. Today its sham romance has been turned into a real romance, for it is the meeting-place of Toc H, one of the noblest legacies of the Great War.

Jack Cornwell and David Livingstone

LEYTON. Here came into the world the best-known boy of the Great War, and here went out into the world the best-known man of Africa. Leyton and its companion Leytonstone have memories of many great folk, but supreme among them are the immortal figures of Jack Cornwell and David Livingstone. In this maze of homes between Epping Forest and the River Lea one lowly house stands out in Clyde Place, Capworth Street, for here was born the boy who won the VC at the Battle of Jutland. We come upon Jack Cornwell at Little Ilford, where he went to school and where he now lies, but it was here that he was born, and the children of Leyton have put a tablet to their hero in the church of All Saints, close to his birthplace.

The church is a storehouse of Old Leyton, with many names of folk famous before Jack Cornwell, and with views and manuscripts and portraits framed in the galleries. It was rebuilt last century except for the tower, which comes from Cromwell's time and has under its domed cupola a bell 600 years old. There is nothing older here, but brasses show us Ursula Gasper of 1483 and the Jacobean family of Tobias Wood, his wife, and their 12 children, with a punning verse about woods and trees. Five members of the Hicks family appear as lifesize figures under the tower, Sir Michael, secretary to Queen Elizabeth's Lord Burghley, lying in his armour with his wife under a double canopy, their heads on their hands, while Sir William, who died in 1688, lies on another tomb with one of his sons beside his wife. Sir Michael has an epitaph which suggests that he wrote it himself, looking back on his happy life as a courtier:

Those things I desired in life I attained; pledges lately deemed the sweetest, a dear wife and a fortune. I was happy in my family; two sons and a daughter call me father. I began to long for Christ, therefore I willingly yield to death; willingly I leave wife, fortune, sons, and daughter.

There is an interesting group of memorials, some by Flaxman. On Sir Robert Beachcroft's stone of 1721 is carved his lord mayor's fur cape, sword, and mace; an 18th century merchant has an angel with folded wings as a tribute to his memory. There is a tablet to William Bowyer, one of 20 printers permitted to follow their trade in Charles Stuart's England, and the print of a lost monument shows Sir William Ryder, the haberdasher who introduced woollen stockings into England from Italy about the time Raleigh was bringing tobacco from America. Another print shows Samuel Kempe, a Leyton vicar, who is wearing the soldier's buff coat he wore when he preached in Cromwell's time, having first placed his pistol on the cushion in front of him, beside the Bible. There is a Flaxman sculpture of a girl reading a book in memory of John Hillerson, and a wall-tablet also believed to be Flaxman's, with the Good Samaritan. Other odd treasures here are a 17th century poor-box with a carving of a lame man, an hourglass brought from Munich in 1693, an old beadle's staff, an ancient map by John Speed, some illuminated and jewelled parchments, and a fragment of a brass discovered in a kitchen.

There is a little medieval glass in a small window in the south-west porch, a beautiful window under the west gallery given by the Girl Guides, and four fine heraldic windows, the one nearest the east having below it a parchment with the autograph of the King of Greece, who was here when the window was unveiled at a Masonic service. Poets and artists have combined to make two beautiful modern windows, inspired by Matthew Arnold and G. K. Chesterton. One is of the Good Shepherd, with a goat in his arms and these lines from Matthew Arnold:

He saves the sheep, the goats He doth not save.
So rang Tertullian's sentence,
And on his shoulders not a lamb, a kid.

The other window of a blue Madonna with the Child in her arms is inspired by these lines of Chesterton:

The Christ Child lay on Mary's lap
His hair was like a light.

In the churchyard lie a soldier and a vicar with astonishing records of service. The soldier was William O'Brian who served 60 years in the Army when it was not much older than he was. He died in 1733 and four years later died old John Strype aged 94, having been vicar here for 68 years, during which time he became famous as an antiquarian, wrote lives of Cranmer and other archbishops, and gave Leyton its church house, with a handsome doorway; he lived in it himself. John Strype's father came to London as a refugee, and John was born at Houndsditch, went to St Paul's School and on to Cambridge, and grew up to divide his time between preaching and writing, becoming vicar of Leyton in 1669 and remaining here till he died in 1737. All the time he was writing history and biography in his own rough way, accumulating a remarkable mass of curious information. His works were reprinted in 19 volumes early last century, but are now of little value. Dying at 94, he outlived his wife and all his children and much lamented that he left so much work undone. He wrote his own Latin epitaph, which has been inscribed on a memorial brass in the chancel floor, and there is a marble engraved with his coat-of-arms which has been remarkably preserved and is now under glass.

Here also lies Sir John Strange, who began life as a solicitor's clerk, and used to carry his master's bag to Westminster, where he saw a judge take his seat as Master of the Rolls, little imagining that he would occupy the seat himself. He sat in Parliament, was one of those who inquired into the conduct of Sir Robert Walpole, took part in the impeachment of Lord Lovat, and was Master of the Rolls for three years before they laid him here in 1754.

Among all these interesting people there lies also in the churchyard Sir John Cotton, who went to sea at 15 and lived through the exciting years of Napoleon. In the days when Trinity House raised 1200 volunteers to safeguard the mouth of the Thames Pitt was colonel and Cotton was lieutenant-colonel. He wrote a book which gives much information about our coast lights at that time, and was awarded a medal for bringing from the East a grass of remarkable fineness and strength. His son William, who lies at Leytonstone, was a director of the Bank of England, and is remembered as having invented the automatic weighing machine for sovereigns; in his day it could weigh 23 a minute, accurate to the ten-thousandth part of a grain. He was the first man to stop the practice of paying men's wages by orders on a public house, and though not very rich was a great philanthropist and delighted in building churches.

Leyton, which has brought Leytonstone within its bounds, has had a delightful mace made for the new borough, modelled on one made for the House of Commons in the time of the Stuarts; it is 48 inches long. In the Central Library is a tablet in memory of the Old Boys of Leyton's schools who fell in the war; it was presented by the teachers of all the schools of the town, and each week a page of the Book of Remembrance is turned over so that the records of all the schools come round in their turn. At a library in Fairlop Road is a bronze plate recording the fact that John Drinkwater was born here. He must have loved these forest scenes in his boyhood, as William Morris used to do, for he, too, was an Essex lad, born at Walthamstow.

Leytonstone has a Roman milestone still standing, and its name comes from it; it gives the distance from London to Epping. There are several 19th century churches, St Andrew's built by Sir Arthur Blomfield, and St John's built largely through the enthusiasm of William Cotton, the bank director who lies in it. It is a white brick structure with stone dressings, a pinnacled tower, and a graceful spire. Its first vicar was a friend of David Livingstone, who came to stay with him on the eve of his journey to Africa. Here he received his last Communion from his friend before sailing for the Dark Continent on a mission which was to bring light to a thousand dark places and to him everlasting fame.

LINDSELL. An out-of-the-way place in beautiful country near Dunmow, it has a church of many centuries hidden among trees and barns, its oldest feature a Norman chancel arch, and its most curious a Tudor tower built as an extension of the aisle. The chancel has 13th century windows used again by 18th century rebuilders, and there is a tiny 700-year-old doorway for the priest, with a mass dial to tell him the time. Just as old are the remains of a saintly figure in glass in the east window, which also has medieval pictures of men and women at prayer, a Madonna and Child with an archbishop, and the arms of Walden Abbey. There are a few old tiles with an eagle among their designs, a panelled 15th century font, a medieval dug-out chest, and a peephole with a carving above it of a solemn man with curly hair. He was probably one of the supports of the roodbeam. Thomas Fytche of 1514 is here in his fur-trimmed cloak, with his wife, six sons, and five daughters, all on brass.

The Nine Roundels

LISTON. Its fine red tower is Tudor brickwork, and stands in a churchyard with neatly trimmed yews, by the side of Liston Hall park. One of the two bells is older than the tower, but far older than both is the Norman nave, which has a small doorway ornamented in the 12th century with zigzags and flowers. The chancel was made wider in the 13th century, but has kept its Norman wall at the east. A Tudor door is still swinging in the porch, and inside are handsome roofs 400 years old, that in the chancel having four angels looking down. A 15th century beam takes the place of the chancel arch, and there is a 15th century font, poor battered thing. The chancel has a medieval wooden seat, and the organist has a 17th century stool. One of the windows is delightful with glass new and old. It has nine charming roundels of Bible scenes, and in the tracery are figures coloured 500 years ago, the clearest being the Madonna holding a palm leaf and an orb. The others are probably St Anne, St George, Mary Magdalene, and St Michael. The church has a pathetic link with one of the most tragic events in the history of the Empire, the Massacre of Cawnpore. We read here how Robert Thornhill, his wife, their two little ones, and a faithful nurse, were cruelly massacred after 66 days and nights of extreme suffering; and how Henry Thornhill and his family had already been murdered at Neetapore in those bitter days of the Mutiny.

LITTLE BADDOW. It has a Nonconformist chapel two centuries old but in the walls of its church are tiles almost 20 centuries old, Roman tiles forming the arch of a door which may be the work of the Saxons. But it is for the treasures it has preserved from the 13th century that the lover of the old and the beautiful comes. Along the nave run richly carved arches with tiny heads peeping out from their massed foliage. Under each of these arches lies a carved oak figure in the costume of the days when the Black Prince went off to the wars. Here is a man in a long gown with hood and short sleeves, with a slit from the ankle to the knee to make walking possible. His companion is a lady with a veiled headdress touching her shoulders and pointed shoes peeping from her long gown to rest on a dog. The sides of their low tombs have carved panels with shields and support an iron railing with fleur-de-lys on the uprights, the work of smiths who may have fashioned armour for soldiers at Agincourt. There are only a hundred oak figures like these in all England.

In glowing colour St Christopher stands out on a wall in all the freshness of the 14th century, the Child holding a little cross from which waves a pennon. To the same 14th century belong the grotesque heads below the parapet of the tower, the hooded men and women forming stops to windows, and two gems of glass with St George on a turret and St Michael striking the Dragon.

In the sanctuary is a splendid tomb of 1639, holding all that is mortal of Henry Mildmay, who fought in Ireland. He lies with his head on his right hand and has a truncheon in his left. His two wives kneel at a desk, one an old lady in scarf and hood. They lived at Graces, a 16th century house a mile away with an avenue of elms a mile long running to the road beside the Chelmer river.

The Saxon Tower

LITTLE BARDFIELD. Its hall is a beautiful Tudor house with overhanging gables, ornamental plaster, and old woodwork within; and the luxuriant elms and chestnuts in its grounds almost hide the church's great Saxon tower. For 900 years this tower has been standing, and a remarkable structure it is, 22 feet wide. All its five stages are Saxon except for the herringbone masonry at the top and the new battlements, and there are Saxon windows cut straight through the pebble and flint walls. A little modern spire rises above the battlements. The nave has Roman tiles and is Saxon too, with a blocked Saxon window keeping company with others of the 14th and 15th centuries. St Catherine, to whom the church belongs, is outside the small medieval porch, and there are 15th century arches from the nave to the tower and to the 600-year-old chancel. There is a Jacobean chest, and a chancel stall about the same age fitted with poppyheads of Henry the Eighth's time; but the most interesting possession of the church is the organ with its carved case, for it is thought to be the work of the famous builder Renatus Harris about the year 1700. He it was who competed with the still more famous Father Smith when a new organ was needed for Temple Church in London, each man building an organ which was tried before the Benchers. Father Smith's won, perhaps because it was played by the immortal Purcell.

LITTLE BENTLEY. A very tiny place, it lies in a well-wooded district, its neat green in front of a churchyard ringed by limes and chestnuts. Both nave and chancel are Norman, with Roman bricks in the chancel walls. The embattled porch was built about 1520, at the same time as the splendid hammerbeam roof of six bays. The handsome 16th century tower has curious gargoyles. An octagonal font of 1500 is ornamented with the arms of the Pyrtons, and there is a brass portrait of Sir William Pyrton, who died in 1490, in the chapel. We found here an old hourglass stand, a coffer of the 16th century, and eight poppyheads on bench-ends 400 years old. The parish register has an entry in shorthand for about 1650.

The Big Barn's Small Neighbour

LITTLE BRAXTED. Here the Blackwater river runs beneath the willows. A timbered house and a huge thatched barn have stood by the tiny church for nearly 400 years. Only 45 feet long, the church walls remain as the Norman builders left them, having completed one of those perfect apses which gave such charm to their early buildings. In the 13th century lancet windows were inserted and in the 15th century the roof was made new. Great beams support the wooden belfry. William Roberts is in brass on the chancel floor, with his two wives in pedimental headdresses and groups of their children. He was one of the precious auditors who served Henry the Seventh in restoring the finances of the nation after the Wars of the Roses. A last-century vicar has left his mark on the walls, which he decorated with his brushes and paints.

As Per Margin

LITTLE BURSTEAD. It looks across the flat country stretching to the Thames, and has two Elizabethan houses, Hatches Farm and Stockwell Hall. The hall has a great clock with a face on which the figures are in blackened bones. The tiny church is 700 years old, built on a knoll and seen from afar. The nave is only 12 yards long, its west end filled with grand old beams supporting the medieval turret and its shingled spire. The tower arch is fashioned from the timbers. There is a brass engraved with skulls in memory of Mary Walton of 1678, and under the chancel lies that Sir George Walton who served under Rodney, captured a squadron of Spanish ships at one fell swoop, and in reporting to the Admiralty wrote, "the number as per margin."

There is a little medieval woodwork preserved from the old screen and worked into the new, a little more in the modern reredos, and the church has treasured a piece of oak with fading colours which formed a background to a little altar before the Reformation. Two windows have delicately coloured glass of the 17th century, one with portraits of Christ and eight Apostles, each in a perfect little landscape. They are gems, probably by an artist from Flanders. One has Philip carrying a rustic-looking cross as he goes out to evangelise the world. The font is 15th century, and so is the roof, and on the doorway are mass dials by which the village told the time in the days before clocks.

A Tudor Masterpiece

LITTLEBURY. Its cottages line two Roman roads by the River Cam, and its ancient stronghold a mile away is hidden among the trees, an oval earthwork of 16 acres with a ditch 50 feet wide. The church is at the cross-roads, and has a 14th century tower, a Norman nave, and 13th century aisles. The two porches have vaulted roofs left unfinished by 15th century builders, and one of them shelters a beautiful doorway made at the great change of style from Norman into English, its capitals showing both the Norman waterflower ornament and the stiff foliage which was to be so popular with 13th century carvers. The other porch has a true 13th century doorway, and in it is a magnificent nail-studded door which has been opening and closing for 500 years. It has a little wicket, and is carved with two pairs of shears to remind us of Littlebury's ancient connection with the wool trade. There is a lectern whose stem and base were carved in the 15th century, two handsome chairs from Stuart days, and an attractive modern screen, the work of a son in memory of his father, a churchwarden. But the masterpiece of woodcarving here is the Tudor structure which completely encloses the 13th century font. Three tiers of linenfold panelling form a case with double doors, the hinges engraved with swords and other devices; and, rising from a carved cornice, is an elaborate pyramid top, with buttresses and pinnacles leading up to a figure of Our Lord. It is of rare beauty, rivalled in Essex only by the font cover at Thaxted. The church has a 19th century wall-painting of the Crucifixion; and a memorial to one of its modern benefactors, Lord Braybrooke, who rebuilt the chancel.

Quite a gallery of Littlebury folk are here in brass, from a man with a long robe and a curious hat, who died just before the Tudor Age began, to Anne Byrd, with a ruff and high-crowned hat from Jacobean times, she being possibly a kinswoman of the immortal William Byrd whom we come upon at Stondon. One of the last priests before the Reformation is shown in his robes, holding a chalice and a wafer; a man and his wife are shown from the same time; a civilian of about 1520 has a portrait not very flattering, perhaps engraved by an unskilled village craftsman; and Jane Bradbury is here in a fine Elizabethan dress, with striped sleeves and a French hood. A brass inscription to James Edwards, who died of the plague in 1522, is interesting as an early example of the use of Arabic figures, the 5 being a curious shape. It is interesting also because he was a bailiff working for the Bishop of Ely, which reminds us of the ancient link between the village and the bishopric. In Norman times the manor belonged to the Bishop, who is said to have had his house where Gatehouse Farm now stands. The farm is a gabled Tudor building, with a roof sweeping down very low.

600-Year-Old Glass

LITTLE CANFIELD. The Romans marched this way along Stane Street, and the Normans began the church set apart among the trees. Their work is in the walls of the nave and in its doorway. The tower and its stone spire are modern, but the chancel and some of the windows are 14th century, and there are fragments of 600-year-old glass. There is a graceful screen richly carved in those days, a porch with handsome tracery of about 1500, modern corbels with striking angel heads, a 17th century chest and a much rarer one probably 700 years old, fashioned of oak boards framed in broad corner posts. Kept in cases in the vestry are the brightly coloured statuettes used here at Christmas time to make up a little scene of the Nativity, Mary and Joseph bending over a crib, a shepherd blowing a pipe, a kneeling king in a green robe, an ox, and an ass. A charming sight they must make by candlelight. Here sleeps Anne Pudsey of 1593, her figure engraved in brass, her son with cloak and sword keeping her company. Another brass to William Fytche of 1578 is complete except for William; he has vanished, leaving a wife on either side and nine children below.

The Old Farmhouse

LITTLE CHESTERFORD. Here among the willows on the banks of the River Cam is one of the oldest farmhouses we have seen. It was built as a manor house at the time of Magna Carta and has kept much from those far-off days, though much was changed in the 16th century when the stack of Tudor chimneys was built in. The oldest part of the house is the kitchen wing, from which two deeply moulded doorways lead into a central hall with something of its ancient timber roof still left. It is astonishing to look up at these oak posts, with their moulded capitals, and to remember that they have been here since about the year 1275.

The little church close by has its nave and chancel under a 15th century roof. The doorway and some of the windows are 14th century, but there are two nave windows which have been letting in the light since the old farm was first built. There is a brass portrait of Isabel Langham as she was in the early days of the Tudors, and a handsome screen carved a few years after she died. On an 18th century monument to a descendant of the great Elizabethan statesman Sir Francis Walsingham is a finely carved figure of James Walsingham in a classical robe, a cherub watching over him. Among some fragments of Tudor glass is a rebus on the name of John Islip, the abbot of Westminster whose beautiful little chapel is in the Abbey. The rebus shows an eye with a hand holding a little branch and the word Slip, as in the front of his chapel at Westminster. Other fragments of glass are 200 years older, and show eagles, fleur-de-lys, and a shield of the Peverells.

LITTLE CLACTON. A neat group of houses lines a wide road running to the sea. Facing the little green at a bend in the road is the plaster-covered church, with a quaint 15th century timber turret containing three bells, one almost as old as Agincourt. A small Norman window in the chancel suggests that the building is as old as St Osyth Priory a few miles away. The font is also Norman.

The Dunmow Flitch

LITTLE DUNMOW. All the world knows it for the Flitch of Bacon which for so long was given here yearly to a married couple who had no quarrels. The custom was as old as anything in Little Dunmow, going back to the days of Robert Fitzwalter, one of the Magna Carta men. It is believed that he built the great white columns with five arches in the nave of the church; certainly he edified the church and adorned it, and a tablet set up in 1915, on the 700th anniversary of Magna Carta, tells us that he was the founder of our civil liberty and marshal of the Army of God and the founder of this Church. He was the leader in that struggle which bore fruit at Runnymede, and one of the executors appointed to see that the provisions of Magna Carta were carried out. He lived for twenty years after seeing the fruits of the struggle of the Barons, and he lies here in an unknown grave.

The story told of the Dunmow Flitch is that Robert Fitzwalter, when lord of the manor, offered the Flitch to the man who had not repented of his marriage for a year and a day, the man having to take an oath to that effect before the prior, the monks, and the townsmen. The custom survived the Dissolution of the Monasteries, and records of the court awarding the Flitch in the 18th century hang on the walls of the church, which is all that remains of the old priory, except that if we call at the cottages or the farms we shall come upon pieces of wood or stone brought from the priory ruins; they are built into the barns and gabled houses of the 15th, 16th, and 17th centuries. In the church also is the prior's chair used in olden days at the court which made the award each year. It is made up of 13th century oak, though the top rail is 15th century. The successful claimants of the Flitch of Bacon were enthroned in the chair, and it is interesting to know that a document of the priory preserved in the British Museum has the names of three men to whom the Flitch was delivered in 1445, 1467, and 1510.

There is a tomb of a Walter Fitzwalter of those days lying with his wife with painted shields about them, he in armour with an elaborate belt and his head on a helmet, she supported by angels at her head and two dogs at her feet and wearing a sleeveless gown, a narrow hip belt, and a corded cloak in the fashion of 500 years ago. A kinswoman of this lady lies in similar costume on an altar tomb under another bay of the old arcade, an attractive figure in alabaster.

The bell-turret of the church rests on the masonry which formed the corner stones of the priory's central tower. There is a wonderful array of beauty in stone on the south wall, delicately carved with animals and tiny flowers; it is set in panels and runs along at the level of the windowsills, and we noticed among the animals a goat, a mouse, a sheep, a pigeon, and a dragon. The font and a beautiful pillar piscina are both 600 years old, and there are two coffin lids of the same time. The shafts of the east window come down to the floor. Built into a wall are about a dozen brightly coloured 14th century tiles, on one of which a man and a woman are exchanging rings under a tree.

In the pulpit are seven lovely panels of 15th century wood tracery, and in the altar rails and reading desk are ten more pieces of medieval carving. A delightful little cherub with its mouth firmly set and its eyes wide open looks out from the back of the priest's chair. In the sanctuary is a mourning figure holding a medallion portrait of Sir James Hallett who was buried here 200 years ago.

One interesting piece of family history we came upon in the register here. There was a John Bull of Little Dunmow long ago, and five of his nine daughters married brothers and cousins named Portway, so that five sisters became Mrs Portway at these altar rails.

A Magna Carta Champion

LEGEND, ballad, and history combine to keep green the memory of Robert Fitzwalter, who has slept here for seven centuries. Divested of fable, he stands clean-cut in history as a dauntless champion of liberty. He was born to great possessions in London and in the counties. As long as his sense of right permitted, he was loyal to John, although, disgusted at the king's infamy, he surrendered a French castle he was defending. For this he was imprisoned and held to ransom.

Restored to favour, he saw the mismanagement of the kingdom

at close quarters, and is believed to have been a party to the appeal to the French king to invade England and dethrone the tyrant John. The plot betrayed, he fled to France, but his pardon was a condition of John's absolution when he surrendered the crown, and became the vassal of the pope. Fitzwalter was appointed "Marshal of the Host of the Lord and Holy Church" which marched to force Magna Carta on the king, and was one of the 25 barons appointed to insist on the execution of its provisions. He was a principal figure in the fighting that followed, and was excommunicated by the pope when the charter was annulled.

One of the two nobles sent to France to call in the aid of the Dauphin, he remained loyal to King Louis after his landing until all was fortunately lost at the Battle of Lincoln, where the Baron was taken prisoner and the charter confirmed. He afterwards went on Crusade, but was back in time to see Henry the Third subscribe to the Great Charter, and he passed to his grave in 1235 with the promise of national rights and freedom fully assured. None had striven harder or suffered more for its accomplishment than he.

The House of a Great Lady

LITTLE EASTON. It used to be rather like a fairyland to the traveller who was happy enough to find himself in Lady Warwick's garden, or having tea with her in the stables. She was one of the great ladies of Queen Victoria's later days, a friend of Edward the Seventh, and, this house being too magnificent for her in the simpler days when she became a Socialist, she fashioned the stables into a beautiful place and lived here with her animals and flowers. In her park not a thing was ever killed or hurt; it mattered nothing if they came into the drawing-room The lawns were like velvet, and delightful it was to walk about the flagged paths, down the stone steps by the lily pools, through the pergolas and along the herbaceous borders. It seemed as if it had all been here for centuries, but Lady Warwick could say as she walked here, "I planted this, I planted that."

But the fairyland of other days has vanished. The great house (Easton Lodge) which stood here with all the grace and dignity of the 16th and 17th centuries about it, and was available for use on behalf of all the good causes Lady Warwick believed in, has been demolished. For 300 years the home of the Maynard family, Easton Lodge had outlived its day as one of the stately homes of England.

Lady Warwick, wife of the fifth Earl of Warwick, was the heiress of the last Viscount Maynard and the monuments of her ancestors can be seen here in the church that has stood here from Norman days, though much refashioned by our medieval builders. There are Roman tiles in the walls, gargoyles looking down from the 15th century tower, and a handsome tower arch leading us into the Norman nave. On one of the walls is a small seated figure painted there by an artist 700 years ago, and fading away are 500-year-old paintings of the last days of Our Lord in Jerusalem.

By the altar is the beautiful tomb of Lady Eleanor Bourchier placed here about 1400, and resting on it, though not belonging to it, is a miniature statue of a 13th century knight in mail armour. In the chancel is the brass portrait of a priest who would know this church 600 years ago, and on a richly canopied tomb between the chapel and the chancel are the brasses of Lord Henry Bourchier and his wife, who were laid here towards the end of the 15th century. Sir Henry's enamelled brass is one of only five in England showing a man wearing the Order of the Garter; his wife has a velvet mantle, faced with ermine, over a scarlet gown, with a coronet and two angels at her head.

Sir Henry Maynard lies in the chapel on an altar tomb of Shakespeare's day, he in armour and his wife wearing a farthingale. The carving on the cushions at their heads and in the detail of their dress is very beautiful. At the side of the tomb kneel their 10 children, five boys with skulls in their hands, the artist having quaintly varied their heights. Sir Henry was secretary to the great Lord Burghley, and on his tomb we read:

> Whence, who, and what I was, how held in court,
> My prince, the peers, my country, can report.

Wearing a loose dress, hood, and ruff, lies Lady Frances Maynard who died in 1613, and there are two other Maynards of the 17th century, one with a fine statue in Roman dress, one with his wife and a group of portraits in busts and medallions showing members of his family who are buried here. In front of this monument is a relief with five symbolical figures. The windows of the chapel are in memory of Lady Maynard of 1857; they are in rich dark colour.

Here are remembered two people famous in their day, one Lady Warwick's great friend Ellen Terry, who loved to worship here and is remembered in a portrait on a marble tablet; the other the fifth Earl of Warwick in whose name his widow placed these lines:

> *And now he rests; his greatness and his sweetness*
> *No more shall seem at strife;*
> *And death has moulded into calm completeness*
> *The statue of his life.*

A Bell's Six Centuries

LITTLE HALLINGBURY. Among many thatched cottages its shingled spire rises from a square wooden turret set up in Queen Anne's day. One of the bells has been ringing 600 years, keeping company all the time with a fine timber porch. The nave and part of the chancel (which was lengthened in the 13th century) are Norman. Roman bricks show the position of a lost Norman window, and form the arch and jambs of a Norman doorway, in which swings a door white with age after 500 years. The nave roof is 15th century, and the chancel roof Tudor. Curious things to find in a church are three Celtic urns from a gravel pit near the River Stort, made before the Romans came. One of the windows has pictures of St Etheldreda reading, and of Alan of Walsingham, the 14th century architect of the wonderful lantern of Ely Cathedral. But of nothing can the village be more proud than of the simple wooden tablet with the names of its heroes, among them G. H. T. Paton, the first Grenadier Guardsman to win the VC in the Great War. With his men only 50 yards from the enemy he walked up and down adjusting the line, and later, before he fell, led a heroic defence which saved the flank.

This village just missed the distinction of having the Charterhouse. The Earls of Essex held the patronage of Little Hallingbury down to Tudor days, when Thomas Sutton bought it with the intention of establishing Charterhouse here. He afterwards chose the old site in London (where his great house remained in dignity till the Nazis bombed it in 1940), but every Carthusian, man and boy, knows the name of this village well, as it comes every year into the service on Founder's Day, when the boys of the school come up from their new home in Godalming to fraternise with the men of the old Charterhouse in the City.

The Oak Figures and the Brass Portraits

LITTLE HORKESLEY. It is a fascinating place in rolling country, with two exquisite timbered houses of the 17th century and a church full of treasures, chief among them the wooden figures and brass portraits of lords of the manor.

An avenue of chestnuts leads through the churchyard, with a lovely view over the wooded valley of the Stour at one end and a 16th century porch at the other. The north wall of the church is three feet thick, probably part of the priory which has left its name to the farm next door. The Normans built this wall, and marks of 14th century masons are on the tower. With the 15th century came the arcade and the south aisle, the beautiful chapel screen with its mysterious holes (perhaps for the children to peep through), the delicate tracery in the lectern, the fragments of glass with glowing suns, and the plain font with a pinnacled oak cover like a little spire, 400 years old, but with new statues in its canopied niches.

Under the altar table is a broken altar stone with three consecration crosses still showing. The ironbound chest with a money slot is 16th century; the iron screen with fleur-de-lys on its standards is 17th; the railed bier with carved brackets has taken nine generations of village folk on their last journey.

The older inhabitants have left a priceless heritage in their memorials. First is a stone coffin lid with a raised cross, and then comes the rare group of three wooden figures. Only three other churches have so many and only Clifton Reynes in Buckinghamshire has more, while no other church has three such figures all from the 13th century. The two men are in mail, the younger one lying cross-legged with a lion at his feet and his heart in his hands, to show that only the heart was brought home for burial. The third is a woman eight feet long, wearing a short mantle looped at the elbows, and with two dogs at her feet. Once these oak figures were gay with paint and gilding, but only a trace of red remains. All three belong to the Horkesley family, lords of the manor till 1322, when they were succeeded by the Swynbornes, whose brass portraits here are unsurpassed in Essex.

Sir Robert Swynborne and his son Thomas are shown lifesize with their shields hung on their triple canopies and lions at their feet.

The father is in mail armour of 1391, and has his monogram on his
sword belt; the son is in plate armour. Only fragments are left of his
brother's brasses and that of the niece whose marriage brought the
Fyndornes here as lords of the manor. The wife of the last of them is
shown in a wonderful brass group on an altar tomb, lying between
her two husbands, Thomas Fyndorne and John, Lord Marney,
whose own sumptuous tomb is by the altar at Layer Marney. She
died in 1549, leaving instructions for this magnificent brass which
shows all three in rich heraldic costume, Thomas on a flowery
mount, Lord Marney on a lion, and Lady Bridget with a beautiful
coif on her head. A great contrast is the little shrouded brass of
Katherine Leventhorp, who died in 1502. The next lords of the
manor were the Husbands, whose brilliantly painted arms appear
on one of their memorials in the chancel.

Yet another precious thing is here, a painting by Van Hoeck, a
pupil of Rubens, showing the Wise Men. One has a rich yellow
robe held up by two delightful children, and two camels poke their
heads into the picture.

His Name Rang Round the World

LITTLE ILFORD. It is part of our great East End, linked to
East Ham, and sharing with Leyton its pride in Jack Cornwell.
There he was born; here he was at school, and in the cemetery of
Manor Park this youngest VC, not yet 17, was laid to rest, with the
First Lord of the Admiralty to deliver his funeral oration.

London has not quite swallowed up the ancient village, for the
church the Normans built for it 800 years ago still stands, only 50
feet long, with walls three feet thick. It has two Norman doorways
and three Norman windows, one opening into the chapel which,
with the chancel and the porch, was added at the beginning of the
18th century.

It was a schoolboy who brought this place fame, and a schoolboy's
brass portrait in the church is its rarest treasure. He is Thomas
Heron, and has in his girdle the pencase and inkhorn he was using in
school here over 400 years ago. Two children of Jacobean England
are also portrayed in brass, the girl with her ruff and lace collar, her
baby brother in swaddling clothes.

Facing each other on a marble memorial kneel the figures of

William Waldegrave, who died in 1610, and his wife, the tiny figures of their seven children kneeling under a ledge. In the chapel are the arms of France and England in 15th century glass, and the taking down of Our Lord from the Cross in a small panel of the 16th century. Here, too, is the great sarcophagus of Smart Lethieullier, the 18th century antiquarian who revealed the vast foundations of Barking Abbey, and whose epitaph tells us, among other things, that "he was a gentleman of polite literature and elegant taste, and richly possessed of the curious productions of Nature, but modestly desired no other inscription than what he had made the rule of his life—to do justly, to love mercy, and to walk humbly with his God." A tablet to William Fry, who died the year before his famous kinswoman Elizabeth, reminds us of another who loved mercy so much that she brought a little of it into our prisons.

Not far from this church is the Council School in Walton Road, now called Cornwell School after the boy who learned here to face death with the courage of a man before he was a man in years.

His name rang round the world. Jack was, of course, a Scout. It was his first ambition to go to sea, but it was his fate to begin life on a tradesman's van. When the war broke out he was allowed to go into training at Devonport, being then 14, and at 16 he became first class boy on HMS Chester, a light cruiser of Admiral Beatty's squadron. He was on this ship at Jutland when the German Navy tried to annihilate the British Fleet. In that great battle on the last day of May in 1916, Jack Cornwell was acting as sight-setter for the gun, and in five minutes his gun was out of action and Jack had received a mortal wound. Of the crew of ten round the gun eight were killed or wounded, but the boy would not take shelter. He stood there as Frank Salisbury has painted him, a noble type of English boyhood, waiting for England's word. He stood at his post till the end of the fight and was landed at Grimsby the next day and taken to hospital. Except for the officers his was the only name mentioned in the original despatches, and he received the Victoria Cross for an example of fortitude and courage that rang through England. His mother arrived in time to see him, but in 48 hours after the battle he had passed to his immortality, and before the nation knew his story this boy, who should have slept in Westminster Abbey, had been laid in Manor Park Cemetery at Little Ilford.

Here he is among the people who knew him as a van boy and a scout. His portrait was hung in thousands of schools. The Cornwell touch has become a familiar phrase, the Scouts have named after him their badge for highest fortitude, and his name is imperishable in the annals of great deeds.

LITTLE LAVER. Its village group clusters about a deep wide pool which would have pleased old Izaak Walton; we found his disciples sitting patiently under the trees. The church, the great barn, and the manor house have all tiled roofs. The church walls are 600 years old and have heads at the windows; the chancel has been rounded into an apse. The wonderful font is famous hereabouts; it was made about the year 1200 and its sloping sides have fleur-de-lys, crescents, stars, and leaves, all perfect.

Fragment of a Paradise

LITTLE LEIGHS. A little place with two lanes and the River Ter between them, it has a great reminder of the world of centuries ago—a church with a Norman nave and Roman bricks in its windows, and the ruins of a priory which are still magnificent. They are all that is left of the paradise set up here by Lord Chancellor Rich out of the vast spoils that fell to his share when Henry the Eighth seized the monasteries and made millions. Here he kept Princess Elizabeth prisoner in the reign of Mary Tudor, and here lived the Chancellor's descendants, worthier men than he, till 1673, when the place passed to the Earls of Manchester, then to the Dukes of Buckingham, and finally to Guys Hospital, whose Governors (we are sorry to say) destroyed it to save its upkeep. Today it is all a cared-for place again. Here flows the River Ter and down in its valley is this gem of Essex, the deep red buildings of the 16th century built on the site of the 13th century priory and with the gatehouses and courtyard of the priory itself. The river still shows us the ingenuity by which the monks filled their ponds, and the view of the medieval and Tudor buildings nestling in the valley is one of the most charming sights in the county.

What remains of the Tudor buildings is a group of two gatehouses and part of two sides of the outer quadrangle. The outer gatehouse has two storeys, and the original doors hang in the outer entrance; the inner gateway has three storeys with four turrets rising above its gables so that they almost hide four rich and lofty chimney shafts. The old doors of the inner gatehouse now hang in the inner archway of the outer gatehouse; they have panels with traceried heads, and at the ground level is a little door for dogs.

Through the inner gateway we pass into the inner courtyard, the cloister of the priory 700 years ago. In it stands a stately conduit built from stones of the monastic buildings; it has a pinnacled parapet. From the roof of the gateway we see the plan of the nave and transepts and tower of the old priory, and the white fragment of the tower remaining shows us how lovely this great white place must have been. Today there are lovely gardens surrounded by old brick walls, and this lovely place is a home again.

The small church, with the light still falling through windows shaped in Roman bricks, has two doorways 700 years old, one with its original door, a font and a roof 600 years old, and a very rare treasure in the 700-year-old chancel. It is the oak figure of a 13th century priest carved out of a log and showing him in his robes with his feet resting on two beasts, his head on cushions held by two angels. He is a very solemn figure and very beautiful, one of the hundred wooden figures that have survived from medieval England. He lies in a setting worthy of him, a recessed arch with a richly carved finial and shafts at each side with little heads at the pinnacles, and heads and acorns in the carving of the arch.

In the nave are ten Tudor pews, and in the chancel a 17th century chair with its rich red cover still unfaded.

The Little Round Church

LITTLE MAPLESTEAD. Here, in a village with gabled cottages 500 years old, stands something to be seen in only three other places in England. This little corner of Essex shares a distinction with London and Cambridge and Northampton, for it has one of our four medieval round churches (the London one, alas, in ruin as this book appears during the Battle for Britain). This is the smallest of the group and the youngest, but as beautiful as any of the others. It was built by the Knights Hospitallers 600 years ago, and has a handsome western doorway ornamented with two rows of square leaves, and with heads of a bishop and a queen. The nave is round, and the aisle goes round it, the entire width of nave and aisle being

30 feet. A most intriguing little place it is, with six very graceful snow-white columns enclosing the nave, and six arches bridging the aisle as we walk round it. There is a 14th century chancel with an apse.

In this remarkable building the Hospitallers worshipped for 200 years, until their preceptory here was dissolved under Henry the Eighth. The font may be nearly 300 years older than the church, and has had its square bowl cut into an eight-sided one. Its ornament includes arches and spirals and a cross. There is a brass tablet to John Harward, who died in 1912 after serving as vicar for 55 years. He was laid in his own churchyard at the great age of 93.

Three Doors of Four Centuries

LITTLE OAKLEY. We come to its cluster of cottages on our way from Harwich; one of them takes us back to the 17th century, while White House Farm is a century older. A cart track over a field brings us to the church in the shelter of limes and elms, and we come into it hardly realising the wonder of the place, for it has three doors four centuries old, the one on the south still with its original strap-hinges. The old west door has moulded battens, and the old tower door has ridged panels. Very few churches are so rich in old doors as Little Oakley. The tiny priest's doorway is cut through a wide buttress and has dripstones carved with Satanic faces. There is delicate stone carving of the 14th century over the piscina, and fragments of old glass 600 years old. The old folk here still speak of George Burmester, who baptised them and their fathers before them, for he came to the church in 1831 and served it till 1892, a span of 61 years.

Here Lies a Slave

LITTLE PARNDON. Here, in this tiny village in the lovely country by the River Stort, lies a slave, poor Hester Woodley, in a grave with elaborate carvings on its stones. She is, we think, only the second slave we have found in an English grave, the other being at Teston in Kent. She was apparently a black woman from Africa, and we have not been able to discover how she came to Little Parndon, but here she was a faithful servant of the Woodleys until she died in 1767. She lies outside the porch of the modern church, and it is explained that she belonged to Mrs Bridget until that lady died, when by reciprocal agreement she passed to her daughter. There is an hourglass on the stone to remind us that the sands of the time of slavery were running out when they laid Hester Woodley here to rest in her 68th year; even then there was living that poet who was to write with truth that slaves cannot breathe in England.

There lies in the church, with a marble monument on the wall, Sir Edward Turnor, who sat for Essex in the Parliament of the Commonwealth and kept his seat after the Restoration, when he was made a judge and took part in the prosecution of the men who tried the king. He became Speaker of the House of Commons. A little while after they laid him to rest there was born in the village another friend of the Stuarts, Charles Radcliffe, who took part in a Jacobite rising and was found guilty of treason. He was only 22 and would probably have been pardoned, but he broke out of Newgate with 13 other men and joined the Stuarts in exile on the Continent, becoming secretary to Prince Charles Edward. In 1745 he was captured on a ship carrying arms and in the following year was beheaded on Tower Hill under the sentence passed on him 31 years before. He bore himself courageously, and his dying speech was printed.

Old Companions

LITTLE SAMPFORD. Through a delightful pine wood we come to its two old companions, the church and the hall. The hall is handsome with windows and gables and chimneys of the 16th and 17th centuries, and has some beautiful old carving. There is a splendid staircase with richly carved pedestals, and an overmantel with heads and grotesques probably by Flemish craftsmen.

The church tower is given an unusual appearance by four octagonal turrets at the corners, and has in its walls the mark of one of the grimmest events in English history. Looking up at this masonry we can see where the 14th century workmen stopped to lay down their tools when the Black Death ravaged the land, the tower not being finished until the terrible days were over. How many of those who began the work came back to finish it, we wonder, for between the August of 1348 and the September of 1349 the pestilence carried away half the population of the land.

A weathervane of 1687 swings on the small lead spire, and the rest of the church looks low behind this tower. Its nave was about, 50

The Timbered 16th Century Wing

The 13th Century Chapter House
BEELEIGH ABBEY, MALDON

St Mary's Church, by the River

The Tower of St Peter's   South Aisle of All Saints

IN THE ANCIENT PORT OF MALDON

years old when the Black Death came, its aisle is 14th century, and its chancel was refashioned by men of the 15th century, who also built one of the porches somewhat askew. The other porch is a little 17th century one of red and blue bricks, and shelters a doorway as old as the nave.

There is a neat 14th century arcade, a plain screen which has kept company with ten oak seats since Tudor days, a chest cut from the solid about 600 years ago, an ancient vestry door with strap-hinges, and a little old glass showing canopy-work and shields. Two carvings by 15th century craftsmen show an angel holding a harp and the head of a lion with a wavy mane; but one of the most remarkable sights is a piece of woodcarving, at least 300 years old, fitted in the back of a chair in the chancel. It shows Christ with 11 apostles in a building, with God the Father above and a dove descending from heaven.

There is a tomb to Sir Edward Grene of 1556, with pillars, heraldic shields, and curious devices; and a monument with the figure of an Elizabethan soldier facing his wife as they kneel at a desk. The change of style which came over our monuments in the next 100 years is well shown by the elaborate tribute to Bridget Peck of Queen Anne's time, who reclines on one arm and holds a book, and is most incongruously dressed as a Roman matron.

LITTLE TEY. The walls of its church remain as the Normans built them, with their diaper work still in the tympanum of their door, and the round apse continuing on the walls of nave and chancel without a break, for there is no chancel arch. The church is so small that 50 paces would complete the round of it, and so low are the windows that a child can peep through them. There is a tiny 16th century turret with a bell dated 1701. Indoors is a hutch-shaped chest of Tudor workmanship, and in the windows are a few fragments of flowers in glass of the 15th century.

In the reign of Charles Stuart the rector was Erasmus Laud, and it is said here that some of the wrath felt by the people of Colchester for his famous namesake, the Archbishop, was poured on his unhappy head.

The Ancient Smithy's Work

LITTLE TOTHAM. The villagers live in a group of cottages a mile north of the old hall, among whose barns and trees the small Norman church is almost lost to view. The central part of the hall is 500 years old and has good timbering. Close by is a pond covered with lilies in due season. Pines, poplars, and young chestnuts give beauty to the spacious churchyard. We come into the church through a magnificent Norman doorway, a lovely example of about the year 1160, the shafts and the three orders of the arch elaborately carved. There is another Norman doorway blocked up. The 15th century font has on all its eight sides miniature carvings of varied styles of window tracery. The ancient craft of the smith, too, is well represented in the ironwork of the doors, foliage work of the 12th and 13th century. On a marble monument lie Sir John Samms and his wife, facing each other in prayer, he clad in his armour of Stuart days.

LITTLE WAKERING. Its church has a surprise indeed, for in it is a pillory, brought in from its old place on the churchyard wall. The village has a row of cottages 300 years old, with neat dormer windows; the hall is 15th century. Facing the old cottages is the church, restored by John Wakering, Bishop of Norwich, about the time of Agincourt. His crest of a pelican preening his feathers is carved on a white stone on the tower. Here was a church long before the bishop's day, for there is a small Norman window in the chancel, with traces of painting on its splays, and a handsome tomb recess as old as Magna Carta.

The Prentice Coat

LITTLE WALTHAM. Many of the farms and cottages round about go back to the 16th and 17th centuries, but a house near Winchford Bridge was built in the 15th century and has attractive woodwork. The church is older still, for its nave comes from Norman England and has kept a doorway and two windows all the time. The chancel was rebuilt about 1400, and the embattled tower is less than a century younger. Its weathervane of 1679 flies as a pennon above the handsome walnut trees in the churchyard. There is a spacious timber porch with beams and cornices and other woodwork by Tudor carpenters; a Tudor door on its old strap-hinges, a fine brass of John Maltun of 1447 who is shown with a dog at his feet and two tiny white cherubs; and an inscription to John Aleyne of 1663. John was a benefactor of the village who left money for the teaching of apprentices, and part of a lad's leather coat worn by one of them is still a curious treasure here. It is kept in a church chest, a magnificent object hollowed out of a sycamore about 700 years ago, and strongly bound with iron straps. Another chest was made in Shakespeare's day, and has a leather coat not in it but outside, the arched lid being covered with leather and initialled with the heads of nails.

The Tale of the Tattered Flag

LITTLE WARLEY. The woods about it rise and fall with the hills, and a row of pretty cottages lines the edge of a breezy common from which are fine views, while the old church stands by the hall on the arterial road to Southend. Built entirely of brick in the 16th century, the hall has great charm, especially the side facing the church, with black bricks making a rich pattern and a two-storeyed porch with a crow-stepped gable. Rising above the high-pitched roof are twin chimney shafts with spirals. The small church is a patchwork of materials, a 16th century chancel and 18th century tower of brick having been added to a nave of grey and white stone. We come in by a 15th century door, and are charmed with two cherubs holding back a canopy over the striking tomb of Sir Denner Strutt, who lies in armour below the figure of his first wife, with his second wife close by. Sir Denner sat in the first Parliament of Charles Stuart. On the wall is the brass portrait of a lady in Elizabethan dress, wife in turn to Davye Hamner and John Terrell. In a niche is a quaint alabaster figure of Father Time.

On the hilltop is the regimental chapel of the Essex Regiment, with Essex saints in the windows and the arms of Essex towns. Attached to the pillars of the nave are carved wooden lecterns preserving the roll of a battalion in the Great War. Flags adorn the church, but the flag most treasured is a faded fragment with Badajos on it, enclosed in a frame on the chancel wall.

It is a fragment with a thrilling tale to tell, the tale of the appalling Retreat from Kabul in the middle of last century. Thomas Alexander

Souter was a lieutenant of the Essex Regiment, one of the 700 men who marched with Indian and Afghan troops in 1841 to restore a ruler driven from his throne by Dost Mahommed. They did their work, and 4500 British troops were settled in Kabul, with 12,000 civilians. Then rose Akbar Khan, son of Dost Mahommed, who led a revolt, murdered the British officials, but promised a safe passage out of the country to the troops and civilians. It was a trick; the whole 16,000 soldiers and camp-followers were massacred except for one man who arrived to tell the tale at the gate of Jellalabad, and a small remnant of fewer than a hundred, with whom was Lieutenant Souter. The remnant made a final stand, and the lieutenant tore the tattered flag from its staff and wound it round his body while a little force of 80 men held the Afghans at bay till their last cartridges were spent. Souter was captured, and was allowed to write home a letter to his wife, in which he said:

In the conflict my posteen (sheepskin coat) flew open and exposed the colour. They thought I was some great man, looking so flash. I was seized by two fellows after my sword had dropped from my hand by a severe cut in the shoulder, and the pistol I had in my left hand missed fire. I threw it then upon the ground, and gave myself up to be butchered.

It happened that one of his captors had found a telescope among the lieutenant's possessions, and on Souter explaining its use to him the captor became friendly and allowed the lieutenant to keep the flag. He was still waiting for death, however, when a relief expedition arrived, and he came home and brought this flag with him.

The Zeppelin Calls

LITTLE WIGBOROUGH. Its medieval stone church has little enough to keep it company—a few cottages, a farm or two in fields running into marshland penetrated by creeks of the Blackwater river, that is all.

Yet it has a memory of something that had hardly ever happened in the world before when it happened here, for one September night in the Great War, when the Zeppelins were striking terror all over England, one of them came down, spread its 680 feet across the farm track leading to this church, and set up such a blaze as was never seen before in these flat Essex fields. It was the L33, one of a fleet of 12 Zeppelins which raided this country on September 23, 1916. Struck while trying to reach London, she at first tried to cross the sea, flying low and chased by our planes; then she came down, thundering like a score of goods trains and settling a few yards from a wooden cottage. The 22 Germans in her shouted a warning to the terrified inhabitants and then set fire to the Zeppelin, using their incendiary bombs; so fierce was the fire that the paint of the cottage was scorched. Carrying one of the crew who was wounded, the Germans threw away their arms and marched on the road towards Colchester, where they met a constable, to whom they made formal surrender.

Village Hampden

LOUGHTON. It is on the edge of Epping Forest, and it must for ever be proud of the Village Hampden who saved the forest from being stolen from the people. It has lost its old church, of which but a stone or two and a fragment of the churchyard wall remain, but on its site a church was built last century "in memory of all who lie in the churchyard."

In the new church are a few things from the old one: a little glass of two kneeling figures older than the Reformation, a charming little cupboard of the 16th century with a tiny painting of the Annunciation three inches deep, and four brasses with 26 people on them. Three of the brasses are 16th century; George Stonard in armour with his wife, John Stonard with two wives, and William Nodes with eight sons whose names are all given. The other brass is 17th century and shows Abel Guilliams kneeling with his wife and their ten children. In one of the windows is a charming figure of St Winifred in memory of a lady of Loughton who died in Samoa.

It was Thomas Willingale who made Loughton famous last century by his brave fight for the rights of the people to the freedom of Epping Forest. He was a poor villager who made a scanty living by gathering wood and grazing animals there. But in the middle of last century, when the lands of the people were being everywhere enclosed, even the Crown rights of Epping Forest were sold and the villagers were robbed of their rights. Willingale was then an old man, but the thought of this injustice was too much for him, and he flung himself into the battle for the preservation of a beauty spot and of customs as old as history. The Corporation of London came to his assistance in the end, and after 15 years of battles in Parliament and the courts a Royal Commission found that the old man was right and that the enclosures were illegal.

A vast sum of money was spent before Epping Forest was declared free for the people again, but in the end Queen Victoria went down and opened 6800 acres as a public place for ever.

Roman Bricks for the Norman Builder

MAGDALEN LAVER. Far from the road stands the ancient church, looking across the trees and fields to a network of wireless masts on the far horizon. The farm is its only neighbour now, but here once stood a Roman house. The Norman builders of the church picked up the red bricks from the ruins and set them in the corners of the nave. In the 15th century a wooden tower was added to the church. Some of the beams are of prodigious size, and it is an elaborate affair, with a pent-roof halfway up and a pyramid over the bell-chamber. The door, decorated with tiny four-leaved flowers, has swung on its iron hinges about 500 years, and the heavily riveted door into the belfry has also been opening and shutting for centuries in its Norman archway. One of two fonts between these doors has rich 15th century carving. There is fine work by a 14th century woodcarver in the screen, which has cusped arches below a row of circles enclosing quatrefoils, linking beauty with boldness; it is a masterpiece.

Facing the midday sun on the outside wall is another carving in marble, the 200-year-old monument over the tomb of William Cole. It has cherubs with torches on each side, and an inscription recording that he was Sheriff of Essex and treasurer of St Thomas's Hospital in London.

A tablet in the chancel reminds us that its remoteness did not save this place from the troubled days of the Civil War, for it tells us that George Kendleton was exiled during the Commonwealth.

The Crowded Centuries

MALDON. It clusters about a hill and looks down on the waters flowing to the North Sea, past the Blackwater islands and the old Saxon church of Bradwell. Its people will tell you that there is no town more picturesquely set in Essex, and indeed it is a captivating place, with old streets and old inns, red roofs and white sails, and three towers that never cease to call us as we saunter through the town.

Viking ships would come this way into the River Chelmer in the early days of our England, and one of our oldest poems tells how Brihtnoth the Saxon fell in the hour of victory over the Danish invaders. Nothing is left of those far-off days, yet Maldon has old and famous places, old houses overhanging the streets, a 14th century inn with characteristic pieces of every century since, a vicarage with ancient doorways and medieval paintings, the old Moot Hall as historic centre of the town, and down in the valley one of the best preserved fragments of an abbey in the south-east of England, 700 years old.

The Moot Hall, built in the 15th century and now used as the town hall, has 17th century panelling on its wall, and in the Council Chamber are portraits of Queen Elizabeth, Queen Anne, George the Third, and the town's great benefactor Thomas Plume, who set up a library on the site of the lost St Peter's church. The library is a fine little place with the atmosphere of Queen Anne's day, solid old tables, photographs of kings and queens, panelled walls, and a Jacobean fireplace, and on the shelves some of the rarest productions of the booksellers of two or three centuries ago. The medieval tower of St Peter's church is all that remains and the library is attached to it with 6000 volumes and a precious register in which are two entries, one of the burial of George Washington's last English ancestor, the other of the christening of the captain of the Mayflower. It is remarkable, surely, that there should remain in this old library a book with these two entries. Lawrence Washington had been ejected from his living at the neighbouring rectory at Purleigh and finally came to Maldon, where he died; he lies in the churchyard. Both his sons emigrated to America, and John became the great-grandfather of George Washington. The boy christened in this church who was to grow up and become the captain of the Mayflower was Christopher Jones; he captained the ship which carried across the Atlantic the little company that was to grow into the United States under the leadership of the great-great-grandson of the man who died at Maldon. One more historic name brought to mind in the church where Lawrence Washington lies is that of the Protector, for here lies the great-grandson of Cromwell's sister Jane.

Among Maldon's ancient buildings are three inns with delightful ironwork in their signs, the White Horse, the Bell, and the Blue Boar. Behind the modern front of the Blue Boar lies an old timber house, which was once the home of the Earls of Oxford; the oldest part of the house is the black and white overhanging storey from the 14th and 15th centuries. We may look down on the three churches of Maldon from the turret of the medieval town hall. St Peter's is only a tower. The second is St Mary's, with a Norman nave and a Norman stringcourse round the tower, and a porch of the 15th century. Norman work remains in the lower stages of the tower, but the rest was rebuilt in the 17th century, and the tower is now crowned by a small wooden spire. The other is the splendid church of All Saints, with the remarkable churchyard in which George Washington's ancestor lies.

The church has an extraordinary triangular tower with Norman stones in its walls, and a group of huge traceried windows looking down on the street. Its buttresses have canopied niches in which stand six men Maldon is pleased to honour: Archbishop Mellitus, Bishop Cedd, the Saxon Brihtnoth, Robert Mantell who founded the priory, Sir Robert Darcy, and Thomas Plume. On the inside wall thus handsomely buttressed most beautiful arcading runs round windows and between them, while below the windows is a masterpiece of 14th century carving, a series of arches in which finely sculptured heads hide the point of meeting.

This is one of the most attractive walls in Essex. Five of these arches form canopies for stone seats, and one is a doorway leading to a crypt. This splendour of decoration, probably unequalled in the county, continues beyond the crypt entrance to another doorway with a door which has been on its hinges 600 years. There is a window in this wall with three 17th century medallions of the Good Shepherd, the woman of Samaria, and the martyrdom of Stephen, and another window by it is of interest because it comes from Maldon's American namesake, a town founded by Essex emigrants about 300 years ago. It is a memorial to Lawrence Washington and it glows with colour and fine figures. St Nicholas is here as the patron of voyagers, St George is wearing a jewelled girdle, Joan of Arc is beautiful in blue and silver carrying a banner, and there are scenes showing the landing of Columbus, the arrival of the Pilgrim Fathers, and George Washington signing the Declaration of Independence.

On a wall-monument with three bays from Tudor days kneels Thomas Cammocke in a central arch with his two wives kneeling, both looking towards him, their 22 children of all ages and sizes being represented in panels below their mothers. Thomas himself is here not unlike Mr Punch, but he was in truth a young adventurer who eloped with his second wife Frances Rich, whom he carried off on horseback. It was one of the romances of the day. Thomas was in the service of Lord Rich, and loved his daughter Frances, and in eloping they found themselves pursued by the irate father and driven to leap into the estuary and to swim half a mile against a strong tide. They reached the boat the other side of the river at Fambridge Ferry, and the father, seeing such an exhibition of courage, relented and allowed them to be married in All Saints, saying "Seeing she had ventured her life for him, God bless them." Thomas lived to be a prosperous citizen of Maldon, and gave the town its first public water supply.

Under the floor of the nave, somewhere near the font, lies a man whose greatcoat might have covered half of Thomas Cammocke's great family, for he was reputed to be the biggest man alive in England, weighing 44 stones. He was Edward Bright, and it is said that when they laid him to rest in 1750 a special apparatus had to be fixed in the church for his burial. It was he who was descended from Cromwell's sister Jane.

Maldon has on its roll of honour not only Thomas Plume, founder of a free school here and a chair of astronomy at Cambridge, but two men who went out to Massachusetts, joined the Parliament there, and helped to found a Maldon on the other side of the Atlantic; they were Samuel Wayte and Joseph Hills, each of whom became Speaker of the Massachusetts Parliament. Here there was born also John Rogers Herbert, who lived for 80 years of last century, became a Royal Academician, and did some of the frescoes for the Houses of Parliament. In the 17th century Stephen Knight, a butcher of the town, was burned alive in the persecution of Mary Tudor, and in the 17th century there came to the town its first Nonconformist minister, a man of great energy and enthusiasm of whom we may truly say that he did things like billio, for he actually was Billio—

Joseph Billio, from whose ceaseless activity sprang the phrase that has now become so familiar.

Outside the town are two legacies from antiquity, a fragment and a monument. The fragment is the roofless but well-cared-for ruin of a Norman leper hospital with Roman bricks in its walls; the monument is the beautiful Beeleigh Abbey in which is all that remains of the great abbey founded by Robert Mantell 750 years ago. It is a charming place, with windows of our three great building centuries, and with the room where the monks would sleep, the room where they would gather round the fire at the end of the day, and the chapter house where they would meet in the morning. It has been thoroughly restored, and all who love these shrines may see it by asking its proud owner. There are graceful columns with bell capitals supporting the vaulted roofs, traces of painting 700 years old, a medieval fireplace with a frieze of angels above it, and panels of beautiful glass 500 years old. There are two rooms 40 feet long and half as wide, and a screen which is almost as old as the Reformation, added when the brick and timber wing of the house was built. The house was filled with treasures when we called—an exquisitely carved bedstead, rare manuscripts and prints, and many fragments from the great church whose foundations lie under the turf outside.

Maldon is the place where those must come who would find that great prophet of our time, Sir Norman Angell. In normal times they will find him seeking the peace he loves in the solitude of a patch of land in the estuary here, called Northey Island. He is lord of it all, but it is an ever-changing kingdom, for at low tide Sir Norman looks out on three hundred acres of green land with a causeway on which he can walk into civilisation, while when the tide is high his kingdom shrinks and he has but a sixth of what it was, with the mainland a mile away and no way to walk. His house is the island's only dwelling-place, a small farmhouse which Sir Norman has made into a comfortable home with stones from the beach, and timbers from wrecks, and the help of a few gargoyles from the Houses of Parliament. His walls shut out the noise of the wind and give him an oasis of quiet in a storm.

The 1000-Year-Old Battle Song

BRIHTNOTH OF MALDON is one of our forgotten heroes, a wise and gallant warrior who refused to surrender to the slothful spirit of Ethelred the Unready when he got rid of the Danes by agreeing to pay the tribute known as Danegeld. Earl Brihtnoth roused the men about him, who trusted him and would follow him anywhere.

He had founded churches and encouraged learning, and his manor at Hadleigh was a safe refuge as well as a delightful meeting-place for friends and comrades. Brihtnoth was filled with fury when he learned that the king was levying the Danegeld, and determined to rouse a nobler spirit in English hearts.

He drew up his will and gave it into the keeping of the Archbishop of Canterbury; then he returned to his manor and set himself to give all the thanes and striplings in his earldom training in the arts of war.

In 991 the terrified people of the East Coast saw a host of sinister shapes drawing near the land. The pale sunlight glinted on their dripping oars as they dipped into the water. There were 93 Long Serpents, and the great sea-king Anlaff was at their head. Sandwich and Ipswich were plundered; the triumphant prows glided swiftly up the Blackwater as far as Maldon. Here the Northmen landed, but during their absence the tide receded leaving their ships stranded. On their return they saw with amazement and amused contempt a little body of armed warriors on the far side of the river. The Vikings sent a messenger who spoke contemptuously to the old earl, but the earl grasped his shield, and answered:

Dost thou hear, seafarer, what this people say? They will give you doubtful tribute, poisonous spears and ancient swords, gear that will profit you naught in the fight. Messenger of the seamen, take word back again, say to thy people that here stands a noble earl with his troop who will defend this land, the home of my prince and people.

Then, with the ebbing of the tide, the proud earl bade the Northmen cross the marshes and engage in combat. The Vikings laughed. Young men and old died fighting. The earl was wounded and bleeding, but he still smote on. Then a Viking, seeing him faint and reeling, leaped upon him to snatch his bracelets and jewelled weapons; but with his dying strength Brihtnoth slew him and then sank exhausted. He exhorted his comrades to fight on, and Brihtwold, an aged follower cast in the same heroic mould, stood over the body of his leader and addressed the throng:

Thought shall be the harder, heart the keener, courage the greater, as our might lessens. Here lies our leader all hewn down, the valiant man in the dust; may he lament for ever who thinks how to turn from this war-play. I am old in age; I will not hence, but I purpose to lie by the side of my lord, by the man so dearly loved.

Night came down gently over that battlefield. The Danes carried off Brihtnoth's head in triumph, and ten thousand pounds of silver from the king, but Brihtnoth did not die in vain.

The Battle of Maldon was immortalised in a poem which is famous in our story because *for the first time in English battle poetry its hero dies with a Christian cry on his lips.*

Professor Freeman translated the 600 short lines that have come down to us, and we know of no better version than his. In the original Saxon the poem reads as if it were written by an actual witness of the fight. We give a few of the stirring lines from Professor Freeman's translation of the poem, beginning with the first clash in the fray:

Waded then the slaughter-wolves,   *The file-hard spears,*
For water they cared not,   *The sharply grounden*
The Viking Host   *Javelins fly;*
There gainst the fierce ones   *Bows were busy,*
Ready was standing   *Shields the point received,*
Brihtnoth with his warriors.   *Bitter was the war-rush;*
Then let they from their hands   *Warriors fell.*

Hard blows are struck on either side, and soon the earl's weapons are stricken from his hands. He stands and thanks God as he yields up his spirit to his Maker:

Yet a word quoth   *That I in world have bode.*
The hoary warman;   *Now I own, mild Maker,*
The daring youths   *That I most have need*
Bade he gang forth,   *That Thou to my ghost*
His good companions.   *Good should grant,*
He to Heaven looked: *That my soul to Thee*
Thank Thee, Nation's wielder,   *Now may make its way.*
For all the good things

Scoundrel

MANNINGTREE. A small town on the banks of the Stour, busy with milling, malting, and timber, it has houses and shops with roof beams centuries old, some built as long ago as the Wars of the Roses. The church, refashioned in the year Shakespeare died, has a curious appearance within, its hammerbeam roof supported on black iron piers. The galleries and choir-stalls and the huge chandeliers are painted black, bronze and silver ornaments on the stalls relieving the monotony.

A tablet set up in 1748 tells the story of a terrible deed of cruelty on the green away up the hill, where Thomas Osmond, a clothworker, was burned for his faith on June 15, 1555. There was a fear that the people would prevent the carrying-out of the sentence, and Lord Rich was appointed to arm a force to subdue the onlookers. So the sentence pronounced on this good man by Bishop Bonner was carried out, this memorial declaring that though his body was burnt to ashes his soul was translated into Heaven.

To this church used to come old Thomas Tusser, whom we meet at Rivenhall, and in the village lived one of the wickedest men of those bad old days, Matthew Hopkins. Son of a Suffolk minister and trained in the law, he decided to earn the twenty shillings paid for every witch discovered. In the reign of Queen Elizabeth and James the First the witchcraft laws had stressed the fear of witches, and in the days of Milton and Cromwell the popular mind was subject to great excitement on this account. The wretched Hopkins set out to exploit the panic of the people and enrich himself at the same time, his method being to prevent a reputed witch from sleeping until she would confess that she had surrendered herself to Satan. He secured conviction after conviction, but his malice roused such antagonism on the part of the educated clergy and magistrates that he had to give up business, and in the end they disposed of the Witch-Finder General as they had disposed of his own witches.

It is pleasant to come from those days to our own times, and to recall that the writer of some of the most charming fiction of the last generation, Ian Maclaren, was born in Manningtree as John Watson. He became a popular minister and wrote Beside the Bonnie Brier Bush, and other works now forgotten but best-sellers then.

Lieutenant of the Tower

MANUDEN. Much beauty has Manuden by the River Stort, whether we look at its white cottages with their timbers, its group of houses with overhanging eaves, its two splendid chestnuts by the gate of an oval churchyard laid out in Saxon England, or its treasure of old woodwork in the church. A sight not to be missed is the superb chancel screen, still almost as it left the carpenter's hands 500 years ago, except for a modern cornice. The tracery at the top is splendid, the double gates are enriched with quatrefoils and foliage, and there are eight bays of lovely old craftsmanship. The church has been much rebuilt, but parts of it are 14th century, the roof has fine 15th century timbers, and there are Norman stones in the transept. Beside a handsome 500-year-old window is a marble tablet to a man who saw much history made in our last Tudor and first Stuart reigns. He was the diplomatist Sir William Waad, who is buried here after a long life of historic adventure. He went on missions all over Europe, and spent eight years as Lieutenant of the Tower, having Sir Walter Raleigh as his prisoner, and helped to investigate the Gunpowder Plot. He conducted many delicate negotiations, such as the attempt to persuade Mary Stuart to come to terms with Queen Elizabeth, and once he was ordered out of Spain by the angry Philip. It was he who led Sir Walter Raleigh from the Tower to his trial at Winchester, the anger of the mob being so great that Waad was astonished that his prisoner escaped alive. Charges were brought against him of tricking his prisoners and even of carrying off the jewels of Arabella Stuart, but there seems to be no authority for all this.

Shining in the east window of the church are figures of Our Lord as Good Shepherd and Light of the World, in memory of John Thomas who built the village almshouses last century. We read here, too, of other benefactors and their gifts, including Robert Bucke the draper, who in 1620 left money for suits and hats and shoes and stockings for three poor men and three poor women.

The Oak Chest

MARGARET RODING. There is a fascination about the little churches on the River Roding, but best of them all is this one dedicated to St Margaret, with its medieval belfry looking so charming against the massed trees. The nave, only 35 feet long, has some of the most perfect craftsmanship left by the Normans in Essex. Here they realised the decorative value of four-pointed stars sunk in a small square panel. They placed these panels outside the round arches of their tiny windows and all round the doorways.

The 14th century masons who rebuilt the chancel have left us some portraits, a man's head on a corbel, and two on the sedilia, where a rude man with his mouth open keeps company with a mitred bishop. The panelled font and the lovely arch over the founder's tomb were their work. The smiths of seven centuries ago also left their handiwork here, in ornamental iron on the door and in the ornament on a chest dug out of an oak tree in the 14th century. The chest has 13 strong bands and fleur-de-lys patterns wrought in iron; it is ten feet long and three feet wide and deep.

On the Roman Road

MARGARETTING. The timber belfry with four bells four centuries old, and a rare Jesse window, give renown to this little village on the Roman road. No lover of beauty passes it by.

The church is surrounded by trees. The thick wall of the nave is Norman, but most of it is 15th century. The timber walls of the porch have lovely open tracery and the door has its original wood and iron. The medieval masons rivalled the woodcarvers; every corbel in the nave is their work, the lion of Mark, the angel of Matthew, the eagle of John, and the ox of Luke, sharing their task with grotesque heads. More delicate are the symbols they carved round the font, rose, crown, mitre, acorns, leaves, square and compass, and a face with a protruding tongue.

The wooden screen must have been very beautiful; the few panels left have five-leaf traceried heads and spandrels with owls and leopards and roses. The two doors still hang on their old hinges, bringing us into the chancel with an east window brilliant with colour and human appeal. It represents the Tree of Jesse, and there runs up through three divisions a vine-stem encircling 12 round panels with 24 figures. Flying freely above Jesse is an angel, in the middle division all wear golden crowns, in the bottom panel are David with a harp and Solomon with his temple, and at the top are the Madonna and the Child. In the side panels are Old Testament figures, Abraham, Jacob, and Joseph and the rest, all with their names.

But the most interesting thing about this group is the record it gives of the life of the time. It was the work of Flemish artists 500 years ago and the men of Jesse's line might very well be burghers of Antwerp or any other town in the Low Countries. Cloak and hat and every detail reflect the life the artists knew, and in pose and colour remind us of the lovely paintings of the golden age of Art.

There is a hint of the rich costume women wore in the 15th century in a brass on the chancel wall, where, resplendent in jewelled headdress, with a pomander box hanging from her girdle, a lady stands by a man in armour, with their seven children below. Farther along the wall in the nave is a family group of 1600, kneeling figures of the Tanfields painted on a small tablet of alabaster.

A door in a 16th century brick arch at the end of the nave leads us to the belfry, with its gigantic timbers. Three posts to right and three to left are linked by arches and made firm by slanting beams, and above go great braces to support the bell-chamber and the shingled spire. In the tower are four bells which rang at all the weddings of our royal Bluebeard.

Roman, Norman, and Tudor Are We

MARKS TEY. It stands on the Roman road near Colchester, ancient enough for its name to have come from the Norman family of De Mark. Its great treasure is in the church, where there is a very unusual 15th century font made not of stone but of wood, something we have come upon only a few times in all England.

The font has eight panelled sides divided by little buttresses, the panels showing throned figures and the symbols of the evangelists. Roses are carved on the bowl and the traceried stem. The cover is pyramid shaped and comes from the 17th century. The tower was rebuilt by the Tudors, and has an oak door as old as itself; the brickwork is said to have been damaged during the siege of Colchester in the Civil War, when it was repaired with timber-work now green with age. There are two doorways and a window shaped by the Normans in Roman bricks, a chancel rebuilt with its arch in the 14th century, and a fine Tudor porch. From the 17th century come a carved chest and two old panels in a modern chair; and there is a tablet to Peter Wright, who was rector for 57 years of last century. Against the wall is a striking peace memorial with brass figures of an archangel and a soldier in khaki.

Old Glass and Old Chest

MASHBURY. A little place, very lonely, it has a small Norman church altered by the 15th century builders, who gave it a

Margaretting   Medieval Tower   **Marks Tey**   Tudor Belfry

Little Maplestead   **The Little Round Church**

Newport   15th Century Monk's Barn

Newport   17th Century Crown House

new chancel arch and a new east wall. Roman bricks are in the walls with two Norman doorways, one sheltered by a handsome Tudor porch, the other framing a remarkable old door which has kept its battens and hinges from the 12th century. There are two small Norman windows, 15th century beams supporting a modern bell-turret, a panelled 17th century pulpit, and a series of paintings over the altar showing the Nativity, Simeon in the Temple, and Our Lord healing the sick, all in watercolour by William Hole, who is remembered for his wall-paintings in the National Gallery at Edinburgh. A 500-year-old chest is strong with bands of iron and seven hinges, and there are fragments of old glass showing a saint from the 14th century and faces of leopards from the 16th.

A mile away we come to Baileys, a Tudor house with three lovely gables, its porch sheltering a doorway bearing the date 1614.

Mr Chimney and the Marriage Feast

MATCHING. Who does not love to think of Mr Chimney and his marriage feast? He was one of the kindliest men who ever lived and had one of the best ideas that has ever brought the glow of humanity into village life.

He was part of medieval England, a Matching man who helped to make the matches of this village pleasant events indeed, and does so to this day. He set up a long building between the church and the green, with a room overhanging four rooms below, and to this upper room the brides and bridegrooms of the village have climbed for 500 years to feast with their friends. The room is called the Marriage Feast Room, and on Sundays it serves as a school for those who may look forward to a feasting when the years have rolled away. It has an open kingpost roof and is in every way a notable survival from the Middle Ages.

Matching is one of the gems of the county, with two greens, a medieval cottage, a lovely gabled house, a 17th century barn across a moat, and a church that hides itself away within field gates. It was founded by the Dean of St Paul's 700 years ago, and its tower was added in the 15th century. There are grotesque corbels in the oldest wall, showing two poor people with toothache; Mr Chimney must have seen them when he came to church. There is more beautiful carving of his time on the font, and a family portrait later than his

S 257

time (1638) showing John Ballett with his wife, two sons, and a lively group of six daughters. It is in brass.

In a modern window is a picture of the first Easter morning in memory of Lord Rookwood, who died in our own century; it shows the three women, two angels, and the hurrying disciples.

The Church of Laud's Friend

MESSING. There are fragments of the Roman Empire in its church walls, and in its cottages huge beams that have supported their roofs four or five hundred years. Its church is one of the few that were enriched in the brief revival of church building in the early days of Charles Stuart. It happened that its vicar was a friend of Archbishop Laud, and in his day many things of beauty were added to the chancel. The vicar was Nehemiah Rogers, a fervent Royalist and "man of good note," as Laud said; he wrote on the parables, and one of his books commands a good price today. He was also rector of Great Tey and Doddinghurst, where he lies. Round the walls is elaborate oak panelling divided by pilasters, with little cherubs peeping out above, and there are fine stalls for the choir. Swinging from a beam in a chapel is a gabled panel with the Royal arms of 1634 and Charles Stuart's Prince of Wales feathers in faint colours on the back. There is an altar table of the same period, and in the tracery of the east window, with 14th century stonework, is 17th century glass by Van Linge, who knew so well how to paint the costumes of his age in vivid yellows, blues, and reds. In the upper lights are figures of Faith, Hope, and Charity, and six scenes below showing six kindly works of charity. This fine window was new when the fury of the Civil War burst over Essex, and we owe its existence today to the fact that it was taken out and buried. In the roof are 15th century angels, and there is a long ironbound chest in which the village documents have been kept for 600 years and are still kept today.

In the Gainsborough Country

MIDDLETON. It clusters under a hill in the Gainsborough country, its small church with the rectory shaded by the fine beeches of the park. The 19th century spire, rising above the old timbered turret, looks down on the Norman walls of the chancel and the nave; we come into them through a doorway much as the

Normans left it, with their round shafts, their zigzag on the arch, and their handsome capitals. Still swinging on its hinges is a door with the beautiful tracery of a medieval carpenter. There is a 16th century chest with quaint ironwork, and a painting of the Annunciation of the same age. In the floor of the chancel is a stone engraved with the portrait of James Samson, a rector of nearly 600 years ago, under a pinnacled canopy. The oak reredos is in memory of a rector who followed him after 500 years and stayed for over two generations. He came in 1823 and was rector till he died in 1889, aged 95. It is one of the most remarkable cases of long service we have come upon, for this rector, Oliver Raymond, followed his father Samuel who was rector for 54 years before him, so that father and son preached in this church for 120 years, through all the life of Napoleon and the French Revolution, through all the rise of modern England till after Queen Victoria's Golden Jubilee.

Richard Corruptible

MISTLEY. It has two ruined churches and a new one, and it has seen trade on the Stour draw its people down from the hill to the banks of the river. One of the ruins is a fragment of a medieval church, the porch alone remaining. Built about 1500, it has a moulded plinth inlaid with panels of flint, and the buttresses and the doorway have much beauty in them. The other ruin is of a 18th century church, forlorn twin towers down in the town. There are memories of the 18th century church in the new one, a handsome place in the park with a spire 140 feet high. Its pleasant interior has been enriched by a carved organ case from Worcester Cathedral and a beautiful window of the Last Judgment.

On the walls is a tablet in memory of Richard Rigby, a notorious politician who was Paymaster-General in the corrupt days of the taxation which lost America for the flag. It is said that he was no better than he should have been, and he is remembered because he raised his voice against the public funeral of Chatham, and because when he died in 1788 he was found to have amassed about half a million of money out of his public services.

MOUNT BURES. It takes its name from a wooded mound where a fortress stood, the silent guardian of a few cottages and an ancient church. Romans and Normans have helped to build the church, the Normans using the bricks the Romans left behind. A Norman doorway here is shaped with them, and others can be seen at the corners of the chancel and transept. Another doorway is 14th century, and both have doors 500 years old. The porch is 15th century; one of its shields has the Sackville arms. There is a Jacobean table, a chest about the same age, and a memorial to a rector for 50 years in the 18th century, Philip Gurdon, whose proud epitaph says that as a minister he was a burning and a shining light.

In a Garden of Roses

MOUNTNESSING. Its houses run along the Roman road to Chelmsford, but the timber spire of its church is a mile away over the fields. The church has been refashioned from the one the Normans built, and the Roman tiles and Roman masonry they used are visible in the walls. We found the church in a garden of roses; it stands on a knoll above a 17th century hall and is renowned for the wonderful timbering set up in its nave in the 15th century. Its massive wooden turret is a wonder, for it is puzzling outside to see what holds it up. The secret is revealed within, where we find enormous beams cut from giants of the forest, supporting trellis work mounting to the roof. Shafts of wood with moulded capitals stand by the stone piers of the arcade, and wooden struts sweep over to rest against the walls of the aisles; it is a mass of woodwork that must weigh tons, yet is so ordered that it wastes no space. It is probably the work of the carpenters who carried the roof of the nave in one majestic sweep across the aisles.

The piers of the nave are strong and dignified, and from the deepcut foliage of one of their capitals peeps out a woman's head with a band across the mouth—some local scold, perhaps, pilloried by a 13th century mason for all time. An angel smiles in pleasant contrast across the nave. There is a 15th century font and two old chests, one with lovely carving of the 17th century, one 700 years old with half a tree trunk for a lid, the original hinges, and rings at the ends for lifting. But the oddest thing we have seen in a church for a long long time is in a glass case here, a fossil rib of a whale.

The village has a windmill whose sails have spun round about 300 years, and a solitary arch 600 years old in the fields beyond it. The arch is part of Thoby Priory, which has medieval walls.

Elizabeth's Four Husbands

MUCKING. It deserves a prettier name, this Anglo-Saxon meadow in the marshes by the Thames, as its name implied in olden days. It has quaint old farms and cottages round about, and a wall of grey stones surrounds the churchyard, probably quarried from a vanished nunnery which stood on the site of the hall. Passing under an avenue of chestnuts we enter the church through a door in a fine new tower. Much of the building is of our own time, but the restorers have left some lovely features of the old one, especially the great round pier supporting the arch between the nave and aisle. The foliage round its capital, from which peep out two wise-looking heads, was carved about the time of Magna Carta. A charming little lady kneels in alabaster on the wall of the chapel; she was Elizabeth Downes, who lived in "matrimonye with four several husbands"; their four coats-of-arms are on her monument.

Barn and Moat

MUNDON. Odd to look at and lonely in its situation, its church gives us an impression of a day that has passed. An ivied elm and a ragged yew grow at its rustic gate, behind a barn of Stuart days keeping company with its great house, and round it all run traces of a moat which must have been filled with water in the days of the Barons. From those days comes the church's oldest possession, the Norman font made square 800 years ago but given the fashionable shape of a later day by cutting off its corners. One of the oldest bells in the county still rings as it has rung for more than 500 years. The timber belfry was erected for it in Tudor days, and a very quaint addition it is, half an octagon fitted round the west wall. The same carpenters may have built the porch, with a gable of moulded bargeboards and spandrels carved with twisted leaves.

Five Days Prime Minister

NAVESTOCK. A colossal barn, tall limes, and a huge chestnut keep company with its church, which has a shingled spire rising from an astonishing wooden belfry. The surprise of it is inside, where 15th century beams and ancient ladders seem to be in great confusion, with masses of woodwork all about us. Looking closer, we see that the four chief uprights are moulded at the capitals, and that four great beams curve up to meet in a boss of carved foliage. The belfry woodwork is oak splendid and unashamed, but the wood in the church is so covered with whitewash that we might think it stone. We see it in the wooden arch of the 14th century chancel, and in another arch across the 13th century chapel, both arches rising from an oak pillar which ends the line of round stone piers built about 1250, when the church was doubled in width.

The oldest masonry is in the north wall of the nave, which has a plain doorway of the 11th century. Four doors in the church are of remarkable age, and have well preserved their ironwork though some of the wood has been renewed. One is in the ancient Norman doorway; others of the 13th century are in aisle and chapel; and double doors of Chaucer's day lead from the aisle into the bell-tower. The porch is 15th century, and in a corner by the modern font are coffin lids of two priests about 600 years ago, one with a raised cross.

On the 17th century gravestone of little Jane Marchant, who was only 15, are two delightful lines:

So fair a blossom, so exquisitely good,
That I want words to make it understood.

In the chancel are two striking 17th century monuments, much in contrast. One has a simple alabaster figure of Ann Snelling holding her baby; the other is the bust of John Greene, a judge who seems proud of his family, for he is shown with a display of heraldry, many of the shields having the stag's head seen again on a helmet above.

The great folk at Navestock have been the Waldegraves, many of whom sleep here. Their old house has gone but its park with a lovely lake is left, and there are monuments to remind us of them. There is a bust of the seventh earl who died in 1846; a relief of the eighth earl's eldest son who fell at Alma; and another relief, carved by John Bacon, to the fourth earl's son, who distinguished himself in Sir John Moore's campaign and was shipwrecked when nearly home. The carving shows a boy unfurling a flag, his mother weeping below.

Two older monuments take us into circles more distinguished still. One is a Latin inscription to a daughter of James the Second, Henrietta, wife of that Lord Waldegrave who, as one of the king's counsellors, had to fly with him at the Revolution. The other is an

enormous wall-tablet telling of the next two generations of Waldegraves, of Henrietta's son James, the first earl, who was an able
ambassador; and of her grandson the second earl, who moved for a
few brief moments in the centre of the English stage. He was James
Waldegrave, too, a friend of George the Second and tutor to the
Prince of Wales. He married a niece of Walpole who was one of
the beauties of her day and was seven times painted by Sir Joshua
Reynolds. Waldegrave is chiefly remembered, however, as the man
who became Prime Minister for five days (June 8–12, 1757). It
happened in the early summer of 1757, and he had no wish to fill the
office, but allowed himself to be nominated to please the king. His
ministry never came into being, however, and nobody can have
been more pleased than he when in place of it was born the famous
ministry of Newcastle and Pitt, during the life of which England
became supreme at sea, in India, and in North America.

Old Timbers

NAZEING. Spread over the low hills above the valley of the
Lea, it has many lovely scenes to show us. There is a breezy
common of 400 acres, groups of pretty cottages, and, away on a
bluff, the church lying in a sacred spot with noble views of Hertfordshire. A bold tower dominates the scene, and high up its turret
is a sundial oddly inscribed with its exact position on the map of
England: Latitude 51 degrees 32 minutes. The tower is 16th century,
the sundial 18th.

A 16th century wooden porch shelters a 700-year-old doorway
cut through the thick wall of Norman masonry. The Norman arches
of two of the original windows are by the door, and facing them is
the arcade of four bays and an aisle added in the 15th century, when
the chancel was made new. About this time the steps were cut in
the wall up to the roodbeam, whose sawn-off end is clearly visible.
The old nail-studded door to the steps is still here.

One or two panels from the old screen have been fixed to two
bench-ends remarkable for the carving of the gruff and humorous
faces springing out from them; and there are other bench-ends with
poppyheads behind the font, which came here with them in the
15th century. An extraordinary ironbound chest is 600 years old;
it has a great lockplate, and it is thrilling to think that it may have

held documents sealed by our last Saxon king, for Harold owned Nazeing and gave it to the monks of the abbey of Waltham.

Four Marys

NETTESWELL. It was given by our last Saxon king to the abbey of Waltham which he loved so well, and there is on the wall of the 700-year-old church a brickwork panel with the emblems of Abbot Rose of Waltham who died in the last year of the 15th century; it shows a double rose between two long-tailed lions, with a crozier and a hare below. In the church is a pair of medieval lancets facing across the nave, with precious old glass in them. One has the angel, lion, ox, and eagle which were the symbols of the writers of the Gospels; the other has three Marys, two fondling little children, and the third a perfect little study of the Madonna in blue and gold. It is a gem of 700 years ago.

There is a figure of another Mary standing by an 18th century monument. She was the wife of William Martin, lord of the manor, a most remarkable lady who sleeps in St Margaret's Westminster. She saw seven sovereigns on our throne and long before she died (at 97) she set up this monument, by which she stands with remarkable portraits of her brother Robert Crosse and his son Thomas.

There are brass portraits of two families of Tudor and Stuart days, one showing Thomas Laurence and his wife and their five children, the other John Bannister with his wife, three sons, and a baby in swaddling clothes. The font at which these children would be christened is 700 years old and still has the staples by which it was locked against witches. On the wall is a mass dial by which the villagers of those days would tell the time.

The church is almost hidden behind a farm, and in finding it we come upon a 16th century barn and a group of fish-ponds.

NEVENDON. It keeps its peace a little apart from the great Southend road. At a bend in the lane we come to its ancient church, with the lychgate between two friendly barns, the vicarage garden next door, all charming with pines and chestnuts and limes. A little wooden bell-turret sits on the nave, which is 600 years old and has had faces watching by its doors all the time. The chancel with its lancet windows is a century older, and the roofs were looking down on the worshippers when Columbus was sailing the Atlantic. The modern pulpit and panelling take their place with a quiet charm; but out of place when we called seemed a big shell-case (though engraved with the names of those who fought in the Great War).

A Unique Piece of Art

NEWPORT. Standing by the River Cam on the Roman road to Cambridge, it has taken toll of the centuries as they passed, and stops us, too, with its display of old houses and its wonderful church treasures, the earliest English oil paintings among them.

Monk's Barn and the Priory are characteristic tributes from the 15th century. The timbered Monk's Barn is a charming house overhanging the pavement on each side of coved eaves, with carving in the wooden arch of its studded door, and under the oriel window a bold bracket showing the crowned Madonna rising from the clouds, a sceptre in her hand, and two angels making music for her Child. The Priory has another wooden-framed oriel window, and close by is the graceful Crown House from the 17th century, with a plaster front and a lovely shell hood over the door. Even the chimney which collects the smoke from four 16th century fireplaces in Martin's Farm is a work of art. Set in a wall by the road are stones carved 700 years ago for the hospital which once stood close by in the park of Shortgrove House, a home old and new, which has been growing for 300 years.

The spacious church on rising ground in the middle of the village has been growing more than twice as long, the chancel and transepts being 13th century, the aisles 14th, the clerestory and the two-storeyed porch 15th, the two doors to the upper porch room 16th. The transept roofs and the angel-borne roof of the nave are 500 years old. The chancel roof, the poppyhead stalls under it, and the panels in the altar table are all 400 years old, the panels of Flemish carving showing the Crucifixion with Mary Magdalene kneeling, and in the background two men in high pointed hats, a crowded Epiphany scene, and Christ triumphant over Death.

The light and graceful screen was made 500 years ago when the cover was made for the 13th century font, and the oak lectern was carved with its double book-rest turning on a swivel, the Old Testament chained on one side and the New on the other. There is a tablet in memory of Joseph Smith of Shortgrove House, Pitt's private secretary, and 16th century brass portraits of Thomas Brond with his wife and four children, and later ones showing Geffrye Nightingale in a Jacobean cloak and ruff and his wife in an embroidered pannier skirt.

But the great rarity here is the portable altar in one of the transepts. It was made 700 years ago to be carried from place to place and set up in camp or battlefield. For this alone it would be remarkable, but on it are the earliest oil paintings on wood known to English art. The altar is made as a chest, with three handles and five locks, and a false bottom with a secret sliding panel. The vestments and books would be kept in the locker and the altar stone in the secret place. A fine band of metal tracery ornaments the outside, and the 13th century paintings are on the inside of the lid, which lifted up to form the reredos as we see it today, with its five panels of the Crucifixion, showing three saints and the Madonna at the foot of the Cross, the heads undoubtedly drawn from life, probably likenesses of the artist's friends. Each saint stands on a mound in a strikingly dramatic pose, delightful representatives of a now old art in its infancy.

Vivid Scenes on Wood and Glass

NOAK HILL. It looks across at the trees in Pyrgo Park, where kings and queens came to stay, and we come to it for a few treasures in its 19th century church, wood and glass about 300 years old, mostly brought here from the Continent. Both in wood and in glass there are strikingly vivid pictures of the Crucifixion by old craftsmen. The one in wood is on the chancel wall, and also shows Christ bearing the Cross. It is sombre and perhaps a little grotesque, but full of quaint realism, and is said to come from a monastery at Florence. The other is in the east window, an intensely realistic scene with Our Lord between the two thieves, the Madonna and three other Marys, John, two horsemen, and soldiers holding the spear and sponge. The window also has full-length figures of Peter and John the Baptist, and a group of the Madonna with Zacharias and Elizabeth. In other windows are French heraldic medallions of the 16th century, panels of Saul with Doeg the Edomite, The Agony in the Garden, The Scourging, and Doubting Thomas. We see also the badge of Jane Seymour, with a bird springing from flowers set in a round tower, and two medallions with the heraldry of Anne Boleyn. All this old colour the church has to brighten it, and it glows too with the vivid hues of coats-of-arms in all the nave windows.

Soldier of Waterloo

NORTH BENFLEET. Here stands a farmhouse of ancient wonder and delight, one of its wings having survived, roof-timbers and all, from the 15th century. The middle block and another wing were made new in the 16th century, and the entrance door has big strap-hinges and many an interesting detail of Stuart times. A great pond, all that is left of its moat, lies between it and a crowd of barns and haystacks. By them is the church, with a few of its original stones still seen, though in the west wall behind the massive timbering is a round-headed window of 1200, now blocked outside by a modern tower. The font is 13th century, the two bells are 15th, and the communion cup, with a band of engraved orna-ment, was first used in the spacious days of Queen Elizabeth. At the entrance to the 16th century porch is a tombstone with this curious inscription:

Sacred to the memory of John Cole, a soldier of Waterloo. At the celebrated command, Up Guards and at 'em, he was wounded by a musket ball but heroically persevered till the victory. He died in this parish April 10, 1836, aged 51, bequeathing his medal to the curate, whose last act was the erection of this tablet.

Sixty Generations of Life

NORTH OCKENDON. Men must have been living here for 60 generations, for there is a Roman burial ground of 16 acres. One of the oldest houses still standing is the timbered post office of Shakespeare's century. The hall is a little younger, but the church which keeps it company has still the fine doorway through which the Normans came into it; it has a striking arch which does not begin to curve until high above its capitals. Indoors each pier of the nave is different, and the pillar between the chancel and the chapel is lovely with 700-year-old carving of oak and vine leaves, all as fresh as if the sculptor had just left it.

The chapel is the shrine of the Poyntz family, and in it lies the proud Sir Gabriel. He is on a magnificent tomb which dominates all others, he and his wife gazing at a painted blue sky on an oak canopy above them. From the canopy look down sun, moon, and stars, and human faces are quaintly painted on the sun and the crescent moon. They are beautiful figures and the embroidery on the wife's dress is elaborately wrought. Sir Gabriel loved old things and set in relief on these walls six monuments to his ancestors. In the armour and dress of their period kneel lords and ladies of the manor from the reign of Edward the Third to Queen Elizabeth, and after that Sir Gabriel added his own monuments and one for his son. All kneeling at prayer in the 16th century way, this group of carvings is one of the smallest sculpture galleries we have seen, none over 12 inches high. After these come greater monuments—one of Sir James with his son Richard, both in armour; Catherine with her husband facing each other; and a bust of Sir Thomas, who lived into Queen Anne's day and has four cherubs lamenting him. There are three brass portraits on the wall facing Sir Gabriel's tomb, one of Sir William Poyntz and his wife (1502), and one of a tall lady of 1532, Thomasyn Latham. Near them is the gravestone of William Baldwin on which is the earliest date in the church, 1316.

It is interesting to look about this place, to see this gallery of monuments, and realise that a lovely wistful figure of a saint has gazed from one of the windows while all these great people have passed to their rest. She is St Helen, holding a book and a staff, clothed in raiment of green and gold as the painter left her 700 years ago. Two centuries passed by and the glassworkers set here another figure to keep her company, Mary Magdalene with her trailing tresses and her pot of precious ointment. Between these ancient figures is now a bishop in his robes and mitre. The window itself is beautiful and its glass of the 13th and 15th century is a remarkable possession. In a window of the 15th century tower are the arms of England and France glowing in glass of the 14th century, so that this fine church adds to its possessions in marble a rare collection of glass of our three great church-building centuries.

About a mile from the church is a house with a 16th century barn and a large fish-pond. Jacobean doors and panelling are in the house, while both staircases were carved about the year 1700.

Here in the early days of the Stuarts was the garden of William Coys, famous among botanists of the time for being the first garden in which the yucca and the ivy-leaved toadflax grew in England. The Hampshire botanist John Goodyer visited the garden and helped Coys to make the first complete English garden list with all the plants scientifically described. Botanists went on pilgrimage to the garden 300 years ago, and it is delightful to know that the garden is maintained by the family which succeeded William Coys.

NORTH SHOEBURY. A few scattered farms and cottages survive on the broad flat acres here, and a road to a gabled farmhouse leads past a dark pond at the edge of a small thicket, behind which stands a Norman tower. It has a wooden spire. The church itself is 13th century. It has fleur-de-lys on its ancient font, and oak leaves in autumn colours glowing in 14th century glass.

The Old Brick Tower

NORTH WEALD BASSETT. Dominated by the bold tower of its church, it lies scattered between Ongar and Epping, named after that Norman Ralph Bassett who was Chief Justiciar to Henry the First, the king who gave us good laws. The tower, 66 feet high, is an excellent example of early brickwork, built in 1500 with a corbel table of tiny arches. The lofty brick tower arch inside frames the west window effectively. Though Roman tiles are dotted about the walls, the church, except for the chancel, belongs to the 14th century. The chief pride of the church is its 16th century screen of five bays. It has moulded posts supporting a fine canopy with traceried heads divided by pendants. The rail has running ornament and a prayer "for the good state of Thomas Wyher, deacon." The door has ornamental hinges 600 years old, and there is some 14th century glass, a 15th century bracket carved with oak leaves and a face, a huge wooden lock, 15th and 17th century carving on chairs, and a curious candlestick.

Engraved on brass are the portraits of Walter Larder, who was laid to rest here in 1606, and his wife and their five children. There are memorials to the Cockerells who lived in the vicarage for nearly a hundred years. The east window is in memory of Henry Cockerell, vicar for 52 years last century; and the glowing glass in the tower window showing the Presentation in the Temple is in memory of his son Louis, who succeeded him.

Made New 600 Years Ago

NORTON MANDEVILLE. Here, facing a spacious modern farm, is one of the smallest churches in Essex, a Norman church made new 600 years ago, built to hold the hundred people of that time and never enlarged. The Norman stones peep out from the flint walls of the 14th century. The children are still christened at the Norman font, a good one with a round shaft carved out of each corner. It has the staples with which it was padlocked against witches. Round about the font are tiles which have preserved their varied pattern under the feet of 25 generations. The nave keeps its original roof with moulded capitals and bases on the kingposts; the end beams support the 15th century bellcot and from their brackets painted carvings of the lion and the unicorn regard each other disdainfully across the nave. The modern screen has eight heads carved for the old screen by a medieval craftsman, and in the nave are six open benches with poppyheads shaped by a Tudor carpenter.

The manor house stands near Norton Heath a mile away, a beautiful timbered and gabled building, with 1613 on its chimney.

Tudor Legacy

ORSETT. Approach it by any way we will, some attraction greets us: an old windmill by a 16th century house at a crossroads London-way, a row of timbered houses on the other side, the Cock Inn towards the Thames, a medieval house with an overhanging storey to the north. A path by the church leads across a field to the earthworks on which stood a palace of Bishop Bonner, the torturer of so many Protestants and chief agent of Mary Tudor's reign of terror.

Close by is another rich heritage from the 16th century, Hall Farm, with an overhanging storey and ancient windows. By this lovely piece of Tudor England stands the village lock-up with a tiny barred window; on a small green under the trees is the village pound; and on another open space is the memorial to the men who did not come back, "in token of pride and affection and respect."

We pass the old Church House, which is now a post office, and a 17th century cottage now a shop, to come to the wooden porch which has sheltered for 500 years the magnificent doorway (with two ancient sundials) set up by the Normans in 1160. The present nave was their whole church. The great tower 16 feet square has on its wall the name of its 15th century donor; its spire is 17th century. The chapel has long been linked with Orsett Hall, a house in a lovely park beyond the village. Its owners have filled it with treasures old and new. A traceried screen of the 15th century divides it from the aisle. An imposing monument covers the grave of Sir John Hart, who died in Cromwell's day and lies between black columns. An angel with a sickle and an angel of the resurrection are on the 19th century tomb of Richard Baker. There are brass portraits in the chancel of Thomas Latham with his wife and their three children in 15th century costume, and a brass of Robert Kinge, a 16th century priest. There is a fine font from medieval days, a Jacobean pulpit, a 16th century chest with linenfold, and another of the 17th century with a lid 700 years old.

The Old Doors

PAGLESHAM. The 17th century inn and its old cottage neighbours lie near the mouth of the River Roche, but the church and its cottages, some of them all wood, stand away in a row looking across the fields to the far horizon. The church has Roman bricks set in Norman walls, but most of the church was made new in the 15th century. The tower is 16th. It is remarkable that all the doors have been opening and shutting since the church was new, still on the same strap-hinges. The oldest bell first rang in Armada year. The work of a Norman craftsman remains in the chancel, on a scalloped capital shaped into a bowl in medieval days for use as a piscina; and there are two elaborately carved chairs of the 17th century in the sanctuary.

PANFIELD. Though it has nothing Norman to show, it has a link with the Conqueror, Great Priory Farm being the 17th century successor of a priory belonging to St Stephen's at Caen, the abbey where William was buried. The church is nearly all 15th century, with a wooden turret, a charming porch, and the original door still on its hinges. Another doorway is 14th century, and has heads of a bearded man and a plump-faced queen. In a little fine old glass are two golden-haired saints, one with an orb and one with a yellow cross; and in a circle the eagle of St John is pecking at its wing. The modern pulpit has tracery 500 years old. Nearly as old as the church is Panfield Hall half a mile away, remarkable for its projecting tower and a group of Tudor chimneys.

PATTISWICK. It is very rich in trees, and has farms and cottages with ancient roofs and chimneys. The nave of the church is 700 years old and the chancel 600, both roofs being medieval. A few of the pews have been here since the time of Henry the Eighth.

Hammer of the Scots

PEBMARSH. Its post office is Tudor and it has many Tudor farms and houses, among them Stanley Hall with a moat and carved beams; Worldsend with two original studded doors; and Greathouse Farm, a modern house with two barns and a granary of the 16th and 17th centuries. But we come to the church for the great attraction of Pebmarsh, for among its treasures is one of the very few brasses in England dating from the first half of the 14th century. There are believed to be only about 16 of them, and this one has the distinction of being among the very earliest to show the plate armour of those days. It is a fine picture of Sir William Fitzralph who fought in the wars of Edward the First and helped to hammer the Scots, dying about 1323. He is lying cross-legged, has armour and chain mail, and wears a long coat tied at the waist. His sword is in an ornamental scabbard, and his feet rest on a hound.

The church is mostly the work of 14th century builders, but from the 16th century come its brick parapets on the tower and aisle, a porch with a niche and a rose, and tie-beams in the nave roof. There is a beautiful 14th century doorway with four animal heads, a modern door with medieval ironwork, a 15th century bell, a pulpit with woodwork 500 years old, two 17th century chairs carved with flowers and leaves and cherubs, and an old chest. In the windows are many scraps of glass as old as the church, shields and foliage, flowers and leopard faces, and a little man standing.

PELDON. It lies scattered on the high ground between Colchester and Mersey Island. The timber-framed house near the church is the wing of a medieval house which has disappeared, and there are two medieval farms a mile away. The inn has panelled doors of the 17th century, and comes into Baring Gould's romance Mehalah.

Prittlewell   A Corner of the Priory, now a Museum

Southchurch   14th Century Manor House, now a Library

Boreham   New Hall

Rochford   Rochford Hall

TWO TUDOR HOMES

The church tower is a bold stone structure of 1400, with flint crosses and two nail-studded doors, both 600 years old. Grotesques jut out from the corners below the embattled parapet. The oldest possession of the church is the Norman font, and there are windows and doorways which have been here 600 years; but the best thing is the 400-year-old hammerbeam roof of the nave.

Faithful Servants

PENTLOW. Its tall tower in the rectory garden was built last century by a son in memory of his rector father, and from the top of it nearly fifty churches may be seen. Many must be in Suffolk, for we are here by the River Stour which marks the county border. Crossing out of Essex we see a charming mill by the water's edge.

Among the old houses of Pentlow are Paine's Manor with a carved beam of Shakespeare's day; Bower Hall of about 1600 with original chimneys and a 15th century barn; and Pentlow Hall of about 1500, with much old woodwork, a fine bay window of Elizabeth's day, and an oriel with 16th century glass showing a hawking scene and shields. It is charming from the churchyard, looking under a great cedar and across the moat still wet. The fine church tower is remarkable as being one of the six round towers of Essex, with walls four feet thick. It was probably added in the 14th century to the nave and apsidal chancel built by the Normans, and protects the Norman west doorway, which is carved at the top with a muzzled bear. The 15th century chancel arch is wide and very high, and a flat arch leads to a chapel of about 1600. There is a 16th century chest, a 17th century table, twisted altar rails a little younger, and scraps of 14th century glass in the east window. But finer than anything is a huge Norman font elaborately ornamented on its four sides, the cover a rich piece of 15th century work with canopies and pinnacles. A Tudor altar tomb in the chancel is the sleeping-place of Edmund and Frances Felton, and a great tomb in the chapel has figures of George Kempe of 1606, his son John who died three years later, and John's wife Elinor in an elaborate headdress and tight-waisted gown. The men are carved in their furred robes, and on the front of the tomb are kneeling figures of the children of John and Elinor, eight daughters with their hair brushed back, and four curly headed sons in cloaks. It is an impressive monument to three generations of an Essex family in the days when Shakespeare was writing his plays.

A window of St Gregory and St George is in memory of Felix Edward Bull who began his ministry in 1877 and preached for 50 years; and a testimonial hanging on the organ tells of Sarah Clark, who played her first voluntary in the year the Crimean War began, and her last two years after the shadow of the Great War was lifted from Europe. For 66 years she was organist, and for 43 she was at the organ while Felix Bull was in the pulpit, a wonderful fellowship of prayer and praise in this small place.

The Greek Maiden

PITSEA. A rapidly growing village four miles north of Thameshaven, it is built on the hills lining the marshlands by the river. At the cross-roads stands a lovely memorial statue, a Greek maiden carrying a torch, a spray of laurel for our heroes.

On a high knoll is perched a church dedicated to St Michael, as are so many churches on hilltops. This one has been rebuilt except for the 16th century tower, with its embattled parapet and gargoyles. In it is a bell which has been ringing 500 years. The plain font is 16th century, and of the same age are the mason marks we noticed on the east doorway of the tower. The chalice was made in 1568 and the paten bears the arms of Sir Thomas Moyer, who lived in the 16th century hall, a timbered building with an overhanging storey.

A Shakespeare Village

PLESHEY. Its great castle was doomed 200 years before Shakespeare wrote the lines which have made it known the world over. He makes the widow of Thomas, Duke of Gloucester, ask that Edmund of York may come to her, saying to John of Gaunt,

> Bid him—O, what?
> With all good speed at Plashy visit me.
> Alack, and what shall good old York there see,
> But empty lodgings and unfurnished walls,
> Unpeopled offices, untrodden stones?

Though but the merest fragment of this old splendour is left this is one of the most famous spots in Essex, with memories of illustrious figures in history.

Far down the corridors of time we travel here, for this beautiful place, with its splendid trees, its Tudor house with an old barn and a dovecot, and its cottage gardens fringed by the waters of an ancient moat, was a fortress almost before our history began. Its very name comes from an old French word meaning an enclosure, and the original Pleshey was ringed in by a rampart and a ditch thrown up by the Britons, a mile round and still to be seen, the ditch sometimes 45 feet wide.

It was within this ancient enclosure that the Saxons laid out a new fortification of a mount and a moated court, and it was upon the Saxon earthworks that the Normans built the castle. The Saxon moat is 100 feet wide and part of it is still full of water; the great oval mount is 900 feet round and 50 feet high, and has its own moat still wet, spanned by the only relic of the medieval fortress, a strongly built bridge fashioned of brick in the 15th century, to which parallel walls of rubble lead down. Norman foundations have been excavated on the mount, but great trees lord over it today. One of the village streets is believed to run along the rampart of still another court, and altogether the earthworks of Pleshey are some of the most remarkable in the land.

King Stephen gave the castle to his rich and treacherous earl, Geoffrey de Mandeville, whose son obtained Henry the Second's leave to fortify it further. It passed to the Bohuns, Earls of Hereford; and it was through Eleanor de Bohun that Pleshey came into history as the home of a royal prince. She was the heiress of her family and married the great Gloucester, uncle of Richard the Second.

Thomas, Duke of Gloucester, and Lady Eleanor founded a College of nine chaplains which we remember as we look at this village church for it began with the noble building they gave at the end of the 14th century. Its end was as sad as the end of the castle, for with the passing of the monasteries it fell into the hands of Sir John Gates, who chose to destroy all the medieval buildings. A flourishing College it must have been, for as many as 137 copes were recorded in an old inventory. Almost everything has gone, but not quite all, for here are three arches which supported the medieval tower, and in the present fine tower are two bells cast in 1400, with medallions showing two birds on a plant.

The church was rebuilt last century by the Tufnells, and here are gathered a few treasures of the old days, among them a monument to Sir William Joliffe of 1749, and one to his kinsman Samuel Tufnell, showing his bust and urns with golden flames. There are two 16th century communion tables, and the tops of two medieval tombs with the shapes of what were once fine brasses. But the most fascinating link with the old days is a stone in the wall, for it probably came from the castle, lay for many years in a garden wall, and is written in Latin with the name of Richard the Second.

It was Richard who brought destruction to Pleshey, bringing the great days of the castle to an end by the foulest of deeds. To this old fortress he came to dine with his uncle Gloucester, but in reality to have him murdered; and by a strange chance it was here, a year or two later, that they brought the king's half-brother, the Duke of Exeter, to have his head struck off for plotting against Henry the Fourth. As for the faithful Lady Eleanor, she went to spend her months of widowhood with the nuns at Barking.

Thomas of Woodstock

PLESHEY in 1397 witnessed one of the strangest scenes in history. Before the castle appeared Richard the Second at the head of a company of nobles and trained bands from London with whom he had marched throughout the night to arrest his uncle Thomas of Woodstock, Duke of Gloucester. He was John of Gaunt's brother, youngest son of Edward the Third, lord of the estate through his wife Eleanor, who was heiress of the last of the Bohuns, one of Shakespeare's tragic figures.

Eleven years older than the king, at whose coronation he carried the sceptre, Thomas, succeeding his wife's father as Constable of England and created Duke of Gloucester, saw service at sea and in France, helped to suppress the Essex peasants who rose in revolt with Wat Tyler, and conspired against his brother Gaunt, whom he did not forgive for marrying his son, the future Henry the Fourth, to Eleanor's younger sister, of whose revenues Gloucester had hoped to remain master by inducing her to enter a convent. Fierce, unscrupulous, and avaricious, Gloucester took advantage of Richard's corrupt and lawless rule to head a movement which threatened the king with dethronement, secured the removal and execution of the royal favourites, and greatly enriched himself.

Richard bided his time for 11 years, then, scenting another conspiracy, struck suddenly, and came with his forces to seize him at Pleshey. Gloucester came out from the castle at the head of the ecclesiastics of the collegiate church he had established, and Richard forced him into the chapel to hear mass. Then the wretched man was seized and shipped to Calais, where he confessed treason and made a moving appeal for mercy. Soon afterwards he was seized at dinner and suffocated. The body was brought to England and lies in Westminster Abbey. In 1808, the grave being opened, the skeleton in its leaden coffin was seen, and was reburied near the faithful duchess.

The Old Priory

PRITTLEWELL. Its tiny group of fishermen's huts at the south end have grown in a hundred years into the greatest Southend of all, the Londoner's seaside, a crowded pleasure place, noisy and happy as a medieval fair ground, but with nothing else from those days until we come to Prittlewell, a mile from the wide open mouth of the Thames.

Here a medieval church stands high at the cross-roads in company with a few odd little cottages, and in a lovely garden to the north of it is the priory and now serving Southend as a treasure-house. The church was here before the priory, for in its chancel wall is an arch built of Roman tiles by a Saxon mason. The Normans and their heirs re-shaped the vast building, and some time about 1470 stone was quarried in Kent for the magnificent tower; it is strong enough still to bear the swing of ten bells, one weighing nearly a ton. Flintwork adorns the top of the tower and the two-storeyed porch, where a 400-year-old door with 20 rich panels and its old iron ring opens on to a 13th century arcade pierced in the original Norman wall. The arcade ends in slender Tudor arches replacing those which once held up a central tower and making the nave now 100 feet long. Tudor masons cut the font with roses and pomegranates, and about the same time a Flemish craftsman carved the two panels framed on the wall, one showing winged beasts with necks entwined; they probably once formed part of a chest. Close by is the stone coffin lid of a 13th century priest.

Painted glass, old and new, adds to its beauty. Above the chapel altar are 20 vivid Bible scenes brought from Rouen and Italy. One showing the Temptation is thought to be by Albert Durer; another shows the three men in a realistic fiery furnace. A lovely modern window close by portrays two bishops over 1300 years apart—Cedd, who brought the Good News to Eastern England, and John Watts-Ditchfield, the first Bishop of Chelmsford, who is still recalled with special affection in the slums of East London. Galahad and King Arthur, St Michael and St George, appear as small glowing figures in the porch.

The church was given to the priory which Robert FitzSweyn founded in early Norman times, and eight centuries later the priory with its 35 acres of garden was given to the town by Mr R. A. Jones, who now rests in the cloister with the monks whose ancient home he lived in and restored. Today their home and his is open to all. We may wander by the River Prittle and come upon the old fish-ponds, and here is a 13th century wall, all that remains of the church the monks worshipped in; though its foundations prove it to have been 180 feet long with great transepts flanking a central tower. The refectory on the opposite side of the cloister has mostly been built up again, but still retains one Norman wall with one Norman window standing out among the rest, and with a doorway still beautiful, though it has needed much patching since the prior first stopped on his way through it nearly 800 years ago to admire the deep mouldings and the leafy capitals. There are beams in the refectory roof 500 years old, and glowing in its windows are modern shields of all who have made their home here down the centuries. Illuminated manuscripts are in cases and frames, and behind a Jacobean altar rail is the memorial to 1350 men of Southend who fell in the Great War.

Passing into the Prior's House on the west side of the cloister we first come to two vaulted 15th century rooms, the first containing part of the lead coffin in which some Roman was buried near the park, a Norman coffin lid, and many a stone from the priory church; the second with some worn timbers from Rayleigh Castle, the home of the priory's founder. Over these vaulted chambers is the timber-framed room where the priors lived and worked, a beautiful room, with the smoke of their fires still left on the magnificent 15th century roof of five bays with two original kingposts. The 16th century put in the fireplace here today, and here is furniture made in the lifetime of the last prior and three things from the end of his story—the seal he had to give up and two documents transferring his priory to avaricious courtiers. The first is a letter from Henry the Eighth, with his portrait and part of the royal seal, granting the priory to Thomas Audley; the second bears the portrait of the boy king Edward and transfers the property to Lord Rich; both documents are superb examples of penmanship.

As we stand where he stood for the last time, looking down on the quiet of the cloister, we can hardly resist a feeling of pity for Thomas Norwich, who saw his priory become the loot of the king and his favourites. Rooms added by later owners are now filled with treasures from the Stone Age onward, and so arranged that we can walk up the corridors of time, past Stone and Bronze Age implements, past a skull 4000 years old, past net-sinkers and loom weights of the Iron Age, Samian ware and Roman coins, pagan swords and a garnet set in gold by Christian Saxons, past weapons and household oddments of the last ten centuries to our own time.

Another beautiful structure which survived in this place is Porters, a red brick house with gabled wings which grew up in the 16th and 17th centuries and still keeps its panelled rooms, the hall with linenfold and carvings of kings, with great beams in the roof and an Elizabethan stone fireplace carved with masks and acanthus leaves. With this house, the priory, and the noble church, Southend's mother village can still draw the crowds away from the sea to wander for an hour or so in another world.

George Washington's Ancestor

PURLEIGH. It is a hilltop village to which Americans come, for here preached Lawrence Washington, the great-great-grandfather of the Father of the United States for ten years, he was thrust out of Purleigh in 1643, and his son John sailed for Virginia in 1657. The 14th century church he knew is a handsome place and has been carefully restored by American friends in memory of the Washingtons. We found a portrait of George Washington and his mother hanging on the walls.

The tower is made beautiful by bands of knapped flints, and little flint crosses ornament the buttresses. Both tower and chancel have bands of 14th century bricks with glazed surfaces, rare examples of early brickwork. The bricks in the porch are Tudor, and the porch shelters a door with iron strap-hinges which has been opening and shutting for 600 years. All this time a leopard has been looking down from one of the windows, shining in the sunlight of 600 summers. A modern window has the portrait of John Wycliffe, and two great oil paintings of Moses and Aaron hang on the walls. The pulpit was made in Queen Anne's reign, and one of the preachers, Provost Hawkins, preached from it for 55 years last century.

Uncle William's Poor Robin

QUENDON. It lies by the road to Saffron Walden, which runs in a valley made by a stream flowing to the River Cam. The road winds past a hundred-acre park in which the deer have roamed for centuries, and in it stands the timbered hall of Tudor days, now faced with red and blue bricks. We see it as the 17th century faced it, a handsome place with a front of six bays divided by pilasters which support a charming timbered cornice. In the grounds is an octagonal dovecot with a lead-capped lantern, and on the walls of the attics are remains of painted figures 300 years old.

The old church stands a little above the road, with six gabled windows and two arcades of the 13th century. Two of their fine columns have niches probably used for holding lights. The chancel was made new 400 years ago, but its arch is 13th century. One of the windows is in memory of John Collin, rector here for 60 years last century, and there is another with two angels in memory of a maid-of-honour to Queen Victoria.

Fine pieces of modern craftsmanship are the lectern, on which is an alabaster angel with flowing hair, and the screen given by Sir William Foot Mitchell in memory of his son-in-law; he was Captain Winter Rose, who gave his life for us, and as he lay dying made a thumbnail sketch of what he would like this screen to be. The font is modern, but the medieval font has been rescued from a ditch and is outside the door. There is a beautiful chalice of Charles Stuart's day in the vestry, where hang two certificates recording burials in wool. From 1621 to 1792 this form of burial is in the register, and among the names of those buried in wool here we found that of Thomas Winstanley, whose son Henry built Eddystone Lighthouse. Henry's uncle William, who also lies here, was famous in his day for his Poor Robin Almanacs. He also sold chap-books, and was a great character towards the end of the 17th century. He is said to have started as a barber in London, and then to have given up the razor to use the scissors for making up his books and almanacs.

The Medieval Decorator

RADWINTER. Here is a woodland setting for delightful old houses, chief among them 16th century Grange Farm with its chimney stack as lovingly finished as a work of art, and the Old Vicarage with elaborate bargeboards carved 300 years ago.

But best of all is the church porch, where 14th century wooden arches hold up an overhanging black and white room, with sunken carving on the great beams forming the outer entrance, and a medieval handle to the new inner door. A door on the other side has more medieval ironwork.

From the black and white of the porch we pass into a church bright with colour. It has 14th century arches to the tower and the chancel, but most of it was rebuilt last century, when the massive tower and spire were taken down and put up again and its old bells re-hung. The tower has kept its 16th century gargoyles and the nave roof its corbels, one open-mouthed with a hand clutching its tongue. Some of the beams are 600 years old.

A medieval decorator painted two arches of the arcades with red and yellow bands, and ever since the church has been turning itself into a gallery of art, some good, some poor. Most impressive is the huge 16th century reredos, which presents the story of the Madonna like a pageant, its six deep recesses crowded with wooden figures in realistic scenes. We see her as a baby and then with her own baby; we see her marriage, death, and funeral. In striking contrast with the many shadows cast on the dark wood by the figures is the case of richly coloured 19th century panels made to fold up and enclose the precious reredos. Each panel is painted with another scene in the Madonna's life, and she appears yet again between two saints in a simple triptych painted by a foreign artist 500 years ago.

Other paintings include a striking 19th century picture of Christ and the Children, a complete series of the Stations of the Cross, brilliantly coloured saints on the organ screen, and a vivid picture of the Ascension in memory of 120 years of service by rectors of the Bullock family, one of whom was here for 51 years. It is mainly due to this family that the village has so rich a church. There is good woodcarving, too, both new and old, including three old chests, a Jacobean chair, and a tall font cover with saints under canopies, a copy of medieval work. Between two huge vestment chests hangs a 12-branched candelabra of the 18th century.

A Passing Curate

RAINHAM. It has stood for many centuries, a compact little place by the Ingrebourne river. Saxons dwelt here, some of their work, among the finest glass drinking horns ever found in Britain, having been discovered in a sandpit close by.

In the heart of Rainham stands a perfect Norman church, chancel, nave, tower, and aisles all built about 1170. The 13th and 16th century additions to the tower have not spoiled the dignity of this charming church. It is impressive to stand under the tower and look up the nave with its massive arcades, each pier with banded shafts and neatly scalloped capitals. The chancel arch is ornamented with chevrons, and through it gleams the light of six east windows. The priest's doorway has a grotesque face above it, and one of the other doors is still hung on an ornamental hinge of the 12th century. A rough Norman font rests on a panelled 15th century base, and the edge of the bowl has the marks of the fastenings of the cover in the days when the holy water was kept locked against witches. The modern screen has a little woodwork from the 15th century screen, but the best carving of that age is in the sanctuary, where a crouching lion from the shoulder of a bench-end is now part of a chair.

There are three brasses, a small one of 1480 showing a woman in a butterfly headdress and two larger ones with a solemn-looking civilian and his wife, whose costume shows how fashions changed in 20 years. Fragments of colour on the walls show us how glowing this church must have been when these people worshipped here.

Charles Churchill, poet and satirist, became curate here in 1756, and of his own preaching he wrote that "Sleep at my bidding crept from pew to pew." But the people of Rainham did not suffer in this way long, for after two years he succeeded his father at St John's, Westminster. He loved the theatre and in 1761 leapt into fame with a masterly satire on the actors of the day. He joined Wilkes's party, wrote many satires, and led a wild life till he died at 34. Cowper called him the "Great Churchill, with a certain rude and earth-born vigour" and Garrick said of him "Such talents, with prudence, had commanded the nation." But he had nothing in him to outlast the popular whim of his age, and his verse is forgotten.

Under Seven Rulers

RAMSDEN BELLHOUSE. Its name comes from the Bellhus family, but it might well have come from the 15th century wooden tower and spire of the church, an example of the astonishing timberwork for which Essex is famous. It is almost the only part of the church not rebuilt, and for over four centuries has kept its huge beams inside, its oak doorway carved with a rose and a shield, its door with hinges older still, and its belfry steps with their unshaped treads. The nave roof is just as old, and a beam in the chancel is enriched with twisted foliage. From the 14th century are the rafters and bargeboards of the porch and a beautiful little piscina arch with tiny quatrefoils in the spandrels. There are three chairs elaborately carved in the 17th century, when the graceful cover was made for the 15th century font; and there is a big medieval chest six feet long, the lid so heavy that it is in two parts each with two handles.

God's Acre charms us here with a cluster of elms higher than the weathercock, and standing in their shade we have a lovely view over rolling meadowland. Under a gravestone carved with an hourglass lies one whom we may perhaps call the most remarkable child in the village, Anthony Child who died an old man in 1726. He had lived under seven rulers, six kings and Oliver Cromwell, and missed the eighth only by a year.

RAMSEY. It stands on the high road to Harwich, with its cottages in the valley, a 16th century farmhouse standing conspicuous by a stream, and the church on a hill towards the sea. The church has a Norman nave and the tower takes us back to the time of Agincourt. At the 500-year-old doorway of the church is a carving of the coronation of the Madonna, a quaint longhaired figure at prayer, and there are crowns, moons, stars, and other small carvings on the mouldings. The door has been on its hinges five centuries, its rich carving much battered by time. The chancel roof is 16th century and the carved pulpit 17th.

The Great Battle

RAWRETH. It lies attractively on a byway, its tower seen afar in the undulating countryside. Except for this old tower, with its lions peering from the corners, and a 15th century arcade, the church was refashioned in 1882 from the designs of Ernest Geldart, rector of the tiny Norman church at Little Braxted. Its font has a modern bowl on a stem which once held a Norman one, and there is a fine screen watched over by a handsome nave roof. A Tudor monument in the south aisle has brasses of Edmund Tyrell and his wife on a stone richly carved. From the porch St Nicholas looks out on this corner of Essex where a foreign king is believed to have fought his last battle for English soil, for we are not far from what is still called Battlesbridge on the River Crouch, and it was hereabouts that Canute, after a long and terrible fight, defeated Edmund Ironside. Where the tall mills now stand by the river the Danish ships are thought to have been drawn up, waiting for the result of a battle which influenced the whole course of our island story.

Stronghold on the Hills

RAYLEIGH. An ancient stronghold on the hills dividing the valleys of the Crouch and the Thames, it has lost its ancient castle but has kept the mound on which it stood. With a ditch all round it, the mound rises 50 feet high and looks down on raised terraces, but of the strong walls raised in the Conqueror's day not a stone remains.

Something remains of the church of his day, for it has Norman work in its chancel walls, the font at which the Normans christened their little ones, and we may see in the outer corners of the chancel the Roman tiles the Norman builders picked up here and used for strengthening their masonry. Near where the road widens in this little town two cottages face each other, one with an overhanging storey four centuries old. Up the hill is the rectory, older still, with two wings giving it charm and beauty, and high on the ridge of a hill is something older than anything else hereabouts, earthworks of a prehistoric race.

A lovely cedar welcomes the climber into the wide churchyard where the massive tower has dominated the church about 500 years. Fine columns support the ancient timbers of the roof, and great windows fill the place with light. A heavy cross-beam with Jacobean ornament spans the tower; it is a relic of the ringing gallery of long ago. A remarkable alms-chest with its original hinges and lock was cut out of a solid block in medieval days. On the arch of the tower are the consecration crosses, and in the tower still rings a bell which may have rung for the victory of Agincourt. There are fine screens old and new; a 15th century one has four traceried bays, and a modern one in memory of a gunner in the war shows the hero stricken on the field gazing at the Cross. In a peace memorial window are the archangels Michael and Gabriel with an angel by the empty tomb.

The splendid tomb of someone unknown has rich carving of niches and pedestals and faces by a craftsman of the 16th century. A brass portrait shows John Barrington, keeper of a royal park here, who was laid to rest soon after his king came home from Agincourt.

A Family Record

RAYNE. Its houses look down on a road where Caesar's legions marched, one of them a 15th century house with a Tudor chimney. Another Tudor chimney rises above the Old Hall, which has kept fine barns from Cromwell's century; and in Rayne Hall by the church there are roof beams possibly 600 years old, with other woodwork and many windows from the 16th century. Out of a barn has been fashioned the village club and library, making, with its old oak rafters, one of the best libraries we have seen in Essex. Here, too, stands one of the best brick towers in the county, built about 1500 by a Lord Mayor of London, Sir William Capel. It has a bold turret, pinnacles and battlements, handsome moulding round the doorway, and panels with shields. Sir William was an ancestor of the Earls of Essex, and the family arms are shown at the belfry door. The Capels lived at the hall, and many of them were laid to rest here. There is a heraldic inscription to Lady Catherine of 1572, great-grandmother of that Arthur Capel of Hadham who tried to rescue Charles Stuart from the Isle of Wight and was beheaded shortly after his king, expressing a wish that his heart might be buried in the royal grave. The chief attraction inside this refashioned church is the rare woodwork in the chancel, some of it by Flemish carvers 300 years ago and some older still. The reredos is a triptych, with 15 panels of scenes from the Annunciation to the Ascension; and near the altar is a beautiful traceried cupboard with figures of saints and an angel. The oak sedilia is carved in the same style, with angels under canopies and weird dogs as armrests; and over the vestry door is a vigorous relief of the death of the Madonna. A high-backed bench is rich with Tudor tracery, and has armrests of quaint men in flat-topped hats with books. The kneeling desk in front is carved with heads and an angel with a scroll; and the work of modern carvers is seen on the panels in the altar rails, where we see Pilate washing his hands. Rather hidden by the altar triptych is an attractive window of our own day, glowing with figures of St Alban, St Edmund, Edward the Confessor, and Charles Stuart. There are two old fonts, a plain 17th century one, and a restored 14th century one with a lovely frieze and symbols of the evangelists. A sacring bell, dated 1520, has been restored to the chancel after an absence of 100 years.

Can any village, we wonder, beat the record of the Hance family in this church? One was churchwarden in Restoration England. His son became parish clerk in 1723, and for nearly 200 years the office stayed in the family. Had we been here in the time of the Stuart Pretenders, of Clive in India, of Wolfe at Quebec, of Napoleon, of the first railways, of Queen Victoria and King Edward and the first years of King George the Fifth, we should always have found a Hance as parish clerk of Rayne. The wheel has turned full circle, for though the last of the Hances to be clerk died in 1916, his son was churchwarden when we called.

A Tragedy

RETTENDON. Its tower is seen for miles on land and looks out to the sea; the walls are five feet thick. It must have been well known to Rettendon's martyr hero, who was burned to death for his faith in 1556; he was John Derifall. The church is from the 13th and 15th centuries, its oldest possession being a stone from a tomb of Becket's time carved with birds and foliage. It was used after the Reformation as a gravestone for an unknown civilian whose family portraits are on it in brass; there are himself, his two wives, and seven children. Close by it is the portrait of Richard Cannon.

On the floor are brass portraits with a tragic tale behind them, those of Richard Humfrey, who died a few years before Shakespeare and is here with his three sons kneeling one behind the other. It was one of these sons who accidentally shot his father, a tragedy which caused great concern at the time, the son being tried and convicted and set free by royal pardon. The actual document of the pardon hangs in the chapel here, with the Great Seal of James the First hanging from it. For a hundred years after this tragedy the family thrived at Rettendon, and then came the time of Edmund Humfrey to pass away, a bachelor and the last of his family. He resolved, apparently, that he should not be forgotten, and he built for himself a vast monument completely filling the east wall of the chapel. Sunday after Sunday he would gaze at his marble figure with sobbing cherubs lamenting him. Above him stands an armoured man and a dignified woman, and there are grey pillars supporting a canopy over which are trophies and a painted shield, while a silver arm holds out a gilded cross.

It is pleasant to turn from this extraordinary structure, the work of an Italian craftsman, to the beautiful woodcarving in the choir, where nine bench-ends have elaborate poppyheads carved with beasts, a bear with a ragged staff, and a child in swaddling clothes on which remain the claws of an eagle. In the backs of some of these benches are traceried panels, probably from an ancient screen; they are of much beauty.

Old Craftsmanship

RICKLING. We come here to see what is left of its Tudor hall, and to admire treasures of old craftsmanship in the church. The hall stands on the site of a Norman castle, and has become a farmhouse with a group of farm buildings. They are set round the sides of a quadrangle, with a gatehouse built early in the Tudor Age. Many of the old windows are left; there is one of the 14th century. A door and a staircase are about 300 years old, and there are massive timbers in some of the roofs. Seventeenth century cottages are grouped round the green, but the church stands apart, near a farm which has a dovecot with more than 400 nesting holes. Except for its Tudor brickwork at the top, the tower is 14th century, and so is most of the church; but the nave has a lancet window suggesting that it was built a century before, and the foundations may be Saxon. There is a 14th century piscina with the remains of a wooden shelf, a 17th century chest still with some of its leather covering, a font of the 14th and 15th centuries, and a splendid modern reredos carved by Flemish craftsmen with saints and angels and evangelists. In the chancel are two handsome arched recesses, one with a marble stone on a 14th century gravestone, the other with a 15th century altar tomb. The shields on the tomb include the Langley arms, and the tomb is said to have been used for the family as late as 1670.

Rickling must be proud of its lovely old screen and pulpit, for both show the splendid art of the medieval workers in wood. The screen is 600 years old and has very beautiful tracery. The octagonal pulpit is a century younger, and has much elaborate ornament.

The Moated Farm

RIDGEWELL. Many little Roman relics of far-off days have been dug up in this village. Its houses today gather about a spacious green. One of the older ones, Ridgewell Hill Farm, was built a year after the Armada and has kept three sides of its moat. It has carved bargeboards, chimney-stacks with eight-sided shafts, and original panelling in the dining-room. Moat Farm and Essex Hall belong to the next century. The church is mostly 500 years old, and has two valued possessions, a screen richly carved by 15th century men and an oak bier made about the same time. Also 15th century are the roofs of nave and chancel (the nave roof fine with leafy bosses, wall-plates, and little figures in niches in the brackets); the base of the lectern with its square flowers; two plain stalls in the chancel; and the font, which has old tiles in the platform by it. The doorway inside the porch is a hundred years older, and so is the north arcade. There is a peephole in the chancel arch, a little 15th century glass made up with a modern scene of the Crucifixion, and a graceful 17th century pulpit with panelled sides and a fluted frieze.

Old Thomas Tusser

RIVENHALL. We come here for some of the finest old glass in England, brought from France by a 19th century rector. In the east window are four roundels of Norman glass showing the Annunciation, the Madonna and Child, the Entombment, and Christ in Majesty. With them are two ecclesiastical figures, one in yellow holding a book, the other an abbot in green with crozier and golden ball. A figure of a knight comes from the 13th century; his name, Robert Lemaire, is in the background. The horse is richly capari-

Saffron Walden   The Stately Tower and Spire

Overhanging Storeys in Bridge Street

The Decorated Gables of the Sun Inn

OLD SAFFRON WALDEN

soned, and the knight, his head hidden by a huge helmet, wears banded mail and is grasping a sword. The rest of the window is filled with 15th century glass, probably Flemish; the most interesting scene is the Adoration of the Magi, in which a dark-faced Moor with gold earrings might be Othello himself. Another chancel window has three 15th century roundels, one of God the Father carrying a golden cross. In the nave are shields and 14th century ornament, with two 16th century medallions.

The church has been rebuilt but has kept some of its old posses-sions, and they still read here from a Bible of 1717. There are two coffin lids 700 years old, twisted altar rails of the 17th century, and a magnificent tomb of alabaster and marble, on which lie Ralph Wyseman of 1608 and his wife Elizabeth, a grand-daughter of the infamous Lord Rich. Ralph wears armour and a ruff, and rests his feet on a seahorse, a quaint creature seen again on a helmet hanging above. Elizabeth is wearing a beautiful headdress; and in front of the tomb kneel three sons and three daughters.

A memorial tells of Samuel Western, who died in 1699; and on the floor, copied exactly from the marbles of its day, is a gravestone of cast-iron, with the family arms. It belongs to Thomas Western of Queen Anne's time, who married a daughter of a London iron-monger. The memory of a more famous member of the family is kept green by an elaborate Gothic monument with two female figures. It is to Lord Western, who died in 1844, having bought Felix Hall at Kelvedon and filled it with treasures collected on his travels. For 42 years he worked in Parliament in the interests of agriculture, and did much to improve our breeds of sheep. He was also a keen worker for prison reform.

Tudor Hall by the church has a chimney-stack of the 17th century; and Rivenhall Place, in a park of 100 acres is partly Tudor too. From the remains of a far older house here Roman pottery and coins have been found; and when the foundations were excavated a corridor with concrete walls 18 inches thick was traced for nearly a quarter of a mile.

At Rivenhall was born Thomas Tusser, a famous small poet of Shakespeare's day whose work was produced in our day in a volume issued at five guineas. He is unique. His long poem on Five Hundred Points of Good Husbandrie, beloved of generations of literary men on the one hand and the practical guide of centuries of reading farmers on the other, is an incomparable picture of agricultural life, a thoroughly competent and exhaustive account of farming, stock-breeding, and husbandry in all its parts, with the tasks for each season and servant, the management of great farms and small, of dairy and household, of men, implements, and animals. Yet Tusser was a failure as a farmer. All the wisdom, pathos, and humour of his Points are born of his own experience, and sad that experience was. He claims good lineage and gentle blood, but was sent by a pitiless father at an early age to serve as a chorister at the chapel of Wallingford Castle, Berkshire, where he was ill-clad and ill-used. It was in the days of the press-gang for choristers, when licensed officers would abduct children for the royal choirs, and Tusser was hustled from place to place where he was wanted. Eventually he reached St Paul's, and from there went to Eton, where the notorious Nicholas Udall was headmaster,

> *Where fifty-three stripes given to me*
> *At once I had*
> *For fault but small, or none at all,*
> *It came to pass, thus beat I was;*
> *See, Udall, see, the mercie of thee*
> *To me, Poor lad.*

Many more stripes of Fate were to fall on poor Thomas, yet he had happy days at Cambridge and for ten years with a lord, whom he served as a musician before the plough became his music, as he used to say.

Twice married, he farmed in Suffolk and Norfolk, but in spite of his comprehensive knowledge he was a failure on the land, though one of its best poets. His poem at first comprised only a hundred points, to which were added as many Poyntes of Huswifery; and from this nucleus sprang the complete work. One of his best compositions is his Ladder of Thrift, in which occur these familiar couplets:

> *To take thy calling thankfully*
> *And shun the path to beggary;*
> *To grudge in youth no drudgery*
> *To come by knowledge perfectly;*
> *To pray to God continually*
> *For aid against thine enemy. . . .*

None of his own business ventures flourished, and this poor

country-loving poet was eventually thrown into prison for debt. He showed others the way to succeed but could not succeed himself, and died in a London prison in 1580.

The Earl Who Loved Cromwell

ROCHFORD. A stately avenue of oak and elm leads us to this small town on the River Roche, and a quiet market square comes as a surprise round the corner. There are many quaint houses with gables and overhanging storeys. In Church Street is a steep-roofed building as charming as when Robert Rich, first Earl of Warwick, built it for poor old folk in the days of Shakespeare.

Rochford Hall, his home, is not far away. Its ancient grandeur has departed, but a turret remains where two gable-windowed roofs meet. Four hundred years ago it had three or four courtyards in which would walk a girl Sir Philip Sidney loved, Penelope Devereux, whose charm he made immortal in his sonnets, where she is Stella and he is Astrophel. Alas, Penelope married Robert Rich, one of the first noblemen to follow the Puritan way of life in an age of gaiety, but deserted him for the frivolous Earl of Mountjoy. Her eldest son was one of the romantic figures of the Civil War.

Rochford Hall is on the site of one of the homes of Sir Thomas Boleyn, father of Anne Boleyn, friend of Wolsey, and friend of the king who was to hound him to his doom.

In the middle of a field is the church which owes much of its stately grandeur to the hall. The tower, a magnificent example of the early brickwork of the Tudor Age, was built in 1500, when an heiress married the grandfather of Anne Boleyn, bringing the hall as her dower. Most of the church was made new in the 15th century, but in the east wall of an aisle is the beautiful net tracery used for windows 600 years ago. A brass portrait of the infant Christ has vanished from the nave, but there is a brass of Mary Dilcock of 1518.

Robert Rich, the second Earl of Warwick, was born under Queen Elizabeth. Educated at Cambridge and knighted at 16, he grew up at court, where he was a gallant figure at tourneys and an actor in the masques of Ben Jonson. He gave his life to the sea, to the colonisation of the Bermudas and of the New World. He was a true founder of empire. With this activity he combined the traditions of Drake and his school by privateering at the expense of Spain, himself sharing the perils of the ventures. The idol of his crews, he was excelled by none of them in the activity with which he climbed the topmost rigging.

But there was a stout Puritan strain in him, and when the persecutions began his home became the sanctuary of displaced ministers, whose unhappy lot was cheered by his unfailing humour, which kept them in roars at his table. He was among the first to resist Ship Money, and boldly to denounce it to the face of Charles; and when the parting of the ways was reached it was he who took over the fleet and kept it faithful to Parliament. When Cromwell became Protector, Warwick, who loved him, bore the Sword of State. It was his grandson and heir who married Frances Cromwell, the Protector's youngest daughter, and died soon after, so depriving the Cromwells of the distinction of the Warwick earldom. In response to Oliver's letter of sympathy Warwick in his grief remembered State affairs, and his reply to Oliver, congratulating him on his "prudent, heroic, and honourable management," went on:

Others' goodness is their own; yours is a whole country's—yea, three kingdoms for which you justly possess interest with wise and good men. Virtue is a thousand escutcheons. Go on, my lord,—go on happily to love religion, to exemplify it. May your lordship long continue an instrument of use, a pattern of virtue, and a precedent of glory.

Warwick left his mark on the New World, where, as at home, he ever urged political and religious tolerance, and, for all his merry spirit and his boisterous laughter, he was one of the most earnest advocates of the religious instruction of the Red Indians.

The Town of the Ancient Forest

ROMFORD. It has trebled its population since our century began and has wiped out some ancient local history which now seems rather quaint, but which nevertheless reaches back to Saxon and even Roman times.

For many centuries its countryside had a government of its own, under the name of Havering-atte-Bower, an independent patch in the midst of Essex, with a royal palace belonging to a succession of English queens. Romford had the chief group of population in this little royal Liberty, where Queens went for retirement, or for hunting in the great Essex forest. When the forest vanished before the advance of progressive agriculture, the Liberty became a typical rural marketing centre, as Romford still is, though now it is also within the residential fringe of London. This century it has been given Raphael Park, with handsome iron gates.

If we would seek visible reminders of Romford's history we must come to the 19th century church of Edward the Confessor, whose 162-foot spire is a landmark all around. It stands boldly in the market place, close to the meeting of the town's four chief roads. The new church has a great monument from the old one showing Sir Anthony Cooke, whose family was dominant in Romford for nearly 200 years. Sir Anthony kneels in Tudor armour facing his wife in a ruff and cloak. Behind him kneel his two sons, and behind his wife the four daughters who are believed to have composed his long Latin epitaph and to have been the cleverest women of their day. They certainly belonged to a remarkable family.

Sir Anthony was the great-grandson of Sir Thomas, a wealthy Lord Mayor of London who built himself a great house in Gidea Park, near Romford, but made the mistake of backing the losing side in the Wars of the Roses and barely escaped the scaffold. Still, he died rich and in Tudor days his descendants flourished, so much so that Sir Anthony rebuilt Gidea Hall, and as Steward of the Liberty of Havering-atte-Bower entertained Queen Elizabeth there.

Sir Anthony Cooke was a student, in love with country life, and a believer in education as the most broadening influence. He acted as tutor to his four sons and five daughters, and their accomplishments were so much admired that he was chosen tutor to the young King Edward the Sixth, who knighted him at his coronation.

The four daughters on the monument all married well. Mildred married the great Lord Burghley, Elizabeth's trusted adviser; Ann became the mother of Francis Bacon; Elizabeth's husband was Lord Russell of the famous Bedford family; Katherine married Sir Henry Killigrew, one of the busiest of Elizabeth's ambassadors. Gidea Hall has gone and the family is extinct, but the alabaster group passed on from the old church to the new church preserves an enduring household.

Another favourite of Queen Elizabeth is on his monument in the church porch. He is Sir George Hervey, with his wife, five sons, and six daughters. He was the Lieutenant of the Tower. On the opposite wall is Anne Carew's monument showing her leaning on her elbow and looking far from attractive.

By the church is an interesting 15th century building originally a home for a chantry priest. Then it became the Cock and Bell inn, now it is once more a Church House. Timbered and plastered, it has old beams and 17th century panelling. When we called the cock could still be seen, on the glass of the door, seated on the bell.

Another link with Romford's past is a picturesque group of 19th century almshouses round a garden in North Street, close to the River Rom winding its way southward through the town to become the Beam River and finally reach the Thames. Their history goes back to 1482 when Roger Reede's will bequeathed his newly-built house of Hoocrofts "to be a dwelling place for five poor men, not blasphemers of the name of almighty God, nor common beggars, but such as have been of good governance and fallen into poverty; the saddest and wisest to be the ruler."

In the manor house of Romford (now vanished) was born in 1592 a poet who for a time was perhaps the most popular English poet in a serious vein. No one is now captivated by reading Francis Quarles, and few have even a nodding acquaintance with him, but he was once a prevailing fashion. Horace Walpole complained that "Milton was forced to wait till the world had done admiring Quarles." The poet's family had associations with the Stuart court, and Francis was an ardent pamphleteer defender of Charles; at the same time he was a Puritan in spirit. His style has annoying contradictory qualities. He followed the fashion of elaborate "conceits," yet no one could write more smoothly and plainly, as we see in this, one of his few famous verses:

> *My soul, sit thou a patient looker-on,*
> *Judge not the play before the play is done.*
> *Her plot hath many changes; every day*
> *Speaks a new scene: the last act crowns the play.*

He had wit and vivacity, but varied it with appalling dolefulness. His obvious piety impressed the serious, but he entangled himself in the literary tricks of his day, and has now been almost wholly excluded even from the most copious anthologies.

Here Lived Francis Quarles

ROXWELL. Here lived for some years the poet Francis Quarles, born in 1592 at Romford. Here he must have written much of his religious poetry, the Emblems which Charles Stuart loved to read. Some of Roxwell's charming old houses and farms were standing in his day, and four of his eighteen children were baptised in this church. It was built in the 14th century and much altered in the 19th, when the tracery of some of its old windows found a strange new home in the churchyard wall. The modern bell-turret stands on 15th century posts, the new screen has 17th century woodcarving from the organcase of Durham Cathedral, and there is an oak settle in which Quarles may have sat. There is interesting 16th century glass in the west window. One picture shows the Nativity, round it being the Annunciation, Mary and Elizabeth, Humility, and other Virtues. Another shows the Resurrection with the soldiers fleeing terrified, and round it like miniatures are scenes from the life of Our Lord. One who died for us in France has the tribute of three heroic figures standing in a window, David and Jonathan and Judas Maccabaeus. A draped marble in the chancel tells of two Sir John Bramstons in the 17th century, the father a distinguished judge, the son a lawyer too. A stone portrait watched over by an angel shows Mary Byng, an 18th century heiress.

A Whisper from Sir Thomas More

ROYDON. It knew the first Englishman of his day 400 years ago, Sir Thomas More; he fell in love with one of the daughters of the moated house whose ruins are still an indication of the grandeur that has passed away. Its streets slope down to the River Stort, some of its shops and houses still looking medieval, the stocks and whipping-post on the green, with the little wooden lock-up close by, reminding us of the rough justice of not so very long ago.

It was to Nether Hall that Sir Thomas More came courting. The towers of its gatehouse still stand above the water of the moat; they were the first defence of a dwelling-house built when the houses of the red and white roses were fighting for the crown. There are still ancient corbels and trefoil arches round the towers.

The hall was the home of the Coltes. A Privy Councillor of Edward the Fourth, Thomas Colte was laid here to rest in 1471, and we see him in his splendid armour engraved in brass, his wife Joan beside him in a collar of suns and roses. In the sanctuary are the brass portraits of his son John with two wives, all in heraldic robes, their sons and daughters in groups below. It was one of these daughters Sir Thomas More came courting—two of them perhaps we should say, for there is a strange little story told of it.

Sir Thomas More's affection was set on the second daughter, yet when he considered that it would be a grief and shame to the elder one to see her younger sister preferred before her in marriage, he turned with a certain pity to Jane the elder, and married her four years before Henry the Eighth came to the throne. The purity of their home life is one of the redeeming features of the pitiless reign of Henry the Eighth, and it is difficult to forget the little story of that dramatic day when Jane Colte sat in church at Chelsea and received a whisper from the Lord Chancellor. Sir Thomas used to carry the cross at the head of processions round Chelsea church and sing in the choir, wearing a surplice like other choristers, and when service was over, and More had left the vestry, a footman would go to his wife's pew and say, "His Lordship is gone." Jane was ambitious and liked such attention, and it is said that after his fall from office the Englishman did not know how to tell his proud wife that he had resigned the Great Seal of England, but in the end he broke the news by going to the pew and saying: "May it please your ladyship, my lordship is gone."

There are two other Tudor brasses in the church, one with John Swift in a fur-lined cloak, and one with the portrait of Elizabeth Stanley who died just after the Armada. There are little panes of medieval glass round a fine figure of Peter gazing across the sanctuary; three elaborately carved chairs three centuries old; and a fine screen carved with the simple tracery of 14th century windows, so that its ten bays look like the windows of a cathedral. The screen is still held together by its original oak pins. The font has been here since the church was new 700 years ago; it is remarkable for having been fashioned out of a square into an octagon by clever sculptors who carved four portraits of their friends at the corners, all four wearing hats with rolled brims, their faces full of character.

The Mark on the Door

RUNWELL. It stands on the low hills near the River Crouch. Its church tower is 15th century but the round columns of the arcades are from a church which was a place of pilgrimage in Thomas Becket's day. The timbering of the porches is enriched with Tudor roses, and the name of one of the benefactors, John Talbot, is on a beam. One of the doors is original, hinges and all, and on the inside is a curious burnt mark looking as if it had been made by a red-hot hand; the old folk will tell you that it is the mark of the devil's hand when he was shut in the church by an ancient priest. On the chancel walls are brasses of Eustace Sulyard and his wife in ruffs, facing each other over a prayer desk, and there are other monuments to the Sulyards, the last of the line being Sir Edmund, who was buried here in 1692. They lived at Fleming's, a farm with a lovely Elizabethan wing still standing. There is a poor-box hollowed out from a block of oak, yellow flowers in medieval glass, and a scratch sundial saved from the earlier church. In a chapel is a vividly coloured oak statue of the Madonna.

The Thread of History Through an Ancient Town

SAFFRON WALDEN. It is the medieval age living on into our century of change, a delightful little town in the Slade valley with a great roll of fame and 100 houses fit to be preserved as national monuments. Life has been going on here for more than a thousand years, and most of the time a thread has been running through it that has found its place in history.

Hundreds of Saxon graves have been dug in the solid chalk, and on the site of the big Saxon cemetery are traces of ramparts known as Battle Ditches, below which were pits in which ancient pottery was found. Looking down from Bury Hill are the ruined flint walls of the Norman castle. In the medieval days after the Normans a poor Walden boy grew up to be Archbishop of Canterbury, and a King of England died in his arms. In the century after these was born that Thomas Audley who became Lord Chancellor and whose grandson built Walden's most marvellous house, Audley End; and in his age Walden produced a Provost of Eton and a poet who had the friendship of Edmund Spenser and yet was good-for-nothing. It produced also John Bradford the martyr, and in one century more it gave to the world that wonderful man Henry Winstanley, who built the first Eddystone Lighthouse. A rich dower it has given to us in the lives of men.

And, as we have said, it is rich in old houses. We find them in every street, with massive timbers, carved brackets, overhanging eaves, and plastered fronts with the dolphins, cornucopias, foliage, and portraits fashionable in the 17th century. Inside some of them are rich fireplaces and lovely screens. One of the houses was once the school and has a Latin phrase on its front which warns us either to learn, or to teach, or to depart. There are not many schools in England with a longer tradition than Saffron Walden's, for it is referred to in the records of 1317, and was endowed in 1522 by Dame Jane Bradbury, widow of a Lord Mayor of London, to support one teacher of grammar "after the ordre and use of teching gramer in the scholes of Wynchester and Eton."

At the corner of Myddleton Place is a 15th century house with closely set timbers in the walls, a richly carved corner-post, and two oriel windows; inside is a magnificent panelled screen. The oak timbers on the house next door come from the house before it, in which the Friends used to meet in the 17th century, a house which came into the history of the town in the year in which the last Stuart king ran away, for we read in the civic accounts that 4d was paid for nailing up the Quaker's door twice. Their door being nailed up, they met in the street, unperturbed by the fact that some of them were arrested. The town is close to the hearts of the Friends, and their oldest school was transferred here from Croydon towards the end of last century. It stands on the hill called Mount Pleasant, a building costing £30,000, in 20 acres of ground.

Splendid and famous and historic too is the Sun Inn, with its captivating gabled front and its story of exciting days in the Civil War. Here Cromwell stayed with Fairfax when they met the Commissioners of Parliament and tried for two or three days to compose the quarrel with the army, trying in vain. The inn, which is in Castle Street, has projecting wings on each side of the 15th century hall, 14th century timbers in its roof, and a plaster front of the 17th century. A cartway has been cut through one wing, and in the gable above it is a big round sun in plaster relief with men on each side wearing long coats, knee breeches, and high-heeled shoes, one man wielding a club and one with sword and buckler. No longer an inn, this historic place now belongs to the National Trust.

Close by the great park of Audley End is a charming group of the 15th century Abbey Farm and Almshouses. It is one of the rarest peeps in Essex. Built of brick with tiled roofs, the almshouses have 20 tenements set round two courtyards, with a kitchen, a hall, and a chapel between them. The chapel has a hammerbeam roof with ornamental work in the spandrels, and the stone-paved kitchen has a great fireplace with an ornamental iron jack. In one of the kitchen windows is a Madonna and Child in glass 600 years old, and in the window of one of the houses is medieval glass with an angel and a pope among other fragments. The town has another group of almshouses which were the gift of Roger Walden in the 14th century, but they have been rebuilt. They stand between Audley Park and the High Street, and preserve from the older building a 15th century brass inscription, two carved corbels of the original windowsills, a Jacobean armchair, and a notice board 200 years old with the rules for tenants.

It should not be forgotten, as we look about at all this ancient beauty, that Walden has a living beauty too. Its name of Saffron comes from the flavouring plant which was once widely grown here, having been brought to England hidden in the staff of a palmer. Today if we come to Walden in carnation time we may see in a nursery a remarkable display of carnations. They are the pride of the town in their season, a riot of colour under one of the widest glass roofs in the world, covering an acre. The town is also rich in trees and in green spaces, for besides the great park it has a wide common and what are called the Bridge End Gardens, with noble cedars. From Audley End runs a double avenue of beeches to Strethall. Walden is perhaps unique among our towns for having two public mazes. One, on the common, is a curious survival of the centuries, a spiral maze cut in the turf. Nobody knows how old it is, but 15s was spent on repairing it in 1699. The other maze is in a corner of Bridge End Gardens, and is a copy of that famous maze at Hampton Court in which ten million people have been lost. As we are visiting it we should peep in at the little picture gallery at the garden gate to see the paintings by Old Masters.

In the castle grounds is the museum, a collection of remarkable interest. The ruins of the castle take us back eight centuries; the contents of the museum go down the ages and across the earth. We see a glove Mary Stuart wore on the morning of her execution, and a grim fragment of human skin which was found nailed to the door of Hadstock church. There are skulls and ornaments from the Saxon cemetery, and the skeleton of an elephant shown in the Great Exhibition of 1851 which was meant to usher in the peace of the world. There is one of the best collections of humming birds to be seen in England. An oak strip has 13th century carving of a mounted knight in mail, a bedstead has 14th century carving, and there is a 14th century altarpiece of alabaster showing Joseph leading the boy Jesus. A Jacobean doll's chair has a padded back. There are two stone mantelpieces from the home of Gabriel Harvey, the ne'er-do-well poet, one with figures of Justice and Truth and one with a pack-horse, a pig eating acorns, bees about a hive, and flowers of the saffron crocus.

Among the most interesting of all the exhibits is one of those rare feather cloaks worn by the kings of Hawaii, made from the feathers of birds that have long been extinct. There are only a small number of these cloaks left in the world, and they are all known, being highly treasured by the people of Hawaii; this one was worn by a king who came to England, who ruled for five years over Hawaii and was so agreeable to the missionaries that Christianity made great progress, and it became possible to pass a code of laws based on the Ten Commandments. The friendly king, Kamehameha, came to England with his queen and unhappily both caught measles and died.

In the castle grounds outside the museum we found the whipping-post and pillory, brought here from the prison of the neighbouring town of Newport.

The stately and impressive church looks boldly across the town. Its tower has 12 bells and dominates the High Street with a fine spire rising nearly 200 feet. There is only one church in Essex bigger than this noble structure of the 15th century, 184 feet long and 80 feet wide. Cupolas and pinnacles rise above its roofs, its parapets are richly carved, and along the north wall run grotesques among which we noticed a chained monkey, a wild man, a saddled beast, and a woman with a cat on her lap. Both porches have vaulted roofs, and the south porch has a priest's chamber above and a 13th century crypt below. In the porch wall is a figure from a 14th century reredos.

The arches of the nave are the solid work of the 15th century mason, the spandrels elaborately carved with familiar devices. Above these arches run 13 clerestory windows in each wall of the nave, filling the church with light. All the roofs are splendid, the chancel roof with the Twelve Apostles and painted bosses 500 years old, the nave roof with angels 400 years old, and the north chapel roof with 16th century saints and angels. Set in the wall of the north aisle are 12 canopied niches 600 years old, with delicate carvings of David playing the harp, St John and the Lamb, the incredulity of Thomas, and Our Lord's last days.

Below this lovely stone carving is a little gallery of brass portraits of people whose names have been lost. They are of the 15th and 16th centuries: a priest of 1430 with a pelican above his head, a woman of 1490, two women in butterfly headdresses leaning gracefully backward, a longhaired civilian and his wife of 1510, a thick-set man in a fur gown of 1530, a woman in a flat cap of the same time, and a 14th century civilian. On a wall are banners and helmets carved in memory of two brothers who died in one week, sons of Lord Braybrooke, one perishing at Inkerman and one at Balaclava. There is a lovely modern window of the Madonna in memory of Lord Braybrooke and his daughter, Augusta Strutt. On one of the screens is a little carving 600 years old. The fine chancel screen was designed by Sir Charles Nicholson, with the gallery above the roodbeam in medieval style. There is a Jacobean altar table, a Jacobean chest, and a plain font of the 15th century. A homely picture of Jerome with the Madonna and Child was above the altar when we called; it is a copy Matthew Peters made of Correggio's famous painting at Parma, and was given to this church by Lord Braybrooke in 1793.

But the chief monument in the church is in the south chapel, where on a fine altar tomb lies the man who was largely responsible for the grandeur about him, Thomas Audley, an Essex man born in 1488 who became town clerk of Colchester and rose to be a member of Cardinal Wolsey's household. On Wolsey's fall Sir Thomas More became Lord Chancellor and Audley took More's place as Speaker of the Commons. He advanced rapidly in the king's favour, and as Speaker allowed himself to transmit to the House one of the most flagrant pieces of royal hypocrisy. He caused two oaths to be read in Parliament to prepare the way for the Act of Supremacy. On Sir Thomas More surrendering to the king his seal as Lord Chancellor, Henry gave it to Audley while he was still Speaker, wishing to retain a Speaker who so well suited his purposes. He helped the king to put away Catherine of Aragon and to marry Anne Boleyn, and then examined Sir Thomas More, whom he could have saved if he would, though he would not. A man of poor character, the willing instrument of his imperious master, he declared that he was glad to have no learning but Aesop's Fables. Having presided at the trial of Bishop Fisher and Sir Thomas More, behaving shamefully at both, this man who had manoeuvred the marriage of Anne Boleyn now conducted her a prisoner to the Tower. He tried the prisoners for the Pilgrimage of Grace, and for all these services he was allowed to have what Thomas Fuller called the carving for himself of the first cut of the monastic properties. He declared that he was always poor till then, but he now became rich enough to build this magnificent tomb at Walden, the town after which he had called himself Baron Audley of Walden. His name is a stain on the Knighthood of the Garter which the king gave to him. He was a tall and impressive man to look at, and these seem to have been his noblest attributes, except that he was loyal as a tyrant's slave.

A man who left us a heroic example and an immortal saying, one of the notable figures of the 16th century, comes into Saffron Walden's story—John Bradford, at one time chaplain to the young King Edward the Sixth. He preached here for two years, and so endeared the people to him that they were in his thoughts as he sat writing his last letter at Newgate, with the prisoners in tears all round him; he called his letter the Dying Martyr's Testament to the Faithful at Saffron Walden. His death was one of the bitterest tragedies of Mary Tudor's reign, and rarely was seen such a crowd as at his burning. Taking a faggot in his hand and kissing it, Bradford looked on the people and cried: "O England, England, repent thee of thy sins; take heed they do not deceive you." It was John Bradford who, seeing a criminal going to execution, used these words which have been quoted a million times since, "But for the grace of God, there goes John Bradford." He was about 45, and a Manchester grammar school boy.

Walden has on its roll of fame two men of the 14th century and two of the 16th. One of its 14th century men began life as a poor boy and rose to be Lord Treasurer of England and Archbishop of Canterbury. He was Roger Walden, probably a butcher's son. He had a curiously adventurous life, advancing rapidly from a rectory to an archdeaconry at Winchester, becoming secretary to Richard the Second, and then Treasurer of England. In 1397 the king banished Archbishop Arundel from Canterbury and gave his office to Walden, but he held it only a little while, for Arundel returned and took the Primacy again. He bore no ill-will against Walden, in spite of the fact that he had removed jewels and six cart-loads of goods from Canterbury. During the public miseries of those times Walden suffered with the deposition of the king and was put in the Tower; he was one of those who fell when King Richard gave up his crown and pleaded for a little, little grave on the king's highway. He came back into favour and was even installed as Bishop of London in the new reign, but he did not long survive this dignity. In spite of his chequered career he is said to have been a gentle character, and even the archbishop whose office he usurped paid high tribute to his qualities.

Thomas Waldensis, who was living at the same time as Roger Walden, is also known as Thomas Netter. He became a monk, and took a great part in the prosecuting of the followers of Wycliffe, being made an inquisitor. He preached against the Lollards at Paul's Cross, and examined Sir John Oldcastle as to his opinions. He became a favourite with Henry the Fourth, and was with him when he died in Jerusalem Chamber, so that he would see that wondrous scene in Shakespeare. Henry the Fourth lay dying, his conscience uneasy, his physical frame in the grip of disease, and the Prince of Wales was by his bed when the king fell into a deathlike trance, and it seemed to his son that the crown had fallen to his lot. Thinking that the king was not to wake again, the prince took up the crown and put it on, and suddenly the king awoke. His dying heart was broken as he felt that his wild son had seized the crown so soon:

> *Dost thou so hunger for mine empty chair*
> *That thou wilt needs invest thee with my honours*
> *Before thy hour be ripe?*

It is said that Henry the Fourth died actually in the arms of

Waldensis, who preached his funeral sermon. He lived through the reign of Henry the Fifth and became confessor of the young Henry the Sixth, with whom he went to Rouen, where he died and was buried, a year before the burning of Joan of Arc in that city.

The two 16th century notables of Saffron Walden were kinsmen, Thomas Smith and Gabriel Harvey. Smith was a Saffron Walden grammar school boy who found favour with Thomas Cromwell, became Public Orator at Cambridge, and had such influence that he was appointed to discuss with Henry the Eighth the point as to whether he should marry an Englishwoman or a foreigner. Smith was a Protestant, and in the reign of the young Edward the Sixth the foul Bishop Bonner was imprisoned in the Tower for his conduct towards Smith. He became Provost of Eton, but lived in retirement during most of Mary Tudor's reign, being made Ambassador to France by Queen Elizabeth. Holbein painted his portrait. He was upright according to the life of his time, was a classical scholar and a writer, and believed in astrology long before the astrological quacks came pouring into Fleet Street. He lies at Theydon Mount, and his kinsman Gabriel Harvey wrote a poem of praise on his death. Both were grammar school boys, but while Sir Thomas Smith lived in the great house Audley End and entertained Elizabeth there, Harvey was but a ropemaker's son, though it is suggested that his father was quite a prosperous man.

At Pembroke College Harvey made friends with Edmund Spenser, who has immortalised him in the Shepherd's Calendar, where he is known as Hobbinol. One of Harvey's poems is also in the group which introduces Spenser's Faerie Queene. Apparently a quarrelsome man himself, Harvey shared with Shakespeare the scurrility of Robert Greene, the forgotten dramatist who imagined that he would live when Shakespeare was forgot, and he assailed Harvey with such vehemence that his offensive references were afterwards expunged from his work. Harvey replied to it in the same unworthy style, and today is forgotten with the rest.

Henry Winstanley Faces the Storm

HENRY WINSTANLEY, genius and dreamer, born at Saffron Walden in 1644 and christened at the font now in the church, built the first Eddystone Lighthouse. Long before he lost his life in that

The West Front from the River Cam

The Hall Oriel and Great Porches

AUDLEY END, SAFFRON WALDEN

The Magnificent Screen in the Hall

THE SPLENDOUR OF AUDLEY END

which the arches, now filled in, are divided by classical pilasters. This enriches one of the two wings, which end in handsome bays, the whole dignified by spacious windows and an open parapet.

The Great Hall is one of the enchantments of the early 17th century. It is 65 feet long, 26 wide, and 29 high. The ceiling is supported by moulded tiebeams, and hammerbeam brackets are elaborately carved, with pendants and strapwork against the walls as if to frame the gallery of portraits above the panelling and the mantelpiece. The ceiling itself is divided into 40 plastered panels, each with a crest or a badge, and banners projecting from the walls recall the illustrious people who have lived here. But all these glories are outmatched by the magnificent oak screen which fills one end of the hall. Its three bays are divided by pairs of figures set on richly carved pedestals, and above and below many other quaint figures stand out from the elaborate ornament of the time. Flying cupids fill the spandrels of the archway in the central bay, and above this arch are two smaller arches filled with pierced arabesques.

At the other end of the hall is a stone screen by Sir John Vanbrugh, from which stairs lead to the long saloon, remarkable for its Jacobean ceiling, a triumph of plaster work with 30 panels of birds and ships and sea-monsters, divided by pendants. Round the wall runs a delicate frieze, and from the overmantel stand out the Howard arms. Framed in arches round the room are portraits of Lord Chancellor Audley (after Holbein) and his daughter Margaret. A smaller door leads into the drawing-room, with a lovely frieze and fireplace, and then on to the two libraries, both with ceilings so perfectly restored that the new cannot be distinguished from the old. The chief library has a double frieze and a Jacobean mantelpiece with grotesque figures enclosing the lower panels, and musical instruments on the pilasters of the upper panels. Here are 10,000 books, most of them collected by the third Lord Braybrooke, who is famous as the first editor of Pepys. A lover of books from his boyhood, Richard Neville went to Magdalene College, whose Masters have been appointed by the owners of Audley End since the days when Chancellor Audley refounded that college, and there he rejoiced in the books Pepys had bequeathed. A few years later John Smith, a member of the college, deciphered the shorthand in which Pepys had written his diary, and Lord Braybrooke published an abridged edition together with letters written by Pepys, a work which held the field for 50 years. It is to the inspiration of this great house that the world owes its possession of the incomparable Diary. Among the treasures in the library now are a Psalter with beautiful illuminations of the 13th century, a Pliny printed by Aldus Manutius, a chair belonging to the poet Pope, and Voltaire's snuff-box.

In the dining-room behind the library is a portrait of George the Second by Robert Pine, believed to be the only portrait of the king painted from life.

The rooms we have been looking at are in the south wing. Those on the north have also much that is beautiful: Jacobean mantel-pieces and Adam decoration. Each wing has an original staircase, the south being remarkable for the decorated newel posts surrounding a narrow well like a cage and rising to the garret to end in delicate arches and pinnacles.

We may all cross the beautiful Audley Park by public paths, and may stand and wonder at some of the classical buildings set on its high points. They were erected by the first Lord Braybrooke. The round temple on Ring Hill is from a design by Robert Adam and commemorates our victories in the Seven Years War. The lofty Corinthian column capped by an urn is a memorial to a lady of the house. The many-pillared Temple of Concord records the recovery of George the Third from his grave malady in 1789. The neat bridge across the Cam by which visitors come to Audley End is the most useful of this group of buildings. We should not miss the stables. Probably too humble to be pulled down in the old days, they remain a delight with their gabled roofs and Tudor brickwork.

When Christianity Came

ST OSYTH. Its quiet charm has attracted men from the days when Britain attracted Caesar, and from then till now the lover of the beautiful has found something at St Osyth.

The pilgrim comes to the broad green which creeps up to the walls of Priory Park, one of the rarest ruins of Norman England, set among spacious gardens and noble trees. The Saxon nunnery of St Osyth has vanished, but here are Roman bricks the Saxons handled when they built it. They are in the walls and in the foundations. A Roman pavement of red and buff mosaic has been found in the park.

It is said that this place goes back to the days of the first Christian king of East Anglia, whose daughter was St Osyth, founder of the abbey here, and it is thought that Canute gave it to Earl Godwin, from whom it passed to the Bishop of London 50 years after the Battle of Hastings, when the priory was founded and these walls were built.

They are magnificent even in ruin. It is recorded that when Henry the Eighth and Thomas Cromwell seized this place the lead on the roof was worth £1000, and among the treasures was a silver casket in which was kept the skull of St Osyth.

By the green is an arched gateway of the 14th century enriched with deep mouldings, big enough for farm carts to pass through yet looking small by the two-storeyed gatehouse, adorned with flints and panels of white stone. In the spandrels of the gateway is St Michael fighting the Dragon, and on each side are elegant niches; in the roof of its arch are little gems of sculpture, among them St Osyth crowned, a hart with a napkin round its neck, and Gabriel bringing the good news to the Madonna.

Through all this we come into a scene of great beauty, the park in which were planted our first Lombardy poplars. It has a heronry of scores of nests and roses blooming where the old monks chanted their praise. Beyond the roses stands the great tower with three turrets, built of chequered stones in the middle of the 16th century. The view from the top is of supreme beauty, the sea and the richly wooded country round giving us a picture not to be forgotten.

By the tower is the wondrous spectacle of thousands of red bricks crumbling away. They were made by the Romans, handled by the Saxons, and built up by the Normans into the great arches which supported the dormitory of the monks and are now slowly crumbling before our eyes.

Behind them is a small chapel made from a vaulted passage, the ribs of its roof springing from marble columns six centuries old; and beyond this chapel a lovely clock tower watches over the site of the old cloisters. Built of chequerwork, it is a little rival of the abbot's tower, and is as old as the house beyond it, both built in the 16th century, though the house has cellars twice as old. The front of the house is dated 1527 and is like a picture book. The wall is patterned in red and black bricks and has a magnificent oriel window overhanging a moulded arch. Round this window 88 shields bear the devices of king and bishop, canon and saint, with the arms of France and many a curious rebus, including that of the Abbot Vintoner who built it, a vine and a tun.

A great national treasure is this group of buildings, and greatly is it cared for. It comes from the days of our Roman masters, through the days of our Saxon forefathers, into the age of our Norman conquerors, and here still stand these venerable walls, rich in history and in beauty, with all the glory of an English garden about them and the story of one of our saints woven into them.

The village has many ancient cottages; Priory Cottage with a projecting hall of the 15th century, one by the cross-roads built in the 16th century, and the moated St Clair Hall built in the 14th century. In the marshes stand Martello towers built to keep back Napoleon, and there is a mill set up long ago to be worked by the tide.

The church, with its massive tower, is a noble structure of Tudor days, seized by Henry the Eighth while the walls were still being raised. We can see the place where the building came to an untimely end, the piers for the new chancel arch standing unoccupied against the walls. Five lofty brick arches run from here down each side of the nave to the west wall, where Norman masonry was pierced by the tower arch in the 14th century. Both the wide aisles, with their brick arches into the transept, are 16th century; so are the brick and stone porch and the wonderful roofs. Lovely white arches nearly 700 years old divide the transepts from the chapels and the chancel. In the chancel is a surprise which the villagers have called The Fold, altar rails curiously shaped like a horseshoe. On an alabaster tomb lies the first Lord Darcy with his wife, he with the Garter round his knee, and by them lies their son John, his wife beside him in a fur-lined mantle. Another John is carved in alabaster wearing the robes and cap of a serjeant-at-law. There is a lovely medieval font with the sword of Paul and the keys of Peter and a portrait of St Osyth carved on it; and St Osyth is also in a lovely modern window. We may compare these portraits in glass and stone with those drawn by medieval artists on 13th century seals, of which some casts are shown in a case by the door.

Among so much that is fine and splendid to look at is one small tribute here that will appeal to many travellers, for it is in memory of a native of St Osyth, Benjamin Golding who founded Charing Cross Hospital. A student at St Thomas's, he became physician for West London Infirmary, which he transformed 100 years ago into the famous hospital at the heart of London.

The story of the village saint takes us back to the day when Christianity began to change the hearts of the rulers of our Motherland thirteen centuries ago. Frithewald and Walburga were King and Queen of East Anglia and were the first rulers to adopt the new faith. Their daughter Osyth loved the religion of hope and joy and made others love it too. As soon as she was old enough she was betrothed to Sighere, son of Sebert, first Christian king of the neighbouring kingdom of Essex. Great festivities took place at the wedding, yet when the feast was at its height Sighere caught sight of a splendid stag passing the house and without a thought for his bride called to his men, rushed out to his horse, and galloped in pursuit. Hunting for him was more important than marriage, thought Osyth, and when Sighere returned from the chase he found that she, too, had left the feast and betaken herself with her maids to the nearest nunnery. An agreement was made by which Sighere gave Osyth the village of Chich, where she founded a nunnery and gave her name to the village.

Years passed and a wooden church was built above the creek; and then Inguar and Hubba, the Danes, came raiding. They sailed up the Colne and burned the nunnery, and, seizing Osyth, commanded her to bow before the images of their gods; and on her refusal cut off her head. The legend is that from the spot where she fell a fountain gushed forth, but for us her life of devotion in those rough days is miracle enough.

Two Brothers

SALCOTT. An ideal place this remote corner of Essex must have been for the smugglers of silks and wines on winter nights, when the tide filled the creek in the marshland here. Old thatched barns and cottages line the quiet street, the post office most beautiful of all. Could any spot be better suited, we may wonder, for a game of hide and seek?

The church would be the nearest building to the creek a hundred years ago, and we may imagine from the holes in the doorway, into which the great beam fitted, that the door was often barred against smugglers and Preventive men. The church takes the place of one which was shattered by an earthquake, but the splendid medieval arch of the tower withstood the shock, and the 16th century doorway still displays its ancient beauty. Propped against a buttress of the tower is a coffin lid 700 years old.

Two brothers of this place were associated with the dramatic quarrel of king and pope which changed the whole history of England. They were John and William Capon, distinguished sons of Cambridge and friends of Cardinal Wolsey. William was his chaplain, and was appointed dean of the famous college established at Ipswich by Wolsey from the funds he obtained from the suppression of religious houses. Ipswich College, however, did not survive its founder and William Capon retained his mastership of Jesus College, Cambridge, till four years before his death in 1550. John rose to higher rank, and as Abbot of St Benet in Norfolk we find him visiting Cambridge in 1529 to persuade his brother and other dignitaries to declare in favour of Henry's divorce with Catherine of Aragon.

The reward for his success was his appointment as Abbot of Hyde, near Winchester, and we find John's name among those who wrote to the pope begging him to consent to the divorce. A year later the king himself wrote to the pope asking him to allow the Archbishop of Canterbury and the Abbots of Westminster and Hyde to pass judgment on the divorce.

Two years later Henry nominated him to the bishopric of Bangor, but the pope refused to consent, whereupon the king assumed papal authority for the second time and told Archbishop Cranmer to consecrate him. A few years later, when the monasteries were being suppressed, John Capon willingly gave Hyde Abbey to his royal master, who made him Bishop of Salisbury, an office he managed to retain until his death in 1557. Foxe calls him a time-serving papist and a persecutor of martyrs under Henry and Mary; and we know that as an old man he sat in Southwark Cathedral and took part in the trial of that courageous and consistent saint, John Hooper.

The Bible and the Pax

SANDON. It has a lovely oak of Old England on its green and a handsome brick tower built when Cardinal Wolsey was lord of the manor. Under its battlements is a row of small arches. There are Roman tiles in the walls, and in the chancel a gem of stone carved by a craftsman who may have come over with the Conqueror. For hundreds of years it lay hid in a buttress, a pillar piscina with beading and fluting carved in spirals round the shaft and beautiful ornament on the hollow capital. A veritable treasure is the medieval pulpit, standing ten feet high on a trumpet-like base of carved wood. It has eight sides with traceried heads and linenfold panels; it has also little buttresses and pinnacled corners. A rich window glows through the tower arch, showing the Madonna attended by angels.

In this pulpit preached a famous scholar who was chaplain to Charles Stuart and lost his living for his loyalty. He was Brian Walton, who gave his leisure to making what is known as the Polyglot Bible in seven languages, a work which cost £8000 to publish. A tablet by his pulpit tells of the death of his wife, and on the wall is a record of a rector of Armada year—a brass of Patrick Fearne and his wife, he kneeling by a table, she wearing a wide-brimmed hat.

But the rarest possession of the church is a medieval wooden pax, a ceremonial tablet such as is mentioned by Chaucer. Our museums have a few examples but otherwise they are extremely rare.

SHALFORD. Its many old buildings include a farm which has an overhanging storey above the porch, and a Tudor door with ornamental ironwork; but for Shalford's treasures we cross a field to the church standing in a quiet valley. Its tower is 15th century, but nearly everything else we see is a hundred years older, the porch with shields and grotesques in its roof, the beautiful traceried door, and the arches and clerestory windows which make the interior so impressive. The handsome altar rails are 17th century, and so is the nave roof, but there are other beams 600 years old, and a splendid chancel screen which has been with them all the time. It has little openings in the lower panels, at which a child might kneel and look through at the altar; and at the back of the screen are two Tudor stalls, and a panelled desk with a pelican on one of its poppyheads.

The east window has fine glass as old as the church, showing shields of arms, lions, and foliage; and there are shields and other fragments in the windows of the aisles. A peephole is 15th century, and so is the font, which has the arms of such famous families as the Mortimers, De Veres, and Fitzwalters. There is much notable stone carving by the 14th century men, the chancel having three handsome sedilia and a very fine recess with an altar tomb. Two other beautiful recesses are in the aisles, and on the sanctuary wall is a brass of William Bigge and his wife, from the England Shakespeare knew.

Rare and Beautiful Glass

SHEERING. Its cottages line the road from Harlow to Hatfield's broad common, but the church stands down a lane behind three huge chestnuts which shade the remains of the whipping-post. It is 14th century, famed for its rare and beautiful glass, and has been lovingly restored and its ancient treasures safeguarded. The tower is 650 years old, and on each side of its arch indoors is a smaller arch forming an arcade at the end of the nave. There is a priest's room over the porch, and in the vestry is a window through which he would watch the altar. He must have been proud of his lovely door and doorway into the chancel, both remaining in all their beauty after five or six centuries. The door has a narrow border of quatrefoils and beads, and the ironwork is shaped into fleur-de-lys for hinges. Original, too, is the woodwork of the doors of the nave, held together by wooden pegs.

The window over the altar was long ago a treasury of glass, and much of it remains. The figures in the tracery are where they were when the chancel was built, revealing to us the eight orders of the Heavenly Host, whose names every monk knew, though they are here set down. Above them is the Madonna, having just received her crown from the enthroned Christ, two attendant angels swinging enormous censers. With their glowing colour and their simple dignity these portraits are among the best in any window in Essex.

Behind a glass frame is another example of medieval colour, a consecration cross with flowered ends, drawn in a red circle on the wall. Still here are fragments of the Norman font, and a stall on which were carved 500 years ago the heads of a king, a queen, and two knights in their helmets. Lost for centuries and found under the straw in a neighbouring barn, this stall is now back in the chancel.

SHELLEY. With such a name it should be a beauty spot, and so it is. There is an Elizabethan rectory with its ancient timbers, a hall among the trees with a door older than the Armada, and a group of farm buildings with a dovecot. By a large pond is the church with a stone tower, a wooden turret, and a shingled spire, all made new. On the wall of the tower is a sculpture on which kneel a family of Charles Stuart's day, John Greene and his wife with six children.

The Oak Arcade

SHENFIELD. Like York's famous Guildhall and a very few other churches we have seen, it has in its church an arcade of wood. The arches are not old, but the fine columns are 15th century, and each is hewn out of a great oak tree which may well have been growing when Magna Carta was sealed. They arc fashioned in the style of stone pillars, with attached columns, and well-moulded capitals and bases. Old timbers are the pride of Shenfield, for the tower is built of them too and rises to a shingled spire, all 15th century, with most of the church. The ancient rood beam is here, the aisle roof is 500 years old, and there are about a dozen pews of the 17th century with panelled ends. The east window has an attractive Nativity scene, and on several window-ledges we found relics old and quaint—a Bible of 1611, two churchwarden pipes of 1670, a cannon ball, and a small anchor. Tucked away in a corner is the monument of Elizabeth Robinson who died in 1652. She lies in alabaster on an altar tomb, a delightful figure of her child with her.

A Thames Headland

SHOEBURYNESS. We gaze from this low headland over the wide Thames estuary toward the hills of Sheppey in Kent, seeing midway the Nore lightship so eagerly longed for by mariners coming home. The Ness is famed for its School of Gunnery, and over its marshes and sands most of our important inventions in artillery have been tested. War and preparations for war have never long been absent here. Stone Age workshops and Roman kilns have yielded their secrets to the antiquarian, and we can trace the rampart thrown up by the Danes who retreated here from King Alfred's men.

The church (at South Shoebury) is a pleasant little place into which we come by two Norman doorways, a trim avenue of chestnuts leading seaward from one porch. The nave and chancel have Norman work, the arch dividing them being carved with chevrons. There is a rare form of window with star-like ornament in the chancel wall. A muzzled bear and a lion-headed monster look down from a window on the passers-by.

The rector here at the beginning of the 16th century was Arthur Dent, a Puritan preacher whose book The Plain Man's Pathway to Heaven was one of John Bunyan's deepest influences. Bunyan's first wife brought with her into the little cottage at Elstow this book and Bayly's Practice of Piety, and Bunyan writes: "In these I should sometimes read with her, wherein I found some things that were pleasing to me." The dialogue style in his Life and Death of Mr Badman is copied from Arthur Dent's book, which is a conversation carried on all day under an oak by four people, an ignorant man being at last convinced of good by the answers of a learned man to questions by an honest man; the fourth man carps and cavils and thus gives the author scope for strong satire against the evils of his day. Published in 1601 Arthur Dent's book was so popular that by 1637 it had reached its 24th edition.

SHOPLAND. A farm in the fields, a row of cottages, and a church deserted except on evenings in high summer, are all that remain of this village. The church is old, with two blocked Norman windows and a roof and timbered porch of the 15th century.

By the 700-year-old font, beautiful with arcading, fleur-de-lys, and other devices, lies a brass portrait of Thomas Stapel, sergeant-at-arms, wearing the armour in which he probably fought at Crecy. The tracery of the east window is filled with fragments of bright medieval glass and there are medieval tiles in the floor of the nave.

The Magnificent Hireling

SIBLE HEDINGHAM. Among its inns, houses, and cottages, some with 15th century roofs, Tudor and Jacobean detail abounds, but the chief interest centres in Hawkwoods, a timbered and plastered 16th century house with a hound and a coronet over its doorway. The house perpetuates the name of a family which, settled here from the time of King John, produced a towering lawless man who became the wonder and terror of medieval Italy.

Roman tiles in the walls of the church tell of the days of Caesar's Britain, but it was a 14th century Hawkwood who raised the present church. Over a window of the grey embattled tower, in which rings a bell 600 years old, a bold hawk is carved as an architectural pun on the family name, a conceit variously repeated indoors. An angel guards the entrance to the 16th century porch, which has roof-bosses carved with the Bourchier knot, and the star of the De Veres, whose great Norman castle is in the next village. In a corner of the tower is a little nail-studded Tudor door leading to the stair turret. The wide nave has two arcades, and a modern font on a 15th century stem. Two bays of the roof spanning the south aisle are 16th century, and have finely carved timbers showing stars and boars. The chancel has two Jacobean chairs.

But the pride of the church is the place in which it is believed lay Sir John Hawkwood, who was brought here wrapped in cloth-of-gold from his tomb in the Duomo, Florence, where we have stood before his memorial. Here in Sible Hedingham, unless our history is false, they laid him in 1394, in a magnificent tomb of which now remains only a canopied recess, resplendent with hawk, boar, pelican, and hunting figures.

It was on the petition of the king that Florence delivered up the warrior who was to her as saint and hero. The name of this son of a tanner was to resound for a generation throughout Europe. He went to the wars with Edward the Third and the Black Prince, and fought at Crecy and Poitiers. Seeking fresh worlds to conquer, he moved on into Italy and there formed what was called the White Company. He lived avowedly to foment war, regular or guerilla, on the widest scale. "God give you peace," was the greeting to him of two gentle friars. "God take away your alms," he answered them; "know ye not that I live on war, and that peace would undo me; and that just as I live on war so do you on alms?" Where rival cities were so many petty republics constantly at war, Hawkwood and his dauntless men-at-arms were almost continuously in demand. He fought for Pisa against Florence, for Perugia against the pope; he fought for this man today and that man tomorrow. When his White Company was taken over by the pope Hawkwood fought for him.

Renowned and terrible, a magnificent hireling, he passed from command to command until in 1390 he settled down permanently as General of the Florentine forces. There as ever he was a brilliant commander, and when he died in 1394 he was given a magnificent funeral, and his portrait by Giotto is in a great procession of figures placed in the cathedral. Tradition has it that Richard the Second brought the body home and that it was buried here.

The Roman Cross

SOUTH BENFLEET. There was a Roman emperor who set himself to stamp out Christianity. Here is the consecration cross of an English church made from Roman tiles. The cross is in the 14th century tower, capped by a shingle spire in which still rings a 15th century bell. By the chancel doorway is a medieval sundial.

It is the church porch that speaks first of beauty here; artists come from far and near to paint it, and architects to study its perfect symmetry. It was built about 500 years ago with its moulded and embattled timbers and its hammerbeams, an amazing mass of carved wood crowded into a tiny space with no suggestion of confusion. The porch has been described as a little miracle of perfection without and within. Indoors the church is handsome with a lofty nave, a modern screen painted with saints, and an organ loft adorned with prints of Fra Angelico's angel choir.

Its oldest part is in the inner wall of the tower, which is pierced by a Norman doorway between two stopped-up Norman windows. The lofty nave has clerestory windows below which are corbels carved 500 years ago, a cat and a pig among them. There is a window and a brass in memory of the village's great hero, vicar during an epidemic of cholera in the middle of last century. He was John Aubone Cook. Dauntless and unflinching in his devotion to his flock, in the end he sacrificed his life to them. The face of the Good Samaritan in his memorial window is thought to be a portrait.

The village lies by a creek of Hadleigh Ray separating it from Canvey Island. Here came the Danes in 893 and set up a fortified camp from which to harry the land. Alfred's men, too much for them, seized their camp and took off to London all the ships they did not burn, and the story of this, told in the Anglo-Saxon Chronicle, has been borne out by the finding of skeletons and charred timbers when the railway was being made. There are old inns of much charm and a few old cottages, and it is a pleasant path in the shade of sycamores that brings us to the ancient tower.

The Perfect Manor House

SOUTHCHURCH. It is proud of its heritage and has adapted its old buildings to modern needs in delightful ways. A perfect manor house of the 14th century is now a public library, and the modern church has made an aisle of the Norman church. The earthworks and the moat which protected the manor house from raiders are in a peaceful park. The main hall, with its high raftered roof and four dormer windows, is the home of books, and housed in its gabled wings are reading rooms and a museum. This lovely place belonged to Canterbury 1100 years ago; the stones used in these walls were handled by men who served Alfred the Great. There is an oak archway which led into a granary more than 600 years ago. The original wattle and daub plaster work lines the walls of the museum.

There are two Norman doorways with zigzag ornament in the church, one in the porch framing a 15th century door with good ironwork, the other reset in the end wall of the new nave with a Norman mason's face keeping watch above it. By two of the chancel windows are medieval scratch dials and, inside, a lancet window of the original church opens into the new nave. There are 14th century tombs and an Easter Sepulchre, and a rare capital of a pillar piscina nearly 800 years old.

Eight great posts brought here in the 15th century still support the turret for a bell which was even then a centenarian, and is still rung. The west window has a fine figure of Christ with the Archangel Michael weighing souls below, and in another window the golden mail of warrior saints gleams vividly in the light of the setting sun.

Cockney Paradise

SOUTHEND. There are hundreds of thousands of people who believe that it is one of England's wonders, and verily it is one of the biggest pleasure towns in England, London's nearest seaside. Actually it is at the mouth of the Thames, but its name is Southend-on-Sea, the south end of its mother village of Prittlewell. It has seven miles of front, and the ships of the world pass it day and night; over 60,000 a year go by. The town is served by two railways, and is so convenient for London that for years it had ten thousand season ticket-holders. It is visited by multitudes of East Enders, many travelling by coach on the great arterial road 100 feet wide and 30 miles long. Others come by steamer to land on the longest pier in the British Empire, riding well over a mile to the shore on an electric tram. There has been a pier here for more than a hundred years, it having been first built to carry Southend across the vast expanse of shallow water which at low tide becomes a sea of mud—yet a not unhealthy sea of mud, for hard footways project from the shore so that people may walk out and enjoy it when the tide is low.

The marble statue of Queen Victoria reminds us that it was the patronage of royalty which brought fame to Southend in the early years of last century. A delightful row of Georgian houses with verandahs overlooking the delightful gardens on the cliff is called Royal Terrace, because Princess Caroline stayed here in Trafalgar year. From here we see the hills of Kent, with the port of Sheerness at the mouth of the Medway, and Gad's Hill where Dickens loved to sit in his garden and look out on the ships as we see them here.

On this sunny walk are acres of lovely shrubbery with rock gardens and waterfalls, bowling greens and swimming pools, and the biggest floral clock in England, 60 feet round and with 10,000 plants in it, the hands being driven by motor. Here also is the peace memorial, a striking obelisk by Sir Edwin Lutyens 40 feet high and with wreaths on the front and back, while on the sides are sculptured the flags for which 1338 men from Southend fought and fell. There are two other obelisks on the beach at Westcliff, the quieter part of Southend; they are the Crow Stones, marking the ancient boundary of London's authority over the Thames. Inland hereabouts is Chalkwell Park, with a beautiful rose garden in its 24 shady acres.

Those who would see Southend as it loves to see itself should come to the carnival in August and join the quarter of a million people who watch the three-mile-long procession. Then Southend's enthusiasm rises to its highest pitch, the consummation of the boisterous fun which all through the summer the amazing Kursaal has kept up. Here hundreds of thousands of pounds have been spent on a gigantic fair, and every year a vast multitude of people know well that here is the matchless Cockney paradise.

SOUTH HANNINGFIELD. It has a few wayside cottages and a small church tucked away behind the big house. The church has the pleasant company of elms and a long red-tiled barn.

Its spire crowns a wooden bell-turret which rests on oak beams in the nave, and there are three windows which make it worth a call. The smallest one is Norman with a wide splay, another is the east window with simple tracery of the 14th century, the third is remark-

The Graceful 16th Century Buildings

The Great Medieval Gatehouse

ST OSYTH'S PRIORY

Sandon

Shenfield

TWO OLD VILLAGE CHURCHES

before she became queen lived the terrible Mary Tudor, and the lodge of the hall is known as Princess Mary's Chapel. It stands by the road for all to see, with tall turrets, a fine doorway, and a broad window of seven lights. There are two old inns of the 15th and 18th centuries, and the 18th century Brook House.

High above the churchyard are the rookeries of the park, old but not so old as the church, which has Norman stones in its walls. It has been refashioned with modern windows, but has a Norman doorway carved with chevron and with old ironwork on its door. The door to the turret of the tower has been opening and shutting 500 years. In a window of the tower is medieval glass with two panels showing the Sacrifice of Abraham, and the Queen of Sheba in white and gold. In the tracery above are 17th century figures of four saints. On the wall of the tower is a medallion portrait of Francis Wollaston, a famous scientist who was vicar here a hundred years ago. He was Professor of Chemistry at Cambridge, where he was famous as an experimenter. The vicar who followed him for 53 years was the remarkable Charles Almeric Belli, a man of great energy who lived to be 95 and called in Sir Gilbert Scott to rebuild this nave and chancel. The oak chancel screen is the work of Scott, resembling a medieval screen. The chancel roof has a choir of angels. In the chapel beyond the gilt iron railings is a wooden cross from Flanders brought from the grave of Christopher Tower, who gave his life for us.

On the wall are brass portraits of an attractive group of children, little Robert Picakis aged seven, and Allen Talbot aged two, a bonny lad with curly hair who died in 1634. There are two groups of children in the clothes they wore in 1500, and a mother with 12 children of half a century earlier.

Lying here is the old owner of the manor, Lord Chief Justice Scroggs, bracketed equal-first with Jeffreys as one of the worst judges who ever disgraced the English bench. The son of an Oxfordshire butcher, he left Oxford an MA, and, preferring the Bar to the Church, escaped conviction for assault and battery during a drunken bout, reached the bench at 43, to become Charles the Second's Lord Chief Justice in 1678.

There centred about this man the chief prosecutions in the bogus Popish Plot of Titus Oates, which, based on some petty Roman Catholic movement towards strengthening the position of that church in England, was magnified by Oates and his creatures into the story of a plot to assassinate Charles the Second and to massacre the Protestants. The part of Scroggs was to convict the prisoners, no matter how lowly or how exalted their status, to rant and roar them into silence, to act as prosecutor as well as judge, to maintain the evidence of Oates as little less than sacred, and to assert that any testimony advanced for the defence was blasphemous perjury.

All England was in a panic, for none doubted the truth of these fictions. Scroggs sent the innocent to the gallows in batches, adding insult and denunciation to the bitterness of the penalty to which he doomed them, asserting that it was better to hang one Papist than three felons. Titus Oates gave a political party its label, naming the opponents of the persecution Tory, after the Irish murderers of English settlers.

When the panic was at its height the accusers declared the queen and her physician to be implicated in the plot to murder the king; and a bill was laid before the grand jury naming the future James the Second as a Papist, to be excluded from the succession, and the king's favourite the Duchess of Portsmouth as a public nuisance.

The tide had begun to turn; Scroggs's heart failed him; he dismissed the grand jury before it could act. He now turned about, and acquitted persons falsely accused, traversed the evidence of Oates and his confederates, and was pilloried in broadsheets and publicly assaulted for his pains. Impeached for his offences, Scroggs was saved by Charles, who dissolved his Parliament and never summoned another; but he no longer dared to continue the unjust judge in office, retiring him with a pension of £1500 a year, to die two years later, in 1683, the scorn of his generation. Scroggs was a witty and powerful speaker, but without conscience or scruple, a paid ruffian of the Court, and a man of infamous private life. He is admirably pictured in Scott's Peveril of the Peak, where he is shown after fear has taken possession of him and he knows not what to do with his prisoners.

Here Was Oliver Goldsmith

SPRINGFIELD. It almost belongs to Chelmsford, but has proud memories of its own. Here walked Oliver Goldsmith, and here we think of one who played his part and gave his life in a deed that will ring through history. It was in a white cottage facing the church that Oliver Goldsmith wrote much of The Deserted Village. He can hardly have been thinking of cheerful Springfield as he wrote of his Sweet Auburn, but we may be sure he knew the sights of this village church, for it was ancient in his day. He would see nearly everything as we see it, the Norman nave with its Roman bricks, the 14th century chancel and vestry, the unusual tracery of the 14th century windows, the Tudor door with its ornamental ironwork. The tower is partly 600 years old; but the parapet, turret, and buttresses are modern. On a doorway to the chancel are three sundials. There is a traceried screen of the 15th century, much restored; a coffin lid 600 years old; a brass portrait of a man in the armour worn at Agincourt; a Tudor funeral helm; and a big 17th century painting of Moses with a censer. The font is one of the best 12th century fonts in Essex, with big flowers and foliage on the bowl and waterlilies below. In the tower are several old gravestones, one of Sir Thomas Stampe who was Lord Mayor of London and died in Queen Anne's time; another with a famous name, an unknown Joseph Chamberlaine of 1692. There is old glass from the 14th century to the 17th, including shields and parts of figures, one a man with a purse and another probably St John drinking from a cup. Panels of Flemish glass show the Descent from the Cross and the Entombment.

But the thing that stirs us most within these walls is a flag of our own day. It flew at Zeebrugge. It was the White Ensign flown on the North Star in one of the most heroic and terrible exploits in the story of the Navy, and it is treasured in this chancel because Lieutenant Charles Paynter, who fell in that great hour, was the vicar's son, only 23 when he died. Moving it is to think that the flag he fought under has come home to the place where his father prayed for him in the darkest hours of the Great War.

Roman Tiles and Norman Windows

STAMBOURNE. Charles Haddon Spurgeon knew its lanes long before he began preaching, for he spent much of his youth with his grandfather at the manse. The medieval Lion Inn was once Moone Hall; it has a 17th century chimney in its moss-covered roof, and a gable with its original woodwork.

The wide and massive Norman tower of the church reminds us of a castle keep. Its walls are four feet thick, and built into the corners are

Roman bricks. Roman tiles form the sides and round heads of five Norman windows, and grotesque gargoyles run round the parapet.

The Tudor porch covers the original doorway of the 14th century nave, which has rafters 500 years old, and but a century later is some brightly coloured glass showing the shield and badge of the Mac-williams, a local family. The lofty chancel arch is 15th century, crossed by a glorious wooden screen over 400 years old. It has five bays of beautiful tracery, some of the lower panels painted in red, green, and gold, with four figures on pedestals. We see St Denis as a bishop holding his head in his hands, St George cheerfully spearing the Dragon, Edmund the Martyr with the arrow which killed him, and that unofficial saint Henry the Sixth, standing on an antelope and holding an orb.

The 16th century chancel has its original roof carved with foliage, and some glorious glass possibly put up by Henry Macwilliam in 1530 to show his pedigree. The east window has two big panels showing a woman in a heraldic mantle kneeling at a prayer desk, with her an armoured man in a tabard. In the tracery are shields held by figures or hung on trees. In the chancel wall is a pointed arch on which one capital is beautifully carved with a helmet, mantling, and shield; below is a delightful little niche. Through the arch is a 400-year-old chapel with its original roof and studded door. The north aisle is 16th century, and also has its original roof. By a window are two lovely niches matching two in the nave, all a feature of the church. The aisle is divided from the nave by a gracious medieval arcade. The dignified pulpit has plain 18th century panels; one richly carved chair in the sanctuary is 16th century, and has an inlaid back. A medieval chest by the tower has three hasps, its little panels deeply sunk.

STANFORD-LE-HOPE. It looks over a creek from which the road winds up to a churchyard beautiful with yew and cypress avenues, shading beds of flowers. From here the radiating roads lead past the Jacobean Hassenbrook Hall with its old garden wall, or the 15th century manor farm with four gables looking out over a pond. Alone in the flat meadows of the Thames, this farm is full of old timber and quaint nooks.

But the church, with a noble tower of modern times, has older work than any house, for there are relics of two windows of the Norman church in its walls. There are 13th century piers and a font of the same time, the font having a cover of Stuart days. In the chancel rebuilt in the 14th century are the heads of two surly monks on the sedilia, and facing them is a charming recess with rich decoration. Beautiful carving enriches the medieval screen round the chapel where the Featherstone family sat apart at worship and were laid to rest. The roofs are massive and the nail-studded door is 400 years old and as strong as ever. Behind the new vestries is one of the extravagant tombs of the 18th century, carved all over with flowers and cherubs in memory of James Adams.

The Unknown David Livingstone

STANFORD RIVERS. A narrow avenue of lofty limes leads us to the door of a church four times as long as it is wide, with Norman windows in the nave and a chancel made new in the 14th century. By one of the nave windows is an old sundial. The bell-turret added 100 years after has a graceful leaded spire. The work of an artist of 600 years ago remains in faint outline on the splay of a window, two figures appearing in colour under gabled canopies. Other medieval craftsmanship is in a gallery with nine traceried heads from the old chancel screen, and about 20 of the old carved pews are still in the nave. Portraits of some of the old inhabitants who sat in these pews are here in brass. Robert Borrow is with his wife, who wears a headdress of about 1500; the infant Thomas Greville is here; and framed in an arch are Anne Napper and her six sons. All these lads would thrill at the tales brought to the village about Francis Drake, who was knighted by Elizabeth three years before this monument was set on the wall.

There is another little tale we remember here, of David Livingstone. While qualifying for his mission to Africa he was sent down to Essex to study for three months; it was a probationary period, and upon the report of his tutor, the Revd Richard Cecil of Chipping Ongar, depended his acceptance or refusal by the London Missionary Society. Part of his task was to prepare sermons and submit them in writing to Cecil, who would read and correct them if necessary, whereupon the student had to learn the sermon by heart and preach it to one of the village congregations round about. The minister of the chapel here being taken suddenly ill, the young Scotsman was called upon to take the evening service, and all went well until the sermon, when Livingstone slowly read out his text—and paused. He said afterwards that it was as if midnight darkness had descended upon him. The sermon, so perfectly memorised until a moment before, had fled, and his mind was filled with blank terror. "Friends," he haltingly said, "I have forgotten what I had to say," and abruptly he left the pulpit, and fled.

Yet the real man showed itself, even here. He had to visit a relative on the far side of London, and, too poor to ride, he set out at three o'clock on a bitter November morning to walk 27 miles. It was so dark that he fell into a deep ditch, but he reached London, discharged his business, and set out on the return journey. A few miles out he found a lady lying unconscious by a trap from which she had been thrown, carried her to a house, made sure that she was not badly hurt, and continued on his way, only to lose himself completely. He was about to lie down in a ditch for the night when he stumbled on a signpost and plodded on, reaching home at midnight after 21 hours of walking, footsore, speechless with fatigue, but triumphant, as he was to be so often in the years to come.

The Lord Mayor and His Wife

STANSTED MOUNTFITCHET. Its houses look down on a Roman road, but its name comes from the Norman family of Mountfitchet, whose castle was destroyed in the year of Magna Carta. There are traces of its earthworks and some rubble foundations. There are Tudor houses here with their imposing timbers, one in Church Road with brackets carved with foliage, and others of the 17th and 18th centuries. A fine tower windmill stands in the background.

The church is a little way off in the 200 acres of Stansted Hall, and has three archways through which men were walking in Norman days, a chancel arch carved with small heads and two doorways with tympanums, all with Norman decoration. The tower is 17th century, but the chancel was refashioned by the 13th century men, and has graceful shafts and a handsome wall arcade. It opens to a chapel by two arches, one of the 13th century, with rich foliage on its capitals, and one of the 14th. Five big linenfold panels are left from a Tudor screen, and from the 17th century are two carved chairs, an attractive cover for the 700-year-old font, and a curious panel carved with the thirty pieces of silver, the Crown of Thorns, a kneeling cherub, and instru-

famous as a historian, his chief works being histories of the Reformation and of the Anglo-Saxon Church.

Fifty Places Centuries Old

STEBBING. Any traveller would stop here for the splendid church, but Stebbing has more. It is as old as Domesday Book and has a moated mound older than the Conqueror and an extraordinary wealth of cottages and farms, at least 50 of them having been here 300 years. The nearest house to the mound is one of Shakespeare's day, and, walking up the village street with its pretty cottages, we come to a group on high ground about the church. One is a little 15th century cottage by the churchyard gate; another is 17th century; and a third is Church Farm, a Tudor building with original carvings round a gabled dormer window. Some distance away is Porter's Hall with its moat still wet, an Elizabethan house with a thatched dovecot. But it is the church that draws all eyes, for it is a magnificent example of the work of the 14th century builders just before the Black Death swept over the land. Its tower has grotesque gargoyles and looks westward at a view of great charm over the valley. Its doorways are handsome. Its interior is spacious with a high tower arch and arcades of five bays. And its glory is a rare and beautiful screen of stone under the chancel arch. The screen has three bays divided by clustered shafts, which rise to form charming lancet arches, enriched with flowers and other ornament. The middle bay has more elaborate tracery, and an arched transom helps to support the Cross and the two pedestals for the attendant figures. Very interesting it is to see that in all this rich carving, set up at one of the most sacred places in the church, the 14th century craftsmen were not afraid to include two of the grotesque figures they loved to carve. Beautiful, too, are the richly carved sedilia in this long chancel, which has on the wall the wooden block of the pulley used for raising the Lenten veil in medieval ceremony, a rare object to find in a church today. The piscina is a double one, and there are two others, one in the 14th century vestry and a beautiful one in the south aisle. The north aisle has something left of an elaborate canopied reredos, with traces of colour, from the 16th century. There is a 15th century font, a chest of the same age, an old oak pulpit said to have been made from a medieval screen, fragments of foliage and tabernacle-work in 14th century glass, and altar rails and a communion table of the 18th century. Two of the roofs are remarkable, that of the chancel being of Henry the Seventh's time with foliage on the wall-plates, and that of the nave a little younger, with wooden angels holding shields. A splendid brass shows the costume worn by a widow who looks as if she might have walked out of Chaucer's Tales.

The Last Baronet

STEEPLE BUMPSTEAD. It has lost the steeple which gave it its name, but it has a group of old houses, farms, and barns, and by the road from Haverhill to Baythorn Bridge are entrenchments of an ancient stronghold. Gone, too, is Bower Hall, though a fine avenue of tall trees still leads to the site. Its six-sided dovecot was built about 1700, its brick walls honeycombed with 220 nesting-holes. Another unusual dovecot is at Claydon's cottage; it is nine feet square and built of mud. It is said that in 1914 something fell down inside it, so frightening the birds that they never returned.

Little Walton's Farm was built about 1500, and has something of its moat still left. Remains of another moat are at 17th century Herksted Hall; and here too is a 17th century weatherboarded barn with a thatched roof. Another thatched barn of the same date is at Latchley's manor house, a timbered and plastered Tudor building surrounded by a moat complete and unusually wide.

One of the finest houses of this countryside is the magnificent Moyns Park, an Elizabethan home in grounds of 200 acres; it has bay windows, pinnacled gables, and three many-cornered chimney stacks. The Moot Hall, a pretty timbered building at the cross-roads in the middle of the village, has a projecting storey, and on the roof is a stone lion holding a shield with the royal arms of the Tudors. The ancient church has a Norman tower, though its upper stage has been repaired with Tudor brick. There are three narrow Norman windows, and a gargoyle below each length of parapet. The porch is 14th century; its roof and a pair of rough and gnarled benches are 16th. The door is partly 16th century and by it is an ironbound almsbox of about 1500 on a traceried post.

The tower arch stands on round pillars and was set up about 1500, a century after the wide chancel arch. In the aisles are six poppyheads 400 years old, attached to modern seats, and in the back of a pew is old panelling which says "Onsel and Thomas Lond, her son, did these stools make in 1568." There are two Tudor stalls in the chancel, a 17th century oak chest in the vestry, an altar table of about 1700, and a cupboard door with Jacobean carving. The font is 500 years old. In one of the windows are fragments of medieval glass, and on a wall hangs a wooden helmet with a Tudor crest.

Near by is an 18th century monument to Sir John Bendish and his wife, with their busts, by which stands a cherub holding a flaming torch upside down. A finer monument against the same wall is to Sir Henry Bendish, the last baronet, showing him reclining in lace cuffs, cravat, and buckled shoes, his curly wig falling over his shoulders. Playing by his pillow lies his infant son, Henry, a lively little fellow.

On the wall near by is a stone to Dick Dare who made his last long journey a few years ago: he, his father, and his grandfather were carriers from Bumpstead to London for 150 years.

We gathered two items of news here from the vicarage, where the greatest treasure of the church was once put to base uses as a shovel— an 8th century bronze boss with panels of ornament and sockets for 18 jewels. It used to be on the chancel door of the church and is now in the British Museum. The other news from the vicarage was that Nurse Cavell was a nursery governess there long before her name was known throughout the world. She was here five years. Often must she have sat in these pews with village folk who can little have imagined that her life would be caught up in the grip of so great a destiny. There is a tablet to her memory in the church.

Here Life Has Been 2000 Years

STIFFORD. It is a quiet place on a hill, with thatched cottages and rich woodlands with the Mardyke in the valley where men lived two thousand years ago. Samian ware of the Romans found here is in the Geological Museum, and a bronze sword has been discovered in the bed of the stream.

The memorial to the heroes of the village tells how they left all that was dear to them, and very dear must have been this church with the shingled spire, a bell projecting quaintly from its side. The plain doorway was built by the Normans; its 16th century door has crescent hinges with scroll-shaped ends, and other ironwork wrought about the time of Magna Carta. Very charming are the lancet windows, but the gems in stone are the heads at each end of the arcade, both delicately carved. The one near the chapel is painted red, with the hair and crown in gilt. The short round column and the moulded capital above this beautiful head is decked with black and red, a glowing note of colour. The face is looking at a window in which is the strongly-drawn figure of a warrior saint in memory of an army officer who died in 1927; it is the work of Leonard Walker.

The simple square font with tapering sides is 700 years old. The oak pulpit was elaborately carved in 1611, and has an hourglass stand. Two lovely chairs were carved at the end of the 17th century.

In bold square lettering in the chancel is recorded the burial of David de Tillebery, who lived 600 years ago, and a portrait in brass shows a rector of 1380, Ralph Perchehay, wearing a collar with the famous Greek pattern, the left-handed swastika. Portraits of later worshippers are in the chapel of the lords of the manor. In a long fur gown lies John Ardalle, who died in 1504, his wife beside him, and shields with bulls and starfish. There are four 17th century members of the Lathum family, Suzan looking very quaint in her conical hat, ruff, and farthingale. Early 18th century cherubs weep in the tower for Sir Nathaniel Grantham, his wife, and his daughter, and there are monuments to the Silverlocks, who lived in a delightful house a mile away, Ford Place, with 1655 on a Dutch gable. Two of the rooms have magnificent plastered ceilings, one of them, with rosettes, bay leaves, and oak leaves, fruits, flowers, and figures of the seasons, being a gorgeous masterpeice of its age.

In the Time of the Conqueror

STISTED. It is one of the places the traveller remembers for the charm of its setting, with moulded chimneys on its cottages, the rookery by the church, rolling meadows toward the Roman Stane Street, and the horizon lined with trees against the sky.

Stisted was a name on all men's lips in the time of the Conqueror, for the overlordship here was the subject of the famous trial on Penenden Heath in Kent between the monks of Canterbury and Bishop Odo. The court sat in the open in the ancient Saxon way and the monks brought their old documents and proved their right. It was the fall of Odo the tanner's son, half-brother of the Conqueror and owner of 200 houses.

There is neither Saxon nor Norman stone here now, but the 13th century columns in the nave show that they were rebuilding here when Thomas Becket was building the choir at Canterbury. The capitals of some of the columns are elaborately carved; on one are three grotesque heads and a dragon with a rose a bird is pecking at. There is much glass in the chancel by 16th century Flemish craftsmen; it is in five lancet windows which almost fill the east wall and two windows facing across the sanctuary; and in it are the two Johns, Elijah in a bright cloak, the Last Judgment, and the Betrayal. The people are quaint and the trees are like those in a Noah's Ark. A panel of the Madonna in a golden and deep blue dress, supported by two women, is of 1554, and in a side window is the Return of the Prodigal, a red-haired lad with ragged sleeves. Engraved in brass below these windows kneels an Elizabethan with her daughter at prayer, members of the Wyseman family.

Most of the wood of the fine roofs of nave and aisles is 500 years old, and the dug-out chest is older, in spite of the date on the lid. There are Tudor linenfold panels in a pew and the Queen Anne pulpit has a carved head very like Pocahontas, the beautiful Red Indian princess who saved the life of Captain John Smith in Virginia, and lies across the river at Gravesend.

The Great Beams

STOCK. On the hills between Chelmsford and Billericay, it has a pleasant green made bright on one side by the vivid red of a row of almshouses, and has at one end one of the most delightful timber spires in Essex. It rises on the belfry of the 14th century church, the belfry being also of wood, older than the church itself. Above the doorway of the belfry are three square windows with lovely tracery, and inside is one of those amazing timber constructions characteristic of this part of England. So huge are the curved beams that the biggest oaks in the forest must have been felled for them. The arrangement of the beams makes a pleasant design, all meeting in a grotesque boss.

The medieval masons were still extending the church in the 15th century, adding an aisle and leaving us the quaint round face of a monk looking down on it. There are four poppyheaded bench-ends from the pews of that period. On the wall behind the pulpit is the brass portrait of Richard Twedye in his 16th century armour, set in an old altar stone with two consecration crosses. It was he who built the almshouses on the green, as a comfort for the declining years of four knights fallen on hard times.

William Byrd's Village

STONDON MASSEY. It is one of the few places with which we can associate the Father of our Music, he whose music is living again, who wrote that

> Since music is so good a thing
> I wish all men would learn to sing.

William Byrd's connection with this scattered village near Ongar has brought a new interest to the place, and a stone has been set in the church wall recording the fact that Byrd lived here. His home was Stondon Place (now made new) and it is believed that he had some difficulty over his possession of it because its previous owner had been involved in a Popish Plot. Though we cannot be sure, it is also thought that Byrd may have died on this site in 1623.

Among the meadows which slope away east of the church still stands a brick and timber house that William Byrd would know, Stondon Hall; he must often have looked at its octagonal chimney stacks. Often also he must have come into this little church, for it has been here about eight centuries, and its flint and stone walls, with Roman bricks in them, were about the first work of the Normans here. Here is their doorway, with a great hole for a bar which fastened it, and facing it on the other wall is the arch of the other door blocked up, like some of their deep-splayed windows. There are 15th century timbers in the roofs supporting the bell-turret, a 15th century font, a screen a little younger, and a reading desk a little younger still. The Jacobean pulpit has a door with the original latch, very neat. In the chancel is the brass portrait of John Carre and his two Elizabethan wives; his merchant's mark is on it. The fragment of another brass on the wall of the nave has been twice used, and what we see is the portrait of the wife of Rainold Holingworth.

It must always be regrettable that Stondon Massey is not able to claim with certainty the grave of William Byrd, but it is highly probable that they would lay him here. At the unveiling of the tablet in the

The Handsome Elizabethan Front

The Timbered South-West Wing

MOYNS PARK, STEEPLE BUMPSTEAD

Thaxted   16th Century Front of Horham Hall

Thaxted   The 15th Century Guildhall

church on the 300th anniversary of his death the Gentlemen and Children of the Chapel Royal were sent by the king to this church to make Stondon ring again with Byrd's old melodies. He was our Shakespeare of music. He wrote masses, services, madrigals, songs, and pieces for the organ, the virginal, and the orchestra.

We had all too little of his work until 1920, when, by a fine imaginative stroke of the Carnegie Trustees, it was made possible to publish all that was available. Then for the first time the world realised that the estimates of Byrd's contemporaries were just, that he was indeed one of the supreme masters of composition in all its forms. Then we realised also that that superb compliment paid him by the Vatican (where his grand *Non nobis, Domine,* is engraved on a plate of gold) was well merited. But there must be more Byrd music to come from private collections; only a few years ago a bundle of his unpublished manuscripts was found in the chained library at Wimborne Minster.

It was at Stondon Massey that Byrd spent the last 28 years of his life; he was a Roman Catholic and lived in the home of a member of his church who had been convicted of treason. The strongest evidence for the probability that he was buried here is the wish he expressed in his will that he might lie here by the side of his wife.

Annunciations

STOW MARIES. It is a small place on the low hills above the Crouch, with a lovely God's Acre of trees and roses. A vivid red cross glows from the wooden bell-turret of the 15th century church, in contrast with the soft red corbel table crowning the nave wall below. Angels are playing viols in the headstops of the windows. There is a medieval niche in the wall now filled by a saint.

In the chancel is a brass portrait of Mary Browne, a village lady of the days of Queen Elizabeth, with little portraits of her three sons and four daughters. The stately wooden reredos dominating the sanctuary is a peace memorial and has three paintings of three Annunciations: the Annunciation of the coming of John to Zacharias, the Annunciation by Gabriel to the Madonna, and the Angel's Annunciation to the women at the Tomb that Christ was risen. They are charming in their silvery colouring, and the setting is helped by the absence of a window in the background. The font is 15th century.

z

Perfect Saxon

STRETHALL. Here stands one of the oldest buildings in Essex, a perfect little piece of Saxon architecture. It is the nave of the church, less than nine yards long, but with the typical long and short masonry of the Saxon builders, and with two of their windows to be seen inside, one a little round opening about eight inches across. The doorway has kept its Saxon jambs and arch, but more interesting still is the low Saxon chancel arch, decorated with the mouldings of Edward the Confessor's day. Through it men and women have been coming to the altar for 900 years. The tower is 15th century, with two bells older than itself; the chancel was partly refashioned when the tower was built. The nave roof is also 15th century, its corbels including heads of angels, an angel with a shield, and a curious carving of a man and a woman kneeling at prayer. Medieval also are two plain seats in the nave; and a door with a huge lock has been swinging to and fro nearly all the time. The bowl of the font is Norman. A canopied altar tomb in the sanctuary is the sleeping-place of a Tudor lord of the manor; and there are two brasses engraved on both sides, one a portrait of a 15th century priest in his robes, on the back being the figure of a lady; the other an inscription to a parson of 1539, the back of this telling of a lady who died in 1450.

Middy From Trafalgar

STURMER. Ancient Britons were buried in the mound we see here in a field, Saxon masons began the building of the little church, and 15th century men fashioned the timber framework of Sturmer Hall, now refaced with modern brick. The work of the Saxons is still seen in the nave and in the little north doorway no longer used, its tympanum carved with squares. The Normans refashioned the chancel and built the doorway on the south, which has weird heads below a tympanum crudely patterned. The porch is of Tudor brick with a crowstepped gable, and there is a studded Tudor door in the chancel. The nave has a double hammerbeam roof, decorated about 1500 with pierced tracery and carved wall-plates. One of the windows has two shields in 15th century glass. This small place is linked with our greatest naval victory, for we read here of William Hicks, who was a middy on HMS Conqueror when she sailed into Nelson's last fight. He was rector here for 44 years, with a tale to tell the village children that must have made their history books seem dull.

SUTTON. A tiny place on the banks of the River Roach, it is bounded on the west by Fleet Creek. An avenue of many kinds of trees lines the road from Southend as it draws near the Norman church, on which is a wooden bell-turret of the 15th century. We come into the church through a timber porch with 1633 in the sunk spandrels of the outer archway. The porch has preserved from the weather a splendid doorway of the 13th century, the age when Lincoln and Salisbury Cathedrals were rising in their grandeur. Six shafts support the deeply cut mouldings of its arch, which is by far the finest possession of the village. Inside, the Norman chancel arch forms a neat frame for three modern pointed windows.

A Craftsman's Work

TAKELEY. It lies on the Roman road near Bishop's Stortford, with 17th century barns and timbered houses, and Roman tiles in the walls of its ancient church. The nave is Norman, the chancel 13th century, and the tower 15th; it has a small spire. The little porch has still its 14th century doorway and the 15th century roof. The treasure of the church is the medieval cover of its modern font. It is six feet high, and rises like an octagonal spire with traceried canopies and pinnacles soaring to a gilded dove which seems to hover among the rafters as the cover is drawn up on the pulley. Perhaps made by the same craftsman is the oak pulpit, standing on a trumpet-shaped base and richly pinnacled. There are traceried bench-ends, also by medieval craftsmen, and a cupboard with Elizabethan linenfold.

TENDRING. A Saxon village is this, with a 17th century hall containing old ceiling beams. By the main road runs a magnificent holly hedge, and from behind the church we have a splendid view over the country to the south. The church, with a tall spire, is entered through a porch with delicately carved tracery in its timbers, foiled bargeboards, and moulded wall-plates. Framing the doorway inside is a great timber arch which, with a similar arch round the facing doorway, supports the hammerbeam of the roof. All this remarkable woodwork is old, set up a few years after the battle of Crecy about 600 years ago. In the 15th century chancel is the tomb of

Edmund Saunder, on which, carved in alabaster, he kneels in prayer in the civilian dress of Shakespeare's time.

Six of England's Highest Honours

TERLING. The Terling countryside, through which the little River Ter flows at times under great forest trees, has a museum piece of its own in a smock mill with fine white sails 66 feet across, still working. It has one of the finest modern houses in Essex, home of the Rayleighs, standing in a magnificent park of 200 acres with the river flowing through it, and scattered about are farms and cottages that were here in our Tudor Age and must have been seen by Henry the Eighth, who had a palace here.

The village is rich in overhanging gabled roofs and Tudor chimneys. A grotesque little man crouches to bear a heavy beam at Eryat's Farm, and the manor house, a dwelling-place of sheer delight, has 15th century foundations, windows of the two succeeding centuries, richly moulded timbering, and a view into the great park across its old-world garden. We do not wonder that here our great Tudor king lived in splendour, or that great folk lived here before him. The palace has vanished, but we know that here was a Norman chapel which was the scene of an act of ingratitude on the part of another King Henry that Bluebeard himself could hardly have surpassed for calculated cruelty. Here it was that Hubert de Burgh was forced from his sanctuary and carried off to the Tower by the young Henry the Third he had befriended.

The ruthless king had drawn his sword on Hubert, who was Justiciar of England, and had called him a traitor, and on Hubert seeking sanctuary in the chapel here had sent men down to fetter him and carry him off to the Tower. On the Bishop of London threatening to excommunicate all concerned, the king released the captive, but, in any case, before the bishop's intervention the village smith, being ordered to fetter Hubert, had stubbornly refused. The king persisted in his persecution of the Justiciar, however, and though he dare not put him to death, finally sent him in chains to the Tower, from which Hubert escaped to Devizes and took sanctuary in the beautiful Norman church of St John, which would then be new. He was ultimately reconciled with his royal master. Far the better man of the two, Hubert is known in Shakespeare as the man who refused to put out Arthur's eyes at the bidding of the ruffianly King John, and in history he is famous, it has been said, for being the first statesman "to convert the emotion of nationality into a principle of political action."

It is one of the few villages that have an ancient chapel. Across the green outside the churchyard stands the little Congregational building which has been here 250 years. It has a 17th century brass candelabra, by the light of which its people have sung their hymns since John Bunyan died; there are 12 branches, and a bird sits on the top. The church stands by the manor house, approached through a porch which has still its medieval timbers. The tower, crowned with a shingled spire with a dove for a weathervane, and carrying its bell outside, is of red brick and white stone, and is one of the 18th century towers, joining a 13th century wall. The church has brass portraits of William Rochester and his wife, who may have seen Henry the Eighth pass by, for they were laid here in the terrible reign of Mary Tudor. Their ten children kneel with them. On another brass 12 children kneel in groups with two mothers and their father, John Rochester, who died in the days of Queen Elizabeth.

In a quiet corner of the churchyard, joining the garden of Terling Place (which has a small gate into it), is a simple monument of red sandstone on which are the words, "For now we see in a glass darkly, but then face to face." It is the grave of one of the most learned men who ever lived in England, John William Strutt, third Lord Rayleigh. He was born at Maldon a few years after the Victorian Era began and lived till the end of the Great War.

He saw science revolutionised and played no small part in the revolution, and for nearly half a century he carried on his work at Terling. Learned as he was, he had the rare quality of making subtle things seem simple. In his collected works are 440 separate papers. They issued frequently and rapidly from his pen, whether he was quietly working at Terling or in the laboratory at Cambridge, whether he was thinking out deep problems or discovering the new gas argon with his friend Sir William Ramsay. He was one of the chief authorities on physical optics, and wrote 150 papers on this subject. We believe that it was he who first suggested that the blue of the sky is due to the shorter waves of light being scattered by the fine particles of dust suspended in the air. He received the Nobel Prize, and was honoured by six of the highest distinctions England can bestow on any man:

the Order of Merit, a Privy Councillorship, the Chancellorship of Cambridge University, the Presidency of the Royal Society and of the British Association, and a tribute on the walls of Westminster Abbey, which tells us with a modesty characteristic of himself that he was "an unerring leader in the advancement of natural knowledge."

The Treasure House With Six Old Doors

THAXTED. The spire of its glorious church guides us from far away, and, no matter which of many roads we take, we are sure to pass some timbered farm before we come to Thaxted's own array of timbered houses, the homes of the cutlers and the wool workers who made this town prosperous in the Middle Ages. For 500 years their Guildhall has been dominating this wide market street, its black and white storeys propped on wooden posts and supported by cross-beams meeting in a great central pillar. All the ground floor is open except where an old lock-up for unruly fellows now houses two massive hooked poles for pulling thatch from burning cottages. In the panelled room above sat the town council in the days of Elizabeth. Close to the Guildhall are many 15th century neighbours, and the Recorder's House a little down the street, two of its bay windows resting on oak coving carved with royal arms. On the way to Broxted is the great Tudor Horham Hall. At the Guildhall the wide street divides, one half to end in a fieldpath to the windmill, the other taking us up the hill to the church.

It is one of the grandest churches in the county, 183 feet long and 87 wide, and so beautiful that it may well claim to be the Cathedral of Essex. Begun about 1340, its growth continued through our great building centuries till the Reformation, and the result is a proud example of English architecture. Perfect balance is achieved with the aisles and transepts, chapels and the two porches, the King's and the Duke's, for Edward the Fourth gave the one with his arms on it, and the Duke of Clarence gave the other marked with his coronet. Both porches are vaulted, and both have a spiral stair leading to a room above and ending in a turret. The north porch room has been turned into a quiet retreat with three charming coloured plaques on the wall by Phoebe Stabler.

It seems to us a fitting thing that a church so beautiful should be guarded by many old doors; there are six about 500 years old and another a century younger. It is the 400-year-old by which we enter, two of the 500-year-old ones are in the priest's doorways in the chapels, and the other four lead us up the spiral stairways and into the rooms over the porches.

The grandeur of the church outside is in its richly traceried windows, the spire and the tower with flying buttresses, and the many panelled buttresses with pinnacles and gargoyles; inside is the pure beauty of birch wood. Two gable crosses are carved with the figure of Christ. The lovely arcades with their host of corbel heads rise to clerestory windows set behind exquisite 16th century panelling, and spandrels of pierced stone give a rare beauty to the chancel. Every main arch has its special beauty. Our eyes are drawn first to the 15th century one, which helps to support the rich stone vaulting of the tower, then to the figures above the transept arches, where St Catherine appears between two wheels on one of the capitals.

In each transept a medieval wheel window admits light from over the chapel roofs, and in the chapels the wide window splays come down to enclose stone benches, except where two little doors have opened to 15 generations of priests. There were stone seats, too, under the rich stone canopies on the transept walls, 11 in the south transept and 7 in the north, where is also a reredos with a grand row of niches, its moulded cornice having the head of Christ between angels in the centre. Many more vaulted niches and dainty recesses are round the church, and adding to all the glory of this stonework is rich colour worthy of medieval days. The church is hung and carpeted with colour, its tapestries, banners, and vestments being the magnificent work of modern craftsmen inspired by the enterprise and fine judgment of the late incumbent and his wife. Some of them we have all seen, for they were exhibited at Wembley. The sea-green shimmering net between the chapel and the chancel is unforgettably lovely.

There remain for us to see the woodwork and the glass, and if there were nothing else these would make the church remarkable. All the roofs are magnificent, both in their strength and their ornament, and here and there are touches of the original colour. The 14th century hammerbeams in the transepts are the oldest. Decorative figures help to support a 15th century roof over the north aisle, where heads and angels look from the bosses. The 16th century added the panelled roofs of the chancel, the nave, and the chapels, with heraldic bosses in the nave and painted emblems in the chapels, where are also two 15th century screens, elaborately traceried, perhaps by the cunning hand that fashioned the woodwork behind the high altar. A staircase with twisted balusters leads to a canopied oak pulpit of 1680, standing on a tall stem with foliage at its angles. There are Jacobean bench-ends, and three fine chests of the 15th, 16th, and 20th centuries, the Tudor linenfold one now serving as an altar to Sir Thomas More, with an old copy of his Utopia open on the top of it.

But we have left the best till last, for here is a font unique in England, for it is encased in wood and the delicate carving of the case is 15th century; the only one at all like it is in another Essex church at Littlebury, with four sides where Thaxted's has eight. Its cover, like a wooden spire, is also 15th century and canopied and finished with remarkable detail to the top of its exquisite finial. The cover does not lift up, but panels in the upper half of the case swing open to reveal the sunken font bowl and the two carved brackets supporting the cover.

The oldest glass here is the armed figure with a spear and the Mortimer arms on his shield in a south transept window; it is late 14th century. Other windows have glass of the 15th, including four Garden of Eden scenes with bishops and angels and St Ursula in the tracery, and more saints and archbishops with the Madonna. The glass in the north chapel is 16th century, like the magnificent stonework framing it.

The church is unusually bare of medieval memorials. Alone in the middle of the chancel floor is a brass portrait of a 15th century priest. There is a small carving of St Francis in memory of Eric Makeham who was killed in the Great War; and Isobel Gloag, who is buried here, is remembered by her painting of St Peter by the south chapel. The work of other modern artists in iron, glass, embroidery, and tapestries adds richness to the rare grace of this church. It is a revelation of beauty.

It is to a Thaxted man that we owe some of the most interesting descriptions of sea journeys in Elizabethan and Stuart days, for there was born here in 1575 Samuel Purchas, the first man to publish Hakluyt's manuscripts. He brought them out in 1625, together with many accounts of voyages by Spanish, Dutch, and English seamen. He spent his all in giving us these treasures, yet he died in poverty, being buried within a few yards of St Paul's Cathedral—in St Martin's on Ludgate Hill, where he was rector.

Miss Buss

THEYDON BOIS. Hereabouts is the most beautiful piece of the forest of Epping; the village has part of it as a great green, round which old cottages stand. In the churchyard are two stately oaks. The church, not yet a hundred years old, was built by Sydney Smirke, architect of the impressive Reading Room of the British Museum, his contribution to the masterpiece of his brother Robert. The low spire is covered with copper, and in the red brick tower are two bells from the medieval church which stood in the valley of the Roding. Also in the tower is a remarkable board painted with the arms of James the First, with the king's head below. A fine example of modern woodwork is the walnut pulpit by Paul Waterhouse, its sounding-board of simple dignity. There is good modern glass with striking portraits of Saint Hubert and Saint Nicholas.

One of the windows is in memory of that noble pioneer woman Frances Mary Buss, who lies in the churchyard. It shows the scene in Pilgrim's Progress in which the Interpreter bids his servant Greatheart conduct Christiana and her companions to the house called Beautiful, "and they went singing." Frances Buss was the daughter of a Punch artist and illustrator of books. In the middle of last century she started a school for girls in Kentish Town and developed a new system which revolutionised the methods of teaching. When she died in 1894 her North London Collegiate School was one of the most famous secondary schools in England.

Triumph of the Carpenter

THEYDON GARNON. A lonely place in a valley between Epping Forest and Theydon Mount, it has a church hidden in the trees, with only a farm and a cottage or two for company. The church has been here about 700 years, but its high brick tower was built by Sir John Crosby, alderman and grocer of London, and his wife in 1520. The door is as old as the tower itself. The nave is remarkable for having one of the very rare timber arcades in England, five bays in oak, the wooden columns having moulded capitals. It was set here in the reign of Charles Stuart and, with the 15th century roof of the nave, is a veritable triumph of the carpenter. An ironbound chest

345

rests on claw-shaped feet in the vestry, a brass plate with his arms stating that it was given in 1668 by Sir John Archer, a judge. In his memory there is a wall-monument on the chancel wall. Facing it on the other side of the lovely east window is an older monument over the grave of Anne, Lady Fitzwilliam, who died a year before Queen Elizabeth, bequeathing to the village the almshouses a few hundred yards away.

Much more beautiful than these classical memorials are two canopied altar tombs in the sanctuary walls. Both are carved in grey marble. One has lost its brasses, but the other has brass portraits of a man in armour with his wife and their five children. There are two other brasses, one of Ellen Branch who died in 1567, and one of William Kirkeby, rector in 1458; he wears a beautiful cope.

Queen Elizabeth's Secretary

THEYDON MOUNT. It has a park on a hill, one of the most delightful hilltop parks that could be imagined, with a great house coming down from the age of the Tudors and a church from the days of Shakespeare.

The glory of the church is in the splendid tombs of those people who lived in the great house, two Thomas Smiths and two Williams. The first Thomas was the great Protestant Secretary of Queen Elizabeth, and we see him a stately bearded man in the mantle of the Garter, looking the scholar he was, lying on his side under an arch round which we read that "What the earth or seas or sky contain, what creatures in them be, his mind did seek to know." His nephew William lies on another tomb with his wife, two sons in armour, three daughters in veils, and two babies kneeling at a prayer desk as high as themselves. This man's son William is gazing upward with his hands on a book and his two wives dominating the tomb. They are kneeling with a plump child in a grown-up dress between them. On the fourth tomb is his brother Thomas, his head on his hand, and cherubs guarding his altar tomb. On the wall above hangs a helmet.

The old house, built by the first Sir Thomas, has changed much down the centuries, but has on both fronts the original windows and the soft red bricks of Elizabethan days. Three gabled dormers looking down on the lawn are original, but the north front has an 18th century portico with four columns. In the windows are many heraldic devices of Tudor times, one glass panel showing a sea fight with ships of Drake's day, and the oldest glass of all having on it the head of a girl of the 14th century.

Sir Thomas Smith was born at Saffron Walden in 1513, his family tracing its descent from the Black Prince. He went to Cambridge at 11, establishing there a reputation as a staunch Protestant. So brilliant was his scholarship that he became Provost of Eton, and reformed the pronunciation of Greek. His scholarship helped Latimer, Ridley, and Cranmer in their reforms, while his tact and judgment were used by Protector Somerset who sent him as ambassador to foreign courts.

When Mary Tudor came to the throne he surrendered all his posts and went into retirement, settling down in marriage and rebuilding the hall here. Elizabeth, who knew his sterling worth, sent him as ambassador to Paris and afterwards made him Secretary. He died in 1577, leaving his lovely home to his nephew, and leaving behind his great work on The English State, an authoritative exposition on government which was not given to the world till six years after his death. The book ran through ten editions in a century and was translated into Latin, Dutch, and German, so that it must be regarded as one of the best-sellers of its time.

The Mailed Knight

THORPE-LE-SOKEN. A little village near the Landermere Creek of Hanford Water, it has a green and an inn with an overhanging storey built 400 years ago.

The church has been made new except for the tower, which has 16th century brick walls. The oldest thing left is the Norman base of the font, and the most beautiful thing left is an oak screen of Shakespeare's day, on which are carved angels holding shields. Under a 14th century arch in the chancel lies the figure of a mailed knight who may have fought with Simon de Montfort, his feet resting on a lion. On the wall of the tower is a tablet to Thomas Wharton, secretary to Charles Stuart's evil genius, Henrietta Maria.

This small place gave two martyrs to the fires, William Hale and Thomas Leyes, both burned in 1555 because they were Protestants.

THORRINGTON. It has farms and other buildings as old as Shakespeare's plays, the best old piece of brickwork being the garden wall of Gatehouse Farm, with its moulded and crowstepped arch. A field gate leads us to a timbered hall with a garden hidden from the churchyard by a row of ash trees. Behind the barn is a splendid grove of oaks. The pinnacled tower greets the tower of Brightlingsea on its hill across the valley. Two medieval sundials are scratched on one of its buttresses. There is one portrait of olden days, representing one of the two wives of an unknown John Clare, who died in 1564; five of their children are here too. A good friend of the church 100 years before the Clares, John Deth, lies in the tower, with a tribute to his generosity. The 16th century font has a carved pomegranate on it, and the 14th century piscina has the head of an ape.

THUNDERSLEY. Swinging in the wind as a weathervane on the spire of its church are gleaming figures of St Peter and the Archangel Michael. They preside over a church with a 15th century roof and a nave and narrow aisles 700 years old. Four great upright beams fill the end of the nave, set here in medieval days to support the bell-turret. On a wall hangs the helmet of some unknown squire buried here about the time the Stuarts came down from Scotland, and by the helmet hangs a sword; but much more beautiful is the Elizabethan chalice with its band of engraved ornament.

The Great Docks

TILBURY. It is the first of the Port of London Docks on coming from the sea, and is 24 miles from the mouth of the Thames. It has passenger traffic facilities equal to any in the world, a floating landing stage 1142 feet long. The biggest liners afloat can come in to it any hour of day or night whatever the tide may be. It has four miles of quays and 45 miles of railways, and daily cargoes arriving from the ends of the earth.

And it has a famous memory, for here, in the stirring times of danger when the battle with the Armada was raging, came Queen Elizabeth to address and hearten her troops. Mounted on a splendid charger, she rode bareheaded, a page bearing her white-plumed helmet. Only two nobles attended her, and one carried the Sword of State ahead of her. Over her bodice she wore a corselet of polished steel, and her words were the words of a veritable Tudor Boadicea.

It was the time of the greatest peril the nation had known since the Norman Conquest, but it was the proudest day of the Queen's life. It was then that she made a marvellous speech which history has preserved. She told her volunteer soldiers (we had no regular army) how others had feared for her to risk coming among them, but she did not desire to live if she could not trust her people:

Let tyrants fear; I have always so behaved myself that under God I have placed my chiefest strength and safeguard in the loyal hearts and goodwill of my subjects; and therefore I am come among you at this time resolved, in the midst and heat of the battle, to live or die among you all, to lay down for my God and for my kingdom and for my people my honour and my blood, even in the dust.

Then followed the famous declaration that history does not forget:

I know I have the body of a weak, feeble woman, but I have the heart of a king, and of a King of England too, and think foul scorn that any prince of Europe should dare to invade the borders of my realm.

The old forge facing the green recalls the busy scene in 1648 when the cavalry for Fairfax halted here on the way to Colchester and the horses were stabled in the nave of the church. There is an old farmhouse which was here then, for it was Tilbury Hall 400 years ago; it has a great thatched barn.

The church (at West Tilbury) stands among elms and chestnuts on the edge of the bold escarpment overlooking the meadows stretching to the Thames, and beyond to the hills of Kent. The rampart and the ditch of an ancient camp are close by, and it is believed to have been here that Queen Elizabeth reviewed her hosts. By the river is Tilbury Fort, with a gatehouse of 1682. There are traces of Norman windows in the nave and chancel of the church, and the walls are among the earliest Norman work in England, being 11th century; but the tower is modern with five 17th century bells hanging in it. On the floor of the nave is a coffin lid 700 years old with a moulded edge and a cross, and there is an ancient piscina and one or two medieval windows.

TILBURY-JUXTA-CLARE. We come to its lonely little church at the end of a narrow lane. It has a tower of Tudor brick, with the badge of the proud De Veres who were probably its benefactors. Much of what we see is 500 years old, the nave and chancel and porch all with their original roofs, the glass canopy-work in the east window, and the fragments of wall-painting, which include a picture of a timbered house with a man and a horse in the foreground. It is partly painted over with 16th century ornament, and there are traces of black-letter texts from the same time. There is a pulpit with

Jacobean woodwork, and a fine old chest heavily bound with iron. Grotesque heads look down from the roof, and above the 17th century panelling in the tower is a crude winged beast in plaster.

TILLINGHAM. Its cottages are delightful; we remember especially the long white timbered house made bright by rose and creeper by the churchyard gate. Some of the neat cottages were built by the Dean and Chapter of St Paul's, who since Christianity came to Essex have owned the land on which they stand. The church, almost lost among the limes, has a plain Norman doorway into the nave, handsome arches of the 14th century, and a square font with foliage carved about the time of Thomas Becket. St Paul's Cathedral has honoured in a window here one of its greatest preachers, Canon Liddon, whose eloquence drew vast congregations to the cathedral in the 20 years he was preaching there.

Norman Walls

TILTY. It still has a few walls from the Norman abbey in the valley of the Chelmer, and excavations have shown that here was once an abbey church with a chapter house and other buildings of the Cistercian monks. Perhaps it was their influence which gave the village church its lovely 14th century chancel where niches adorn the buttresses, an elaborate cross stands on the gable, and the east wall is nearly filled by a window with exquisite tracery, a great stone wheel crowning the five tall lights. Curious heads look out from the gables. Another lovely window is in the side wall, and within is a perfect row of four linked arches for the sedilia and piscina with heads, one of a man in a curious hood. The belfry with its handsome cupola is modern, but the nave began as a little chapel beyond the abbey walls and was built about 1220. It has a row of graceful lancets, a double piscina, and a timber-framed porch of the 17th century. Timbers of the 14th century are hidden by the plaster of the roofs, and a massive embattled beam crosses the church where the chancel meets the nave.

One of the old abbots is remembered by a brass inscription with four Latin verses, and there are fine brass portraits of one of Henry the Eighth's counsellors, Gerard Danet, his wife, five sons, and six daughters. With four heraldic shields and an inscription running round, they make a perfect group. Very well preserved is the brass of George Medeley in Tudor armour, with his family of six.

TIPTREE. Where the great forest of Essex spread hundreds of years ago, fruit trees now stand in ordered rows. We came in spring, and found the 200-year-old windmill looking down on a pink and white cloud of cherry and plum and apple blossom, a lovely scene. It is said that smugglers brought their contraband from the creeks, up the long hillside road, to conceal them in the brick tower of this mill. The great sails still jut out from its dark cone-like cap, an eerie landmark in the winter twilight.

Away beyond the heath towards Great Braxted stands an Elizabethan house with fine transomed windows. It has a great Tudor fireplace and a rubble wall from a medieval priory.

Swear Not At All

TOLLESBURY. Lying near the Blackwater estuary, a centre of the oyster fisheries, its streets have many quaint old buildings. The green has become a paved square, and round it stand tiled cottages of many ages and the long, low brick walls of the churchyard. A battered wooden building with an acorn-shaped finish was the lock-up for the village ne'er-do-wells. Sloping down to the south wall of the churchyard is the tiled roof of three houses into which the 15th century hall has been divided.

The square is dominated by the massive tower which rests on the oldest stones the village has, a rubble foundation of Saxon times. Indoors above the 14th century tower arch, is a course of Roman tiles the Saxon builders used, and over the 15th century doorway is a lofty arch of similar tiles. A Norman window close by has a representation in modern glass of St Cedd, the Saxon bishop who built the first churches in Essex. In the modern chancel is a richly carved monument to Jane Gardiner, who died in 1654. On a wall-brass in the nave are 400-year-old portraits of Thomas Freshwater in a fur-lined gown, with his wife and their nine children.

The small font may pass unnoticed, yet it has an odd little story. It was obtained for the church in 1718 by a strong-willed church-warden, Robert Joyce, from a certain John Norman, who came into church cursing and talking loudly during service. To prevent his being prosecuted he paid five pounds, and out of this sum the font was bought, the churchwarden having these wise words put boldly round the bowl:

> *Good people all, I pray take care*
> *That in the church you do not swear*
> *As this man did.*

A Man and His 30,000 Days

TOLLESHUNT D'ARCY. Winding roads with cottage doors opening on to them give a charm to this old-world place under the elms. We come into its church by a porch of 500 years ago, with carved figures on the corners of the parapet and angels at the door. The door into the nave has still the draw-bar which bolted the door when it was new, 500 years ago.

It is in the chapel that we find the treasures linking this place with the great days of the Tudors, the chapel of the Darcy family who lived at the hall next door and gave the village its name. Their portraits are in brass. Here lies Antony, in the armour he wore before the Armada. Here is Philippa, wearing a French hood, her daughter beside her. On the wall is a brass which is a spoil of the monasteries, for on the other side is an abbot of 1400 in mass vestments. Unnamed brasses of a man in the armour of Agincourt and of a woman in a veil are on the wall, and earlier still is a gem of Flemish work from a brass of about 1375. It is a rare fragment with the Madonna and Child, St Bartholomew, St Philip, the lion of St Mark, and the bull of St Matthew on a rich background of grape vine. Both sides of it are engraved.

The sculptor has added to the treasures here, with an armoured figure of Thomas Darcy kneeling face to face with his wife Camilla, an elderly woman in ruff and gown. They built the bridge which leads across the moat, and on the brick piers are their sculptured coats-of-arms and the date 1585. Inside the timbered house are doors of great beauty and a room lined with panels carved with a mermaid, an eagle, and a child. In the grounds is a dovecot with a quaint roof.

There has passed away in this village in our own time a man who had been its physician and friend for 67 years, the wonderful John Henry Salter. He left behind him a diary covering about 30,000 days written in eighty volumes and running to about ten million words. He had a wide practice in the county, and in the old days would take long journeys, sometimes using two or three horses a day.

Thaxted   The Noble Church

Thaxted   The Medieval Nave

He was a volunteer soon after the Crimean War, he served as a major in the Great War, he had shot big game in Russia, he performed scores of operations before anaesthetics were known, he loved dogs and painted them, he loved flowers and painted them, and this was one of the notes in his diary:

I have discovered how to keep well. I never have more than two meals, with nothing to eat or drink between. I go to bed at night, and wake up five hours later as sure as clockwork. The rest of the day I work.

We see his natural history collection in the Chelmsford Museum.

TOLLESHUNT KNIGHTS. It has one knight all forlorn. We found him at the end of a lane running by the railway to a farm and a church, the church in the shade of a cluster of tall trees. The knight is in the 14th century chancel, a curious stone figure in plate armour holding a heart in his hands, as he has done for five and a half centuries and more.

TOLLESHUNT MAJOR. Whoever loves stone must here love brick, for the 16th century builder has shown us what he could accomplish in decorative moulding in bricks in a country house and a village church. The two-storeyed gatehouse and the boundary wall of the courtyard of Beckingham Hall were set up in the reign of Henry the Eighth, when the tower was added to the neighbouring church. The mouldings of the windows in the upper stages of this tower are as neat as stone could be, while blue bricks make patterns up the tower. There are vaulted brick canopies over niches in the walls of the nave, and by the altar is a 13th century coffin lid carved with a cross. The church stands in open country facing a pond, and from the battlements of its tower is a glorious view of the Blackwater estuary and the trees on Mersey Island across that sparkling band of water.

Dorcas Smyth's Books

TOPPESFIELD. True to its name, it stands high, with wide views over Essex and Suffolk, and with a rich heritage of old houses round about. Toppesfield Hall, close to the road, is 300 years old and has much original woodwork. Berwick Hall has kept some of its moat; Bradfield's Farm is 15th century and has a Tudor barn; and parts of the rectory are thought to be 500 years old. The most striking sight in the village is a pinnacled brick tower built in the last year of the 17th century, the guardian of a church much older. Both its

A A

porches are 15th century, one timbered and weatherworn, the other with an embattled parapet and a grotesque gargoyle. The doorways are 14th century and so is the chancel, which leans out of line with the nave. The south aisle roof has been here 500 years, and the nave roof has a beam carved about 1600. There is some 17th century panelling, and a little 15th century glass probably from a picture of the crowning of the Madonna. Under a canopy is a panelled tomb with a cross in bold relief, thought to be the sleeping-place of the founder of the chancel 600 years ago; but the surprising monument is one with two piles of carved books supporting a broken pediment with a beehive. It has a lamb crouching on a book below the inscription, which is to Dorcas Smyth who died in 1633.

TWINSTEAD. Here is a family from the England of Shakespeare and Raleigh, their portraits engraved on enduring brass. Isake Wyncoll is bareheaded in a long-sleeved cloak, his wife Marie has a richly embroidered dress and a ruff, and below are their five daughters, two in round hats. They are in the nave of a church they would fail to recognise, for it was refashioned 250 years after their day, its companion a giant old cedar in the corner of the churchyard. There are three high chancel arches, a carved chair of about 1700, a panelled chest of the 18th century, and a marble stone to Robert Gray who was rector of the old church for 44 years. His successor Henry Shortland stayed 40 years, and he it was who made the building new.

Beautiful Ugley

UGLEY. It deserves a better name, for with beautiful cottages and farms, splendid barns, and an ancient church, it is one of the most charming villages in Essex. Someone has suggested that its old name was Oakley, which the Normans mispronounced. One of the old houses, Parsonage Farm, has Tudor carvings on a fireplace; another, Orford House, has a square dovecot with 350 nests. Ugley Hall of the 16th century has a noble barn of 11 bays, with aisles and three entrances. Bollington Hall of the 17th has another fine barn with eight bays and two gabled entrances. A little way off, among fine chestnut trees, stands the church, its Tudor brick tower said to be the last in Essex to keep a flock of pigeons, which were turned out not long ago. The chancel is modern, but has masonry from the ruins of Bollington church, including niches carved 600 years ago. The nave is 13th century, the chancel arch and the porch are 15th century. Part of a medieval screen stands under the tower arch, and there is a hoary chest of about 1600 with four fastenings and a great lock. A sombre cherub looks out from the chancel wall in memory of Isaac Whittington of the 18th century; and a delightful figure of Charity shines from a window to remind us of a lady who loved her village.

ULTING. It lies by the part of the River Chelmer which was made into a navigable canal at the end of the 18th century. A few of its houses are 300 years old, and the church beside the tree-shaded canal is more than twice as ancient. It is a little building 45 feet by 18 feet almost entirely 13th century, but with a tiny turret and spire of the 15th century. The font, on six short pillars, has been here since the church was built; the nave roof and the piscina carved with a flower are 600 years old; the wall-plates of the chancel roof are a century younger; and two bench-ends fastened to a chest in the vestry were made when the Tudor Age began.

Brass and Glass

UPMINSTER. Its fine windmill greets us as we come; if we like to climb to the top of it we can see a sweep of 40 miles of Essex and the hills of Kent. The old-world village has grown into a garden suburb of London; its gabled Elizabethan hall has become the home of a Golf Club; but it keeps one of the most charming 15th century houses in Essex, Great Tomkyns, with lovely windows and project-ing wings and a hall open to the roof. By it is a 17th century thatched barn with three bays.

Two avenues of yews which have been growing in three centuries bring us to the church with a 13th century nave, a 14th century arcade, and 15th century beams in its tower. The door to the turret stairs hangs on hinges 700 years old, and has been opening and shutting 500 years. There are fragments of woodwork of the same age in one of the medieval screens.

The church has an interesting collection of brass and glass, six brasses having portraits of Tudor and Stuart times. An unknown man in civilian dress is of Henry the Eighth's day, and Elizabeth Dencourt has a horned headdress and heraldic mantle of the century before. Nicholas Wayte and his wife are on a stolen medieval brass which has an abbot on the back, and above them is a brass of a lady of 1560 with a book in her hand. Dressed in elaborate armour is Geerardt d'Ewes with his feet on what looks like a wolf, and in a beautiful dress with a wide collar is Grace Latham of 1626.

St George appears twice in the chancel, once in a modern statue and again in the east window in memory of one of our heroes. Another chancel window has Our Lord and eight saints, one of them holding a model of the oldest church in Essex. In a smaller window is a medley of old and new glass, with the year 1630 standing out from heraldic devices and little butterflies giving it charm. We noticed in it the figure of a child in swaddling clothes.

A sword hanging on the wall belonged to one of the sailors of the Holden family who have long been distinguished in Upminster. They have been rectors since 1780, one of them for 63 years. Here is the grave of Dr Henry Holden who died at 95 after being Headmaster of Uppingham, and by it is the tomb of Luther Holden who died at 90, having been President of the Royal College of Surgeons.

Life Comes to the Marshes

VANGE. Here the Langdon Hills come down to the drained marshes of the Thames estuary, through which flows Vange Creek. The Thames is now away from the village, but for hundreds of years man fought a losing battle with the floods, landowners having to repair the embankment walls or forfeit their lands. So sadly beaten were they that in 1620 the Government sent for expert Dutchmen to set up stout walls, and gave them these forfeited lands as their fee.

So it was that Cornelius Vandenanker came here with hundreds of his countrymen, reclaiming the marshes from Dagenham to Canvey by transporting tons of chalk from the quarries at Grays, and in some places constructing three walls, one within the other. He amassed a great fortune by selling the marshes he had redeemed. There is a record that his wife was buried in Downham church in 1692.

Vange is now a fast-growing place, for though the Thames is away Thameshaven is spreading in. Its small church is solitary on a hillock projecting toward the Thames. No road approaches, a few elms shading the long path across the fields which brings us to the churchyard. The church, less than 60 feet long, is crowned with a tiny wooden turret perched on the nave. The manor was held for Bishop Odo, the Conqueror's stepbrother, and the church was apparently begun about his time if we judge by its solid chancel arch. There is a blocked Norman window and a Norman font, its solid square bowl with rough zigzag lines on one face and foliage on the top.

WAKES COLNE. One of its houses, Crepping Hall, was mentioned in Domesday Book and was the seat of the Creppings. We see it as a timber and plaster house of the 15th century, much altered in 500 years, but with its original doorway, and with some of its original kingpost roof inside.

Several Tudor homes are hereabouts, one with a 16th century chimney stack, another with a moat. The oldest part of the church is the Norman nave, which has kept a doorway all these years. It is in a 15th century timber porch, and frames a Tudor door with straphinges and a domed handle-plate. The chancel and its arch are 14th century. The bell-turret rising on fine timbers is 15th, and one of its bells may have rung in Tudor days. A charming little font bowl is the oldest possession of the church, its sides panelled by 12th century carvers. A curious doorway, about 400 years old, opens to a stair in the thickness of the chancel wall, and may have been connected with the use of the Lenten veil. Remains of ancient wall-painting by the chancel arch show something not often seen, black roses.

The Bells Ring Out the Storied Past

WALTHAM ABBEY. Every Scout knows it, for here is Gilwell Park, the 70 acres in which Scoutmasters are trained; and every English boy should know it, for it has sometimes been called Harold's Town, because the last of the Saxon kings founded a church and was long believed to have been buried here.

In a field at the back of the church is a primitive bridge with a single arch which the boys call Harold's Bridge, though it is younger than it looks, being only 600 years old. Of the old monastic buildings of the Normans there is little to see except a vaulted passage; there is also a 14th century gateway. The 15th century inn has an overhanging storey making a lychgate into the churchyard, and a shop in the market square has timbers carved by medieval artists showing a crouching woman with a jug and a man with his tongue out. There are many 16th century buildings in the town, and a square near the abbey is still known as Romeland because the rents from its houses supplied the papal dues. It was in a long-fronted house of this square that the seed was sown of one of the decisive movements of the world, for in it Cranmer met Bishop Gardiner on that day when he "struck the keynote of the Reformation and claimed for the Word of God that supremacy which had been usurped by the popes for centuries." It was a hundred years after this that Thomas Fuller was vicar here, and he never ceased to be proud because Waltham itself "gave Rome the first deadly blow in England."

One more link with the Reformation Waltham has, for behind an ivied wall in Sewardstone Street we may see a 16th century chimney of a house which has in it the walls within which John Foxe wrote his immortal book of martyrs, the poignant story of hundreds of the bravest men and women ever living in these islands, who walked into the fire to be burned rather than surrender their faith in God.

But it is, of course, the church and the cross that the traveller comes to see. They stand a mile or so apart, the church a fragment of its former self but without an equal in the county. It has the noblest Norman nave in the south of England. One arch of the great Norman tower remains, having been filled in to form the east wall, and standing at the east end of the churchyard we may see the herringbone masonry of the transept wall which Harold must have seen; it has a blocked up Norman window above it. The south doorway is magnificent with the rich carving of a Norman craftsman. When King John signed the Charter at Runnymede there was rising here a church as long as Norwich Cathedral, being built as part of the penance John's father performed after the murder of Becket. Waltham Abbey was one of the three monasteries Henry the Second then founded, and it has only been realised in our time how magnificently he carried out his vow. For on this abbey alone he spent over £1000, a huge sum in his time, when a labourer's wage was a penny a day. The spade has revealed that Henry's church was at least 400 feet long, and had two central towers linked by a nave as long as the nave still standing. Beyond the eastern tower stood the choir before whose high altar it was long believed that Harold's body lay. Each tower had its transepts, those next to the choir being 140 feet across.

The ten acres under which the foundations of this great church and many monastic buildings lie were market gardens until a few years ago, when they were bought and divided between the Office of Works and the church authorities, who have laid out five acres as a Garden of

Rest. Fragments from forest and mine far across England must lie below this quiet plot, for national records have been searched and we know the story of the stupendous task the repentant king put in hand. In the roofs 265 cartloads of lead were used, brought from the Peak and the Pennines to Boston and to Yorkshire ports, and thence by sea to London, where it was shipped on to the River Lea. The timber came, not from Epping Forest hard by, but from Brimpsfield in Gloucestershire and Bromley in Kent. We learn that William of Gant was the builder, and first abbot of the new foundation. Waltham Abbey remained the pride of our kings for three centuries, and even Henry the Eighth must have felt some reluctance about spoiling it, for he left it to the last. Then the vast building became a quarry for all, the only glory left being the western nave, which was used as the parish church.

We approach this great place through a deeply recessed doorway 600 years old, which was refashioned when the west tower was rebuilt in 1558, and we pass in through another beautiful 14th century doorway which was the west entrance to the abbey. It has vaulting rising from beautiful capitals, a running pattern of flowers, and carved niches on both sides. If we come at service time we shall hear the bells in the tower which inspired Tennyson to write his famous New Year verses, "Ring out the old, Ring in the new." He was living at High Beech close by when he heard the bells of Waltham Abbey and sat down to write these stanzas of In Memoriam:

> The time draws near the birth of Christ;
> The moon is hid, the night is still;
> A single church below the hill
> Is pealing, folded in the mist;

and then these more familiar verses of Old and New Year:

> Ring out old shapes of foul disease;
> Ring out the narrowing lust of gold;
> Ring out the thousand wars of old,
> Ring in the thousand years of peace.

> Ring in the valiant man and free,
> The larger heart, the kindlier hand;
> Ring out the darkness of the land,
> Ring in the Christ that is to be.

A place of great splendour is the nave, its Norman pillars impressing the eye with equal grace and strength. Above them runs the triforium, and above that the clerestory, with its array of columns supporting the round arches through which the light floods in. So thick is the wall up there that a vaulted passage runs through it all the way. All these arches are adorned with zigzag and some of the columns have zigzag and spirals cut into them, once filled with gilt metal, as we see from the rivets still here. All this great work is Norman except for a few piers at the west end, where the 14th century architects adapted the Norman work to their pointed style.

Columns fifty feet high run up to the ceiling of this wondrous nave, and we are brought at once from the 12th century to the 20th, for the painted roof is a mass of colour by one of our own famous artists, and the light by which we see it comes in through Burne-Jones windows. On the ceiling are painted the signs of the Zodiac, the labours of the months, and other symbolical subjects, all the work of Sir Edward Poynter before his days of fame—and the roof is lit by a rose window below which are three windows designed by Sir Edward Burne-Jones before fame came to him. The rose window shows Creation, and below is a Jesse Tree with the patriarchs on one side and the prophets on the other.

The oldest tomb here is the imposing wall-monument of Sir Edward Denny, resting on a shelf in his armour, with his wife in her Elizabethan ruff and hood below him, and their six sons and four daughters round the tomb; the last little girl is holding her sister's arm. Standing by the wall is the alabaster figure of Lady Elizabeth Greville, cousin of Lady Jane Grey. Two 16th century families are in brass, Edward Stacey with his wife and son, and Thomas Colt with his wife and their ten children. On a realistic altar tomb of white marble is a sculptured panel of a ship at sea and mourning angels with tears on their cheeks; the tomb is to Captain Robert Smith of 1697, but resting on it is a bust of Henry Wollaston, a 17th century magistrate in Roman dress.

Out of an aisle we mount up to a beautiful chapel 600 years old; it has a crypt beneath it with fine vaulting. The chapel is lit by great windows with exquisite tracery, and has low stone seats round the walls divided by stone columns. It may be reached from outside through a beautiful doorway carved with flowers, and is charming without and within. Two of its windows have in them the Archangel Gabriel bringing the good news to the Madonna, and three lovely

Waltham Abbey   The Great West Tower

South Ockendon   Rochford

Rayleigh   Layer Marney

FOUR OLD ESSEX TOWERS

Blackmore

Stock

Laindon

West Hanningfield

TIMBER TOWERS AND SHINGLED SPIRES

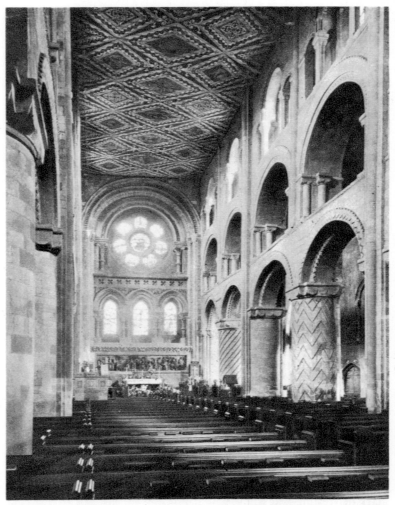

Waltham Abbey   The Wonderful Norman Nave

figures at the Presentation in the Temple, one of the windows being in memory of Francis Johnson, who was curate and vicar 56 years. Above the altar are scenes at least 500 years older, a 14th century painting of Judgment Day: Christ is seated in majesty with outstretched hands, and Peter stands with other figures in front of a group of medieval buildings, while on the other side are angels receiving the good and the fires of hell receiving the wicked.

In this chapel are such memories of old Waltham as the stocks and whipping-post and pillory, the works of a clock which ran in this church for 260 years, a portrait of Thomas Tallis who was organist in the last days of the abbey, two Jacobean chairs, Roman remains, and casts of the abbey seals. Two other odd things we found in this museum; one a 16th century waterspout wrongly claiming to be part of Harold's tomb, the other a grim relic of the days when suicides were buried at the cross-roads, for it is a stake which was found piercing the skeleton of a man buried there.

Such is Waltham Abbey as we see it. It lives in history and in legend, for legend tells us of one Tovi, standard-bearer to Canute, who found a piece of the Holy Cross at Montacute in Somerset and built a church here to preserve it; to this day this Waltham church is dedicated to St Lawrence and the Holy Cross. It was given its name in the presence of Edward the Confessor, who was here in 1060. Here on its way to Westminster Abbey rested the body of Queen Eleanor for one night, and 17 years after lay the body of her King Edward, waiting in this abbey for three months during the preparations for his funeral at Westminster.

It is in memory of Queen Eleanor's last ride that Waltham Cross was built. It is perhaps the best of all the crosses that bear her name, and was set up to mark the place where the body of the queen rested on that sad procession from the Notts village in which she died to Westminster Abbey where she lies. Twelve crosses were set up to mark her resting-places, the first at Lincoln, the last at Charing, and this, the one outside Northampton and a third at Geddington, are the only remains.

Waltham Cross stands actually in Hertfordshire where the road from the abbey joins the Roman Ermine Street, at the spot where the abbot and his monks met the sad procession from St Albans on a dark December day in 1290. Today it is in a busy street; then it stood with nothing but a chantry and a wayside inn to keep it company. Of the chantry not a stone remains, but the inn is still close by; it was probably the abbey guest house, and has as its sign four swans which recall the swans on King Harold's shield at Hastings.

It is believed that this cross was designed by William Torel, the goldsmith who made Queen Eleanor's tomb in the Abbey. Much of his cross has survived the ages, though it has been twice refashioned from his materials. It has six sides and three tiers all richly adorned. The lower tier is solid, and each of its six faces is decorated like a window, with two trefoil panels under a quatrefoil, shields hanging from knots of foliage in the panels. Round the top of this tier runs a richly carved cornice, battlemented and pierced with crosses, and above this rise eight pinnacles supporting the lovely canopies of the second stage. In these canopies are three statues of Queen Eleanor holding her sceptre, all three original except for one head. Above the canopies rises the third tier of the cross, solid like the ground tier, carved like a lancet window and with rich finials on the six corner shafts. In the centre of these finials rises a daintily carved crown, from the heart of which springs a pinnacle topped with a stone cross.

A Hundred Miles of Crowded Streets

WALTHAMSTOW. With Epping Forest on the east, and on the west reservoirs and the River Lea with its marshlands, it is an attractively placed town, and has for its motto the inspiring words that Fellowship is Life. We found an old man on the bridge across the marshes of the Lea who has seen Walthamstow grow from a village into one of the forty biggest towns in England, with 100 miles of crowded streets and about 150,000 people.

If we come to it over the bridge across the marshes (here still called the Lammas Lands), we tread where its oldest inhabitants trod in the days before history, for in the excavations of the river banks have been found a pile dwelling of the Bronze Age and a British canoe of the 5th century, dug out from the trunk of an oak. The boat is in the British Museum. Here also has been found a Viking ship 45 feet long, lying keel upwards in the mud with a skeleton under it.

By the road across the marshes stands a quaint old inn which was once the haunt of Izaak Walton, and the road brings us to an old copper mill which struck copper coins to relieve the distress in the Napoleon wars.

Essex Hall, the old school with wooden pegs on which Disraeli would hang his coat (and Granville Sharp before him) has gone, but in Lloyd Park, which now belongs to the town, stands the Georgian house where William Morris lived as a boy, boating and fishing in a moat running round a little island there. It has attained a new dignity in our time, for it is to house a rare collection of pictures given by Arthur Mackmurdo and Frank Brangwyn, including many of Brangwyn's own works. The house is the chief link the town now has with William Morris, his birthplace having disappeared.

At Walthamstow lived Sir William Penn, the father of the Quaker; he was sent out by Cromwell to start the Empire in Guiana, and succeeded only in the capture of Jamaica, so setting up the flag between the two Americas. Lady Penn lies in the churchyard. Salisbury Hall Farm, built about 1600, stands on the site of the house in which the old Countess of Salisbury was arrested before her butchery by Henry the Eighth; her death was probably the foulest stain on his name. Forest School has two old windows from Howden Church in Yorkshire, with 13th and 14th century glass, in which are eagles, acorns, and a priest. Woodford County High School for Girls is housed in a fine 18th century manor called Highams, and in the charming grounds is a great lake.

The pride of Walthamstow is the 200-year-old Vestry House, once the workhouse and now transformed into a museum. Over its doorway remains the old inscription, If any would not work, neither should he eat. It is one of a group of buildings gathered on a hill near the church in the middle of the town. As we walk through it the past history of Walthamstow is gradually revealed to us by a case of prehistoric objects found in the marshes, or by photographs, drawings, and plans of buildings, and people. Set up within this building is the old parish lock-up, with the ring to which refractory prisoners were fastened. Round one of the rooms runs a series of 40 painted brilliant coat-of-arms. There is some panelling and a doorway from Essex Hall and the bell which may have called Disraeli and Granville Sharp to their lessons. There is an original drawing by Burne-Jones, a portrait of William Morris by G. F. Watts, a parish chest with eight locks, a magnificent piece of 17th century smith's work, and a motor car which claims to be the first ever made in England with an internal combustion engine.

In the group of buildings about the Vestry House stands the old armoury, goal, and Volunteer Centre. Like the Vestry House, it was built about 1700 by a master carpenter, Thomas Turner, who lies in a plain tomb with a yew at each corner. There is here a tomb (that of Jesse Russell) carved by Chantrey and in a plain tomb near it lies Ann Pearce who died in the home of Sir Robert Wigram, and was the faithful nurse of his 23 children for nearly half a century.

The tower of the church, with the porch, aisles, and chapels, are all from the reign of Henry the Eighth; the chancel is modern. On the walls is a fine brass of Sir George Monoux wearing his chain as lord mayor, and by him is his wife in her 15th century dress; Sir George was the founder of the delightful group of red brick alms-houses (with the original grammar school) seen in the churchyard. There is a palimpsest brass of 400 years ago, one side with an Eliza-bethan in a fur coat, the other with a civilian. Lady Lucy Stanley kneels in a cloak and coronet under a kind of triumphal arch, with four daughters dressed as in Stuart days; there is magnificent heraldry on her tomb. A monument by the famous Nicholas Stone has busts of Sir Thomas Merry and his wife, with richly detailed por-traits of their four children. A Jacobean wall-monument with fine ironwork in front of it shows Sigismund Trafford in Roman dress with his wife and their little one.

One of the odd things we found here was a beadle's stick carved with a crown and mitre over 250 years ago, and on the wall is a memory of the Maynards who were for 300 years lords of the manor.

The Craftsman Who Transformed the English House

WILLIAM MORRIS came into the world on a spring day in 1834, and for nearly fifty years he was fighting for the causes he had at heart. As artist, poet, reformer, printer, and manufacturer, he stands among the giants. His father was a bill-broker in the City, his mother a member of a musical family. It was a lucky parentage for William, for he inherited his mother's gifts, his father's business instincts, and he had immeasurable gifts of his own. He had a happy childhood, running wild in Epping Forest and grounding himself in that passion-ate love for trees and flowers which never left him. He went to Marl-borough and then to Oxford. At that time he was determined to be-come a clergyman, but at Oxford he fell in with a group of undergraduates who formed a friendship that was only broken by death, young men full of ideals reaching out toward a wider inheritance and development of culture than Morris had dreamed of.

He developed a great love for art and history, particularly that of the Middle Ages. He read everything of Ruskin and Carlyle that he could lay his hand on, and he travelled. He took up architecture, becoming the articled pupil of G. E. Street, and soon another influence came into his life, that of Dante Gabriel Rossetti, who persuaded Morris that he would be much better as a painter than as an architect. His giant intellect had already grasped the principle and history of architecture, and in his spare time he was writing poetry. Well it was for Morris that he had a father with a purse behind him while he battled between professions, developing his gifts, enriching his genius. A poor man could not have taken such a course. It was Morris's peculiar destiny to be a Jack-of-all-Arts and master of all. His poetry, in particular his Earthly Paradise and Death of Jason, placed him high among the English poets. He also wrote a great deal of prose.

When he was 25 and about to marry beautiful Jane Burden, he wanted a home, and set to work to build a palace of art of his own at Bexley in Kent. He designed the house himself, and a nice time the builders had getting their foundations in, for Morris would allow no trees to be felled! Then, when the Red House was built, he set about the finishing and furnishing, and found that there was no ironmongery, no carpets, curtains, or furniture to be bought in the shops that he considered fit to be put into a palace of art. The search for his own home-fittings made him realise in horror to what a depth the applied arts had sunk in England. He could find nothing that did not offend an artist's eye. "I will make them," said he; and it was good for the country that he did, for now the giant Morris began to get into his stride. With the cooperation of a group of friends, chief among them Burne-Jones, he started a business at Merton Abbey in Surrey to produce painted windows, furniture, metal and glass work, artistic tiles, hangings, tapestries, printed material, jewellery, embroideries— a vast workshop wherein the ideals and the pure beauty of medieval art came to life again.

William Morris built up in English home life and in our art schools an influence which has never died. It was largely through him that people came to see the horrible little meannesses of design and colour which were carried out by manufacturers and seen everywhere in ordinary houses. He spent his life sweeping such rubbish out of our lives. He mixed up politics and art and ideals in a delightful way, and became a convinced Socialist. He felt that art should be the great and purifying power in all men's lives, as it was in his; and how could that be if man lived in squalor and poverty?

As time went on he concentrated his energies on weaving, dyeing, and printing. He considered that, like all the applied arts, the trade of printing was in a bad way. He had left his small palace of art and bought a lovely 17th-century Manor House at Kelmscott, a small village on the Thames, where he set up the Kelmscott Press and printed books from type cut by himself, illustrated with woodcuts by Burne-Jones and other artists of the day. He also found time to write and illumine manuscripts in the manner of the Middle Ages.

It is impossible to estimate the purifying influence of William Morris on his day and generation, or on ours. He died all too soon, in 1896, recognised as one of the greatest creative geniuses, and perhaps the most perfect craftsman, that modern England has known.

Overthrown

WALTON-ON-THE-NAZE. Old Walton has been swallowed up by the sea, its church having vanished in 1798. The estates about this church belonged to St Paul's Cathedral and over one of the stalls we found the Latin words meaning *Overthrown by the Sea* instead of the customary name of the manor. Today Walton is a watering-place with smooth wide sands and a pier which we understand is the second longest in England, the longest also being in Essex, at Southend.

The geologist will find many fossils in its Red Crag beds; the archaeologist will find traces of a factory in which men of the Stone Age shaped their tools and weapons; the historian must note that hereabouts (in what we now call Frinton) was established the first telephone communication with a lighthouse.

On the bold promontory of the Naze stands a lofty tower built by Trinity House as a seamark in the days of the Napoleon wars.

The Royal Refugee

WANSTEAD. London has flowed into it, but has not been able to engulf this ancient place, for it is protected on all sides by forest land and open spaces, Wanstead Park and Wanstead Flats, and a lake-filled corner of Epping Forest.

A colony of over a hundred herons has settled in the park, of which 200 acres belong to the City of London; we could scarcely have believed in these cockney herons had we not seen their nests, 60 of them. The park was beautifully laid out by Richard Child, first Earl Tylney, whose father and brother we find in the church, but the gorgeous house he built has gone these hundred years. Louis the Eighteenth and his queen lived in it, refugees during the Napoleon wars, when they lived chiefly at Hartwell in Bucks. In an earlier house standing on this site took place the marriage of the Earl of Leicester and the Countess of Essex, of which no one dared tell Queen Elizabeth for a year, so much had she wished to marry the man herself.

Among the new shops in the High Street are some 18th century homes, one the manor house with a beautiful hooded doorway; and for contrast there is a tiny timbered cottage of the 17th century 14 feet by 7. The Spanish chestnuts on the green are much older than the church they lead us to, a classical building of 1790 with a pillared porch and a cupola. Under a richly carved canopy is a rare three-decker pulpit. There are some Chippendale chairs, a beautiful lectern, and a modern candelabra presided over by a two-headed eagle. A portrait in relief shows George Bowles, a lover of art who died in 1817.

Almost filling a wall of the chancel is the monument of Josiah Child and his son Bernard, who both appear in Roman costume, one lying on a shelf, the other standing on a pedestal with angels blowing trumpets above his head. Sir Josiah, a City merchant and economist (but not the banker) died in 1699. He was for a time Governor of the East India Company, one of whose chaplains lies in the churchyard. The chaplain is James Pound, whose account of the mutiny of Indian troops on the Pulo Condore Islands is treasured in the Bodleian. He lost all in the insurrection, returned to England, became rector of Wanstead, and soon made a name as an astronomer. The Royal Society lent him a telescope, and Sir Isaac Newton procured the maypole from the Strand for him to mount it on. He fired his curate, James Bradley, with the same enthusiasm, and had he lived he would have had the joy of seeing this much-loved nephew succeed Edmund Halley as Astronomer-Royal.

Pass, Friends

WEELEY. *Pass, Friends, All's Well,* says its memorial cross; but it is worth while to pause a little, if only to glance at these old cottages and farms they left behind. It is worth while, also, to walk down the lovely lane leading to the red brick church, looking out of place among the old trees overhanging two wide ponds and a quaint thatched barn. Yet the tower is of bricks baked 400 years ago, rare large bricks being used at the bottom and standard ones at the top. Inside hangs a bell of 1400. The rest of the church is modern, but it has a 15th century font, and a Norman shaft with a scalloped capital is used in the sanctuary as a table.

WENDEN LOFTS. Its church, which has splendid trees around it, was refashioned a century ago but has kept a fine Norman doorway with chevron ornament, a three-decker pulpit, and several other old possessions. In 18th century glass we see a sundial and Jacob's Ladder, with a symbolical snail; and in foreign glass a little older is a figure of Charity, scenes of the Nativity, the Crucifixion, and a group of armed men with a camel. William Lucas of 1460 is here in brass with his wife and eight children. One of the sons was Abbot of Waltham, and is shown in his robes carrying a crozier. The daughters are wearing headdresses fashionable 500 years ago. A wall-monument tells of the Wilkes family who worshipped here for a century, one of them bearing the whole cost of rebuilding the church.

Middy Under Nelson

WENDENS AMBO. A charming village near Audley End Park, its Norman tower stands by one of the most picturesque farms in Essex, Wenden Hall. Part of the hall is 15th century, and with it are two big barns, one of them splendid with three gables and a thatched roof. The tower doorway is from the earliest Norman days, and was probably set here in the Conqueror's lifetime; it is arched with Roman tiles and has a plain stone for a tympanum. Just above is a Tudor window, with three Norman ones higher up. The rest of the church is a medley of the centuries, its nave walls being the Norman ones taken higher in the 15th century, its chancel and south arcade 13th, its north arcade 14th, and its vestry 15th with a Tudor door still letting the parson in. There are weird and expressive heads

Waltham Abbey   Harold's Bridge

Waltham Abbey   The 14th Century Gateway

Stock   Rainham

Margaret Roding   South Ockendon

FOUR ANCIENT DOORWAYS

on the arches, and fastened to one of the pillars is a font of about 1400 with a handsome domed cover 200 years younger. A piscina in the aisle is 14th century, and a very fine one with a trefoil head in the chancel is a hundred years older. The chancel has some 14th century wall-paintings illustrating the story of St Margaret, the Martyr of Antioch. The church also treasures a remarkable amount of woodwork by craftsmen of 500 years ago. There is a screen with elaborate tracery, two fine kingposts among modern timbers in the roof, a door and a staircase leading up the tower, seven benches, and a pew carved at its end with a tiger resting his paw on a mirror. Best of all, perhaps, is a 15th century pulpit with rich tracery in great variety; it has nine sides, and stands on nine square legs. A splendid brass shows a man in the armour worn at Agincourt, perhaps a portrait of one of the Lovedays.

A little link with our greatest sailor is in the churchyard, for here is the gravestone of William Nicholson who had many tales to tell before he died at the great age of 104. He was a middy under Nelson in the Mediterranean, his ship being the Vanguard, on which Lady Hamilton and her husband took refuge when the French captured Naples at the end of the 18th century.

A Chest Older Than Parliament

WENNINGTON. It is in the level country of Rainham marshes. The arch of a Norman doorway reset in a refashioned aisle is the oldest part of its church, but the 13th century has much to show: a nave and chancel with narrow windows still in place, a handsome round pillar supporting an arcade, a low marble font, and, most remarkable of all, a hutchlike chest of wood, on which the slots for the hinges remain; it is one of the old chests which guarded the documents of our villages before a Parliament sat in England. The small tower and the pier of the other arcade were built in the 14th century, when the kingpost roof was set over the chancel. The best examples of woodwork here, both belonging to the 17th century, are the pulpit, with delicately carved pilasters and arched panels, and the elaborate oak font cover. By the pulpit is a 17th century hourglass stand with leaf-like ornament. On a wall is a curious little monument to Henry Bust, who kneels at prayer near the pulpit in which he preached in the days before the Civil War. With him is his son.

WEST BERGHOLT. Stone Age men dropped implements here which our own generation has picked up, and signs of the Romans have come to light, so old is this village near Colchester. One of its farms has been using two doorways for 500 years, and another is 16th century. The church stands near a fine red house and most of it is 600 years old. Its wooden turret may be 15th century, but the work of the 14th century men is seen in the arches of the nave, the timbers of the porch, and the moulded plates in the roofs. There is an old door with ironwork by a long-forgotten smith, a font bowl possibly 700 years old, a quaint little gallery with the royal arms, a few scraps of glass as old as the church, and a big Tudor chest with six hinges. At each end of the building is panelling of the 17th century about the same age as the fine lectern with its elaborate decoration.

The Birthplace of Lord Lister

WEST HAM. This big and densely peopled part of Greater London has great docks and great industries, and a population of nearly a third of a million. It includes Forest Gate and Silvertown, and is divided from London by the River Lea, crossed by the wide successor of the famous Bow Bridge. This is said to have been the first arched stone bridge in Essex, and was kept in repair by the monks of Langthorne Abbey, of which some 13th century window stones are built into a wall near the Adam and Eve inn.

Chaucer would gaze on the abbey from his rooms on the City gate, and did not his tender-hearted prioress pronounce her French after the school of Stratford-atte-Bow? The borough boasts a poet of its own, whose name was Thomas Lodge. He gave up law for letters, and his sonnets and elegies, lyrics and plays, brought forth the praise of Edmund Spenser and Robert Greene (the forgotten man who was jealous of Shakespeare).

Thomas Lodge's father was the Lord Mayor of London whose ships from Africa are said to have begun our trade in slaves, at that unhappy time when Stratford was burning men and women at the stake. The site of their martyrdom is at the busy cross-roads, and here in a churchyard is a lofty spire capped by a martyr's crown. On one of the six sides is a relief of the burnings from Foxe's Book of Martyrs, and the other sides give the names and dates of all the local victims who are known. Behind rises the tall pinnacled spire of plain-looking St John's church, one century old, and opposite is the high tower of the town hall, its dome 100 feet above the street, brooding over a balustraded roof with many statues.

Another statue stands outside the public library, for Stratford must have its Shakespeare, be he ever so small. For years the little figure stood in the vestibule of Drury Lane Theatre, and was saved when the building was burnt in 1809. The poet is stroking his beard in meditation, and bids us "Come and take choice of all my library." The rest of the block is used as a college and museum, and there are symbolical figures carved in relief on its many gables. Along the front stands a row of pillars on a frieze decorated with cherubs.

The museum owes much to the Essex Field Club and John Passmore Edwards, the philanthropist whose bust faces us as we enter. The collections illustrate the natural history and antiquities of Essex, and there are many models for teaching children. This was possibly the first museum to stage a living exhibit of wild flowers and grasses, and these have been renewed without a lapse since the beginning of our century. The survey of the animal kingdom starts with the tusks and teeth of mammoths and the skulls and horns of bison, all from Essex, and with fossils from all over the world. One fine exhibit is a wonderful panorama of Epping Forest, complete with stuffed animals and birds and models of toadstools.

The works of man start with cumbersome flint implements dropped at Leyton thousands of years ago, and next we see how he learned to put handles on his tools. There are relics from his dwellings, and his implements of bone and bronze. One exhibit deals with the mysterious low mounds, about a foot high, which are found along the high water mark of the Essex coast. We see their contents, red earth and rough red pottery, supporting the theory that at these mounds earthenware was made for evaporating salt. Soon afterwards came the Romans, and we are shown various types of the pottery they introduced. Finally there are prints and photographs of old Essex abbeys and priories.

The fossils and birds in the museum would have delighted George Edwards, born here in 1694. He went to a clergyman's school at Leytonstone, and read incessantly while he was apprenticed in the City. He travelled in Holland and Scandinavia, where he was seized as a spy, but he returned home to make coloured drawings of animals.

He studied fossils, corresponded with Linnaeus, and spent 21 years writing a great History of Birds. He gave to the world 500 bird scenes never pictured before, and he worked on to the end; then they laid him to rest from his labours in the crowded churchyard of West Ham.

The church has a big square sundial of 1803 which bids us Remember, and for sunless wet days is a long cloister joining the south aisle to the road. The tower of about 1400 has been liberally patched with brick: at the top is a turret and at the bottom a doorway with traceried spandrels.

There are signs in the clerestory that the Normans built no mean church here, probably a dignified building with transepts; now the nave has round piers of the 13th century, and above them are many Tudor beams. The chancel roof was built about 1500, a century after the chancel arch. Medieval arcades divide the chancel from its flanking chapels: the south chapel is probably 15th century and the other 100 years younger, a brick turret rising above its walls.

All forlorn lies the disused bowl of a font of 1707, and very gruesome is a 15th century stone on the tower, carved with skulls.

On the chancel arch is an Elizabethan brass of Thomas Staples faced by four women. Beneath are 20 verses, one for every shilling he left as an annuity to the poor. In a round-headed recess in the chancel wall are kneeling figures of John and Francis Faldo who died 300 years ago, looking very small beside the later monuments. In the north chapel is a memorial with rich pilasters framing the armoured figure of Captain Robert Rooke and his two wives, with their seven children. In a niche is James Cooper with his wife; he has been reading a book for nearly 200 years. Below the arch of the chapel is a 15th century altar tomb, but who lies in it we do not know. Angels hold shields in carved panels round the sides, and the beer barrel and maltster's shovel suggest an unknown brewer. There is no mistake about Sir Thomas Foot, who stands with his wife on a fine monument with a festooned urn. He was Lord Mayor of London in Restoration days, and wears his chain. Near by are cherubs adorning the monument of one of his successors, Sir James Smyth, who died in the reign of Queen Anne.

On the wall of the other chapel is a quaint 300-year-old group in a recess flanked by columns, showing a woman kneeling at a prayer desk with one of her husbands, while another husband reclines contentedly reading a book. A pathetic story must lie behind another monument in this chapel, where Nicholas and Eleanor Buckeridge set up their own tomb after losing five children. A kneeling girl on the cornice is flanked by busts of four infants, and below kneel their parents, who died over two centuries ago. They are descendants of that Thomas Buckeridge of the last Stuart reigns who wished to have his bones mingled with the ashes of his "dear and innocent child" at West Ham church. He was a friend of Godfrey Kneller and the Duke of Buckingham, and wrote the Lives of the English Painters.

Near the church is West Ham Park, 80 acres of green beauty, with many cedars over 150 years old. At the house called the Cedars lived Elizabeth Fry. West Ham Recreation Ground is a delightful park, its lawns gay with flowers, and in the middle plays a fountain surrounded by irises, a band plays under the trees, and children play everywhere.

But the name that shines above all others is Lord Lister's. Here he was born, and his house facing Upton Park is marked by a tablet.

He Saved Millions of Lives

LISTER was one of the greatest benefactors of mankind, born in 1827, son of a gifted Quaker. He took his medical degree at 25, was professor of surgery at Glasgow eight years later, and returned to London to give the last 16 years of his working life to King's College.

It was as a prince of surgeons that he devised the methods associated forever with his name. He worked in hospitals where 80 per cent of deaths followed operations, even minor breakings of the skin, and he saw the imperative need of surgical cleanliness. When Pasteur announced his discovery of fermentation from germs Lister realised that germs were responsible for the frightful consequences of operations. He sought out sterilising agents and prevented contact with the wounds by anything calculated to create septic conditions. Almost at once he reduced mortality by 65 per cent, and today his disciples feel it little short of a crime to lose life after an operation which before his day was almost certain to be fatal.

A brave and noble spirit, Lister worked patiently on in face of professional doubt and jealousy, content with the results and the gratitude of his patients. What he meant to them is tenderly expressed in a sonnet by W. E. Henley, who was for two years in his care. We give some lines from this poet's proud homage:

His brow spreads large and placid, and his eye
Is deep and bright, with steady looks that still.
Soft lines of tranquil thought his face fulfil—
His face at once benign and proud and shy.
If envy scout, if ignorance deny,
His faultless patience, his unyielding will,
Beautiful gentleness, and splendid skill,
Innumerable gratitudes reply.
His wise, rare smile is sweet with certainties,
And seems in all his patients to compel
Such love and faith as failure cannot quell . . .

He was raised to the peerage, and long before he died was acclaimed throughout the world as the greatest healer of all time. Prejudice had died down and he was acknowledged the saviour of millions of lives. The first doctor in the House of Lords, he was President of the Royal Society and of the British Association, was one of the original members of the Order of Merit (the highest distinction the King bestows) and was laid to rest among princes and poets in Westminster Abbey.

Queer Belfry

WEST HANNINGFIELD. The long grass of the churchyard was aglow with primroses when we called to see the treasure of the village, the amazing dug-out chest which has been here 600 years. It is bound with iron and has two lids, both very hard to lift, and is over eight feet long. It would come here about the time the new font was set on the Norman base, the carvers giving it trellis work and roundels on the stem and ballflowers and quaint heads round the bowl. There is a charming portrait in brass of 1361, the oldest brass but one of a lady in all Essex. It shows the head and shoulders of Isabel Clouville in the delightful veiled headdress of her time. There is a shield of the family arms in 15th century glass and an altar tomb in which lie a 16th century John Clouville and his wife. In the window above the tomb are two little heads of women with a Tudor rose between them.

A very curious feature here is the 15th century wooden belfry at the end of the nave; it is planned like a cross, each arm two stages high, the centre rising a stage higher and crowned with a spire. The interior is a medley of old beams and, mounting a rough 16th century ladder, we find the curved braces meeting at a grotesque face. It is all a little like some goblin barn rather than a belfry.

From a Roman House

WEST MERSEA. There are Roman tiles in its Saxon tower and Roman fragments appear wherever men dig about the churchyard. We must believe that this mouth of the Blackwater river was a Roman centre of importance. Here a mosaic pavement about 20 feet square and gay with roses and ivy leaves was laid bare 200 years ago, and smaller pavements have since been found. A little way from the church men digging a sawpit exposed a mass of concrete resembling a six-spoked wheel 200 feet round, with 12 little buttresses spaced on the rim. The nature of the round building these foundations supported is a mystery; some antiquaries think it would be a monument like those on the Appian Way, others that here stood a lighthouse or a watch-tower.

It was richer booty that fell to the excavators on opening a barrow on a farm a mile along the road to Colchester. Just below the level of the farmyard they found a small tiled chamber in which was a lead casket, 13 inches square and deep, containing a bowl of pale green glass. In this bowl were the ashes of a Roman who had been cremated in the first century.

From ruins of those days the Saxon builders of the tower picked up the masonry for the corners of a massive tower over 12 feet square. In its walls are their round openings with narrow splays, while the arch opening into the nave is shaped by Roman tiles and is nearly four feet thick. Made new in the 14th century, the Saxon church has two red consecration crosses still on the wall, and there is a marble font brought here by the Normans, resting on a round marble pier which some believe to have been found among the Roman ruins. Under the tower are two worn chests. Bright and shining is a 16th century lunette fixed in an aisle; it is a piece of Della Robbia ware in green and blue and white, with a reverent sculpture of Christ after Calvary, angels supporting him.

The Solitary Tower

WEST THURROCK. It lies by the Thames, and its neighbour Grays is spreading its industries over its borders. The great chalk quarry cut into the steep hill behind it is a grand foreground of a magnificent view of the Thames towards Gravesend, the walls of the quarry rising in grey tiers above a green pool. In the distance sweeps the majestic river with barge and hurrying tug and stately liner on its gleaming surface. Standing out, solid and solitary in the waterside wastes, is the 15th century tower of the church, with flint bands round it. It was one of the churches at which pilgrims would call on their way to Canterbury.

In a hole by the tower can still be seen the foundations of the church of Norman times; it had a round nave 25 feet wide, a very rare feature in our ancient buildings. The present nave was the chancel of the round church. The aisles were added about 1200, and the chancel with its two chapels 50 years after, rapid expansions suggesting considerable pilgrim traffic. The arcades of the chapels and the higher roofs belong to the 14th century, when the jolly curly-haired head of a king smiling over a door was carved.

A great stone under the altar lies over the grave of one who shared in these busy scenes. His lost brass, showing him resting on a beast, can only be imagined from its impression on the stone, but the deep lettering round the edge has preserved his name, Nicholas Ferobaud. He died 1315. Close by are portraits of Humphrey Heies, who died in 1584, and his young son, who wears a ruff. Latin scholars enjoy the many puns in this inscription.

There are alabaster figures of Sir Christopher Holford and his wife in a chapel, brought back into the church from a rubbish heap. He is in armour and his lady in rich clothing. Below him is a stone coffin of the 13th century, and worked into the wall are rare 14th century tiles with eagles and leopards and other rare patterns. Many fragments of glass of that century gleam from the windows. The font is rare because it is of chalk, carved in the 15th century with shields, a rose, a four-leaved flower, the sun, and a holy lamb.

He Saw Captain Cook Struck Down

WETHERSFIELD. Some of the houses of this big village are very old, projecting over the street with gables enriched by carved bargeboards. They have a quaintness all their own; in a thatched cottage which was a chapel in medieval days is the relic of a piscina, now used to make a window.

The tower of the church begins with Norman windows and grows younger with pointed ones as it rises to a square wooden lantern, then to a copper-covered spire, adding to the curious effect by hanging one of its bells outside. Part of the nave wall is so thick that it may be Saxon, but nothing else so old is left. Two doors have been swinging here 600 years, one in a 15th century porch; the nave has round columns of the 13th century and octagonal ones of the 14th; the clerestory is 15th century with a Tudor roof; and on each side of the 14th century chancel are stone seats in recesses with pointed arches. With them are two sedilia and a finely decorated piscina. A remarkable corbel was first carved as a woman's head, but her face has been turned into a flower. The traceried screen is 15th century, and so is a font no longer used. Among fragments of old glass in the windows is a striking head with a yellow beard and the name of Daniel above it; it has been here 600 years.

The most striking monument is a richly panelled tomb with sleeping figures of Henry Wentworth and his wife as they were in the 15th century. He is in armour with his feet on a unicorn, and she wears an elaborate necklace of roses; but the tomb is pathetically disfigured with names and initials scratched on it by louts, some as long ago as the 17th century. We have seen few monuments so wantonly disfigured. Hanging on the wall above is a Tudor funeral helmet, with the head of a bearded unicorn.

Among memorials to families worshipping here is one to Mark Mott, who founded a charity in the 18th century, and of much interest is the big tablet to the Clerkes, for it records the name of Captain Charles Clerke who must have seen as much of the globe as any man of his day. Three times he sailed round the world, meeting his end in attempting to go a fourth time with Captain Cook. He had the poignant experience of lying helpless on his ship, and seeing the natives kill the immortal captain. He saw the tragedy through his glasses and could do nothing. He was senior officer and took charge of the expedition in place of Cook, but his health grew worse and before he reached Kamchatka he was dead, only 38. They buried him under a tree, a man mourned by all his companions, for he was a frank and merry sailor, a fine seaman, and an honest kind-hearted Englishman.

A window of Our Lord appearing to Mary Magdalene is in memory of Captain Gordon, who died in the Indian Mutiny, and of his wife, who lived on for half a century without him. A brass tells of General Gordon of the Black Watch, who fell in the Great War.

Three miles from Wethersfield stands one of the oldest houses in the county, Great Codham Hall. One of its wings is 16th century, the other is 17th, and both have 17th century chimneys; but the main part of the house is 600 years old and its original kingpost still supports the roof of its 14th century hall.

WHITE COLNE. Its two best possessions are a pulpit and a chair, treasured in a church whose walls are probably 800 years old. The chair is 16th century, rich with flowers, a shield-of-arms, and a lamb with a flag. The pulpit is a splendid piece of Jacobean work, finely ornamented with figures in three panels. We see St James the Great with a staff and a gourd, St Augustine of Hippo with a mitre and crozier, and Charity carrying a babe who holds an orb in one hand and blesses us with the other. Between the panels are pilasters enriched with jewel ornament, and among the decorations of the cornice are two human masks. The church has Roman bricks at its corners, and a high and narrow chancel arch 600 years old. Its companions in the churchyard are several handsome oaks.

Here stands Fox and Pheasant Farm, built in Cromwell's time, with a fox and a pheasant on one of its fireplaces. It has sent treasures of the soil to Colchester Museum, urns and other fragments from a Celtic burial ground discovered in 1924.

Roman, Saxon, and Norman

WHITE NOTLEY. It has lost the great water mill which stood by the lovely Tudor hall, but there is still its big pond, with a deep ditch beside it. The brick and timber house has a delightful aspect with irregular gables, fine windows, and Tudor chimneys.Yet the village has something more remarkable than anything it has lost, for its church has come from three of our historic ages; it is Roman and Saxon and Norman. We come into it through a 14th century porch and a pointed wooden arch fronted with a decorated bargeboard, and the aisles, the nave arcades, and the end of the chancel are by the first English builders of the 13th century; but the Normans had made so effective a chancel arch with Roman tiles that the rebuilders left it for us, though they did demolish the tiny apse of which traces have been discovered.

The Norman masons shaped a Saxon headstone into one of their window-frames, and it has been made into a window-frame now in the vestry, with one of the rarest glass portraits in the county set in it. The portrait is of a crowned saint holding a book, a gem of colour

ESSEX

preserved for 700 years; it has yellow fleur-de-lys as a background. The villagers are also very proud of two 16th century roundels in a modern dormer window, one showing a lovely child. The 14th century tracery in some windows is of elaborate design, and the stone faces are perhaps of local celebrities. The font is by a craftsman of the 15th century, who panelled its stem and set bearded faces, foliage, and shields on the bowl.

The oldest woodwork is a dug-out chest with a heavy lid older than Magna Carta. The door, with a traceried top, is 14th century, and so are the rafter roof of the chancel and the pent roofs of the aisles. Both aisles have traceried screens of great beauty, one 15th century and the other 16th, each only eight feet wide but with five bays. The end of the nave is filled with the massive beams set up in the 16th century to support the bell-turret, which rises without a break into a short shingled spire.

From White Notley in the persecuting days of Mary Tudor went forth its great hero George Searles, to die in the fires of martyrdom at Stratford-le-Bow. There had just been laid in the churchyard when we called a parish clerk aged 92, who was believed to be the oldest parish clerk in England, having served White Notley as clerk and sexton for 70 years. He was Joseph Challis.

What the Centuries Gave It

WHITE RODING. It has something from every century since the Conqueror; all of them have given some little thing of interest or beauty to the simple church by the mill. It has something, indeed, much older than the Conqueror, for a walk under a bower of trees with their roots beneath the rectory moat brings us to walls with Roman bricks in them; they are at the corners of the nave. This is how we may put the time-table of the centuries in this interesting little church.

11th. Then were built the arches and the tiny windows.

12th. Now the font was carved, a hoary square bowl with rough zigzags, and perhaps a Norman mason carved the five consecration crosses on the altar stone.

13th. The ironwork of the south door was wrought with the drop-handle which twenty generations have used.

14th. During this century were carved two weird figures looking

379

down on the sanctuary, one resting his chin on his arms, one gripping his hair as if distraught.

15th. The carpenters of this century fashioned the roof, and the glass workers gave a window a roundel of coloured glass.

16th. The villagers realised that they had a splendid chance for a tower, and up it went, three stages of it with battlements from which a lead spire rises.

17th. The old men gathered for a chat in their handsome new porch, listening to the five bells at the time of the Great Fire of London, the bells that ring today.

18th. The curious chest and the altar table came.

19th. Now was added a new vestry, and the church was restored.

20th. To this time we must be grateful for the lovely roses blooming in the churchyard.

A constant friend to its church this village has been, and an old friend to the village has been the medieval house known as Colville Hall. It is half a mile away, one of those red brick homes which began to spring up over the countryside when the devastating Wars of the Roses ended at Bosworth Field. It has a low gable and pinnacles, and has been enriched by mullioned windows in which are ten roundels of glass painted with the occupations of the months.

The Little Thatched Shrine

WICKEN BONHUNT. Its church, with a dainty spire, watches over a charming cottage group, with fine elms close by and Wicken Hall next door, an Elizabethan house with a handsome chimney stack. But those who come from Newport will pass an older shrine at Bonhunt Farm, a little Norman chapel with a roof of thatch. It was called St Helen's, and is less than 40 feet long, its chancel only 10 feet wide. Here still are five Norman windows, one of them circular, a filled-up Norman doorway, a scratch dial close by, and a pillar piscina built into a window.

Nothing in the village church is quite so old as these simple walls, unless it be the rough square bowl of the font. But it has a 13th century chancel, and two of its old possessions are like those of the chapel, a scratch dial and a piscina. The chancel has also kept some of its lancet windows, a small seat for the priest, and a monument with a figure of a woman and cherubs in memory of little John Bradbury who died in 1693. He was the heir of his family, who lived not far away at Brick House, a handsome Tudor building with two imposing gables. A sculptured figure in Roman dress is at a corner of one of them, and a stone bust is over the entrance. With the house is a thatched barn of the 17th century.

WICKFORD. A compact village round which the River Crouch swings under three bridges, it has kept in its rebuilt church a font and two bells of the 15th century. A window as old is in the vestry, and all who come will be glad that Wickford has used again its old chancel roof, handsome with carved bosses and shields. In the doorway are gates adorned with leaves and scrolls; and an attractive window to a doctor shows Christ as the healer of the sick, with a lad on crutches and a child in its mother's arms.

The Deserted Church

WICKHAM BISHOPS. In the fields, a few yards from the 15th century doorway of a cottage, we came upon an ill-used and deserted church with a shingle spire on a wooden turret. The Normans built it, using Roman bricks for the corners of the chancel and Roman tiles for a doorway. The doorway has been replaced with a medieval brick porch, and there is still hanging in it a door 500 years old. We found the tiebeams of the 15th century roof still strong, but the rest was a picture of desolation, with the pavement broken round the font, which had a lid 500 years ago to prevent the holy water from being stolen for black magic. On the altar is a gravestone with the word Resurgam, and we may hope it will be prophetic for the old church. Only its 600-year-old chest has been moved to the new church with the lofty spire.

Still ringed round with its moat is Wickham Hall, a timbered Stuart house with 15th century glass painted with lively little birds.

A Link with St Paul's

WICKHAM ST PAUL. It has belonged to St Paul's Cathedral for a thousand years, a little link in Essex with the heart of London. Its houses are round a pleasant green, but its church is half a mile away by a farm, and we come to its porch beneath archways of roses. It was standing much as we see it before old St Paul's perished in the Great Fire. Its fine brick tower is Tudor and has a door to the stair turret, which has been opening for 400 years. Part of the nave is

12th century, and the chancel was refashioned in the 14th century. One of the bells has been here about 500 years; and just as old are the nave roof and the great treasure of the church, a fine chancel screen with much delicate tracery. There is a 13th century chest bound with iron, a Jacobean altar table with a new top, and fragments of 15th century glass including a lion's head.

WIDDINGTON. A small village with a pleasant green near the source of Cambridge's river, its oldest possession is a Norman window in the church, opening to a 15th century vestry. The church has been much restored, and its tower has been rebuilt with bold gargoyles and handsome pinnacles, but it has kept treasures from all the great centuries. Behind the altar is a 14th century window with fine carving about it, a grotesque head with foliage coming from its mouth and a bird eating fruit. Another window has the shields of France and England in 14th century glass, and a medallion of 1664 showing a sundial and an hourglass. There is a piscina 700 years old, and a brass portrait of a civilian who lived before America was on the map. The oak doors and their ironwork in the porch are notable, and are said to be 15th century.

Widdington Hall not far away is now a farm, and goes back to the 15th century. Beside it is a Tudor barn; but an even finer barn belongs to Prior's Hall, a farmhouse whose stone walls behind the plaster are believed to be almost as old as Magna Carta. The barn has eight bays, side aisles, and gables with foiled bargeboards.

WIDFORD. Its great house and its church are 19th century, the house in the splendid 600 acres of Hylands Park, the church remarkable for its imposing spire rising 145 feet. A window in the tower has fine figures of the Madonna in white, St George in a rich red cloak, and St Nicholas in purple carrying a sailing ship. A big sycamore guards the churchyard, where we see the tomb of Lady Falkland, who was a benefactor of the village in the 18th century.

His Six Sons

WILLINGALE. It is Willingale Spain and Willingale Doe, probably the villages of rival Norman knights whose friendliness is all forgotten but whose rivalry remains, for still their two churches are in one churchyard, a curious sight.

Willingale Doe has one thing left from its Norman builders, the capital of a pillar piscina set in the 14th century wall of the nave; Willingale Spain's walls stand much as the Norman knight built them, with a rugged simplicity and patches of red Roman tiles at one of the corners and in two doorways.

Willingale Doe, if we count its 15th century tower, is bigger by 20 feet. It has an ancient curly head on the gable outside, and, inside, the medieval font at which would be baptised the children of Thomas Torrell, whose portrait is in brass in the chancel; his little dog is at his feet. On a wall-monument of Charles Stuart's time rests Richard Wiseman and his wife, he bearded and in plate armour minutely carved in alabaster; the sculpture is framed in marble columns, resting on lions with a quaint sea-horse between them. We noticed also a comic sea-horse on a 16th century helmet hanging on the chancel wall. The pulpit has linenfold panels, a worthy rostrum for old John Swain, a rector of our own time who died at 91, lying here with his wife who died at 94.

Willingale Spain has always been proud of the work of its smiths on two of its church doors. The grotesque heads of serpents on one door in the nave have survived the timbers on which the Normans fastened them, and the strap-hinges on the priest's door are fine examples of medieval forge work. The posts for the timber turret piercing the high-pitched roof are 15th century, and one of the bells is older still. The chancel, made new 500 years ago, has a curious home-made monument of wood and parchment, more appealing than much of the pretentious alabaster of its day. It is a simple wooden frame with folding doors on which are crudely painted two shields-of-arms with the record of the six sons of Edward Bewsy. They lived in the days of Charles Stuart, and here their father set their names, the dates of their deaths, eagles on their coats-of-arms, and a rhyme which ends:

> *Six lie here shaken from the tree;*
> *Where eagles frequent are, dead bodies be.*

The Moated Farm

WIMBISH. It has many fine farm buildings round about; one of them, Tiptofts, has remarkable timbers 600 years old and stands within the waters of a moat. Inside its hall are wooden columns to support the massive tiebeam of the kingpost roof; and the original 14th century roofs are also over the buttery and solar wings. With its great brick chimney added 200 years later, the house is a rare example of an ancient English home. Broad Oaks is a moated manor house of Tudor brick, with graceful chimneys and handsome windows of stone. Within are doors and panelling of the 17th century, and a stone fireplace of about 1560.

The church is in a lovely setting of trees, and has nave walls and a little window of the 12th century. Of about the same age is the handsome doorway, protected by a 15th century porch whose upper room is reached by a stairway in the thickness of the wall. The double door has been opening and shutting since Henry the Seventh was on the throne. Handsome columns have been standing in the nave for 700 years; a board painted with texts and commandments was here before the Spanish Armada sailed; and the Tudor roof of the aisle has a fine rose in one spandrel, balanced by the arabic figures 1534. Two 14th century screens are very finely traceried, and from the same age are some glass flowers and shields and yellow leopards. Here are two of the oldest brass portraits in Essex. They show Sir John de Wautone of 1347 and his Ellen, he looking much as a warrior at Crecy must have looked, his lady very gracefully dressed. The portraits are set in the head of a cross, the only impress of a brass cross in the county; and below is the impress of an elephant, the badge of the Beaumont family.

The Ancient Timbers

WITHAM. It has old barns, old inns, and old cottages, and it lies on the Roman road to Colchester at the point where the River Brain crosses it. On one of the timbered houses by the bridge are brackets carved with a cock and a hen. The 14th century church has Roman bricks in its walls and a doorway carved with chevrons by the Normans; in it swings a 15th century door with traceried panels, companion through the ages for a door older still leading out of the chancel into the vestry. Here are still the roofs made by the carpenters who made these doors, for all the roofing of the 14th century aisles and the 15th century chapels is original. The handsome chancel screen is also 15th century, carved with Tudor flowers. In the chancel are two oak seats of about 1500, and on the wall are painted figures of Francis Harve and his wife, an Elizabethan couple facing each other at a prayer desk. By it is a bust of William East, who died

Ugley   Village Beautiful

Willingale   The Two Churches

White Roding   The Old Mill

in 1726. On an altar tomb lies John Southcotte in his judge's robes with his wife in her Elizabethan ruff and cloak.

Hanging over a doorway are four helmets, one 15th century and one worn by a trooper in the Civil War. The elaborately engraved almsdish is Jacobean, a chest with three locks is 16th century, and one of the two coffin lids in the chapels is Norman.

The hill on which the church stands is known as Chipping, the old name for market, and the name of the Woolpack Inn close by recalls the sort of goods sold there. Some alterations in a cottage here a few years ago showed that it was the ancient guildhall. Four oak arches span the width of both rooms, upstairs and down, and it is probable that this little hall was built at the end of the 14th century. Tudor fireplaces were afterwards put in, but they are now hidden.

The old barns are at Powers Hall a mile away, one with seven bays, aisles, and gabled porches being 15th century, the other with five bays is 17th century. Ages before they came the old earthworks were here through which the railway has been cut, for they were built by Edward the Elder as defence against the Danes.

The Splendid Brass

WIVENHOE. An oldfashioned little town five miles down the Colne from Colchester, it has a quay facing the River Roman, a tributary from the west. Here they cultivate oysters and build yachts. The High Street has houses 300 years old, one or two with elaborate plaster decoration of foliage and trees. Overhanging storeys, gables, and carved bargeboards give charm to these old buildings, though it was sad to see Wivenhoe, a member of the Kent Cinque Port of Sandwich, fallen on hard times.

In the churchyard is a magnificent group of chestnuts. Most of the church was made new after an earthquake in 1884, but the bold tower of 1500 stood firm in the shock, and the 14th century arcades of the nave, some brasses, and a few old gravestones, and many moulded stones remain.

A splendid monument in the church is the brass portrait of Lord William Beaumont, who was buried here in 1507; his head rests on a helm bearing a lion crest and his feet are on an elephant which carries a castle. An elaborate triple canopy with gables and pinnacles shelters this great armoured figure. His widow married John, Earl of Oxford, and was laid to rest here in 1537. Her figure is also in brass, resplendent in a heraldic cloak and a pedimental headdress with a coronet; it has a triple canopy and an embattled super-canopy as well, a magnificent brass for so late a period. The countess lived in Wivenhoe Hall, and the wing with crowstepped gables built in her lifetime still stands. Toward Colchester is Wivenhoe Park, a well-wooded estate in which deer wander over 200 up-and-down acres.

WIX. It lines the road from Colchester to Harwich, and has a 17th century inn. Not far away stands an Elizabethan house with a three-storeyed porch under a crow-stepped gable; it is on the site of a priory founded in the reign of Henry the First and abolished by Cardinal Wolsey. The church is by the old house, ivy climbing its walls toward the little turret which holds a small bell. We found a much bigger bell, itself covered with ivy, hanging in a detached wooden turret in the middle of the great churchyard. The church has been made smaller, for we can see from the outside a bricked-up arcade with capitals moulded 700 years ago.

A Great Ambassador

WOODFORD. We come to it by one of the most impressive roads near London, a mile of trees marching with the highway from Wanstead. Around its approach are remnants of the great Essex Forest and beyond it the still delightful glades of Epping. It has memories of a lost church; it has known great days as a fashionable watering place; it has beyond Woodford Bridge the garden city of the older boys of Dr Barnardo's homes; but it has passed through the changes that come to any place into which population flows by tens of thousands. In the changing present it will forget its past.

Yet some associations Woodford is not likely to forget, for it was the scene of the boyhood of William Morris, it was the birthplace of Sydney Smith and Coventry Patmore, and in its earth there lies one of the first and best of our ambassadors, Sir Thomas Roe. Strange it is that he should lie with no memorial.

One memorial there is in the churchyard, a draped urn which must bring many pilgrims to the grave it marks, for in it lie the father and the mother of William Morris. In this grave they laid his father in 1847 and nearly half a century later they laid the widow beside him. Here at Woodford Hall, within an arrow's flight of the spot where his parents rest together, the poet passed the most sensitive years of his youth.

The father was a wealthy bill-broker in the City. The boy was born near by at Walthamstow, over the ridge which parts the Lea and Roding rivers, and when he was six they came to live at Woodford Hall. The park was separated only by a fence from the Forest, and the hall had a doorway into the churchyard. By the roadside, on a green space now enclosed, stood the village pound and stocks. Fifty years later Morris wrote of the Epping Forest he loved, "I was born and bred in its neighbourhood and knew it, yard by yard, from Wanstead to the Theydons and from Hale End to Fairlop Oak." His life centred elsewhere in later years, but here it was that he received his primal impulses.

The old church has given place to a new one. A tombstone preserves the memory of a man who fell from the tower when it was being built in 1708, but the tower is the only part as early as that date. All the rest is modern, yet the list of rectors comes from 1177. The churchyard has a yew tree 17 feet round, still strong and healthy after its 400 years and more.

There is a beautiful wall-monument of Rowland Elrington and his wife, kneeling in Tudor dress under an arched recess, and a tall urn-capped column in memory of the Godfrey family, whose most famous member, Sir Edmund, was a magistrate of the highest repute, honest, public-minded, and generous, yet was murdered in connection with the so-called Popish Plot of the infamous Titus Oates, the mystery of his fate being one of the strangest chapters in the history of crime.

From the chancel arch hangs a flag which has been here since the Territorials came into being and which had been before them the flag of the Woodford Company of Volunteers raised to meet Napoleon if he came. A bright window with figures of Peace and Victory is in memory of the men who did not come back, and there are two windows in memory of two scouts among them, one showing David and Jonathan for Arthur Quelhorst, the other showing St Michael and St Denis in memory of Charles Eastgate. Of its witty dean and its sentimental poet Woodford has small remembrance; and of Sir Thomas Roe it had none that we could discover.

Sydney Smith won social fame as a brilliant talker until he became too much of a professional in that vein. A very hearty man and "good fellow," he was too free in expressing his opinion to attain high dignity in the church, but his writings remain breezy even when their themes have become out-of-date. Coventry Patmore was a sentimentalist who won a public of his own by his simple style, and then bewildered his customary readers by exercises in more complex forms of expression. His general tone was feminine. A greater man than either of these two sons of Woodford was Sir Thomas Roe, one of the most successful ambassadors England ever sent to a foreign land.

He came of the London merchant class, his grandfather being a lord mayor. His education was by travel, though he went to Oxford and also had legal studies. When Queen Elizabeth was old he was a young squire at her Court, and James the First knighted him, while the Prince of Wales sent him more than once to explore the great South American rivers. His first experience as an ambassador was to the Mogul Emperor of Hindustan, to open up trade, and he succeeded in laying trade foundations in the Bombay region. On his way home he made a successful call in Persia and introduced England there.

After that his journeys abroad were frequent. First he went as ambassador to Turkey, and was so successful that he was kept at Constantinople against his own wishes for seven years. While there he negotiated a peace treaty between Turkey and Poland and liberated hundreds of English captives from Algerian pirates, secured the famous Codex Alexandrinus copy of the Bible now in the British Museum, and collected 29 manuscripts for the Bodleian. His next mission was to mediate on peace between Sweden and Poland, and he was successful in arranging a truce. On his way home he made trade treaties with Danzig and Denmark. James had a gold medal struck in his honour. Again he was sent abroad as the English Ambassador Extraordinary to a conference for settling a general European Peace, and similar visits continued until his death in 1644.

His intervals at home were occupied in Parliamentary work, he representing the University of Oxford. The charm of his manner and conversation was admitted wherever his duty carried him. In short, at that early period England had in Sir Thomas Roe an ideal ambassador with a European reputation, but there is no advertisement in such work, and so this successful worker for peace and helpful trade lies still without a monument in the place where he lies.

Cecilie Sandys

WOODHAM FERRERS. Its houses line a winding uphill street, and the church stands behind with a good view of the valley of the Crouch. It is a wide open building of the 13th and 14th centuries, having lost its tower. It has a 14th century font and four 15th century benches. The wall over the high chancel arch shows in a faint pink all that remains of a medieval Doom painting, in which Christ sits on a rainbow; and there are bright yellows and blues in the 14th century shields of France and England in a window. A delightful monument is a son's tribute to his mother; it shows Cecilie Sandys, who survived her husband, Archbishop of York, living in the Elizabethan house he had built a mile away, still standing. She kneels in painted alabaster, a lady of Jacobean days, below a graceful trellis covered with flowers, Father Time with an hourglass in his hand lurking in the shadow of a column behind her.

Along the road is Bicknacre, where a solitary arch stands like a shadow of the priory which stood here from the 12th century until 1507, when its last canon died in it.

Little Imp

WOODHAM MORTIMER. Whoever peeps into this church on the road to Maldon will make the acquaintance of a delightful Elizabethan maid, engraved in brass and wearing a pleated gown. This is from the inscription they wrote for her, little Dorothy Alleine:

> *A little imp here buried is,*
> *Her soul to Christ is fled.*

The church in which she lies has been rebuilt save for one wall, which is Norman and has an arch with remains of red colour. The capital of the pillar piscina is Norman, and possibly the round font, which stands on a medieval stem. The altar table is 17th century and there is carving of that age on the pulpit and the organ case.

The hall by the church is a fine three-storeyed building with a 16th century wing framed in timber at the back, and made imposing by four Dutch gables added to the front 300 years ago.

The Doctor

WOODHAM WALTER. It has an Elizabethan inn among the cottages in the hollow, and a complete Elizabethan church on the side of the hill; and the wild common on the high ground inland has a romantic beauty.

The inn has carving of oak leaves and acorns and the tendrils of the vine on the woodwork of the overhanging storey, and the bargeboards on the gable add to its old-world charm.

The 16th century church is aglow with red bricks and has a red-tiled roof and crowstepped gables; and it has some treasures saved from its predecessor. The most valuable of these is the font, tall and light with traceried panelling of the 15th century. There is medieval glass in the windows, seven roundels with glowing suns and the figure of a reaper in a green cap bending at his task. The reaper is the symbol of man's labour five centuries ago; against the wall is a bronze symbolical of the work of our own century. It shows a doctor looking through a microscope, and is in memory of Henry Ayrton Chaplin, of the West African Medical Staff, who died in 1905 at Salaga while engaged in research. Over the design are these lines of Kipling:

> Take up the white man's burden,
> The savage wars of peace:
> Fill full the mouth of Famine
> And bid the sickness cease.

One day this century the villagers had a great surprise. They received news that Henry Thompson, who had been their fairy godfather ever since he had come from Aberdeen to live among them at Warren Farm, had left £50,000 for the playing-fields which he had established on his farm. He was one of the men who have made it impossible for honest folk ever to repeat the silly jokes about Aberdeen; he had lived here 30 years and laid out cricket pitches and football grounds on his own estate, and by his will he desired to carry on his benefactions for all time.

Mound and Moat

WORMINGFORD. A century ago they moved its mysterious mound and discovered hundreds of urns in parallel rows, grim relics, perhaps, of the 9th Roman Legion cut off at the Stour while marching to support their army against Boadicea. Moated houses bear witness to the troublous times of a later era, and even the 17th century homestead Garnons has traces of an outer enclosure. This house has five neighbours as old as itself, and there are many pretty cottages amid beautiful scenery. Church House is Tudor, and so is Church Hall, a delightful building with brick chimneys looking on the entrance to the beautiful churchyard.

The church has a 15th century bell in its Norman tower, which has a 17th century parapet but Roman tiles in the corners. The Norman nave has two of its original windows blocked with Roman bricks. The porch has a 15th century arch through which we come to a fine little nave arcade 200 years older, its pointed arches on eight-sided pillars. The aisle is 13th century, but has a Tudor roof. The chancel was made new in the 14th century, its arch crossed by a modern screen into which has been worked some 500-year-old carving. A window on the sunny side has a tiny Tudor shield and a 14th century roundel, and in the opposite wall is some delightful 14th century glass with floral borders and nine roundels.

In the floor of the tower is a 15th century brass of a civilian in long gown and pointed shoes, and of the next century is the brass of a praying man with his two wives in big hats and frilled sleeves. By the chancel arch hangs a thankoffering for those who safely returned from the Great War, a painting of a ship being welcomed to harbour, "the haven where they would be."

In the churchyard is a font bowl filled with fuchsias, foreign flowers which would have astonished the medieval maker of the font.

WRABNESS. It pushes itself out into the estuary of the Stour and has long views of Suffolk across the water. It has ancient thatched barns, a timbered cottage of Stuart days, and a hall with a wing 600 years old. As it has no tower the bell which summons the village to prayer hangs in a wooden turret in the churchyard. We come to the church by a porch with a 700-year-old coffin lid in the wall, through a doorway carved with flowers and shields in the 15th century. There are Norman stones above the door and facing us as we enter is a Norman doorway used no more. The font is 500 years old and has saints sitting on the bowl, with angels supporting.

The Cradle of the BBC

WRITTLE. Now that the world is one vast whispering gallery it is difficult to remember that as far as we are concerned it all began in this small Essex village, for Writtle was the birthplace of British Broadcasting.

We remember standing on a hilltop in Kent and hearing a man cough at Writtle, and time itself will not efface that memory or destroy that thrill. It was in the days when the wireless telephone was making its way and the wonderful Marconi men were sending out concerts for fifteen minutes every night. After the telephone a series of telegraphic signals was sent out on carefully measured wave-lengths to enable amateurs to test their coils, and it was announced that those within 20 miles of Writtle could receive the programme on a crystal receiver. One of the papers reported that "in addition to the Writtle concerts, time signals from the Eiffel Tower, ships working wireless at sea, aeroplanes talking to aerodromes, weather reports, and many other interesting and useful messages were passing through space unheard and generally unsuspected by the public."

Seven hundred years before Marconi came into the world Writtle, it is believed, was famous for a palace of King John, and half a mile from its church is a dry moat with a fish-pond still called King John's Palace. The great charm of Writtle, however, is in the pond and the cricket pitch on the village green, with houses of all ages framing its great triangle. Two 17th century houses stand by the churchyard, and the best and oldest of all, built about 1500, with its old timbering exposed, overhangs the path which brings us to the church. Here still are both the original porches, probably built when the church was completing its first century.

Most of the walls have stood about 700 years, but the tower was made new last century, two 600-year-old grotesques having been built into it. The much-weathered font is Norman, the roof borne on musical angels is Tudor, and there are poppyhead pews of the 15th and 16th centuries and modern stalls with a 17th century frieze let into them. We found on a windowsill carvings of a man in a hat and a woman in a crown, both 600 years old.

On a striking sculpture by Nicholas Stone in memory of Edward Pinchon and his wife is a winged reaper, with arm upraised, standing on a rock amid sheaves of wheat with mourning angels about wearing wide-brimmed hats. On the wall kneel Edward and Jane Eliott with their 10 children, dressed as Elizabethans, and in the sanctuary is the bust of Sir John Comyns in his robes as Lord Chief Baron of the Exchequer in the 18th century.

A remarkable group of brasses ranges over two centuries to the closing days of Shakespeare, and among them is a wife with three husbands, and a husband with four wives. The four wives belong to a civilian of 1510 and are all looking admiringly at him, three groups of children being with them; the three husbands belong to Thomasin Thomas, who wears a dress of the early 15th century. Two of the husbands are in armour, the third is represented only by his shield, but the lady has a second brass of herself.

Set in small stones near her are brasses of Elizabeth Pinchon in a Tudor cap and widow's hood, with six kneeling children, and Constans Berners with her hair flowing down below her waist. A man and woman and eight children of the Bedell family are wearing 15th century dress; Edward Bell of 1576 is with his family; and Edward Hunt kneels in a ruff facing his wife at prayer, she in a tall hat.

The village has two greens with old houses round both, and on St John's Green the dwellers in olden days paid a tax known as Green Silver, a halfpenny a year for the privilege of looking out on the green. We have come upon a knight of our own time who pays a duke a shilling a year for the privilege of opening his window on a village green in Sussex.

It was at Writtle that there was born a most remarkable man named John Eastwick, who became a doctor at Colchester and wrote pamphlets against abuses in the church. For this his ears were cut off and he was thrown into prison, but the Long Parliament released him and granted him £5000 compensation from the Archbishop of Canterbury's estate. He fought for Parliament in the Civil War, but after the king's execution he became a pamphleteer once more, this time against the Independents.

ESSEX TOWNS AND VILLAGES

In this key to our map of Essex are all the towns and villages treated in this book. If a place is not on the map by name, its square is given here, so that the way to it is easily found, each square being five miles. One or two hamlets are in the book with their neighbouring villages: for these see Index.

394

INDEX

This index includes all notable subjects and people likely to be sought for, and a special index of pictures appears at the beginning of the volume.

INDEX

INDEX

INDEX

INDEX

INDEX